Con

GW00708101

Continued on next page

Contents at a Glance

Continued from previous page

PART V: ADMINISTERING THE SYSTEM

Mac OS® X Tiger™

Brian Tiemann

SAMS
**Teach
Yourself**

Sams Publishing, 800 East 96th Street, Indianapolis, Indiana 46240 USA

Mac OS X Tiger in a Snap

International Standard Book Number: 0-672-32706-6

Library of Congress Catalog Card Number: 2004093743

Printed in the United States of America

First Printing: May 2005

08   07   06   05   4   3   2

Trademarks

Warning and Disclaimer

Bulk Sales

Sams Publishing offers excellent discounts on this book when ordered in quantity for bulk purchases or special sales. For more information, please contact

> U.S. Corporate and Government Sales
> 1-800-382-3419
> corpsales@pearsontechgroup.com

For sales outside of the U.S., please contact

> International Sales
> international@pearsoned.com

Acquisitions Editor
Betsy Brown

Development Editor
Scott Meyers

Managing Editor
Charlotte Clapp

Project Editor
Andy Beaster

Production Editor
Benjamin Berg

Indexer
Erika Millen

Proofreader
Paula Lowell

Technical Editor
John Traenkenschuh

Publishing Coordinator
Vanessa Evans

Designer
Gary Adair

Page Layout
Bronkella Publishing

Graphics
Tammy Graham

About the Author

Brian Tiemann is a freelance technology columnist and software engineer who has written extensively in online magazines about the Macintosh, Apple software, and the philosophy of user-friendly design that has always been synonymous with them. A creative professional in the graphic arts and web design world as well as in networking and software quality, he uses Mac OS X because of its Unix-based stability underlying the powerful built-in creative tools that let him bring his graphics, music, movies, and photography to life.

Having been a Mac user for nearly 20 years, Brian has observed Apple's growth from a maker of simple personal computers to the powerhouse of film production, digital music, online lifestyle, and publishing that it is today. A graduate of Caltech, author of *Mac OS X Panther in a Snap*, and coauthor of *FreeBSD Unleashed* and *Sams Teach Yourself FreeBSD in 24 Hours*, Brian enjoys animation, motorcycles, photography, technological gadgets, the outdoors, and writing about them all. He lives in Silicon Valley with canines Capri and Banzai, who posed for pictures used throughout this book.

Dedication

To my parents, Keith and Ann; my brother, Michael; and his wife, Julie.

Acknowledgments

Time marches on, and with it Mac OS X. The team of editors at Sams Publishing deserves great acclaim for wrangling this book into shape, consisting as it does of at least as much new or changed material as was present in the Panther book. I'd like to thank John Traenkenschuh for being a voice of moderation against my Mac fervor while at the same time keeping all the technical details in line; Ben Berg for formalizing the vocabulary and making everything tidy; Scott Meyers for helping us all keep apprised of the ever-changing face of Tiger under development; Andy Beaster for tying all the content together and putting up with last-minute changes; and Betsy Brown for keeping everything on track. These and the rest of the Sams staff—especially the art and illustration department—have my deepest thanks.

I would also like to thank all those who have served to hone my passions both for writing and for the Mac: James Lileks for bolstering my ego with his very presence; Steven Den Beste for toughening me up; Mike Hendrix for keeping that torch lit and that flag flying; and Paul, Mike, Damien, Kevin, Aziz, and J for always keeping me on my toes. Lance, Kris, Chris, David, John, Van, Trent, Marcus, Paul, and all the rest: Thank you for understanding once again during these past three months, and for making sure that I didn't completely lose touch with reality while sequestered with the G5. You do remember me, don't you?

We Want to Hear from You!

As the reader of this book, *you* are our most important critic and commentator. We value your opinion and want to know what we're doing right, what we could do better, what areas you'd like to see us publish in, and any other words of wisdom you're willing to pass our way.

You can email or write me directly to let me know what you did or didn't like about this book—as well as what we can do to make our books stronger.

Please note that I cannot help you with technical problems related to the topic of this book, and that due to the high volume of mail I receive, I might not be able to reply to every message.

When you write, please be sure to include this book's title and author as well as your name and phone or email address. I will carefully review your comments and share them with the author and editors who worked on the book.

Email: **consumer@samspublishing.com**

Mail: Mark Taber
          Associate Publisher
          Sams Publishing
          800 East 96th Street
          Indianapolis, IN 46240 USA

Reader Services

For more information about this book or others from Sams Publishing, visit our website at **www.samspublishing.com**. Type the ISBN (excluding hyphens) or the title of the book in the Search box to find the book you're looking for.

PART I

Understanding Mac OS X

IN THIS PART:

1

✔ Start Here

Ever since the very first days of the Macintosh, Apple Computer, Inc. has prided itself on building computers that were "different." Back in the early years, Macs were marketed on the principle of being graphical, easy-to-use alternatives to the arcane, command-line-driven DOS computers that then were most common. Later, Apple's "Think Different" campaign presented the Mac as a stylish and elegant niche machine for the artists, writers, and free thinkers of the world. Today, the computing world is unarguably dominated by Windows PCs, but the Macintosh holds an indomitable (if small) percent of the market—an unbending cadre of loyalists, their numbers bolstered by newcomers attracted by the stability and modern design of Mac OS X.

The original Macintosh.

The Macintosh's operating system, known as the "Mac OS" since version 8.0 (Mac OS 8) in 1996, has often seemed to be quirky, oddly designed, even clumsy—particularly to those people who were used to Microsoft Windows (and before that, MS-DOS). The first Macintosh hit the shelves in 1984; at that time, before Windows had become widely used on PCs, the Mac—"the computer for the rest of us"—was often derided as a "toy" because its operating system was graphical—using icons and menus and multiple windows for different applications, when many computer users preferred to think of computers as being something that only a privileged few ought to be able to understand, something that should be controlled only with austere keyboard commands.

When Windows 95 was released, however, it incorporated many graphical features that seemed to mimic features of the Macintosh, and Windows users found themselves using their computers in ways that Mac users had been accustomed to doing for years. Still, Microsoft implemented the features of Windows in such a way as to be *just* different *enough* from the Mac that Windows users came to think of Windows's way as the more common and natural, despite the Mac's long-standing claim to have been specifically designed, through thousands of hours' worth of human interface study, to be the most intuitive system for controlling a personal computer that could possibly be created. Reality seemed to have outpaced Apple's theory.

Meanwhile, open-source Unix operating systems such as Linux and FreeBSD had come onto the scene, bringing their own ideas about how computers should work, as well as their much-vaunted advantages of stability, security, and networking versatility. Windows grew to incorporate many Unix concepts as the Internet age dawned. By the time the translucent iMac was released in 1998, the Mac OS had fallen behind the technological curve, despite its fans' insistence that it was still the most pure and elegant operating system on Earth.

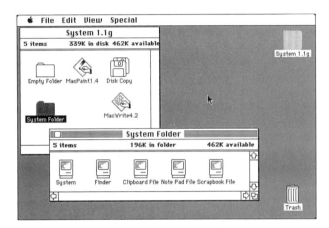

The Macintosh System 1.0, the operating system of the original Macintosh, is the distant ancestor of Mac OS X.

When Apple co-founder Steve Jobs returned to Apple after being exiled from the company for more than 10 years, he brought with him an infusion of ideas from the company he had been running in the meantime, NeXT, which made a line of computers based on the BSD flavor of Unix. Apple put all its efforts behind turning NeXT's system into a new generation of system software, which was released to the public in 2001 under the name Mac OS X, with the "X" pronounced "Ten." This new operating system replaced the aging Mac OS 9's core technology with the BSD Unix undercarriage derived from NeXT, and laid on top of it a redesign of the familiar Macintosh operating system that boasted many new features and deep alterations to the venerable user interface. The goal was to create a hybrid operating system with industrial-strength networking features and stability, that would be as intuitive and elegant as the old Mac OS, but immediately familiar to users of Windows or people brand-new to computers altogether. With Mac OS X, Apple gave Macintosh users a platform they could again be proud of using, one that gave them bragging rights over the competition. Now, the world's most easy-to-use computer was also a true Unix workstation, and compatible in most important ways with a Windows-dominated computing world.

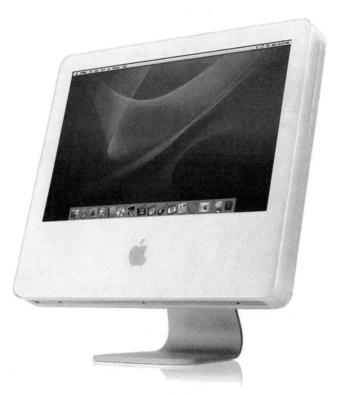

Following the tradition of the original all-in-one Macintosh, the components of the 2004 G5 iMac are all contained inside the hanging display unit.

Whether designed to be superbly intuitive or not, Mac OS X—in its current incarnation, version 10.4, code-named "Tiger"—is not guaranteed to be easy for a new user to figure out. Depending on whether you are used to Windows, familiar with Mac OS 9, or new to computers altogether, Mac OS X offers a specific set of unfamiliar metaphors and technical challenges to overcome. Nonetheless, Mac OS X enables the user to accomplish very nearly everything that a user of any other operating system can do, if in a slightly different way. This book explains how to do those tasks, step by step, introducing the concepts fundamental to Mac OS X along the way. Whether you are a Windows user, a longtime Mac user, a Unix geek, or a first-time computer user, the procedures in this book should leave you with an understanding of why Mac OS X is designed the way it is, which in turn should enable you to accomplish things far beyond the scope of this book.

Coming from Windows

If your exposure to computers has only been through the various flavors of Microsoft Windows, Mac OS X is likely to seem strange and non-intuitive at first, even backward. However, with an introduction to a few basic concepts, you should be able to find your way around the system with ease.

The first major difference between Windows and the Mac OS is that on the Mac, applications are *modal*. This means that whatever application you are currently using is in the foreground, and its controls effectively take over the entire area of your screen, though you can still see everything around and behind the current application window and interact with some of it. The menu bar across the top of the screen changes to reflect the controls provided by the current application. For instance, if you are using TextEdit, the menus shown at the top of the screen are TextEdit's menus. By contrast, Windows is designed so that each application fits within a single window, which can be any size up to the full size of the screen, blocking other applications from sight. Each application window in Windows contains its own set of control menus, and nothing outside the application window applies to any given application.

▶ KEY TERM

Modal—A style of computer interface in which all of your input, using the keyboard or clicking the menu bar, is interpreted by a single application, until you switch to a different "mode" or application (using the Dock, or by clicking on another application's window). In Mac OS X, you can run dozens of applications at once if you wish, but the menus at the top of the screen all belong to whichever application is currently active in the foreground.

▶ NOTE

Because applications in Mac OS X take over the entire screen context, there is no such thing as "full-screen mode," as Windows users are accustomed to having. All applications are effectively full-screen, even if the window you're working with is very small. This is why there is no "maximize" button in Mac OS X, but rather a **Zoom** button. You will learn more about the **Zoom** button later in this chapter.

Mac OS X has no "Start" button. How do you launch applications, then? Applications are started by double-clicking them where they reside on the hard disk, typically in the systemwide **Applications** folder. Because it can be time-consuming to open the **Applications** folder each time you want to access an application, Mac OS X provides the Dock as a shortcut. The Dock is a broad horizontal strip across the bottom of the screen that stores the icons representing commonly used applications, documents, and other items; it allows you to control these objects with a single click. You will learn more about the Dock later in this chapter.

Quitting applications is a little different in the Mac world. In Windows, you might be accustomed to quitting an application by simply closing its main window. On the Mac, however, because of its modal interface in which an application consists of the entire screen space and not just its main window, it's possible for you to close all of an application's windows and the application will still be running. When this happens, applications continue to run invisibly, taking up memory and other system resources that you might need for other tasks. The correct way to completely exit an application in Mac OS X is to choose the **Quit** option from the application's primary menu. See **2** **Find, Launch, and Quit an Application** for more details.

Finally, if you're a Windows user sitting down at a Mac for the first time, you might notice that there is only one mouse button. You might be used to two or three buttons, a scroll wheel, and other such features. However, all Macs ship with a single-button mouse. You might find this to be absurdly limiting; you might be so used to using the mouse's scroll wheel that you can't imagine computing without it. Don't worry—the good news is that Mac OS X supports scroll wheels, multiple buttons, and all the rest of the advanced mouse features. However, the Mac OS has always been designed with the new computer user in mind: a single mouse button is much easier to understand than multiple buttons. Everyone has been confused by which mouse button to use at some point in their life. Apple's solution is to stick with the one-button mouse, and to design Mac OS X and all Mac applications to use no more than one mouse button. If you have a second or third mouse button, it's a bonus, and provides shortcuts to many common tasks, as in Windows; but it's never, ever *required* to properly use the computer.

Coming from Mac OS 9

Many die-hard Macintosh users see Tiger's predecessor, Mac OS 9, as the ultimate expression of the purity of vision that was the original Macintosh; they claim that Mac OS X is a travesty, a sellout, a mongrel that never should have been. Although there is something to be said for some of the classic Macintosh's admirable design goals, it has to be acknowledged that times have changed. It's not the same computing world that it was in 1984. Most people know basic computing concepts nowadays, such as files and folders and dragging-and-dropping. Moreover, it's a Windows world now; and although no dyed-in-the-wool Mac user will admit to Windows having any technical advantages over the Mac, there is one Windows advantage that cannot be denied: ubiquity. That being the case, the Macintosh must evolve or die.

Fortunately, the compromises that Mac OS X has had to make are of minimal impact, and the advantages it provides are very tangible. For instance, Mac OS X no longer uses the venerable Type and Creator codes to identify (respectively) what kind of file a document is, and what application created it. Instead, Mac OS X uses filename extensions to determine the file type (the extension can be hidden, simply by renaming the file, or by using a check box in most **Save** panels). Mac OS X also provides a global "opener application" framework that allows you to specify the application in which a file will open. This might seem less symmetrical and elegant than the old way, but in practice it's a lot more flexible.

▶ **NOTE**

If you have a JPEG image file with the **.jpg** extension hidden, you never have to see the extension (nor does any other Mac user with whom you share the file), but if you send the file to a Windows or Unix machine, the extension is visible and tells that operating system what kind of file it is.

More visible and less technical differences are, of course, present between Mac OS 9 and Mac OS X. The Dock is the biggest one. In Mac OS 9, you had to launch applications from their locations on the disk or create aliases to them to place on your Desktop, or use a tool called the Launcher. That approach is no longer necessary now that you can simply place application icons directly into the ubiquitous Dock. For the same reason, there is now much less need to keep important documents and folders on the Desktop; they can be kept filed away in your **Home** folder, while simultaneously appearing in the Dock for one-touch access. The Desktop can be kept much tidier this way.

The Control Strip is gone. Quick one-touch actions that once resided in the expandable tab at the bottom of the screen are now incorporated into the *system menus* that occupy the right half of the menu bar. Other functions from the Control Strip now appear in the **Apple** menu, which is now a global control menu with fixed content, rather than the free-form list of user-defined shortcuts that the Apple menu was in the old days. (Those shortcuts now go into—you guessed it—the Dock.)

▶ **NOTE**

The **Apple** menu contains global controls such as logging out, shutting down, putting the computer to sleep, getting system information, controlling various global interface settings, and launching key applications such as **System Preferences**.

The old Control Panels are now consolidated into the **System Preferences** application. Users of Mac OS 9 and earlier will probably not miss the ever-lengthening list of Control Panels that caused interminable conflicts, lockups, and other incompatibilities; also gone are the Extensions, which were incremental additions to the operating system such as device drivers (and not to be confused with filename extensions). Mac OS X still has Extensions, but they're much more tightly controlled and much less user-accessible in the new, security-conscious Unix architecture of the system.

Finally, because of the multi-user nature of Mac OS X, your starting point in the system is no longer the Desktop, but the **Home** folder inside **Users** on the startup disk. Rather than placing all your files in folders on the Desktop or in the top level of the disk, the new way to keep things organized is to start at your **Home** folder and use the labeled subfolders inside it: **Pictures**, **Music**, **Documents**, and so on.

▶ **NOTE**

The idea that the entire disk is no longer your playground for placing files wherever you please can take some getting used to, but in the long run, especially if you share your computer with other users, you'll find that a Mac OS X system is typically far better organized and easier to navigate than any well-used Mac OS 9 system.

The Nickel Tour of Mac OS X

Switch on your Mac. The first thing you will notice—apart from the musical chime that tells you the system is starting up—is that unlike Windows, Mac OS X is graphical from the very first moment the computer begins to *boot*. A gray screen with the Apple logo signifies the first phase of booting, in which Mac OS X examines the computer and its devices, makes sure that they're all in working order, and prepares to start. After this phase is complete, the Mac OS X logo screen appears with a progress bar, along with informative statements about which parts of the operating system are being started. Finally, depending on whether you have enabled automatic *login* or not, you will either be presented with the Login Window or be taken directly to the Desktop of your account.

▶ **KEY TERMS**

Boot—The process of starting up your computer. The term comes from the early tongue-in-cheek concept of the computer "pulling itself up by its own bootstraps."

Login or *Log in*—Mac OS X is a multiuser operating system. This means that each person (or *user*) can start a session with the computer with personalized settings and security privileges. Starting one of these sessions is known as *logging in*, and the window from which you begin a session (by picking a username from a list and typing in a password) is the Login Window.

▶ **NOTES**

If this is the first time you have started your Mac, after it finishes booting, you are guided through a one-time initial personalization process. Enter your name, address, and other personal information into the system for use in many of Mac OS X's convenience features. If you're worried about your personal data being collected by Apple or third-party companies, don't; Apple has one of the best track records in the industry for treating its customers' private information with confidentiality.

During initial setup, if you're using a brand-new computer, you may also be given the opportunity to upgrade from an older Mac. If you want to move your documents and settings from an older computer to the new one, be sure that both computers are equipped with FireWire, and that you have a FireWire cable handy (6-pin to 6-pin). The instructions on the screen will guide you through the process of transferring your data.

The Desktop

As has become traditional in the computer world, your entire screen area is known as the Desktop. This virtual work area contains files (usually referred to as *documents*) and folders, which can be scattered anywhere on the screen, as is true with a real-life desktop. However, Mac OS X's Desktop has numerous features that aren't likely to be found on any office desk.

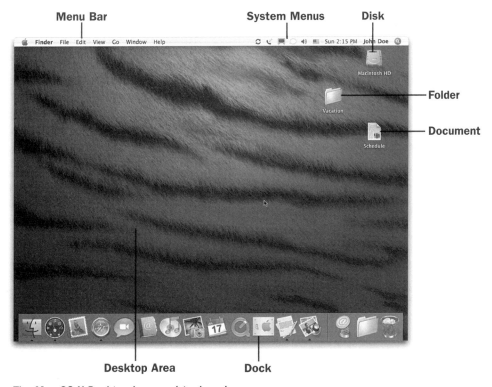

The Mac OS X Desktop is your virtual work area.

In Mac OS X, the Desktop contains nothing but the files and folders you choose to put there. There are no "standard" fixed items, as with **My Computer** in Windows or the hard disks in Mac OS 9. (Disks may appear there, depending on the settings you choose.) The whole Desktop area is yours to scatter with documents and folders; however, considering the ways Mac OS X provides for you to organize your stuff, you shouldn't have to keep documents on the Desktop except for those files you're currently working on.

The Menu Bar

The permanent bar across the top of the screen is the menu bar; it contains all the menus for whatever application is currently active, as well as the **Apple** menu at the far left and the **Spotlight Search** icon at the far right.

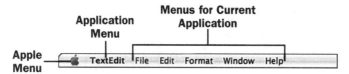

The menu bar changes based on the application that's currently open.

The **Apple** menu contains global options and controls for the entire system; these options are always the same no matter what application is in the foreground. Its contents include general information about your Mac, shortcuts to the controls for the Dock and the **System Preferences**, and controls for shutting down or sleeping the computer.

Next to the **Apple** menu is a menu in bold, labeled with the name of the current application. This menu always contains certain controls for the application, such as the application's Preferences, the "About" information, and the **Quit** function.

▶ NOTE

The rest of the menus are defined by the application and can vary a great deal; usually there are **File** and **Edit** menus, dealing respectively with file management and manipulation of text and data. At the far right is typically the **Help** menu, which contains the application's documentation.

The System Menus

The right side of the menu bar is taken up with the system menus. These are a series of specialized informational icons, each conveying some useful piece of data about the system, and each containing a menu with further information or options.

Shown here are only a few of the possible system menus that can be displayed by the various parts of Mac OS X. Each can be turned on or off at its appropriate place in the **System Preferences** or the application associated with it.

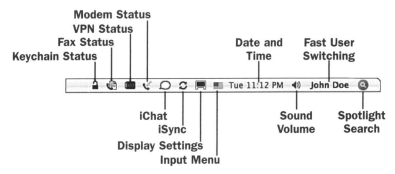

The system menus are iconized to give you visual cues about what functions each controls.

The Dock

At the bottom of the screen is the Dock, a unique feature of Mac OS X. The Dock is a flexible combination of taskbar and document holder. Items in the Dock are all shortcuts or representations that point to real items—applications, documents, or folders—residing anywhere on your disks. You can place anything you like into the Dock by dragging it into place; applications go on the left side of the vertical dividing line, and documents and folders go on the right side. The Dock is anchored on the left by the icon for the **Finder**, which is how you navigate the Mac OS X system; the rightmost icon is the **Trash** can.

▶ NOTE

You can place as many applications or documents in the Dock as you want. As you put more items in the Dock, it expands in width until it fills the entire screen. If you add even more items, the Dock shrinks vertically so that all the icons scale to fit.

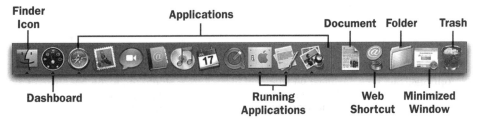

The Dock contains whatever you want it to; applications go on the left and files and folders go on the right.

When an application is running, a black triangle appears underneath its icon in the Dock. You can launch an application from the Dock by clicking its icon once; after the application is running, clicking its icon switches you from whatever else is in the foreground to that application.

On the right side of the Dock are the documents and other items you place there. If you click a document in the Dock, the document's designated opener application launches and opens that document. Click and hold on a folder in the Dock to see a list of the folder's contents from which you can open individual documents.

You can remove any document or any non-running application from the Dock by simply clicking its icon, holding, and dragging it off the Dock. The item disappears in a puff of smoke when it is successfully removed from the Dock; however, this does not mean the item is deleted from the system. It's just no longer shown in the Dock. Think of the Dock as your quick-access system, a collection of shortcuts to whatever resources you use frequently.

▶ NOTE

Hold the **Control** key and click the vertical divider line in the Dock; from the menu that pops up, select **Dock Preferences**. With the dialog box that opens, you can play with some of the Dock's coolest features—size, position on the screen, automatic hiding, and magnification.

The smiley-faced **Finder** icon at the far left of the Dock is what you click to open a new **Finder** window, with which you can navigate your Mac's disks and the surrounding network.

On the far right, the **Trash** can is where you put items you want to delete. Drag documents, folders, and other items from the Desktop or **Finder** windows into the Trash to throw them away; you can retrieve these items by clicking the Trash and dragging them out of the window that appears. You can retrieve thrown-away items until you empty the Trash (using the **Finder** menu at the top of the Desktop). After you empty the Trash (which you should do periodically to regain disk space), the items in the Trash are gone for good.

▶ TIP

Items from different disks can be in your Trash. Until you empty the Trash, thrown-away items will still take up space on whatever disks they're stored on. If you need to free up space on a hard disk, it isn't enough to merely throw unneeded items into the Trash— you also need to empty the Trash before the space is recovered.

The **Trash** icon is also used for ejecting removable disks, burning writable CDs or DVDs, and disconnecting from remote servers. When you drag one of these items to the **Trash**, the **Trash** icon changes to an **Eject** symbol or a **Burn** symbol as appropriate to the kind of item you are dropping onto it.

The Finder

The **Finder** is the built-in application that allows you to navigate through the disks in your Mac. If you click the Finder icon at the left end of the Dock, you will get a window that shows you the items in your **Home** folder.

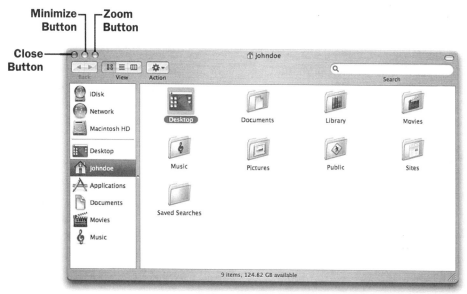

A Finder window.

Clicking the folder icons in the **Finder** allows you to move from one part of the system to another, or from one disk to another, and to view and manipulate your documents. More on navigating the disk later in this chapter.

The Finder window shown here exhibits a crucial part of Mac OS X: the window control buttons. These three buttons, colored like a traffic light (red, yellow, and green), appear on every window of every Mac OS X application:

▶ NOTE

If a window exhibits the colored control buttons in the top left, it's the foremost, or active window, of which there can only be one at a time in the system. Other windows, floating in the background, have their control buttons grayed-out to indicate that the window is not active. However, you can click the control buttons to manipulate even an inactive window—the buttons' colors appear when you move the mouse over them, and the buttons can be used to close, minimize, or zoom the window.

- Clicking the red **Close** button closes any window. If the window contains a document that has been changed (such as a text file in TextEdit), and therefore cannot be closed without either saving the changes or discarding them, a dot appears in the middle of the close button to show that if you click it, you will be prompted for what to do.

- Clicking the yellow **Minimize** button sends the window to the Dock, getting it off your screen so that you can retrieve it later.

- Clicking the green **Zoom** button, in any window, causes the window to automatically size itself to the most efficient size possible—the smallest it can be while showing all the contents of the window, if possible.

Your Disks

Disks, including the built-in hard disk inside your Mac, appear in the upper-right corner of the Desktop. When you *mount* any new disk on the system (a CD-ROM, or an external hard disk, for instance), the new disk's icon appears on the Desktop as well. Double-click any disk to open a **Finder** window showing the disk's contents.

▶ KEY TERMS

Mount—When a disk is connected to the system and can be opened up for navigation, it is *mounted*. Remote network servers can also be mounted by connecting to them as described in Chapter 4, "Networking Your Mac." External storage devices, such as USB memory card readers, typically mount automatically and appear on the Desktop when connected and powered on.

Eject—The opposite of *mount*; ejecting a CD-ROM is the same as "unmounting" it. Remote network servers and external storage devices must be properly ejected before disconnecting them to avoid the risk of data loss.

When you insert a disk, such as a CD-ROM, it appears on the Desktop. To *eject* the disk, you drag it to the **Trash**, which appears at the right end of the Dock. While you're dragging a removable disk, the Trash can icon turns into an **Eject** icon to show that the disk will be ejected when you release the disk icon on top of it.

▶ TIP

If you don't want to see your disks on your Desktop, you can customize their behavior in the **Finder Preferences**. From the **Finder** menu at the left end of the menu bar, choose **Preferences**; under the **General** tab, enable the topmost check boxes to select which kinds of mountable items to show on the Desktop.

Your Home Folder

When you open a Finder window, it opens by default to your **Home** folder. This folder has the same name as your account's "short name," and it resides in the **Users** folder at the top level of your startup hard disk. To learn more about the Home folder, see ⓲ **Add a New User.**

Your **Home** folder is where you spend the majority of your time when organizing and navigating your documents and folders. Inside your **Home** folder are several more folders, each with its own special purpose. Many of these folders are used by applications to store documents of the appropriate types for your quick access.

▶ **NOTE**

There's nothing stopping you from putting, for instance, a Word document in your **Movies** folder, or an MP3 file in the **Pictures** folder. The folders are intended to help you keep your different kinds of data organized, but they don't force you to do so.

- **Desktop**. This special folder is an alias to your actual Desktop space; any documents or folders that appear on the Desktop are actually stored in this folder.

- **Documents**. Any saved files from applications, such as word processing or text documents, project files, spreadsheets, and HTML or PDF files, can be stored in this folder. Many applications default to this folder for saving documents.

- **Library**. The special **Library** folder contains items you install to enhance the system, such as fonts, screen savers, **System Preferences** panes, and plug-ins for applications; it also stores automatically generated items such as application Preferences (in the **Preferences** subfolder), web bookmarks, and logs.

- **Movies**. Keep your video files in this folder.

- **Music**. Store digital audio files here, such as MP3 and AAC files. iTunes keeps your music files organized within this folder.

- **Pictures**. Image files are typically stored in this folder; iPhoto keeps its photo collections here.

- **Public**. Place files in this folder that you want to share with other users over a network.

- **Sites**. Files placed in this folder are accessible to remote Web users accessing your computer through Personal Web Sharing.

Applications

The **Applications** folder sits at the top level of your startup disk and contains all the applications you have installed. *Applications* in Mac OS X are nearly always single objects, like folders or documents, and can be moved to any place in the system without any ill effects; however, it is usually best to keep all your applications in their designated folder. You can quickly access your applications from the icon directly below your **Home** folder in the Sidebar of any Finder window.

▶ KEY TERMS

Application—Also known as a *program*, an application is any piece of software you run within Mac OS X. Adobe Photoshop, Microsoft Word, any game, and the Finder are all applications.

Utility—An application designed for a small, specific purpose. Often, when you close a utility's single window, the entire application quits.

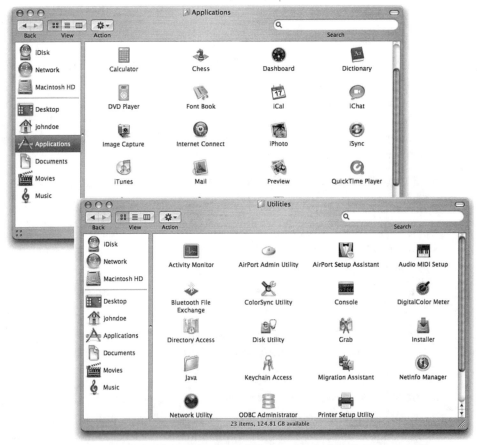

The **Applications** and **Utilities** folders contain all the programs installed on your Mac.

Within the **Applications** folder is a folder called **Utilities**. Tools essential for the management of Mac OS X are kept in this location. Over the course of this book, you will become familiar with many of the *utilities* in this folder.

The Library

There is a **Library** folder at the top level of the disk, as well as one inside your **Home** folder. You have two **Library** folders because of the hierarchical, multiuser nature of Mac OS X. The global and user-level **Library** folders contain much the same sort of items, but the difference is that items installed in the global **Library** apply to all users, whereas the ones in your **Home** folder apply only to you. For instance, you can install a new font in the global **Library** folder, and all users in the system can access it; but if you place the font in your own personal **Library** folder, only you will be able to use it.

A third **Library** folder exists in the **System** folder; this folder's contents apply only to Mac OS X itself, and should not be tampered with (it could destabilize the operating system).

▶ **NOTE**

Generally speaking, you will not need to manually work with the files in either **Library** folder. These folders are mostly maintained by the applications you run. Some items in these folders, such as the **WebServer** folder (the document root for the included Web server), are intended for modification by advanced users.

System Preferences

The central control system for Mac OS X is an application called **System Preferences**. The quickest way to access **System Preferences** is to select it from the **Apple** menu, which is available no matter what application you are currently running.

*The **System Preferences** application is the control center for managing how your Mac looks and acts.*

System Preferences is subdivided into a number of sections, each of which controls a certain area of system configuration, such as **Network, Appearance, CDs & DVDs,** and so on. In this book, according to Mac OS X convention, the individual sections of the **System Preferences** application are referred to as *panes*. Subdivisions of a single pane, which are accessed by clicking a labeled tab at the top of the window, are referred to in this book as *pages*.

▶ **KEY TERM**

Pane—A conceptual section of a **Preferences** window, with its own specialized icon, which controls a certain area of configuration for the system or an application.

▶ **NOTE**

Most applications also have **Preferences** windows that you can summon to control how the application behaves; these windows are often divided into panes just as **System Preferences** is. An application's **Preferences** window is always accessible under the application's primary menu.

The "preference panes" that make up **System Preferences** are grouped into conceptual arrangements. Some preferences apply only to you and the customizations you want to apply to your own login sessions; other preferences apply to the entire system. Some preferences control how certain hardware components will behave, such as the sound system and the display hardware; others manage networking and Internet access.

▶ **TIP**

Feel free to explore the many preference panes and see what kinds of options are available to you; this book explores nearly all of them in the course of explaining the myriad specific tasks that Mac OS X enables you to do.

The Mac's Keyboard

Understanding how the Mac keyboard is laid out, and what its special keys do, is a crucial part of understanding how the Mac works. If you're new to the Mac, the special keys at the bottom of the keyboard might seem weird or esoteric; however, there is a method to their apparent madness.

Modifier Keys

First of all, the Mac has three special modifier keys, found at the bottom of the keyboard. These keys are **Control** (sometimes spelled **Ctrl**), **Option,** and **Command** (also known as the **Apple** key and represented as ⌘). These keys, like the **Ctrl** and **Alt** keys on Windows keyboards, are used in combination with other keys on the keyboard to accomplish certain common functions in the operating system as well as in most applications. However, unlike the modifier keys in Windows, the Mac's modifier keys each have their own specific meanings, which are usually carefully observed by application developers. The keys are also each expressed by their own special symbols, as shown in the following chart.

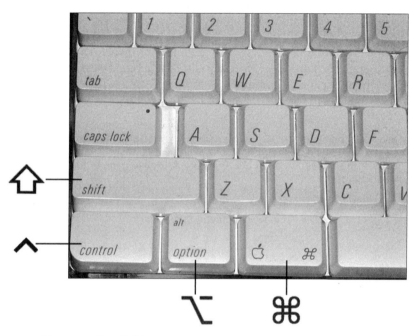

Key	Symbol	Purpose
Command	⌘	In combination with alphanumeric keys, ⌘ (also often called "propeller," "Apple," or "splat") creates shortcuts to actions that are available from the menus in an application.
Option	⌥	The "magic" key. The **Option** key combines with letter keys to allow you to enter special accented or alternate letters or symbols. When combined with mouse actions or graphical buttons, **Option** changes the meanings of common functions to a less-used "alternate" version.
Control		This key simulates the second (right) mouse button of a two-button mouse. Normally, if you click and hold the mouse on an item for a second or two, you will get a contextual menu with shortcuts and other options; however, if you hold down **Control** while clicking, the contextual menu pops up immediately. If you're used to right-clicking things in Windows, **Control**+clicking does much the same thing. Also, **Control** is used for compatibility with Unix applications designed with the PC **Ctrl** key in mind.
Shift	⇧	**Shift** is usually used for capitalizing letters or creating common special characters; however, it is also often used similarly to **Option**: to trigger an "alternate" version of some function.

Key Combinations

The Mac has function keys—**F1** through **F16**—along the top of the keyboard; however, unlike the function keys in Windows, the Mac function keys are hardly ever used for any strictly predefined purpose. In Windows, for example, you can press **Alt+F4** to close a window; this does not work on the Mac. Functions such as closing windows have different, carefully chosen key combinations, based on regular alphanumeric keys and designed to be easily remembered and consistent across nearly all applications. Most of these key combinations involve the **Command** key, although the **Option** or **Shift** key can be combined with other keys to create a secondary, related command.

▶ **NOTE**

On laptop Macs, you have to hold down the **Fn** (**Function**) key to use the **F1** through **F12** keys, as these keys are primarily mapped to functions such as brightness and sound control. You can reverse this configuration in the **Keyboard & Mouse** pane of the **System Preferences** application.

Common Key Combination	Meaning
⌘N	New (window, document, and so on)
⌘W	Close window
⌘Q	Quit application
⌘S	Save document
Shift+⌘+S	Save document as (with a new name)
⌘P	Print
⌘;	Preferences
⌘H	Hide application
⌘C	Copy
⌘X	Cut
⌘V	Paste
⌘.	Stop (interrupt or cancel)

▶ **TIP**

Mac OS X and its applications have many more key combinations than these; you can find them all by looking in the menus, which show the key combinations along with the commands to which they correspond.

▶ **TIP**

You can configure which keys perform which special modifier functions by going to the **Keyboard** tab in the **Keyboard & Mouse Preferences** pane of the **System Preferences** application, and clicking the **Modifier Keys** button. This is also a good way to remind yourself which symbols indicate which modifier keys.

Return and Enter

It must be noted that, on the Mac, the **Enter** key and the **Return** key have different meanings. **Return** is a text-editing key, using the original "carriage return" meaning from the days of typewriters. When you press **Return**, the cursor moves down a line and to the left end of whatever window you're typing in.

The **Enter** key (which in Windows has the same meaning as the Mac's **Return** key) is a little more specialized. When you press **Enter** (usually found on the numeric keypad), Mac OS X interprets the keystroke to mean "Perform the default action in the current window." A window typically has a single flashing blue button in the lower right, which represents the default action for that window; pressing **Enter** simulates clicking that button. In other words, if you're typing in a text box, pressing **Return** will start a new paragraph; pressing **Enter** will cause the program to accept the changes and close the window, as though you had clicked the **OK** button. Some applications don't behave exactly according to this rule, but most do.

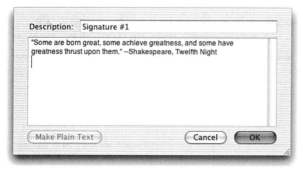

In this application window, press **Return** to start a new line of text; press **Enter** to accept the changes and close the window (as if you'd clicked the **OK** button).

Concluding the Tour

Now that you have seen the highlights of Mac OS X and have a basic understanding of what features do what, a few final notes are in order.

Put the Computer to Sleep

To put your Mac into a state of suspended animation, select the **Sleep** option from the **Apple** menu. The computer will appear to shut down, the fans and hard drive will spin down, and the display will go dark, but the power indicator light, which varies from model to model but which is usually purple, will pulse gently. This means that you can immediately wake the computer from sleep at any time by pressing a key or moving the mouse. The computer will immediately become usable again, without having to go through the entire boot cycle.

Because a Mac uses almost no power during sleep, it is the preferred means for turning the computer off for the night; Sleep mode is especially well suited to laptops, which automatically go to sleep when you close the lid. However, a sleeping Mac must still be connected to power; you can't unplug a sleeping iMac or remove an iBook's battery, or the computer will shut off entirely. (PowerBooks can remain running in sleep mode for a few minutes with the battery disconnected, allowing you to swap out an exhausted battery for a fresh one.)

▶ NOTE

If your computer does not shut down cleanly—for instance, if the power cord is pulled, there is a power outage, or a sleeping laptop runs out of battery power—it may take longer to boot the next time you switch it on. Mac OS X has to repair the fragmentation on the disk that is caused when the machine shuts down unexpectedly, and these repairs can take a minute or more.

Log Out

To end your computing session, select **Log Out** *<Your Name>* from the **Apple** menu. This will automatically quit all your running applications and return you to the **Login** window. If you use a Mac that is shared among several users, you will want to *log out* each time you're done using the computer. Logging out protects your documents and settings from being altered or even seen by any other users (to see your documents, another person must have your login password). It's always a good idea to log out if there's any chance of someone else using the computer or of the computer being lost. If someone steals your laptop, logging out protects your sensitive documents even from a thief's prying eyes. To learn how to make your files even more secure, see **136** **Secure Your Files with FileVault**.

▶ KEY TERM

Log out—To end a login session. When you log out, you are returned to the **Login** window.

Shut Down

If you want to completely shut down your Mac, choose **Shut Down** from the **Apple** menu. As with the **Log Out** option, the Mac automatically quits any open applications and ends your session; however, it will then proceed to clean up the system and then methodically power down. There is no need to press any switches—the computer will shut itself off completely. This is the safest method for deactivating your computer when you're done using it; it's safe to unplug the Mac or open it up to change the internal hardware after it has shut down. However, because shutting down and then *restarting* (a "warm boot") takes much longer than simply waking from sleep (which is almost instantaneous), it is usually not desirable to shut down completely unless you have a good reason to do so.

▶ **KEY TERM**

Restart—To shut down the entire system and immediately boot it again, as though you had turned off the power and switched it back on. This process is also known as a *reboot* or a *warm boot* (a *cold boot* is when you start the computer after it's been shut off completely), and is typically necessary only if something goes badly wrong with the operating system—an unlikely occurrence in Mac OS X.

Navigating Mac OS X

Particularly if you're already familiar with another operating system (Windows or Mac OS 9), navigating through the structure of a Mac OS X system can be a challenging and unusual task. Mac OS X isn't any more complex than these other operating systems, but it's *different* enough from them that if you don't know what to look for, you could find yourself at a loss for what to do next.

Following this chapter, this book is filled with step-by-step demonstrations of useful tasks you can accomplish with Mac OS X. However, before we can proceed to those tasks, it is necessary to provide some detailed background on the **Finder**—the application that allows you to move through the system and find the resources you're looking for.

Structure of a Disk

Without disks, Mac OS X is nothing. The system must boot from a "startup disk," which is a disk with a full installation of Mac OS X on it. A startup disk (or startup *volume*) can be a hard disk, a CD-ROM or DVD, an external drive connected with FireWire or USB cables, or even a remote disk accessible over the network—anything with a readable *filesystem*. The entire operating system (which consumes about three gigabytes of disk space) must be available on a mounted disk for the Mac to function.

▶ **KEY TERMS**

Volume—Any disk (or portion of a disk that has been partitioned) is a volume, a discrete storage resource that can appear on the Desktop or in the Finder.

Filesystem—A term that refers to the software architecture that allows the operating system to read from and write to a volume. It also can mean simply a volume; for instance, your startup disk is both a volume and a filesystem.

▶ **NOTE**

Every item in the system can be located by describing its *path* (the names of the folders you have to open to get to that item). You will seldom see a path written out in text, but if you do, it is described as a series of folder names separated by slashes or colons. For instance, the **Home** folder for a user called **johndoe** is inside the **Users** folder of the startup disk; its full path is **/Volumes/Macintosh HD/Users/johndoe**, though it may be shown only as **/Users/johndoe**, depending on the context. Some applications might show the path as **Macintosh HD:Users:johndoe**.

Beyond just the operating system, however, is the part of the disk that you will be using. As you saw earlier in this chapter, your **Home** folder also resides on the startup disk of the operating system, in the **Users** folder. As you use the system, the applications you run will create files, all of which will be stored within the **Home** folder; this goes for documents you create, files you download from the Internet, and preference files and other supporting data for your applications. To use all these files, you must be able to find them; that's where the Finder comes in.

Know the Finder

Click the **Finder** icon at the left end of the Dock. A window opens up that should look like the one shown here.

▶ **NOTE**

To hide or show the labels on the Finder's toolbar buttons or customize which control buttons are available, choose **View**, **Customize Toolbar** while a Finder window is open.

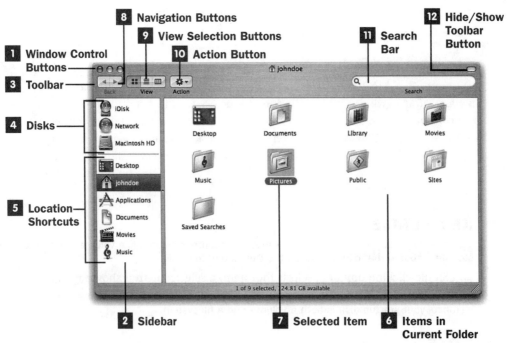

A Finder window.

▶ **NOTE**

Removable disks—such as CDs, DVDs, card readers, network servers, external floppy or optical drives, and iPods—have an **Eject** button next to them in the Sidebar. Clicking this button ejects the disk in the case of truly removable media such as CDs or floppies, or unmounts it in the case of fixed USB, FireWire, or network devices.

❶ Window Control Buttons

Use these buttons to close, minimize, or zoom the window.

❷ Sidebar

The entire Dock-like section on the left side of the Finder window is the Sidebar. It provides starting points for you to use in navigating the disk.

❸ Toolbar

The buttons across the top of the window are all part of the toolbar, which provides controls that apply to all Finder windows. You can customize which buttons appear in the toolbar, using the **Customize Toolbar** command in the **View** menu.

❹ Disks

This area shows all the disks and other data sources available in your system. Click on any disk to show its contents.

❺ Location Shortcuts

Each item here is a link to a folder in the system; clicking an icon takes you to that folder's contents. You can add folders to this pane by dragging them into position, much as you can with the Dock.

❻ Items in Current Folder

Depending on the view you have selected (using the **View** selection buttons), icons representing the contents of the current folder are displayed arbitrarily or in organized listings. Double-click any folder to open it in the same **Finder** window; double-click any document to open it in its default opener application.

❼ Selected Item

Single-clicking any item selects that item; a selected item is shown with a darkened box around it and its label highlighted in a colored oval. You can select multiple items by clicking and dragging a box around them.

❽ Navigation Buttons

As you move through the system of folders, you can move back and forth through your navigation history using these buttons.

9 View Selection Buttons

Choose Icon view, List view, or Column view. Each view has its own advantages and specialized options. You will see each of these views in detail later in this chapter.

10 Action Button

Use this button to perform specific actions on any documents or folders you have selected. Available actions include opening documents or folders, setting color labels, getting detailed file info, or moving items to the Trash.

11 Search Bar

Type in this field to perform an instant search on whatever text you type. See **12 Find an Item** for more on searching with Spotlight.

12 Hide/Show Toolbar Button

This button allows you to hide or show the toolbar (the row of control buttons) and the Sidebar.

The Finder is a flexible piece of software that can be tailored to however you are most comfortable using it. Let's take a look at what some of its controls do. First we have the three different view modes, which you can switch between at any time. Each view mode has a particular strength—speed of navigation, amount of information, configurability of presentation—and is weak in others. You will find that different view modes are appropriate for different areas of the system.

▶ TIP

You can assign a different view mode to every folder in the system. One folder can be in Icon view (with large icons), another might be in List view (with small icons), and a third can be in Column view. Each folder stores the view settings that were in effect when you closed the window in which you were viewing that folder; if you then open that folder directly, it opens with the same view settings it had when you last closed it.

Icon View

The first view option is Icon view. Each document and folder in the window appears as a pictograph or icon, with a label underneath it or to the right. Depending on your settings for the folder, the icons can be arranged in a strict grid pattern or scattered arbitrarily around the window. You can click and drag icons from one part of the window to another; some application developers create artistic presentation folders this way, as you will see in **1 Install an Application from Disc or Download**.

Icon View Button

*A Finder window in Icon view, and its **View Options** panel.*

Icon view is the most configurable of the views. To configure the view, choose **Edit**, **View Options**; a panel opens in which you can select your viewing preferences, such as the background color or picture, or the icon arrangement.

▶ **TIP**

Hold down the **Command** and **Option** keys, then click and drag to pan around a window in Icon view.

To open a folder shown in Icon view, double-click it; the new folder opens in the same Finder window, its contents replacing those of the folder you were in previously. Alternatively, you can have the new folder open in a new Finder window, by holding down the **Command** key while you double-click. If you hold down the **Option** key while double-clicking a folder icon, the new folder will open in a new window *and* the old window will close.

▶ **TIP**

Hold down the **Command** key and click the title of the Finder window to see a pop-up menu showing all the folders in the path to your current location. This action lets you easily jump to any point along the folder path.

Icon view is aesthetically pleasing and very useful for displaying folders with a few special items in it, but for easier sorting or quicker navigation, the other two views are often preferable.

▶ **TIP**

If you've got an Icon view window that has icons scattered haphazardly all over the place, select **View**, **Clean Up**. The icons all snap to an organized grid layout.

List View

List View Button

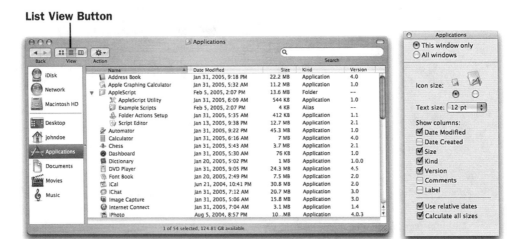

*A Finder window in List view, and its **View Options** panel.*

List view provides the most information about the items in a folder. Documents and folders are listed alphabetically (if you're accustomed to Windows, you might be surprised at first to see that folders are alphabetized right along with documents, instead of being shown first in the listing as in Windows). However, several additional columns show extra information about each item. You can click the column headings to sort the items based on whichever column you choose. These columns include the time of last modification or access, size, kind, version, and label color; in the **View Options** panel, you can enable or disable these columns according to your taste.

Navigating in List view is more flexible than in Icon view. To the left of each folder is a small triangular arrow pointing right; if you click the arrow, it turns downward, and the folder's contents are displayed, indented under the folder. This arrangement allows you to open branches of the hierarchy of folders underneath the current folder. However, to see folders higher up in the hierarchy, you must use another method to move back along the path, such as clicking the **Back** button at the top of the window or holding down **Command** while clicking the window title.

List view is tailored for showing the maximum amount of item information possible, at the expense of the prettiness of Icon view. However, it's still not the easiest mode for fast navigation; for that, you need Column view.

▶ TIPS

You can select a set of items in the same spatial area by clicking and dragging to create a selection box around the items.

You can click to select one item, scroll to another item further down the list, and press **Shift** while clicking to select the entire intervening range of items.

Hold down **Command** while clicking individual items in succession; each additional item you click is added to the selection. **Command**+click individual selected items to deselect them while leaving the rest selected.

⌘**A** is nearly always a key combination for **Select All Items**.

Column View

Although Icon view and List view have been in the Mac OS for many years, Column view is a new addition to Mac OS X—but not a new idea. It first appeared in the NeXT operating system, which also pioneered features such as the Dock, which eventually made their way—in heavily altered form—into Mac OS X.

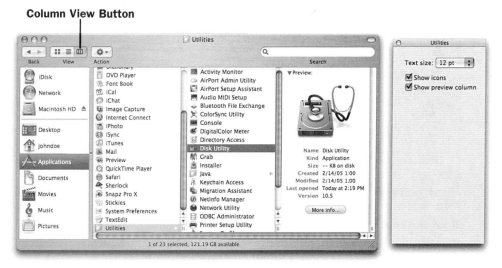

A Finder window in Column view, and its **View Options** *panel.*

The idea of Column view is pretty simple: your window contains a series of columns, each of which represents a folder. The columns can be scrolled left and right, and picking a folder from any column causes that folder's contents to be shown in a new column to the right. This way, the entire path through a folder hierarchy can be represented in a single left-to-right view, and you can scroll horizontally to any point along the path.

If you select a file in a folder, the column to the right displays that file's preview and vital information, along with a **More Info** button that opens the item's familiar info panel. However, you don't get to see much else in the way of item information in Column view. All that's visible in a folder list are the icons and item names, which are always sorted alphabetically. Column view is designed with easy navigation as its primary goal, and the tradeoff in this case is information visibility. If you need to move quickly up and down through the folders on a disk, but you don't especially need to see the detailed information on all the items along the way, Column view is the most efficient way to do it.

The Action Button

In a Finder window, there are several things you can do to a document or folder directly without need for any extra applications; these include labeling items, creating new folders, getting detailed information on items, duplicating items, and moving items to the Trash. These operations are all grouped into the **Action** button.

The Action button and its contextual menu.

If you click the **Action** button without having selected any items, you will see only two options listed in its context menu: **New Folder** and **Get Info**. However, if you select one or more items first, the menu is filled with options.

▶ **TIP**

Most of the actions that can be launched from the **Action** button are described in 🔢 **Find an Item,** 🔢 **Create a New Folder,** and 🔢 **Set a Color Label.**

Use the Second Mouse Button

Contrary to popular belief, the Mac does not limit you to a single-button mouse, even if that's all Apple sells; you are perfectly free to plug in a two-button or three-button mouse, or one with a scroll wheel, and Mac OS X will support the extra features without any need for extra drivers. The operating system is designed to require no more than a single mouse button, but if you have more mouse buttons, they can provide you with shortcuts to commonly used functions.

The contextual menu resulting from right-clicking an item.

For instance, in the Finder, right-clicking a document or folder opens a contextual menu that matches the one you get from selecting the item and then clicking the **Action** button. (You can also get the same menu by holding down **Control** while clicking on the item.) The right-click context menu lets you perform an action on the item with two clicks in the same general vicinity, rather than three or four clicks and drags that require you to move the mouse all around the window. The **Action** button provides all the functionality available in the system, so a single-button mouse can accomplish everything the system offers, but a multi-button mouse saves you time and effort.

Hide the Toolbar and Sidebar

The elongated white button in the upper-right corner of the Finder window is an interface element that appears in the Finder and a handful of other applications; its purpose is to let you shrink the window to its bare minimum components, hiding the toolbar and Sidebar from view so that all you see is the window and its contents.

A Finder window with the toolbar (at the top of the window) and the Sidebar hidden.

▶ TIP

Double-click the vertical divider between the Sidebar (on the left) and the document pane (on the right) to hide the Sidebar. You can also drag the divider back and forth to adjust the size of the panes.

If you hide the toolbar, be aware that you won't be able to change view modes or navigate back and forth using the mouse; you can use keyboard shortcuts for navigating (⌘[and ⌘]), and you can change the view mode using the **View** menu. But actions from the **Action** button's context menu must be selected from the **File** menu or by right-clicking the item you want to work with. A window with the toolbar hidden can be more streamlined and take up less space, but it's missing many amenities you might decide are too useful not to have available.

▶ NOTE

In Icon view with the toolbar hidden, if you double-click a folder, the new folder opens by default in a new window; if the toolbar is shown, double-clicking a folder opens the new folder in the same window. It's assumed that if you have the toolbar hidden, you expect to have your navigation path available in the form of the windows you have opened to get to your current position.

The Get Info Panel

Each document or folder has a wealth of information associated with it. On the Mac, documents can have custom icons, version numbers, opener applications, access permissions, comments, and other bits and pieces of data that are normally useful only to applications. The **Get Info** panel lets you examine that information for each item in the system.

*The **Get Info** panel for a document.*

The **Get Info** panel consists of several subpanels, each of which can be expanded or collapsed by clicking the triangle arrow in the left corner of each one. You can use the **Get Info** panel to change many of a file's attributes: You can show or hide the filename extension (or remove it entirely), you can change the opener application, you can set a comment, and you can modify the access permissions. Some of these processes are covered in **7 Assign an Opener Application to a File**, **17 Change an Icon**, and **18 Set a Color Label**. For now, remember that the **Get Info** panel can always be accessed for any item by selecting **Get Info** from the **Action** button menu or by pressing ⌘I.

Customize the Finder

The control buttons you see in the toolbar at the top of the Finder aren't all you get; there's actually more to the toolbar than you have yet seen.

One of the unique features of Mac OS X is that many applications have toolbars that can be customized with whatever set of control buttons you like. The Finder is one of these applications. Select **Customize Toolbar** from the **View** menu to see a sheet full of controls you can place in the Finder's toolbar.

*The **Customize Toolbar** sheet for the Finder.*

▶ **TIP**

⌘+click the **Hide Toolbar** button (at the top right corner of the Finder window) to cycle through the various types of icons and labels you can use—small or large icons, with or without labels. Adding the **Option** key (⌘+**Option**+click) opens the **Customize Toolbar** sheet.

To add any of the listed controls to the toolbar, simply drag them into place where you want them to appear. To remove a control from the toolbar, drag it off the window; it will disappear in a puff of smoke. If you put too many items on the toolbar for them all to be visible simultaneously, the ones that can't be shown are accessible by clicking an arrow at the right end of the toolbar.

Feel free to experiment with these controls; you can arrange them any way you like, and you can always go back to the way it was before by dragging the "default set" of controls into the toolbar; this resets the controls to their factory settings.

You can also use the controls at the bottom of the sheet to control whether the toolbar controls are shown as icons, as text labels, or as both. You can reduce the size of the buttons by enabling the **Use Small Size** check box.

You can control another set of global Finder options in the **Finder Preferences** window. Open this dialog box by selecting **Preferences** from the **Finder** menu.

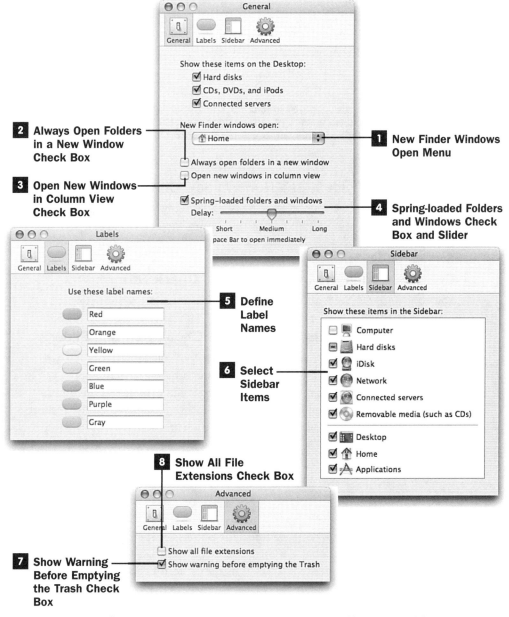

The *Finder Preferences* window, showing the *General*, *Labels*, *Sidebar*, and *Advanced* panes.

Options you can configure in these panels include (as you have seen earlier) which types of storage devices you want to display on the Desktop as well as the following behaviors:

1 New Finder Windows Open Menu

You can select whether opening a new Finder window starts you in your **Home** folder (the default behavior) or with the entire **Computer** view, which lets you see all the available disks and resources attached to your Mac. Because the Finder already shows you all the disks in the Sidebar, it's probably best to leave this option set to **Home**.

▶ NOTE

An older Mac that has been upgraded to Mac OS X might have a lot of data folders at the top level of the hard disk. Instead of moving all these folders into your **Home** folder, you might prefer to configure the Finder to use the **Computer** view to access them more easily.

2 Always Open Folders in a New Window Check Box

You can select to have each new folder open in a new window. Enabling this option is equivalent to holding down the **Command** key while you double-click a folder icon.

3 Open New Windows in Column View Check Box

You can choose to have all new folder windows open in Column view.

4 Spring-loaded Folders and Windows Check Box and Slider

Spring-loaded folders is a convenience feature that allows you to navigate through the folders in your disk while dragging a file at the same time. While holding down the mouse button and dragging a file icon, hover the mouse over a folder in the Finder; regardless of what view you're using, after a short delay the folder blinks and then pops open. You can then drop the file into that folder (and it will close), or you can drive still deeper into other folders using the same method. The slider in the **Finder Preferences** dialog box lets you control the length of the delay before the folder pops open.

5 Define Label Names

In the **Labels** pane, you can customize the names for each of the seven different colored labels available. For instance, if you like to use red labels for items that are urgent, you can change its name from **Red** to **Urgent**. The new label name will appear in all textual representations of the label in the Finder, such as in the **Label** column in List view. For more about labels, see **18 Set a Color Label**.

6 Select Sidebar Names

The **Sidebar** pane lets you select which kinds of media (disks, servers, and other data sources) as well as which folders or documents will appear in the Finder's Sidebar. Use the check boxes to enable or disable the indicated items. The options you select here do not affect items you drag into the Sidebar manually.

7 Show Warning Before Emptying the Trash Check Box

In the **Advanced** pane, you can turn off the warning that appears when you empty the Trash, permanently deleting whatever items are in it.

8 Show All File Extensions Check Box

If you want, you can choose to show filename extensions under all circumstances, even if the extension is hidden. This can be useful if you do a lot of cross-platform work and don't want to be confused about whether a file has a hidden extension that will appear when transferred to a Windows or Unix system, or whether it has no extension at all. However, because the hiding of a file's extension can be toggled on and off simply by renaming the file and adding or removing an extension as appropriate, this option is probably not likely to be useful unless you're a hardcore purist.

2

Working with Applications

IN THIS CHAPTER:

Without applications, all you can do with Mac OS X is move files around and change their names, or customize your work environment. Applications are what make a computer into a tool for accomplishing useful tasks, which is what this book is all about.

Mac OS X comes with many applications bundled by Apple as part of the operating system. Indeed, it is entirely possible to live the Digital Hub life (as promoted by Apple's marketing team) using only the applications that come with your Mac; after all, Apple produces more cutting-edge software for more diverse purposes than just about any other technology company in the world. Software such as iTunes, iMovie, and Safari that come with your Mac have one thing in common with high-end third-party applications such as Adobe Photoshop and QuarkXPress: They're all *applications*, which is to say they're self-contained programs you run to accomplish some task and quit when you're done using them.

This chapter addresses the skills necessary to manage your applications, install and delete them, and make them interact with your files so that they do what you need them to do.

1 Install an Application from Disc or Download

→ **SEE ALSO**

3 Add an Application to the Dock
9 Uninstall an Application

Installing an application under Mac OS X is considerably different from the way it's traditionally done under Windows. Because Mac OS X has no central Registry for storing application data (as Windows does), and because Mac OS X applications are single monolithic "bundles"—which can be moved around from place to place or from disk to disk as though each application is a single file (rather than being folders full of DLLs and config files, as it's traditionally done in Windows)—oftentimes installing an application involves nothing more complicated than dragging an icon from one disk window to another.

Some applications under Mac OS X do use installer programs, as is typical of Windows; this is usually the case with large and complex software, such as Adobe Photoshop or Microsoft Office. When an application uses an installer program, it's usually because the installer has to add resources to the system, such as Library frameworks or kernel extensions, or because it allows you to perform a custom installation, containing only a subset of the complete package. (Microsoft Office, for example, allows you to choose between either a drag-and-drop complete install, or an installer program which allows you to select just the parts of Office that you need.) The more complex the software, the more likely you will need to run an installer.

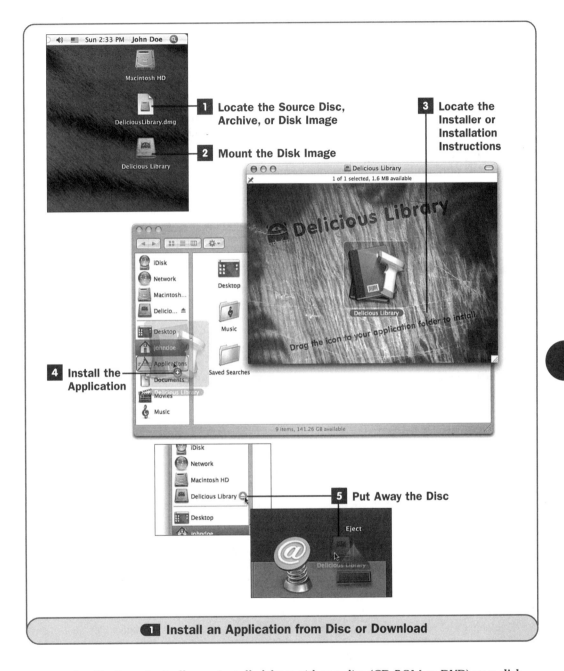

1 Locate the Source Disc, Archive, or Disk Image

2 Mount the Disk Image

3 Locate the Installer or Installation Instructions

4 Install the Application

5 Put Away the Disc

1 Install an Application from Disc or Download

Applications typically are installed from either a disc (CD-ROM or DVD) or a *disk image*. In either case, the process for installing the application is generally the same: You must *mount* the source disk, then open it up to see what the installation procedure is. We will look at both an application that requires an installer program (iTunes), and one that must simply be dragged from its disk image to your **Applications** folder (Delicious Library, an excellent organizational tool for DVDs, CDs, and books).

▶ KEY TERMS

Archive—A collection of documents, folders, or applications that are packed into a single file, which is usually compressed so it can be easily downloaded. On the Mac, archives can be Windows-style ZIP files (with **.zip** extensions), **.sit** (StuffIt) files, **.tar.gz** files (for Unix utilities), or disk images.

Disk image—A specialized kind of archive file, a disk image is a file that when opened acts like a regular disk that you mount on the system. Disk image files end in **.dmg** or **.img**; if you double-click on one, the Disk Utility application opens up and expands the disk image into a virtual disk mounted in the Finder. You can then browse it or manipulate its contents just as you would any real disk.

1 Locate the Source Disc, Archive, or Disk Image

An application downloaded from the Internet is usually in the form of an *archive* file. This file can be either a compressed folder (usually with a .zip, .hqx, or .sit extension) or a disk image.

Downloaded files usually appear directly on the Desktop. If you don't see your file there, your browser might be using a different location for its download files. Many web browsers provide a "download manager" tool that allows you to locate a downloaded file and open it automatically.

If you're using the Safari web browser, many downloaded applications will unpack, mount, and copy themselves automatically, and even clean up after themselves, leaving only a single icon for the application sitting on your Desktop. If this is the case, you can skip the rest of this task and simply move the icon into your **Applications** folder for best organization, or just run the application from where it is.

▶ TIP

Check the **Preferences** of your web browser to see where it is configured to save downloaded files. Safari, the built-in Mac OS X browser, is normally set up to save downloads to the Desktop, but if you can't find files you've downloaded, the browser might be set to save them somewhere else.

▶ TIP

Beginning with Mac OS X Tiger, StuffIt Expander (which is used to open archive files in the popular .sit format) is no longer included with the operating system. Visit **http://www.stuffit.com** and download the free StuffIt Expander to ensure you'll always be able to open downloaded application archives.

2 Mount the Disk Image

If your application is on a CD-ROM or DVD, insert it into the drive. Its icon will appear on the Desktop, or in the Finder's sidebar (if you have configured the Finder to show removable disks in the sidebar).

If the application is an archive file downloaded from the Internet, double-click its file icon. If it's a ZIP or SIT archive, StuffIt Expander launches and expand the file into a folder. If it's a disk image, however, Disk Utility launches and transforms the file into a virtual disk, mounted on your Desktop or in the Finder's sidebar.

▶ **TIP**

Many browsers, such as Safari, automatically expand archive files when they're done downloading. Safari launches StuffIt Expander to unpack SIT archives; if the downloaded file is a disk image (with a **.dmg** extension), or if a SIT archive expands into a disk image, Safari opens the disk image and mounts it as a disk on the Desktop. When downloading an application from the Internet, wait until the browser finishes unpacking it to either an application folder (as with GraphicConverter) or a mounted disk image (as with Delicious Library), and then use that item to install the application.

3 Locate the Installer or Installation Instructions

At this point, you have the application source disk mounted—whether it's an inserted disc or a disk image. Navigate to the disk's contents in the Finder or double-click its icon on the Desktop. A Finder window opens, showing the disk's contents.

▶ **TIP**

It's a good idea to keep the download page open in your browser even after you've downloaded the archive or disk image file; the page often contains useful installation instructions.

The window should contain instructions for installation, a "Read Me" document, or a "package" file (which is an installer application that you must double-click). Each application is distributed differently. The Delicious Library disk image, for instance, has clear instructions for what to do next, whereas the installer folder for iTunes contains nothing but a package file. If it's not clear what you need to do, look for a "Read Me" file or other similar instructional document.

4 Install the Application

Delicious Library's installation instructions are clear enough: Simply drag the application icon from the disk image folder to your **Applications** folder. To do this, open a second Finder window by clicking the **Finder** icon at the far left of the Dock or by pressing ⌘**N**. Then drag the Delicious Library folder from the first window to the **Applications** folder icon in the second window.

1

Many other applications, however, have an installer program. To install iTunes, for instance, double-click the **iTunes.pkg** file icon to launch the installer. Follow the onscreen instructions, which direct you to choose an installation disk, accept the user agreement, and restart the computer at the end (if necessary).

⑤ Put Away the Disc

A disk image can be unmounted (or ejected) just like any other disk. Drag its icon to the **Trash** in the Dock (which turns into an Eject symbol, labeled **Eject**), or click the **Eject** button next to its icon in the Finder's sidebar. The original disk image file is still there; you might want to create a special folder to keep it in, such as one called **Downloaded Software** in your **Documents** folder, in case you need it later (for instance, to reinstall the application or review the installation notes). See ⑬ **Create a New Folder**.

If you're installing from an inserted disc, when you eject it (using the same method) the drive door opens, allowing you to remove the disc.

1

2 **Find, Launch, and Quit an Application**	
✔ **BEFORE YOU BEGIN**	→ **SEE ALSO**
❶ Install an Application from Disc or Download	❸ Add an Application to the Dock

---

In Mac OS X, applications reside primarily in the **Applications** folder. The most basic way to launch an application is to navigate to that folder and double-click its icon.

❶ Open a Finder Window

Click the **Finder** icon at the far left end of the Dock, or press ⌘N while in the Finder to open a new Finder window.

▶ NOTE

Old Mac hands may be accustomed to the ⌘N keystroke creating a new folder, not a new Finder window. In the Mac OS X tradition, though, ⌘N is used for creating a new instance of whatever the standard window is for the current application, and that applies to the Finder, too. **Shift** invokes an "alternative" function; use ⌘+**Shift+N** to create a new folder.

▶ TIP

You can tell what application you're currently in by the boldfaced menu name to the right of the **Apple** icon in the menu bar at the top-left of the screen. If you aren't in the Finder, click anywhere on the Desktop to switch to the Finder.

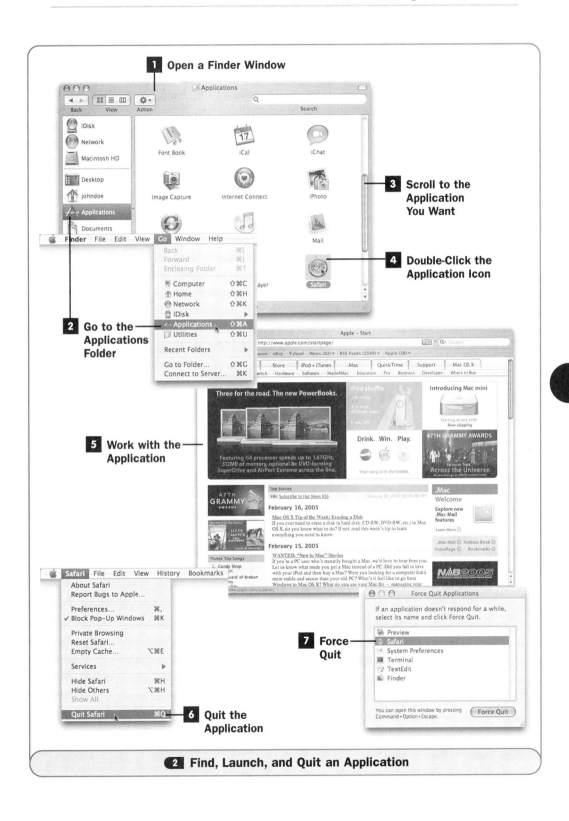

1 Open a Finder Window

3 Scroll to the Application You Want

4 Double-Click the Application Icon

2 Go to the Applications Folder

5 Work with the Application

7 Force Quit

6 Quit the Application

2 Find, Launch, and Quit an Application

2 Go to the Applications Folder

The lower-left pane of the Finder window contains a shortcut icon to the **Applications** folder. Click this icon to open the **Applications** folder. Alternatively, select **Applications** from the Finder's **Go** menu, or press **Shift+⌘+A**. (With this key command, you don't even have to open a Finder window first.)

3 Scroll to the Application You Want

Depending on the view mode you're in, the applications in the folder will be arranged differently—generally alphabetically, but Icon view and List view allow the applications to be sorted by many other criteria. Use the scroll bars to search through the window until you find the application you're looking for.

▶ TIP

If you know the application's name, try using the **Search** bar at the top of the Finder window. Click **Computer** in the resulting Spotlight view to ensure you're searching all local disks.

4 Double-Click the Application Icon

When you double-click the application in the Finder, the application icon appears in the Dock, bouncing up and down. It will keep bouncing until the application has completed launching; after that, a black triangle underneath the icon shows that the application is running.

▶ TIP

Almost every application has **preferences** you can set. Preferences (which under Windows are often variously called **Options** or **Settings**) control the application's behavior, appearance, and interaction with the rest of your system. By convention for consistency, every Mac application's **preferences** are accessible from the bold-titled application menu. The keyboard shortcut to reach **Preferences** is typically ⌘, (comma).

5 Work with the Application

When the application has launched completely, you can begin to use it. With most applications, you can choose **File**, **Open** from the menu bar to select an existing document with which you want to continue working or editing. To open a new document in most applications, choose **File**, **New**, or press ⌘N.

6 Quit the Application

In Mac OS X, just because all the application's windows have been closed does not mean the application is no longer running. (This may surprise Windows users, as a Windows application whose main window has been closed is typically understood to have been completely quit.) An application can be running with no windows open; it's still taking up memory and system resources. If you want to quit an application, you must explicitly tell it to quit.

Under the bold application menu, no matter what application you're running, the last option is always **Quit**. Switch to the application you want to quit, open the application menu, and select **Quit**. You may be prompted to save changes in whatever document windows you have open. The standard key combination for the **Quit** command is ⌘**Q**.

▶ TIP

After you launch an application or open a document, it is entered automatically into the **Recent Items** submenu of the **Apple** menu. You can access these recently opened items quickly from that menu without having to navigate to their disk locations again.

2

7 Force Quit

Sometimes, an application might misbehave, crash, freeze, or otherwise become unresponsive. Mac OS X is robust enough that if this happens, you can generally switch to another application and continue using the rest of the system; but to stop the misbehaving application and get it to stop using system resources, you might have to force it to quit. This method immediately terminates the application without saving any changes in memory; it's sort of messy, but it gets the job done.

Press ⌘+**Option+Escape** or select **Force Quit** from the **Apple** menu. The **Force Quit Applications** dialog box appears, showing a list of all currently running applications. Select the one you want to quit and click the **Force Quit** button. The misbehaving application is immediately terminated.

▶ TIP

If your Mac becomes unresponsive or extremely slow, and you don't know which application or process is causing it, a handy tool is the **Activity Monitor**, located in the **Utilities** folder (if you're able to get to it). It shows all currently active processes, and if you sort them on the % **CPU** column, you can determine whether one process has gone haywire by taking up all the processor's attention. Select it and click **Quit Process** to end it; your system's performance should return to normal.

3 Add an Application to the Dock

✔ BEFORE YOU BEGIN	→ SEE ALSO
1 Install an Application from Disc or Download	**4** Control an Application from the Dock
	5 Minimize and Restore a Window
	106 Change the Dock's Position and Behavior

Navigating to the **Applications** folder every time you want to launch an application can be tiresome. Fortunately, the Dock is there to act as a combination launch bar and task manager. You can add shortcuts to as many applications as you want to the Dock; after an application is on the Dock, your access to that application is just a single click away.

▶ **TIP**

You can add all kinds of items to the Dock—not just applications. Right of the vertical dividing line, you can place documents, folders, aliases, and even whole disks if you like. You just can't put them to the left of the dividing line, and you can't place applications to the right of the line.

3

1 Open a Finder Window

Click the **Finder** icon at the left end of the Dock, or press ⌘N while in the Finder to open a new Finder window.

2 Locate the Application You Want

Navigate to the **Applications** folder using the shortcut in the lower-left Finder pane, or choose **Go, Applications** from the menu bar at the top of the Desktop. Scroll to the frequently used application icon you're looking for.

▶ **TIP**

It's even simpler to add an application permanently to the Dock if the application is already running. Click the application icon in the Dock and hold; after a moment, the contextual menu appears above the icon. Select **Keep In Dock**. The application icon will remain in the Dock even after you quit it.

3 Drag the Application to the Dock

Click the application icon in the Finder; holding down the mouse button, drag the icon into the Dock, to any position left of the vertical divider bar. Move the icon between any two icons you like, and they will separate to make room for the new icon. Release the mouse button, and the icon settles into position. After that, a single click on the Docked icon launches the application.

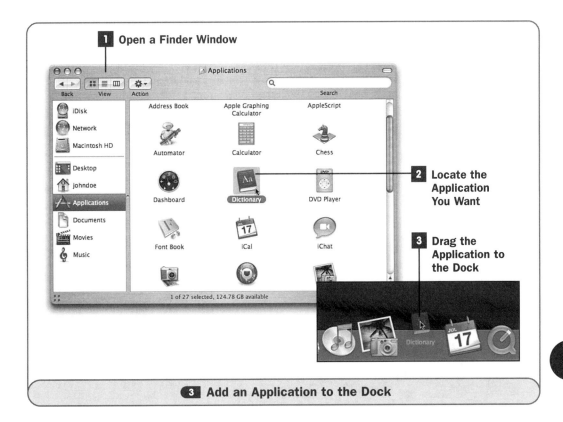

Add an Application to the Dock

▶ **NOTE**

A translucent "question mark" symbol in the Dock signifies an item that had previously been placed in the Dock, but that no longer exists on the disk. If you see one of these question marks, hover your mouse over it to see what it's labeled; if the name is that of an application or document that you know you have on your system and you want to keep in your Dock, locate that item in the Finder and drag it to the Dock again. Then remove the question mark by dragging it off the Dock.

You can place the application anywhere you like on the left side of the Dock; if you don't like where you put it, drag it to a new position in the Dock. You can also remove it altogether by dragging it upward off the Dock so that it disappears in a puff of smoke.

▶ **TIP**

Try adding the entire **Applications** folder to the Dock! Open a Finder window, then select your disk from the Sidebar; drag the **Applications** folder icon from the main Finder window down onto the right side of the Dock. Now you can click and hold, **Control**+click, or right-click the **Applications** folder in the Dock and have immediate access through a pop-up menu to all the applications installed on your system.

4   **Control an Application from the Dock**

✔ BEFORE YOU BEGIN	→ SEE ALSO
2 Find, Launch, and Quit an Application	**5** Minimize and Restore a Window
3 Add an Application to the Dock	**106** Change the Dock's Position and Behavior

The Dock gives you the ability to control certain basic behaviors of all applications, whether they're running or not. Some applications are designed so that you can control more specific functions from the Dock without even needing to switch active applications.

1 Show an Application in the Finder

Although having an application icon in the Dock is convenient, the icon is just a shortcut to the original application. Sometimes you have to access the original item, for instance if you want to view the **Get Info** panel for the application to find information such as its version number. Fortunately, any application in the Dock—whether it's running or not—can be traced back to its original location.

Click and hold the icon in the Dock, or **Control**+click or right-click it. A contextual menu pops up. Every contextual menu for items in the Dock has, at the very least, a **Show In Finder** option. Select this option, and a Finder window appears showing the original item in the folder where it resides.

2 Select from an Application's Open Windows

Some applications allow you to have more than one document window open at once. When this is the case, you can switch from one window to another using the Dock.

Click and hold, **Control**+click, or right-click the application icon in the Dock to open the contextual menu. At the top of the contextual menu, for any running application, is a list (by name) of all the open windows for that application. Select the window you want, and that window will come to the foreground.

▶ **TIP**

You can switch between applications using the ⌘+**Tab** and ⌘+**Shift**+**Tab** key combinations, which rotate respectively forward and backward through your open applications. When you use either of these keystrokes, the icons of the open applications appear floating in the middle of your screen, and remain there as long as you hold down the **Command** key. Press **Tab** or **Shift**+**Tab** repeatedly to select the application you want.

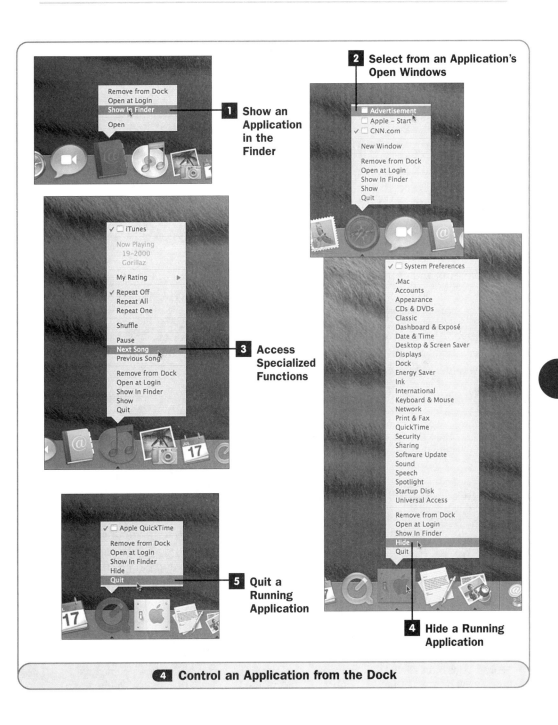

2 Select from an Application's Open Windows

1 Show an Application in the Finder

3 Access Specialized Functions

5 Quit a Running Application

4 Hide a Running Application

4 Control an Application from the Dock

3 Access Specialized Functions

Some applications, such as iTunes and Mail, allow you to perform certain specialized actions without bringing the applications to the foreground. This can be very useful when you want to perform an action in the background while you continue to work on something else.

Open the contextual menu for the application; under the list of open windows are any special functions that the application has available. iTunes, for instance, has controls that allow you to play or pause the music, skip forward or backward, or toggle Shuffle mode. Simply select from the menu to perform these functions.

4 Hide a Running Application

Any running application can be hidden—in other words, all its windows can be made invisible. Hiding an application can be useful if you want to keep an application open but also want to clean up your work environment.

Open the contextual menu and select **Hide** from the bottom area of the list of options. All the application's windows will disappear; if the application is currently active, the previously active application becomes active.

▶ TIP

With the application's contextual menu open, press the **Option** key. The **Hide** option turns into **Hide Others**. Selecting this option allows you to hide all applications *except* the application you're controlling.

5 Quit a Running Application

Quitting an application terminates its execution, closing all its windows and removing it from memory. You can do this by switching to the application and choosing **Quit** from the application menu; you can also quit using the Dock's contextual menu. Open the contextual menu and select **Quit** from the bottom of the list. The black triangle disappears from under the application icon in the Dock as the application quits.

▶ TIP

If you press the **Option** key while the contextual menu is open, the **Quit** option turns into **Force Quit**. If an application is misbehaving or not responding, the Dock's contextual menu will have a note to that effect at the top, and the **Force Quit** option will be available at the bottom.

5 | Minimize and Restore a Window

✔ BEFORE YOU BEGIN	→ SEE ALSO
2 Find, Launch, and Quit an Application	**6** Grab the Window You Want

Minimizing an application's windows shrinks them to thumbnail-sized versions sitting at the right end of the Dock, near the **Trash**. Minimizing windows allows you to get certain windows off the screen while keeping others active. A minimized application is still running; it just takes up none of your Desktop space. You can easily restore a minimized window at any time.

1 Minimize a Window

The yellow control button at the top left of any window minimizes that window. Click the button, and the window shrinks into the Dock using the "Genie Effect"—the window morphs into a flexible shape that condenses as it "flows" into an icon in the Dock.

You can also minimize a window by selecting **Minimize** from the **Window** menu, or by pressing ⌘**M**.

A minimized window in the Dock is marked with the icon of the application it's a part of, such as Safari's "compass" icon for web pages, or the Finder's "Mac face" icon for Finder windows.

▶ NOTE
Some kinds of windows, such as QuickTime movies, will continue to play even if minimized into the Dock.

2 Restore a Window

A minimized window can be restored by simply clicking its icon in the Dock.

3 Use a Different Minimize Effect

The Genie Effect looks cool the first few hundred times, but eventually you might want to use a minimize effect that's a little quicker and less ostentatious.

You can select the minimize effect from the Dock Preferences. From the **Apple** menu, choose **Dock, Dock Preferences**. In the dialog box that opens, select **Scale Effect** from the **Minimize using** drop-down list. The **Scale Effect** option simply scales the window directly into its Dock position, rather than following the smooth curved path of the Genie Effect (which takes a little bit longer).

5

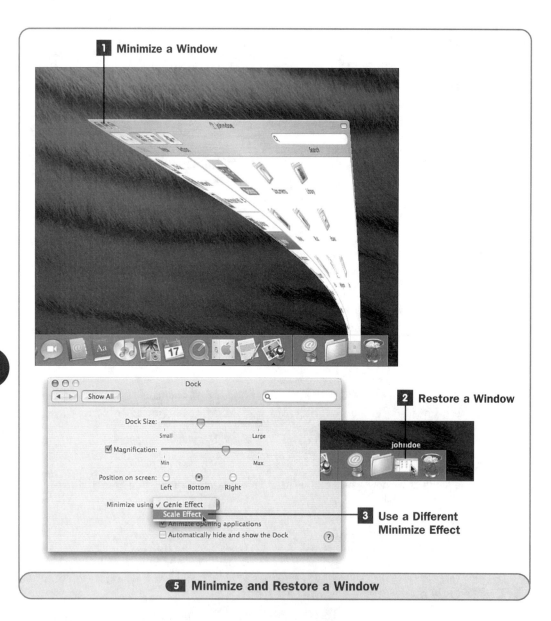

1 Minimize a Window

2 Restore a Window

3 Use a Different Minimize Effect

5 Minimize and Restore a Window

5

▶ **TIPS**

You can also select the minimize effect from the Dock's contextual menu. **Control**+click (or right-click) the vertical dividing line in the middle of the Dock; from the contextual menu select **Minimize using**, and then choose the effect you want.

If you like showing off Mac OS X's graphical talents to your friends and co-workers, you can run the Genie or Scale Effect in slow motion by holding down the **Shift** key as you minimize the window.

6 Grab the Window You Want

✔ BEFORE YOU BEGIN	→ SEE ALSO
2 Find, Launch, and Quit an Application	**104** Select a Screen Saver
5 Minimize and Restore a Window	**94** Access Your Desk Accessories (Dashboard)

Exposé is an innovative feature, unique to Mac OS X, that allows you to instantly and temporarily "tile" all your open windows across your screen—smoothly shrunk so that they all fit—and select the one you want to work with, without having to shuffle through hidden applications and windows piled on top of each other. Instead of painstakingly resizing or moving your windows around, you can simply press a key to see all open windows at once, pick a window with a click, and get right back to work; none of your windows' sizes, shapes, or positions are affected. Exposé is set up by default so that certain function keys invoke it, but it can be configured to use other keys or even simple mouse gestures. After a few days using Exposé, you'll wonder how you ever got along without it.

▶ **TIP**

In most Mac OS X applications, you can cycle between all the application's open windows by repeatedly pressing ⌘` (backquote). Cycle through your running applications by pressing ⌘+**Tab**.

Exposé has three modes:

- **All Windows.** All the currently open windows scoot out from underneath each other and tile across the screen so you can visually pick the application or document you want.

- **Application Windows.** All the open windows in your current application, such as all open images in Photoshop, are tiled; windows belonging to other applications fade into the background.

- **Desktop.** All the windows slide off the screen so you can see your Desktop and access the files on it.

For the first example, let's look at a usage case where you want to place all your relevant windows side by side so you can pick the one you're interested in.

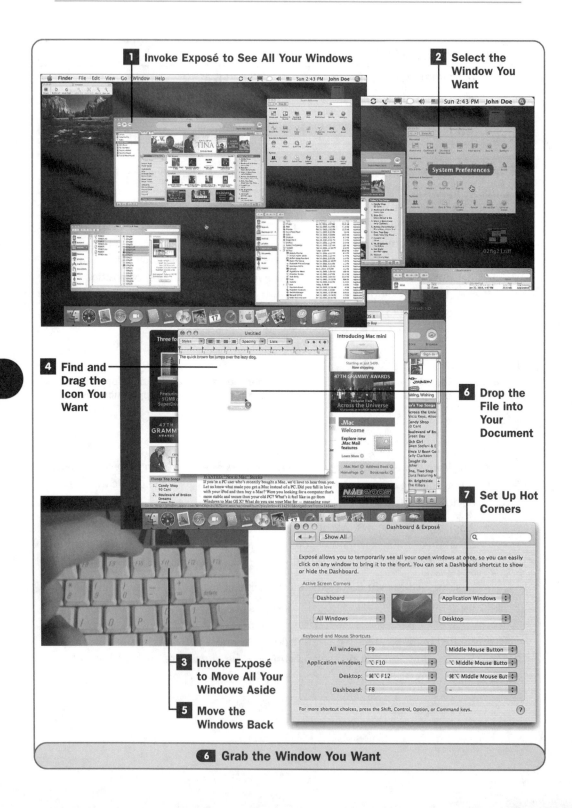

1 Invoke Exposé to See All Your Windows

2 Select the Window You Want

4 Find and Drag the Icon You Want

6 Drop the File into Your Document

7 Set Up Hot Corners

3 Invoke Exposé to Move All Your Windows Aside

5 Move the Windows Back

6

6 Grab the Window You Want

■ Invoke Exposé to See All Your Windows

Press the **F9** ("All Windows") key. This key is set up by default to tile all the open windows in the system, no matter which applications they belong to.

Press the **F10** ("Application Windows") key to tile only the windows that belong to the current application.

▶ TIP

If you've accidentally invoked Exposé when you didn't want to, or you want to cancel it, press **Escape**—or press the function key you pressed to invoke Exposé (**F9**, **F10**, or **F11**).

■ Select the Window You Want

Hover the mouse over each tiled window to dim the window with the window title superimposed over it. Use this approach to help you choose which window you want; then click the desired window. The selected window jumps to the foreground, and all the rest of the windows return to their original positions.

■ Invoke Exposé to Move All Your Windows Aside

Suppose that you want to embed a picture file in a document you're writing in TextEdit. The picture you want is on the Desktop, but there are so many windows open that you can't see it. Exposé allows you to brush all the open windows out of the way instantly, grab the file, bring all the windows back, and drop the file into TextEdit—all without having to minimize or hide any applications or disrupt your working window layout.

Press **F11** to move all the windows offscreen and show the Desktop, and all its icons, free of window clutter.

■ Find and Drag the Icon You Want

Find the picture file on the Desktop that you want to embed in the TextEdit document. Click and hold the picture file icon, as though you're going to drag it.

■ Move the Windows Back

Without releasing the mouse button, press **F11** again to recall all the offscreen windows back into place. Your mouse pointer should still be dragging the picture file's icon.

6

▶ TIPS

Briefly tap one of the function keys (**F9**, **F10**, or **F11**) to tile the windows and leave them tiled until you select the window you want; press and hold a function key to tile the windows only for as long as you hold down the key, so that they snap back to position as soon as you release the key.

Exposé's tiled windows are "spring-loaded," in much the same way that folders in the Finder behave. If you're dragging a file icon when you invoke Exposé, you can hold the mouse on top of a tiled window until the window flashes and springs to the front. Use this method, for example, to drag a document from a Finder window into Mail or TextEdit.

6 Drop the File into Your Document

Drag the graphic file icon to wherever in the TextEdit document you want to embed the file, and release the mouse button.

7 Set Up Hot Corners

If you don't like using the **F9**, **F10**, and **F11** keys to access the Exposé tiling modes, select **System Preferences** from the **Apple** menu, then open the Exposé pane. Here, you can choose different trigger keys for the various tiling modes. See **94 Access Your Desk Accessories (Dashboard)** for information on Dashboard, the new Exposé-related system for accessing desk accessories in Mac OS X Tiger.

Furthermore, you can configure the four corners of the screen to trigger Exposé using "mouse gestures." In other words, you might configure the upper-left corner of your screen so that if you move the mouse into that corner, all the windows will tile; you can specify that if you move the mouse into the lower-right corner of the screen, all the windows will move offscreen.

▶ TIP

Use the menus in the **Keyboard** section to choose different function keys or key combinations to invoke the three Exposé modes, if you find them easier than the default settings. For instance, if you want to invoke "Desktop" mode using **Control+Shift+F3**, simply hold down **Control** and **Shift** while opening the menu for **Desktop** mode.

Similarly, if you have a multibutton mouse connected to your Mac, you can configure special mouse clicks to invoke Exposé with almost no physical effort. For example, hold down **Option** while choosing the **Middle Mouse Button** option from the **All Windows** menu in the **Mouse** section to make **Option**+clicking the middle mouse button invoke Exposé's "All Windows" mode. If you don't have a multibutton mouse connected, the **Mouse** section does not appear.

7 | Assign an Opener Application to a File

✔ **BEFORE YOU BEGIN**

1 Install an Application from Disc or Download
2 Find, Launch, and Quit an Application

Navigating to the **Applications** folder and picking an icon from the Dock aren't the only ways to launch applications. Perhaps even more useful is the fact that you can automatically launch an application simply by double-clicking a document created by that application.

Mac OS X allows you to assign a certain *opener application* to any individual document, or to all documents of a given type. This is the application that will launch when you double-click the document, opening the file so you can work with it.

▶ KEY TERM

Opener application—The application you set a document to open with. When you double-click the document, this is the application that will launch to open the document.

1 Find the Document You Want

Open the Finder and navigate to a document to which you want to assign an opener application. For instance, if you want to open a JPEG image file in Adobe Photoshop, first use the Finder to locate the JPEG file in question. Select the JPEG by clicking it.

▶ TIP

If you want, you can select the opener application for a given document on a one-time basis. In the Finder, **Control**+click (or right-click) the document; from the contextual menu that pops up, select **Open With**. All the installed applications capable of opening the selected document appear in the resulting list. Select the application you want to open the selected file in, and the application will launch.

2 Get Info

Select **Get Info** from the **File** menu or from the Finder's **Action** menu. Alternatively, press ⌘I, or **Control**+click or right-click the file and select **Get Info** from the contextual menu that appears.

7

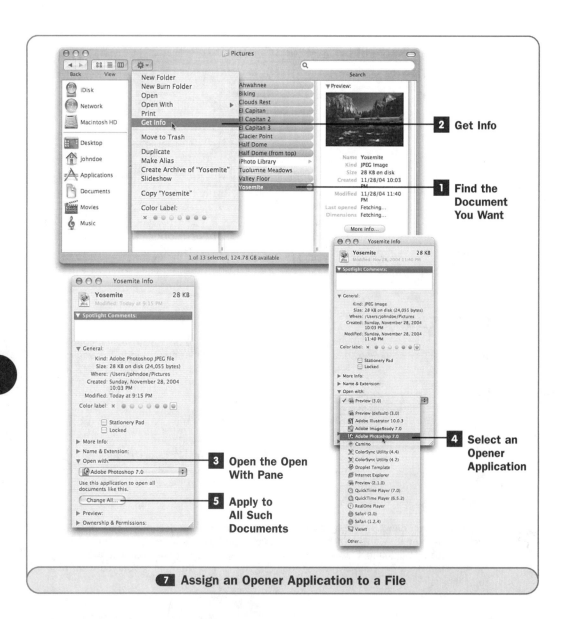

7 Assign an Opener Application to a File

3 Open the Open With Pane

In the **Info** panel, click the gray triangle next to the **Open with** heading. All the applications capable of opening documents of the same type as the selected document (in this case, a JPEG image) are listed in the drop-down menu.

4 Select an Opener Application

Select the application you want the document to open in. The document is immediately associated with the application you choose, and you can close the **Info** panel. You will know that the document's application has been changed because its icon will now reflect the new application. In the example shown, the **Yosemite** picture file was originally associated with the Mac OS X **Preview** application; now it is associated with **Adobe Photoshop**.

5 Apply to All Such Documents

If you want to open *all* JPEG images in Photoshop, click the **Change All** button. Be careful with this option—if you have previously set up a lot of different JPEG images to open in different applications, that information will be overridden and lost when you click **Change All**.

8 Revert an Application to Factory Settings

✔ BEFORE YOU BEGIN	→ SEE ALSO
1 Install an Application from Disc or Download	144 Move Your Data to a New Mac

There are times when an application simply stops working properly—every time you launch it or try to execute some action, the application will *crash*, freeze, or otherwise misbehave. An operation that worked perfectly fine when you first installed the application might suddenly stop working for good, with no apparent reason. This might be the result of the computer not being shut down properly (as the result of a power outage or a laptop battery running down), or of physical corruption on the hard disk's surface.

It's possible for the entire system to crash; if this happens (a rare occurrence in Mac OS X), the mouse freezes and the screen becomes dimmed and overlaid with an instructional message saying that you must restart the computer using the power on/off button.

▶ KEY TERM

Crash—When an application quits unexpectedly (and typically puts up a dialog box explaining that it has done so), it is the result of something in the application happening in a way the programmer didn't intend, and from which the application cannot recover.

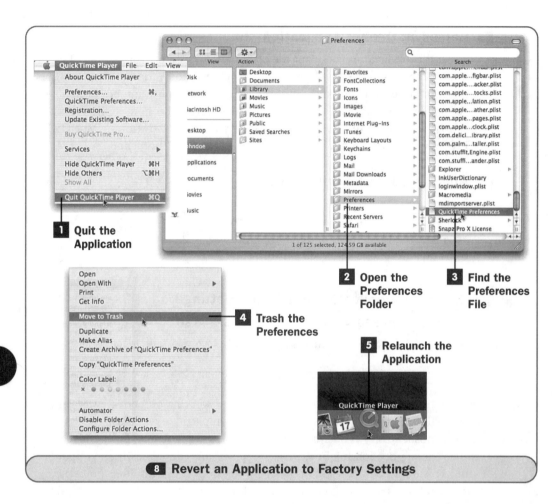

8 Revert an Application to Factory Settings

Because applications don't "decay" over time, and neither do they malfunction out of spite (although the evidence for this belief might seem overwhelming), there is often a simple explanation for such a malfunction: The application's configuration file has become corrupted, and must be replaced. The most common reason for this to happen is that the application itself contains flaws (or "bugs") that prevent it from dealing properly with certain configuration options that you might set during perfectly normal operation, leaving the configuration in a corrupted state.

If you have a misbehaving application, the following procedure might help. Because every application is different, this procedure might not work, but the architecture of Mac OS X is such that if you follow this procedure, the application will effectively be returned to its pristine, just-installed state, and should work the same as it did when you first installed it.

▶ **TIP**

The process of returning an application to its factory settings is typically known in Mac circles as "trashing the Preferences."

1 Quit the Application

Make sure the application is not running, if it is capable of running at all. If the crash is related to a certain command that you use, but it otherwise runs properly, you will need to quit the application if it's running before you can restore it. Choose **File**, **Quit** or press ⌘**Q**. An application typically writes out its configuration to the **Preferences** folder at the time you quit; so you should quit the application before messing with the Preferences.

2 Open the Preferences Folder

Click the **Finder** icon in the Dock to open a new Finder window; then navigate to your **Library** folder inside your **Home** folder. Inside the **Library** folder is a folder called **Preferences**; open this folder.

3 Find the Preferences File

Inside the **Preferences** folder is a list of documents, each one associated with an application installed on your computer. Every application keeps its Preferences in one of these files and writes changes to it as you change the settings of the application.

Some applications' Preferences are in the form of an XML "plist" file, with a filename in the form **com.<*company*>.<*application*>.plist**. Other preference files are named more clearly, such as **QuickTime Preferences**. Locate the file associated with the application you're trying to repair. (There might be more than one such file; there might even be a folder with several files inside it. If this is the case, just to be thorough, select all of the likely candidates whose name suggests that they belong to your application. Remember, you can always move these files back to their proper location, so don't be shy about moving more files than you need to.)

▶ **TIP**

If you're not sure which Preference file is the one you want, try viewing the **Preferences** folder in List view and sorting the list on the **Last Modified** column. The most recently modified file probably corresponds to the application you most recently quit or that most recently crashed.

8

4 Trash the Preferences

Drag the file (or files) from the **Preferences** folder onto the Desktop (if you want to experiment safely) or directly into the **Trash**. You can also select **File**, **Move to Trash** or open the contextual menu for the Preference file (**Control**+click or right-click) and choose **Move to Trash**.

5 Relaunch the Application

Start the application again, and try the operation that was previously misbehaving. If it works, great! You can move the old, faulty Preference file from the Desktop into the **Trash** and discard it if you want.

If the application is still misbehaving, you can move the Preference files back into your **Preferences** folder (after quitting the application) to ensure that when you do get the problem resolved, your old settings will be preserved.

▶ NOTE

Because you have now reset your Preferences for this application, you will now need to examine the application's settings and adjust them to your liking again.

9 Uninstall an Application

✔ **BEFORE YOU BEGIN**

1 Install an Application from Disc or Download
8 Revert an Application to Factory Settings

Removing an application from your computer is one of the easiest things you can do, and one of the nicest advantages of the Mac over Windows. Because Windows operates based on the Registry (a complex database of pieces of information installed by applications), you usually have to run uninstaller programs to remove an application from a Windows machine (even then, it's rarely a clean operation—a badly written uninstaller can leave conflicting data in the Registry). A Mac OS X application, however, is just a single item you can simply throw away.

1 Locate the Application

Open a Finder window and navigate to the **Applications** folder. Most applications are found in this folder; if the application you want to remove is in a different location, navigate there instead.

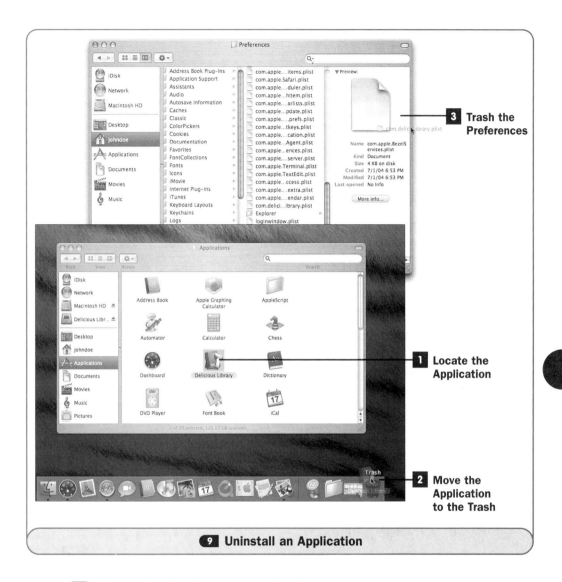

9 Uninstall an Application

2 Move the Application to the Trash

Drag the application icon from the Finder window into the **Trash** in the Dock.

3 Trash the Preferences

Technically, you're done uninstalling the application. The only thing that remains from it on your computer is a file containing the preferences for that application as you have personally configured it. That file can't hurt anything. If you want to be really thorough, though, go into your **Preferences** folder (inside the **Library** folder, under your **Home** folder), locate the Preferences file for the application you just deleted, and throw it away, too. This step is generally unnecessary, because the Preference file won't do any harm if the application it relates to is no longer present on the system.

10 | Run a "Classic" Application

✔ **BEFORE YOU BEGIN**

1 Install an Application from Disc or Download

Most Mac applications are designed to run "natively" in Mac OS X, meaning that they are programmed specifically for the architecture of the Mac OS X operating system. However, some older applications are still in use that were designed to be run on Mac OS 9 or earlier versions, and are therefore very different from Mac OS X applications in a number of key ways.

You can run these so-called "Classic" applications only within an environment called Classic (which is, in effect, a copy of Mac OS 9 running inside Mac OS X). If you launch a Classic application, the Classic environment launches automatically, and from then on you can use the application just as you would any other, but you can also launch the Classic environment separately, for instance if you want to save time by launching it at the beginning of your session so that Classic applications can later be launched quickly.

1 Open Classic Preferences

Open the **System Preferences** (select it from the **Apple** menu) and open the **Classic** pane.

2 Select a System Folder

Most installations of Mac OS X have a single **System Folder** (the folder containing the complete Mac OS 9 system that comprises the Classic environment). If you have multiple copies of the operating system installed, however, you must select which one to use for Classic. Select a disk or volume (and expand it using the triangular arrow), and select the **System Folder** corresponding to the installation of Mac OS 9 that you want to use.

3 Start the Classic Environment

Click the **Start** button to launch the Classic environment. Classic starts up in a window you can expand to show the boot procedure of a Mac OS 9 computer (the one that's effectively being booted from within your Mac OS X system).

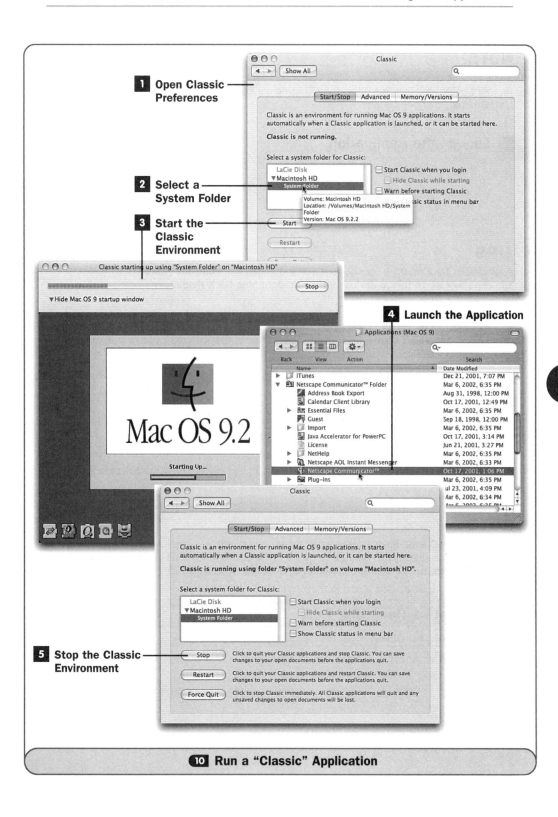

1 Open Classic Preferences

2 Select a System Folder

3 Start the Classic Environment

4 Launch the Application

5 Stop the Classic Environment

10

10 Run a "Classic" Application

▶ **NOTE**

If you receive a notification that Mac OS X must update some files in the Classic environment before proceeding, allow the OS to do so; this is expected behavior for new installations.

4 Launch the Application

Open the Mac OS X **Finder** by clicking the familiar **Finder** icon in the Dock, and navigate to the application you want to run. Double-click the application icon as you would any application in Mac OS X to start the Classic application.

▶ **TIPS**

Applications for Mac OS 9 can be found in the global **Applications (Mac OS 9)** folder. You can navigate to this folder using the standard Mac OS X Finder.

A Classic application can often be identified by the way its icon looks. Mac OS 9 supported icons only up to 32×32 pixels in size (Mac OS X icons can be 128×128 pixels and can incorporate 24-bit color with transparency.) Thus, a Classic application's icon might look blocky or drab.

10

5 Stop the Classic Environment

After you quit the Classic application, it's a good idea to shut down the Classic environment as well, because the environment takes up resources you might need for other tasks. Repeat step 1 to open the **Classic Preferences** dialog box again and click the **Stop** button to shut down the Classic environment.

▶ **NOTE**

If you stop the Classic environment while there are still Classic applications running, the applications are shut down. Be sure to quit your Classic applications cleanly, just as you would before shutting down the computer altogether!

11 Automate a Recurring Task

✔ BEFORE YOU BEGIN

1 Install an Application from Disc or Download
2 Find, Launch, and Quit an Application

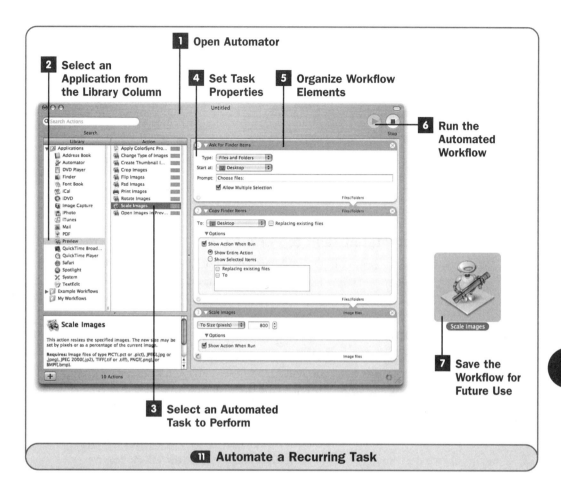

1 Open Automator

2 Select an Application from the Library Column

4 Set Task Properties

5 Organize Workflow Elements

6 Run the Automated Workflow

7 Save the Workflow for Future Use

3 Select an Automated Task to Perform

11 Automate a Recurring Task

Mac OS X Tiger contains a new application called **Automator**. This tool is designed to simplify your work by giving you an easy way to script the operation of any applications you use frequently. You can set up an automated workflow that runs through a predefined procedure, driving your various applications, any time you need to do so. For example, if you frequently need to apply a set of processing operations to groups of image files, you can use Automator to create a workflow that performs these operations automatically without any interaction from you.

1 Open Automator

Automator is found in the **Applications** folder at the top level of the hard disk. Double-click its icon to launch the application.

2 Select an Application from the Library Column

The **Automator** application consists of two columns of hierarchical tasks on the left, grouped by the application to which they pertain, and a pane on the right where you visually set up the workflow by linking together a series of component tasks.

First, select the application or saved workflow you want to use from the **Library** column. For example, if you want Automator to apply a series of image processes to a selected group of picture files, start by selecting **Finder** from the list (because you will need to use the Finder to select the image files in question).

3 Select an Automated Task to Perform

The **Action** column shows all available actions associated with your selected application or saved workflow from the **Library**. For our example, locate the **Choose Files** action and drag it to the workflow pane.

4 Set Task Properties

The action expands into a visual workflow element with several properties that you can set. In this case, the **Ask for Finder Items** action begins with a **Type** option (to specify what kind of items the task can accept as input), **Start at** (the folder in which the file selector will begin), the text for a prompt (used in the title bar of the file selector), and the option to allow selection of multiple items. Set these items according to your needs. For instance, in this example we need to get a group of image files, so select the check box for multiple selection of files.

5 Organize Workflow Elements

Next, repeat the process thus far to choose the next task in the workflow. A label at the bottom of the workflow element shows what kind of results to expect from the action. In our case, the **Ask for Finder Items** action gives us files or folders. Other kinds of actions might return images, web URLs (addresses), Mail messages, or just about anything else. Make sure that the next action that you choose can take the same kind of input that matches the output of the previous action. If two consecutive tasks are not compatible, the first is treated as the end of the procedure that passes data from one task to another, and the next begins another series of tasks.

▶ TIP

You can see what kind of input, output, and options are available for each action by selecting the action and then viewing its description in the pane in the lower left.

Drag as many actions into the workflow as you need in order to complete the procedure. If you need to change the order of the workflow elements, you can click and drag them by their title bars up or down. To remove a workflow element, click the **X** in the upper right.

▶ **NOTE**

Automator helpfully suggests tasks that you might wish to add for convenience or safety. For example, if you add a task that performs image operations on a group of selected files, it asks you whether to add a **Copy Files** task to create duplicates of the original items, to make sure you don't overwrite them with your procedure.

6 Run the Automated Workflow

You can run the procedure from within Automator by clicking the **Run** button in the upper right (a "Play" triangle). Each task shows a "progress" spinner as it runs, which changes to a green circle when it's complete. Use this method to test your workflow as you build it. If you detect a problem, or you don't want the workflow to continue all the way through, click the **Stop** button to interrupt it.

7 Save the Workflow for Future Use

After the workflow is complete, you can save it in one of two formats (select **File, Save**). Saved as a **Workflow**, the procedure becomes a WFLOW file, which reopens Automator if you double-click it, letting you then run the workflow using the Run button. However, for the most streamlined product, choose the **Application** format when saving. This converts your workflow into a self-contained application with its own icon (featuring the little Automator robot, known as Otto); when you double-click this new icon, the workflow immediately executes, without needing to open Automator. This is the best way to create a procedure that you'll use a lot in the future.

▶ **NOTE**

You can transfer an Automator-created application to another Mac to use there; however, that machine must be running Tiger or a later operating system version for it to work.

Automator is an application large and intricate enough to merit a book of its own; there are vast possibilities for how to create workflows, define new tasks, save workflows as "plug-ins" for certain applications, and extend the capabilities of your most frequently used applications beyond their original design. This brief tour should be enough to get you started, though; feel free to experiment and explore what's possible!

3

Keeping Things Organized

IN THIS CHAPTER:

Mac OS X, like all operating systems, is designed to help you organize data. This data is represented using the industry-standard "desktop" metaphor, originally pioneered by the first Macintosh and its precursors. In the desktop metaphor, any meaningful grouping of data under a single name—a picture, an audio recording, a shopping list—is represented by a *document* (also known as a *file*, a term that will be used interchangeably with *document* in this book). Documents can be sorted into *folders*, which are simply containers for documents. Folders can contain other folders as well as documents, and thus you can organize all your information into a hierarchy that resembles a large, ungainly filing cabinet.

Mac OS X gives you the ability to manage these documents and folders, to move them around, change their names, create new ones, and get rid of the ones you don't need anymore. In the context of modern computing hardware, this means that Mac OS X must enable you to manipulate disks—hard disks, CD-ROMs, DVDs, and other such devices that store your documents. In this chapter, you will see how to use the tools that Mac OS X gives you to accomplish these tasks.

Furthermore, as your computing needs grow, so does the need for Mac OS X to adapt to them. Over time, you will probably feel the need to add memory, new hard disks, and even second displays in order to keep up with the pace of the technology you interact with at home and at work. This chapter discusses how to add a new hard disk to your system and configure it to hold your expanding data; it also covers how to add a second display and configure it to your liking. Finally, because keeping your Mac's internal clock accurate is so crucial to the internal system functions as well as to applications such as iCal that keep track of your schedule for you, this chapter discusses how to set the time and date, and how to set up your computer to configure them automatically.

12 Find an Item

→ **SEE ALSO**

14 Create a Smart Folder That Contains Certain Types of Items

16 Make an Alias (Shortcut)

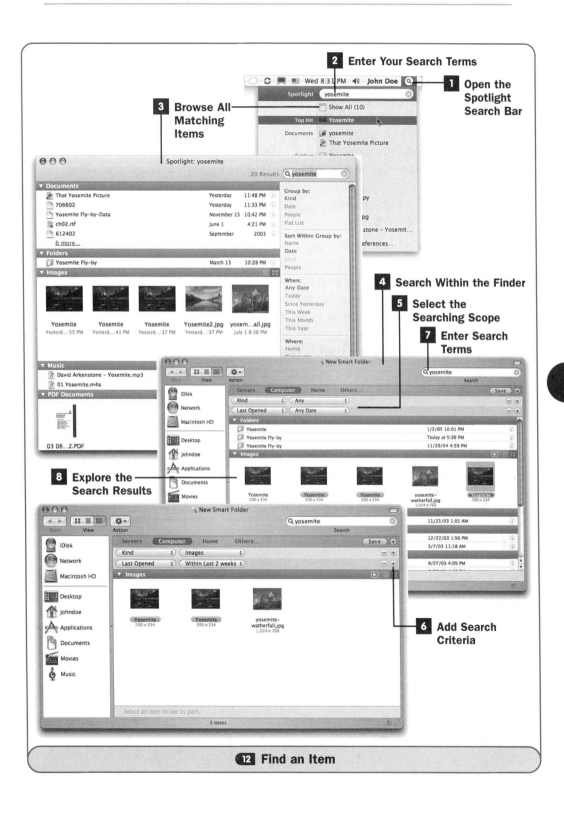

2 Enter Your Search Terms

1 Open the Spotlight Search Bar

3 Browse All Matching Items

4 Search Within the Finder

5 Select the Searching Scope

7 Enter Search Terms

8 Explore the Search Results

6 Add Search Criteria

12 Find an Item

12

The Macintosh Operating System has always excelled at finding your stuff; after all, they don't call its navigation system the Finder for nothing. In Mac OS X Tiger, however, Apple has brought searching technology to a whole new level, with a feature called **Spotlight**. This technology is a database subsystem overlaid upon the filesystem, invisibly, that constantly indexes every new item added to the computer on the basis of kind, creator, last-opened date, and a litany of other criteria. Whereas the Finder in previous versions of the operating system only allowed you to search the names of files looking for a match to a text string you typed in, Spotlight expands this functionality to allow you to search documents' contents, authors, comments, media-specific attributes, and just about any other associated pieces of data.

Furthermore, Spotlight is integrated into the Finder, as well as into applications such as Mail and Address Book. Within the Finder, you can create create sophisti- cated "canned" searches based on detailed query criteria, and save the results of those queries into what are known as *Smart Folders*, as you will see in **14 Create a Smart Folder That Contains Certain Types of Items**.

1 Open the Spotlight Search Bar

Click the magnifying-glass icon at the far right end of the Mac OS X title bar. The **Spotlight** search bar appears, prompting you for text terms on which to search.

▶ NOTE

If this is your first time using Mac OS X Tiger, Spotlight has to index your entire disk (or disks) before making its contents available for searches. Opening the **Spotlight** search bar during this process tells you how long it will take before it's ready (usually no more than an hour or two, for disks with a lot of data).

2 Enter Your Search Terms

Type a word (or a few words) of text that matches the name of a document you're looking for, the author, or the document's contents. As you type, a list of matching items immediately expands below the Spotlight bar. These results are grouped by kind: first the "top hit," or the item in which your search terms matched most closely or frequently; then Chats in which the terms appeared, text or Word documents, folders whose names matched, HTML (web) documents, and so on alphabetically. Only a few results are shown—two or three per category. If you see the result you want in this list- ing, simply click its title in the list, and it will open in its designated opener application. If the file has no application associated with it, see **7 Assign an Opener Application to a File**.

▶ **TIP**

The Spotlight pane of System Preferences allows you to define what kinds of data Spotlight should index, as well as what disks and volumes should be included in searches and what users of the system should have access to search results. Make sure to visit this pane if you have sensitive information on your computer that you don't want other users seeing, or if you want to shorten the time it takes Spotlight to become ready to use by excluding certain volumes from indexing. **The Spotlight settings defined by an administrator apply to all users of the system.**

3 Browse All Matching Items

Chances are that there won't just be one or two matches to your search terms—there'll be hundreds. Click the topmost item in the Spotlight results menu, **Show All**, to reveal a new application window with detailed and navigable results of everything that matches your search terms. This full-featured **Spotlight** window lets you select how the results are grouped: by Kind, Date (the time each item was last opened), People (authors and artists, according to how each kind of document defines them), or a flat list of all matching items regardless of category, sorted by date of last access.

▶ **TIP**

Use the **Sort Within Group by** links to choose how items are sorted within a category. You can also use the **When** links to filter out files that haven't been accessed within the past day, past week, or other time periods, or the **Where** links to confine the search to a particular disk or area of the system.

12

Within a category, several options are available for revealing more information about the items that Spotlight returned. Click the **i** icon next to any item to show detailed information about it. Each category by default shows only the top five matches (sorted by the date of last access), and you can click a link at the bottom of each category to see all the matching items of that type. In some categories, such as **Images** and **Movies**, you can choose between List or Icon view modes to see larger previews of each item. Movie files can even be played right in this window, just as **Music** files can be played in their expanded **Info** panes.

When you've located the item you're looking for, double-click it to open it in its designated opener application.

4 Search Within the Finder

The Spotlight search mechanism is great for quickly finding an item with textual characteristics that you can match by typing search terms. However, Spotlight integrated with the Finder presents an even more powerful way to search. What if you wanted to craft a very specific search query for, say, image (picture) files created within the last two weeks, with size greater than one megabyte, and with dimensions greater than 1000 pixels wide? With the Spotlight database working its magic, you can.

Choose **File**, **Find** or press ⌘**F** while in the Finder. A new **Finder** window appears, with its document pane in New Search mode.

5 Select the Searching Scope

Use the names at the top of the window to define where you want the Finder to look for your items. The **Servers** option searches any network volumes currently mounted, **Computer** uses all available disks and volumes in the computer, and **Home** confines the search to the folder hierarchy within your **Home** folder. You can add more searching scopes using the **Others** button.

▶ NOTE

Because Spotlight operates by creating a local index of the contents of all volumes mounted on the computer, every time you mount a new network volume, you must wait for Spotlight to index it before its contents are available for instant searches.

6 Add Search Criteria

The Finder's search mode allows you to specify as many different searching criteria as you want; *all* the criteria must apply for the results to match. For instance, you can search for items whose filename contains **art**, whose filename begins with **A**, whose kind is **audio**, and whose last-modified date is after last Christmas. You make room for new criteria by clicking the + icon after any criterion line; then use the drop-down menus to define what kind of criteria they are and what sort of comparisons to use. Use the – icon on any criterion line to delete that criterion.

The criteria in the first drop-down menu aren't the only ones you have to work with. Select **Other** from the menu; a sheet appears with a long list of specialized search attributes that apply only to certain kinds of data, such as the aperture size for photos, the authors of a text document, the headline of a news item from the Web, or the pixel width and height of image files. Select one of these attributes and click **OK** to add it to your search criteria. If you click **Add to Favorites**, the attribute will be added to the drop-down menu for easy access later.

7 Enter Search Terms

Optionally, enter text in the **Search** bar in the Finder's toolbar (next to the magnifying glass). This text is added to the search criteria—all results must match the entered terms as well as whatever criteria you've set up so far.

8 Explore the Search Results

As you add search criteria, the results are shown in real-time in the Finder window, organized as in the Spotlight results window. You can click the **i** icon next to any item to view detailed information about it, as well as a **More Info** button, which reveals the item's **Info** pane. You can list certain kinds of files in the interactive Icon view. Click any item in the list, and its location on the disk is shown in a path listing at the bottom of the window. You can see the series of folders (in a horizontal layout) you'll have to navigate through to get to the item, or double-click any one of the listed folders to go to that folder's Finder window.

▶ TIP

While building your search, use the Finder's **View, Show View Options** command to select how items should be sorted within the results listing. Note that the third view mode selector button has changed from Column view to a new icon indicating Grouped view, the view you use when browsing Spotlight search results.

You can double-click a file anywhere in the search results window to launch it in its opener application. You can also drag any listed item from the results window to the Desktop or another Finder window to copy it, or hold down ⌘ while dragging to move it.

12

13 Create a New Folder

→ SEE ALSO

14 Create a Smart Folder That Contains Certain Types of Items
15 Rename a Folder or Document
17 Change an Icon
18 Set a Color Label

The basic unit of document storage is the folder. A folder can reside in any place in on a disk, and folders (and folders within folders within folders) are what make up the hierarchical organization of any Mac OS X system.

Mac OS X provides you a number of special-purpose folders inside your **Home** folder for storing certain kinds of documents. You can always create new folders to suit your purposes, and you can keep those new folders anywhere you like. For instance, you might create a folder on your Desktop to hold Word files for a project you're working on, and then move that folder into your **Documents** folder when you're done with it, so you can easily find it later. The first step in all this organizational wizardry is creating that new folder.

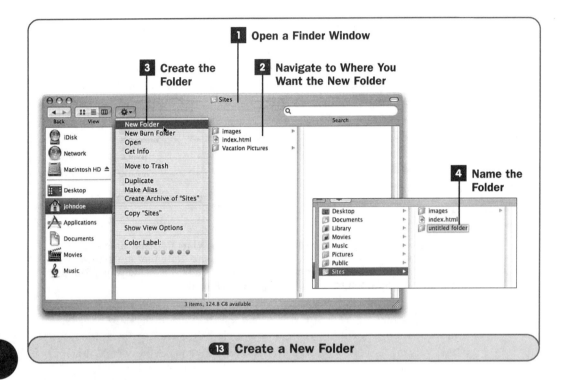

13

Create a New Folder

◆ Open a Finder Window

Click the **Finder** icon at the far left end of the Dock. Alternatively, click any-where on the Desktop to switch to the Finder, and then press ⌘N to open a new Finder window.

◆ Navigate to Where You Want the New Folder

Using whichever view modes you find most convenient, move through the folders in your **Home** folder until you're at the position where you want to create the new folder.

▶ TIP

Press ⌘ and click the title of the Finder window to see the path to your current location.

◆ Create the Folder

Select **File**, **New Folder**. Alternatively, press **Shift+⌘+N** or select **New Folder** from the **Action** button menu in the Finder window. A new folder appears in the listing, with the name **untitled folder**.

4 Name the Folder

The new folder's name is selected as soon as it's created, so you can immediately type a new name for it. You can use any name that doesn't duplicate the name of any other item in the current folder. When you're done typing the name, press Return to commit the change.

---

14 Create a Smart Folder That Contains Certain Types of Items

✔ BEFORE YOU BEGIN	→ SEE ALSO
12 Find an Item	15 Rename a Folder or Document
13 Create a New Folder	17 Change an Icon
	18 Set a Color Label

New in Mac OS X Tiger, *Smart Folders* are really just a way to save a Spotlight search as a "canned" query. You can't put items into a Smart Folder the way you would a regular folder; rather, the Smart Folder's contents are dynamically updated to match the results of a saved search.

▶ KEY TERM

Smart Folder—A dynamic listing of items matching a saved Spotlight search, presented as a "folder" with the search results inside.

When you define a search using the Finder, the criteria you use to create the search can be saved to a new Smart Folder, which you can store anywhere you like, and open as you would a regular folder to view its contents. There are several ways to create a new Smart Folder, but they all center upon the process of defining a query from Spotlight search criteria within the Finder.

1 Open a Finder Window

Switch to the Finder by clicking the **Finder** icon in the Dock, or by clicking anywhere on the Desktop. Creating a new Smart Folder begins with defining a new search for items in the system; there are several ways to do this once you're in the Finder.

2 Create a New Smart Folder

From the **File** menu, choose **New Smart Folder**. This command brings up a new Finder window with a blank Spotlight query in the navigation pane, with blank criteria for **Kind** and **Last Opened** already set up for you to use if you want. The new folder is not placed anywhere until you have saved your search.

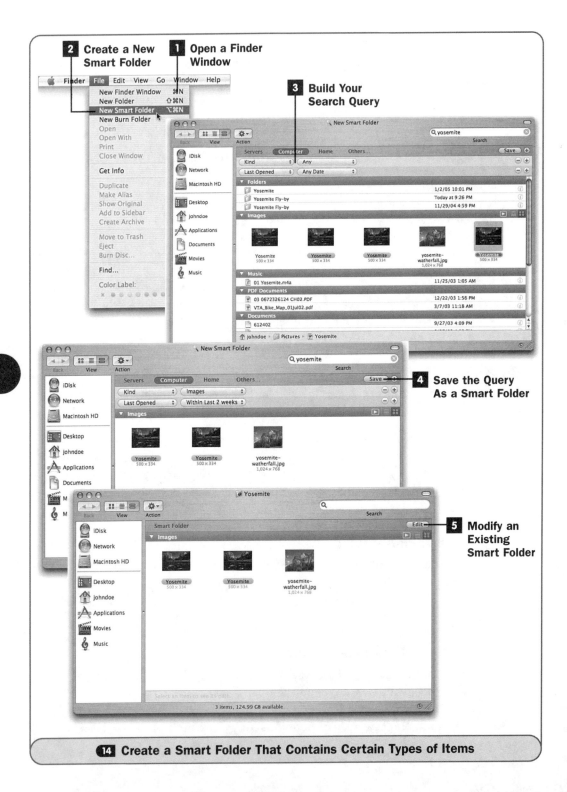

14 Create a Smart Folder That Contains Certain Types of Items

Alternately, choose **File**, **Find** (or press ⌘**F**) to bring up a **New Search** window. This method differs from **New Smart Folder** only in that it starts at the global level, and thus does not have the current Finder location among the searching scope buttons at the top of the pane.

▶ **TIP**

You can save any Finder search as a Smart Folder, even one that you started by entering text into the Search bar. All these methods use the same Spotlight workflow described in this task and in ⬛**12** **Find an Item**.

⬛**3** Build Your Search Query

Build up your query terms according to the steps in ⬛**12** **Find an Item**. Be sure to select the correct search scope, and to add textual search terms if necessary by entering them into the Search bar. As you add query terms, the list of matching files is shown in the Finder window.

▶ **NOTE**

The technology underlying Spotlight and Smart Folders is very similar to the database used in iTunes, and Smart Folders are modeled on iTunes' Smart Playlists in concept. If you know how to set up a Smart Playlist (see ⬛**84** **Create a Playlist or Smart Playlist**), then you know how to create a Smart Folder—as well as Smart Mailboxes and other Spotlight-based groupings throughout Mac OS X.

⬛**4** Save the Query As a Smart Folder

When you're satisfied with your search terms and results, click the **Save** button. You are prompted for a name for the new untitled Smart Folder, and for a location to place it. The default location for Smart Folders is the **Saved Searches** folder in your **Home**, and you can also choose the Desktop or your **Home** folder; however, once the Smart Folder is saved, you can move it anywhere you like. Select the **Add to Sidebar** check box to make the new Smart Folder appear in every Finder window's Sidebar for quick access.

After the Smart Folder has been saved, you can navigate into it as you would any other folder. Smart Folders are indicated with a "gear" symbol on the folder icon. As you add new files to the computer, the contents of the Smart Folder are automatically updated to reflect all files that match the search criteria.

⬛**5** Modify an Existing Smart Folder

If the search criteria in a Smart Folder turn out not to be what you need, you can adjust them at any time. Open the Smart Folder; click the **Edit** button at the top of the document list. The search criteria are then shown at the top of

14

the navigation pane. Use the + and – buttons to add or remove search criteria and modify them to fit your needs. When you're done, click **Save**; the Smart Folder is now redefined upon your revised criteria. To cancel modifying a Smart Folder, simply close the Finder window.

15 Rename a Folder or Document

✔ BEFORE YOU BEGIN	→ SEE ALSO
13 Create a New Folder	**16** Make an Alias (Shortcut)
	18 Set a Color Label

14

Renaming a folder or document in Mac OS X is a seemingly simple process that hides some surprising complexity. On the face of it, there's really nothing to it: Select the item, type in the new name, and you're done. However, there are a few hidden complications to watch out for.

One of these complications is that of filename *extensions*. In Mac OS X, these extensions are usually (but not always) required to define a document's type—but you don't have to see them. Extensions can be turned off on a per-document basis. If you rename the document in the Finder so that the extension is removed, for example by renaming **Picture1.jpg** to **Picture1**, the extension merely becomes a hidden attribute of the document. Similarly, if you add the appropriate extension to a document, it merely becomes "un-hidden." If you add an incorrect extension (such as **.txt** to a **.jpg** file), Mac OS X warns you that proceeding can cause the file to become associated with the wrong application or stop working properly, and gives you the option to proceed with the extension change or stick with the old one.

▶ KEY TERM

Extension—The often cryptic final few letters in a filename, after the dot. Originally popularized by **MS-DOS** after the example of Unix, the extension is a simple way to designate a document as being of a certain type; this way, an application could know what kind of file it is just by looking at its name.

▶ TIP

Use the **Get Info** window to see whether a document has a hidden extension or not; you can also hide a document's extension or show it, using the **Hide extension** check box.

By hiding documents' extensions, Mac OS X guarantees that the extension will be there if you transfer the file to a Windows machine, where extensions are required for documents to work properly.

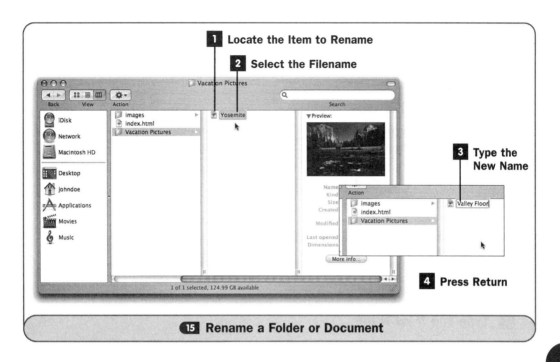

1 Locate the Item to Rename

2 Select the Filename

3 Type the New Name

4 Press Return

15 Rename a Folder or Document

A few common extensions are listed here:

Extension	Kind of Document
.jpg	Picture (Joint Photographic Experts Group)
.gif	Picture (Graphics Interchange Format)
.doc	Microsoft Word document
.rtf	Rich Text Format document
.txt	Plain Text document
.mov	QuickTime movie
.html	Web page (Hypertext Markup Language)
.pdf	Page layout (Portable Document Format)
.dmg	Mountable Disk Image file
.zip	ZIP archive (Windows-style)
.sit	StuffIt archive (Mac-style)
.cwk	AppleWorks document (originally ClarisWorks)
.pages	Pages document
.key	Keynote presentation

15

1 Locate the Item to Rename

Open a **Finder** window and navigate to the folder containing the document or folder you want to rename.

2 Select the Filename

For the item you want to rename, click the filename underneath or beside the icon. The item becomes selected (a darkened box appears around it) and the filename turns into an editable text field. Alternatively, click the icon to select it and then press **Return** to activate the filename as an editable field.

▶ **TIP**

In Mac OS X, if you click a text field (such as the name of a file in the Finder) and drag the mouse down, all the text to the right of where you clicked becomes selected. Similarly, if you click and drag up, everything to the left of where you clicked becomes selected.

3 Type the New Name

Type whatever name you like into the name field. Filenames can be any length up to 255 characters.

You can use almost any letters, numbers, or symbols in filenames, including characters in Japanese, Russian, and many other languages. However, there are a couple of exceptions to this freedom. Colons (:) are not allowed in filenames because the internal architecture of Mac OS X uses the colon to signify the separation between folders in the path to an item. You similarly can't use a period (.) as the first letter of a filename, because that has special meaning for Mac OS X.

Some applications may also prevent you from creating files with a slash (/) in the name, or names longer than 31 characters. These are limitations in the applications, though (caused by the merging of Unix and the old Mac OS), not in Mac OS X.

▶ **TIP**

If you've accidentally started renaming an item that you don't actually want to rename, simply press **Escape** (**Esc**) to cancel the operation.

4 Press Return

Press **Return** to commit the change. Alternatively, click anywhere on the Desktop or the folder window to deselect the item and make the name change stick.

16 Make an Alias (Shortcut)

✔ BEFORE YOU BEGIN	→ SEE ALSO
11 Find an Item	**17** Change an Icon
15 Rename a Folder or Document	

Sometimes you will have need to keep a document (or folder, or application) in more than once place at once. You might have a Word document in your **Documents** folder or a song in your **Music** folder, but you might also want to have it on your Desktop for easy access. The Dock provides some of this convenience, but sometimes what you really want is to create an *alias*—a shortcut to a document, folder, or application. This is helpful in situations where an application or another user expects to be able to find a document in a certain folder, but you want to have it in a more convenient place for yourself—but you don't want to make a duplicate that can get changed independently of the original. An alias lets you access one item from two, three, or as many locations in the system as you want, while leaving the original item unmoved.

▶ KEY TERM

Alias—A pseudo-file that, when opened, instead opens a real file, application, or folder elsewhere in the system. An alias can even point to files on external disks or remote servers, and it will mount the disk or server (even dialing up to the Internet if necessary) to access the original item.

An alias looks just like the original item, but has no contents of its own; it's just a pointer to the original file. If you double-click the alias, the original item opens. You only ever have to make changes in one place (the original file), rather than having to keep two copies of the document in sync. Unlike shortcuts in Windows, aliases in Mac OS X continue to work even if you move the original item from one place to another.

▶ NOTE

To delete an alias, simply throw it away. Trashing the alias will not damage the original item!

▮ Select Item to Alias

Open a **Finder** window and navigate to the folder that contains the item to which you want to create an alias. Click the item so that it becomes selected, with the darkened box around it.

16

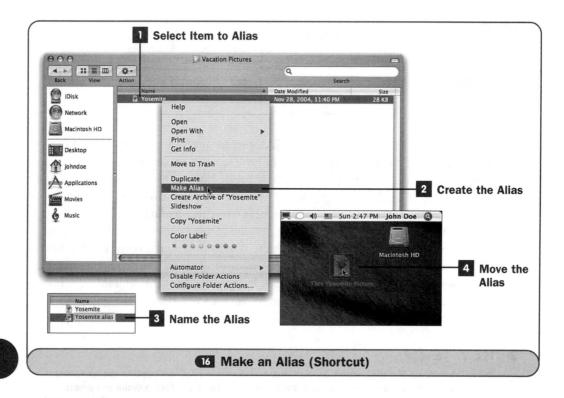

16 Make an Alias (Shortcut)

2 Create the Alias

Select **Make Alias** from the **File** menu. Alternatively, press ⌘L, or select **Make Alias** from the **Action** button menu in the Finder window. A new item appears next to the selected one, with the same name as the original and **alias** appended to the end of the name.

▶ NOTE

The ⌘L key combination seems to have no relation to the term "alias"; however, it is likely named for the Unix "link" concept, which is very similar to the aliases of the Mac OS. Mac OS X introduced the idea of minimizing windows, which was given the old ⌘M key combination that used to be used for **Make Alias**.

3 Name the Alias

The new alias becomes the selected item, and the name becomes an editable text field. You can type whatever name you like for the new alias, as long as it doesn't have the same name as any other item in the folder it's in. Press **Return** to commit the name change.

4 Move the Alias

Open another **Finder** window, navigate to where you want to move the alias, and drag the alias from its original location to the new window. If you want the alias to reside on the Desktop, just drag the newly renamed alias from the original Finder window to the Desktop.

▶ **TIP**

An even faster way to create an alias is to hold down ⌘ and **Option** as you drag an item from one Finder window to another. The curved arrow icon next to your mouse pointer indicates that you will create an alias rather than moving the file or creating a duplicate.

---

17 Change an Icon

✔ **BEFORE YOU BEGIN**	→ **SEE ALSO**
13 Create a New Folder	**18** Set a Color Label
15 Rename a Folder or Document	

One of the convenient and unique features of the Mac OS is that you can apply your own custom icons to individual documents, folders, and volumes (disks). You can copy an icon from one item to another, create your own icons from picture files, or remove custom icons from items to return them to their generic appearance.

1 Locate the Source Image

An icon can come from either of two places: a picture file copied to the Clipboard, or an existing icon copied from another document or folder. Decide where the icon is going to come from; open a **Finder** window and navigate to where that source item is.

2 Copy the Source Image to Clipboard

To create an icon from a picture file, first open the picture in Preview (or any other picture-viewing application that allows you to copy image data to the Clipboard). Copy the picture to the Clipboard by choosing **Edit**, **Copy** or pressing ⌘C.

▶ **TIP**

You can view the contents of the Clipboard by switching to the Finder and then choosing **Edit**, **Show Clipboard**. If the picture has been successfully copied to the Clipboard, it will appear in the Clipboard window that opens.

16

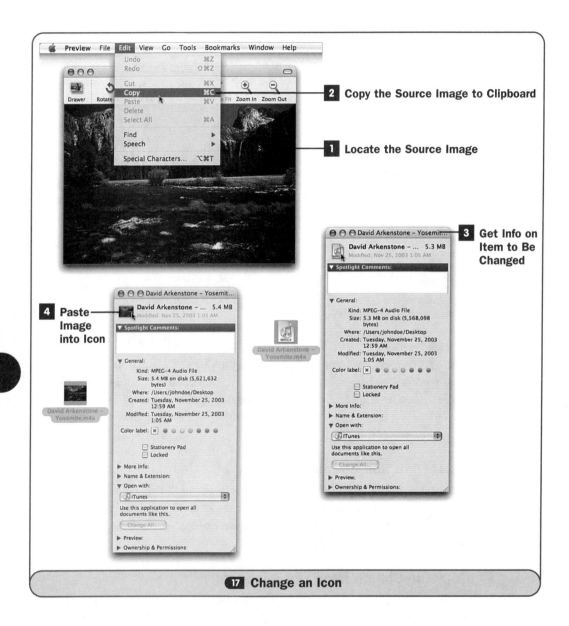

2 Copy the Source Image to Clipboard

1 Locate the Source Image

3 Get Info on Item to Be Changed

4 Paste Image into Icon

17 Change an Icon

To copy an existing icon from another item, select that item and then choose **File, Get Info** (or press ⌘I). Use the mouse to select the icon in the top-left corner of the **General** pane of the **Info** window, and choose **Edit, Copy** or press ⌘C to copy the icon to the Clipboard.

3 Get Info on Item to Be Changed

Select the document or folder whose icon you want to change. Choose **File**, **Get Info** or press ⌘I. Click the icon in the top-left corner of the **General** pane of the **Info** window.

4 Paste Image into Icon

Press ⌘V to paste the Clipboard's contents onto the item as its new icon.

▶ NOTE

In Mac OS X, icons can contain 32-bit picture data—red, green, blue, and alpha (transparency) channels, with 8 bits each. If a part of the icon image is transparent (the alpha channel is at maximum), that part of the icon will not be clickable—clicking on that region will not select the icon. This means that if you apply a custom icon that's got a weird shape and not much non-transparent image data, it will be difficult to click the icon in the Finder.

For icons in the Dock, the whole square region of an icon responds to a click, whether it's transparent or not.

Icons in Mac OS X can be arbitrarily scaled to any size up to 128×128 pixels, so technically you only need a single image for an icon; however, icons often look best at 32×32, where some icons switch to a "lower-resolution" version for better readability at smaller sizes. Use an application like Iconographer (http://www.mscape.com) to create these multi-sized icons.

17

18 Set a Color Label

✔ BEFORE YOU BEGIN	→ SEE ALSO
15 Rename a Folder or Document	**11** Find a File
17 Change an Icon	**14** Create a Smart Folder That Contains Certain Types of Items

In Mac OS X, you can assign different colored "labels" to documents and folders. The meanings of these labels are up to you to define—a blue label might mean "Incomplete projects" or "Items I haven't looked at yet," and red labels might signify "Documents from the Thompson account." Labels appear in the highlight color of an item's name, in an oval around the text. You can sort items in the Finder based on the label color, allowing you to group items conceptually without having to fiddle with their names or put them into folders. You can also use the color label as a search criterion in a Spotlight search or Smart Folder.

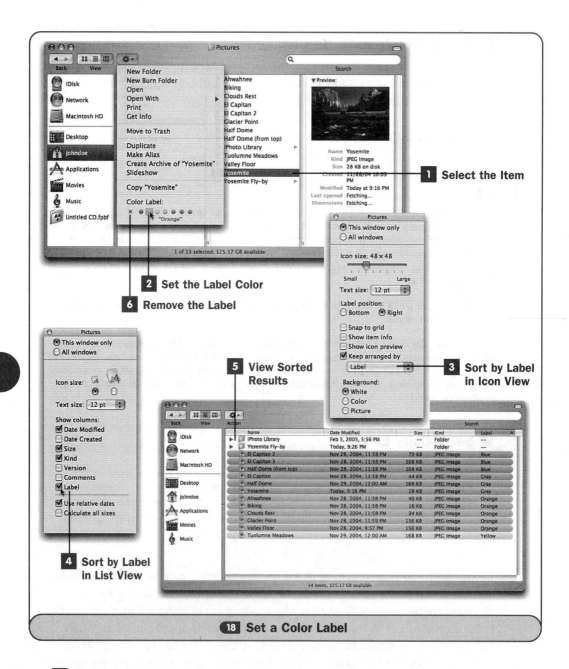

18 Set a Color Label

1 Select the Item

In a Finder window, select the item you want to label.

▶ TIP

You can label multiple items at once. Select as many items as you want, using the **Shift** or **Command** key in conjunction with mouse clicks, and then set the label color.

2 Set the Label Color

From the **File** menu or the **Action** button menu, choose the **Color Label** you want to use. Seven colors are available to choose from; click the appropriate colored dot. You can also set the label by right-clicking (or **Control**+clicking) the item and selecting the label color from the contextual menu.

3 Sort by Label in Icon View

In the Finder's Icon view, you can sort items by label color. After you have set different colored labels for several items within a folder, select **View, View Options**. In the **View Options** panel that opens, select the **Keep arranged by** check box and select **Label** from the drop-down menu to group items by their assigned label colors.

▶ TIP

In Icon view, choose **View, Arrange** and then choose **by Label** to arrange the contents of a folder immediately into a well-organized grid sorted by the files' labels.

4 Sort by Label in List View

You can also sort items by label colors in the Finder's list view. First make sure that the **Label** column is shown by opening the **View Options** panel (choose **View, View Options**) and selecting the **Label** check box. Then, in the Finder window, scroll to the far right of the window and click the **Label** column heading to sort the list based on the assigned colors.

▶ TIP

You can also make use of color labels when finding files. While building a Spotlight search in the Finder or creating a Smart Folder, create a criterion based on the **Label**; you can then specify which color labels you want to look for, or which ones you want to avoid (using the **is not** clause). Create as many of these criteria as necessary to match the correct files.

5 View Sorted Results

Although these examples are shown in black and white, the names of the label colors in the Finder's list view show how easily you can sort items in a folder based on label colors.

6 Remove the Label

To clear a label you don't need anymore, select the item with the colored label you want to remove. From the **File** menu or the **Action** button menu, click the **X** under the **Color Label** option to remove the color. You can also access the **Color Label** options by right-clicking (or **Control**+clicking) to open the contextual menu.

You can assign special meanings to the various color labels. In the Finder **Preferences**, click the **Labels** tab; then, next to each color, type a new name for each label. For instance, you might make red signify "Overdue," and yellow signify "In-progress," to help you keep track of documents that you're working on over a long period of time. Without color labels, writing the chapters of this book would have been much more difficult!

19 Move, Copy, or Delete a Document or Folder

✔ **BEFORE YOU BEGIN**

- **11** Find an Item
- **15** Rename a Folder or Document
- **18** Set a Color Label

Moving a document or folder from one place to another is one of those fundamental tasks that make up the core of using an operating system such as Mac OS X. If you ever decide to organize your files or clean up your system, you've got a lot of folder manipulation and document-moving ahead of you.

When you *duplicate* a document or folder, you create an identical copy of it in the same folder, with all the same properties except for the word **copy** added to its name. You can then use this duplicate to make changes, create a backup, or any number of other uses. Unlike an alias (which is just a link back to the original file), a duplicate is actually a second file that exists separately from the original and shares nothing with the original except for its name.

▶ **NOTE**

If you drag an item from one volume or disk to another (such as from a CD-ROM to the hard disk), the item is duplicated rather than moved. The green + icon next to the mouse cursor indicates that the operation will be a duplication. To duplicate rather than move an item directly into another location, hold the **Option** key as you drag a document or folder from one Finder window to another.

Because *deleting* a document or folder is by nature a destructive action, Mac OS X makes it a two-step process to protect your files. First you move the item into the Trash (analogous to Windows' Recycle Bin); later, you empty the Trash to delete the items in it permanently. You might think this an unnecessary precaution, but sooner or later you will have an experience where you wish you hadn't deleted something. If you haven't yet emptied the Trash, you can easily retrieve the deleted item.

18

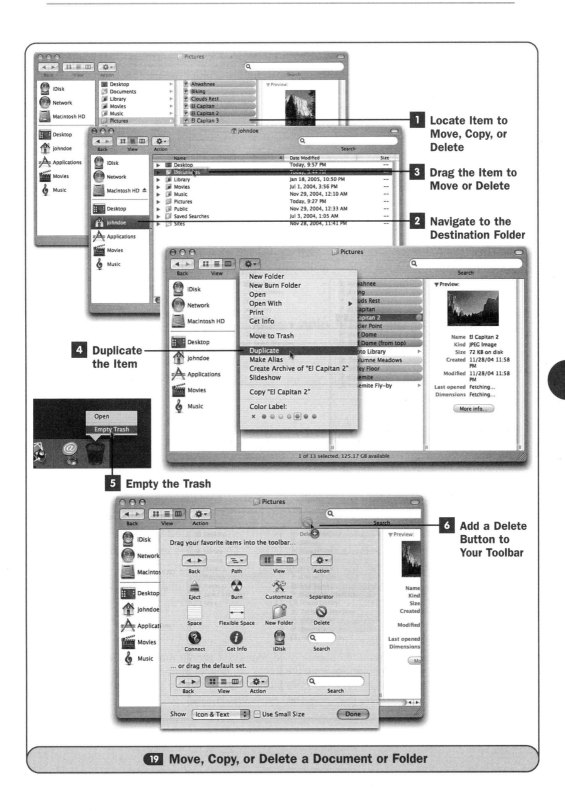

1 Locate Item to Move, Copy, or Delete

3 Drag the Item to Move or Delete

2 Navigate to the Destination Folder

4 Duplicate the Item

5 Empty the Trash

6 Add a Delete Button to Your Toolbar

19 Move, Copy, or Delete a Document or Folder

1 Locate the Item to Move, Copy, or Delete

In a Finder window, navigate to the document or folder that you want to move, copy, or delete. If you're working with an item on the Desktop, you don't have to open this first Finder window.

▶ TIPS

You can select multiple items at once by dragging a selection box or by using modifier keys—hold down **Shift** to select a contiguous block of files, or ⌘ to select multiple individual files. To move or delete these multiple items, click any of the selected items and drag.

You don't necessarily have to open a second, "destination" Finder window. If you have spring-loaded folders enabled, you can drag the item onto any folder, hold it there, and the folder will spring open into a new Finder window. Keep repeating this process—without letting go of the mouse button—until you're at the destination. Then release the button to move the item.

2 Navigate to the Destination Folder

If you're moving an item, open a second Finder window, and use it to navigate to the folder to which you want to move the document or folder. If you're moving an item to the Desktop, you don't have to open a second Finder window.

3 Drag the Item to Move or Delete

To **move** the item, click and drag the document or folder from the first Finder window into the second one.

To **delete** the item, drag the item to the **Trash** can at the right end of the Dock. Alternatively, select the item or multiple items, then choose **File, Move to Trash** (or right-click or **Control**+click the item and select **Move to Trash** from the contextual menu), or simply press ⌘**Delete**. The items are now in the Trash, and can be retrieved by clicking the **Trash** icon to open a window that lists all the items in the Trash, and then dragging the items back out again.

▶ NOTE

When deleting items on a remote network drive, Mac OS X cannot move the items to the **Trash** on your own computer; instead, the items are deleted immediately (after you confirm in a dialog box that this is what you actually want to do). Be careful deleting items on a remotely mounted drive—you can't undo the action!

4 Duplicate the Item

Choose **File**, **Duplicate** to create a copy of the selected item. Alternatively, select **Duplicate** from the Finder's **Action** menu, press ⌘D, or right-click or **Control**+click them item and choose **Duplicate** from the contextual menu that opens.

▶ **NOTE**

If you duplicate a folder, all of the folder's contents are duplicated as well.

A new item is created next to the original one; the new item has the same name as the original with the word **copy** appended to it before the extension (if any). This default naming convention allows the duplicate to appear next to the original when you sort by name.

To give the new item a more descriptive name, click the item's name and type a new one. Press **Return** when you're done.

5 Empty the Trash

Periodically, you should empty the Trash to clear out the list of items you have thrown away and free up disk space (which is not recovered if you simply throw items away). Emptying the Trash is a permanent, one-way operation; afterward, items that were in the Trash can't be recovered. Choose **Empty Trash** from the **Finder** menu; alternatively, press **Shift+⌘+Delete**. A confirmation message appears (which you can turn off in the **Finder Preferences** window). After you confirm the operation, the Trash is emptied.

19

▶ **NOTE**

If you simply empty the Trash, there's a possibility that the deleted items can be recovered by the right kind of special software. If you've thrown away sensitive data that you want to make sure can never be retrieved, Mac OS X provides a **Secure Empty Trash** option. From the **Finder** menu, select **Secure Empty Trash**, and confirm at the dialog box that you want to proceed with this operation, which scrambles the data where the deleted files were, making it impossible to retrieve them.

6 Add a Delete Button to Your Toolbar

If you want, you can put a button on the Finder toolbar that lets you immediately move all selected items to the Trash with a single click. With a Finder window open, choose **View**, **Customize Toolbar** and drag the **Delete** button from the **Customize Toolbar** dialog box into the toolbar where you want it to appear. Then click **Done** to close the dialog box.

20 Burn a CD/DVD

✔ BEFORE YOU BEGIN	→ SEE ALSO
19 Move, Copy, or Delete a Document or Folder	**85** Create (or Burn) a Custom Audio CD

Most modern Macs come with drives that can *burn* CD-ROMs, and many can also burn DVDs. If you have such a drive, you can take advantage of the modern physical method for transferring documents from one computer to another: writable optical discs.

▶ KEY TERMS

Burn—To write documents to an optical disc (a CD-R, CD-RW, or DVD-R).

CD-R—Writable compact disc. A CD-R can be burned once, and after that its contents cannot be changed. A CD-R or CD-RW can hold 650 or 700 megabytes of data, depending on the format.

CD-RW—Rewritable compact disc. A CD-RW can be burned multiple times, usually up to a few dozen times.

DVD-R—Writable digital versatile disc. A DVD can hold 4.7 gigabytes of data and generally costs significantly more than a writable CD. Data on a DVD is heavily compressed, making the format much more complex than that of a CD. Some DVD formats, such as DVD+RW and DVD-RW, can be written to more than once.

Burn Folder—A special kind of folder that can be used to set up a collection of items to burn onto a disc. When you insert a writable disc, you can associate it with an existing Burn Folder to immediately burn its contents to the disc.

Floppy disks used to be the medium of choice for storing or transferring data. With the advent of the iMac, however, floppy drives vanished from the Mac in favor of external Zip drives and other competing forms of auxiliary storage, as well as the newly popular method of transferring files over the Internet. Although this provided much of the same functionality as floppies did (without the 1.44-megabyte size limitation), many people still had a need for a way to store large documents, as well as to create better media for installing software. Writable CD and DVD drives, with their versatility and inexpensive media, have stepped into that niche in the computing world.

Mac OS X makes the process of *burning* a CD or DVD straightforward. You insert a blank disc, move documents to that disc in the Finder, and then drag the disc's icon to the Trash to burn the documents onto it. You can also use *Burn Folders* to create collections of data that can be set up before you insert a writable disc, and that can be easily burned more than once.

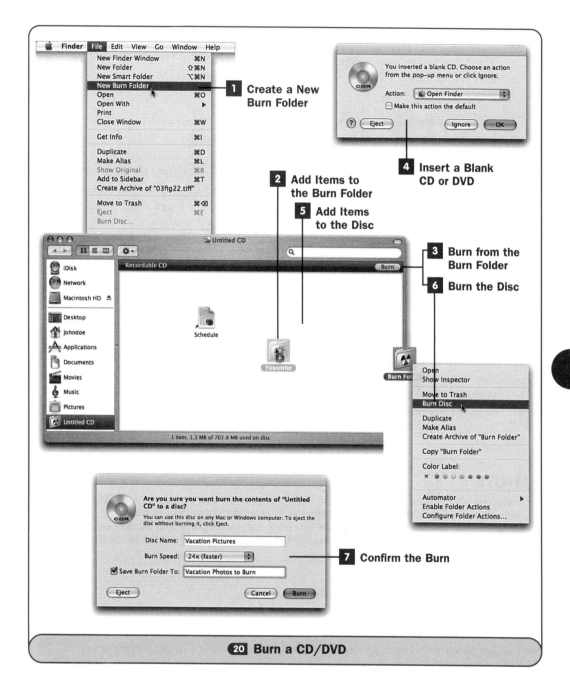

1 Create a New Burn Folder

2 Add Items to the Burn Folder

4 Insert a Blank CD or DVD

5 Add Items to the Disc

3 Burn from the Burn Folder

6 Burn the Disc

7 Confirm the Burn

20 Burn a CD/DVD

1 Create a New Burn Folder

These first three steps are optional. If you have a *CD-R* or DVD ready to burn, and you don't need to burn the same collection of files repeatedly, you can skip to step 4.

A *Burn Folder* is a way to create a saved collection of items that you can burn multiple times to make many identical copies of a disc. In the Finder, choose **File, New Burn Folder**. A new folder appears in the current Finder window (or on the Desktop), marked with a "Burn" symbol on the folder icon and with a name of **Burn Folder**. A Finder window showing the contents of this empty folder also appears. You can see from the dark and shiny header bar on the navigation pane that this is a special kind of folder: It's a container for items to burn onto a disc, complete with a **Burn** button at the top.

Rename the Burn Folder to give it a name descriptive of its contents. When you burn a CD or DVD using this folder, its volume name will be that of this Burn Folder.

2 Add Items to the Burn Folder

Drag items into the Burn Folder to set up the collection of data to be burned. Use folder hierarchies and customized folder window presentations however you like; the way the contents of the Burn Folder appear is the way they will appear once burned onto a CD or DVD. You can close the **Burn Folder** window and come back to it later; its contents are preserved just as with any folder.

▶ NOTE

Note that as you drag items to the Burn Folder, the curved arrow on your mouse pointer indicates that you're creating aliases rather than dragging the original items. This ensures that the original items won't be moved or lost in the process of burning the disc. When the disc is burned, complete copies of the original items are written to the disc, not just aliases.

3 Burn from the Burn Folder

When you're done adding items to the Burn Folder and ready to create the disc, choose **Burn Disc** from the **File** menu or from the contextual menu that appears when you right-click or **Control**+click the Burn Folder's icon, or by clicking **Burn** in the header bar of the folder's Finder window. You are prompted to insert a blank disc; a dialog box reports the minimum size of the disc to hold the contents of the Burn Folder.

4 Insert a Blank CD or DVD

Many Macs have an optical drive with a tray you must eject before you can insert a disc. Press the **Eject** key on the keyboard, place the blank disc in the tray, and press **Eject** again to close the drive.

Most newer Macs, such as PowerBooks, newer iBooks, the Mac mini, and the iMac G5 have slot-loading drives. On these Macs, simply insert the disc into the slot and press until the drive pulls the disc in.

Unless you're burning from a Burn Folder, Mac OS X automatically tries to mount the disc. When it finds that the disc is blank, the operating system presents you with a dialog box that asks what you want to do with it. For CD-R discs, you can choose whether the disc is intended for documents or for music. To create a disc for music files, select **Open iTunes** from the **Action** drop-down list. You can then use iTunes to burn a music CD that can be played in any CD player, or an MP3 CD that can be played on modern MP3 CD players. To create a disc for documents, choose **Open Finder** (the default) from the **Action** drop-down list. If you mistakenly choose the wrong application, just eject the disc and insert it again.

▶ **NOTE**

20

Another choice you have is to click the **Ignore** button. If you do this, the blank disc is not mounted for burning and does not show up anywhere in the system; you must use the **Eject** key to get it out. The **Ignore** option is available so you can have a blank disc in the drive before you begin a task such as burning a CD or DVD from the Finder, iTunes, or Disk Utility, and thus save having to be prompted to insert one.

If you are burning from an existing Burn Folder, Mac OS X automatically prepares to burn and presents a dialog box asking for a disc name presenting burning options. Skip to step 7 if this is the case.

If you are not burning from a Burn Folder and have simply inserted a new blank disc, Mac OS X places the disc on the Desktop (with the name **Untitled CD**) and opens a Finder window similar to the one you see if you're working with a Burn Folder. (Burn Folders and mounted blank discs work the same way in the Finder.) A Burn Folder representing the blank disc is also automatically added to the Finder's Sidebar.

▶ **NOTE**

Refer to **85 Create (or Burn) a Custom Audio CD** for more information on creating audio CDs and DVDs.

5 Add Items to the Disc

You can now fill the disc with documents. Drag items into the disc's Finder window or onto the disc's icon as you would a Burn Folder or any mounted volume. Organize items in folders the way you want them to appear each time you or anyone else inserts the disc; if you try to put more data on the disc than it can hold, you will get an error message. (As with a Burn Folder, the items you drag to the blank disc are just aliases, not the originals or duplicates.)

▶ **TIP**

You can change the name of the blank disc volume just as you would rename a folder, by clicking its name and typing a new one, anytime until you burn the disc.

6 Burn the Disc

When you're happy with the contents of the disc, it's time to burn it. In the Finder, click the **Burn** symbol next to the disc's icon in the Sidebar, or click the **Burn** button at the top of the blank disc's Finder window if it's open; alternatively, drag the disc's icon from the Desktop to the **Trash** can icon (which becomes a **Burn** symbol while you're dragging the disc).

7 Confirm the Burn

A dialog box prompts for some final burning options. First, specify a disc name, which can be different from the name of the disc as it appeared while you were building its contents. Then, choose the burn speed, which can range from slower but more reliable speeds (**4x**) to faster but potentially more unreliable speeds (**24x**); it's generally safe to use the fastest speed available, but if you encounter errors, try slower speeds. Also, select the **Save Burn Folder To** check box and specify a folder name if you want to save a Burn Folder of the disc's contents, in case you want to burn more copies of the same disc in the future. When you're ready, click the **Burn** button. (You can also choose to **Eject** the disc, discarding all the changes you've made.)

20

▶ NOTES

Be aware that Windows PCs sometimes cannot read a volume name longer than 16 characters; keep your disc name concise and descriptive if you intend the disc to be used on different kinds of computers.

While you have a writable disc mounted, if you have **Fast User Switching** enabled (see **112** **Switch to Another User**), other users who are logged in at the same time as you won't be able to access the optical drive or the disc in it. You must either burn or eject the disc before other users can use the drive. (If you don't have Fast User Switching enabled, other users won't be able to be logged in at the same time you are.)

The disc will now be burned; this process can take several minutes, including the verification process after the burn is complete (which you can skip if you want, by clicking the **Stop** button that appears in the **Burn** progress dialog box). After the burn is complete, the disc is mounted in the Finder (or in iTunes, if it's a music CD), and can be accessed like any other CD-ROM or DVD.

After the disc is burned, a Burn Folder with contents identical to the disc's is saved on the Desktop, if you so chose; you can burn another copy of the same disc by skipping back to step 3.

▶ NOTE

Some software, such as open-source operating systems like Linux and FreeBSD, can be installed from CD images that you download for free. Before you can install the software, however, you must create an actual CD-ROM or DVD using the disc image that you have downloaded. Similarly, you can make a duplicate of an installation CD or DVD (for safekeeping) by creating a disk image of the original disc.

Use the **Disk Utility** application (found in your **Utilities** folder) to create a new disk image. Insert the CD or DVD, then choose **Images**, **New**, **Image from <*disc name*>**. Disk Utility then creates a **.iso** disk image file from the disc's contents.

Choose **Images**, **Burn** to select a **.iso** disk image file to burn onto a new CD or DVD. Be sure to have a blank CD or DVD-RW disc handy! (Mac OS X supports the ***DVD+RW*** format as well, but less enthusiastically.)

21 Add a Newly Installed Hard Disk to the System

→ **SEE ALSO**

22 Partition a Hard Disk

No matter how large your Mac's disk might seem when you first buy it, the computing world has a way of coming up with new ways to use up disk space. Just a few years ago, it was difficult to imagine a 10-gigabyte disk. Now, most people's digital music collections exceed that size easily. With digital video editing becoming ever more popular, even 60GB or 100GB disks are starting to look small.

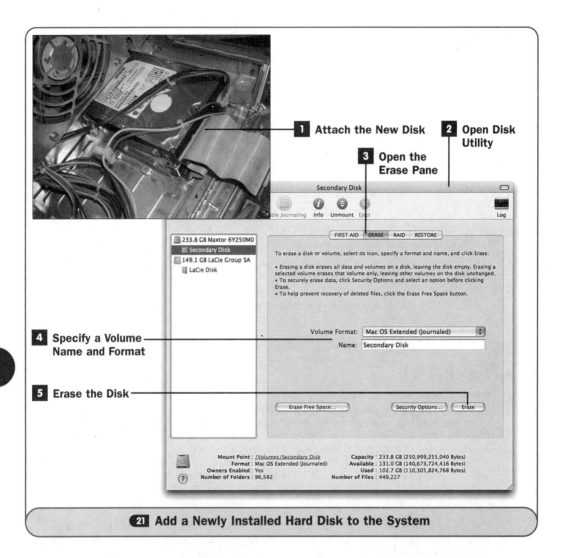

21

21 Add a Newly Installed Hard Disk to the System

The expandable Power Macs allow you to install new internal hard drives; even with iMacs, Mac minis, and laptops, you can hook up new storage devices over USB or FireWire connections. When you buy a new disk, however, you must properly prepare it before it can be used.

1 Attach the New Disk

For an internal hard disk, follow the instructions provided with your Mac for adding a new disk. Generally, you will have to remove your computer's cover (with the power off, of course), remove a metal caddy, mount the drive in the caddy, and replace the cover so that the disk cable and power cords can be attached.

▶ **TIP**

Be careful when working with the interior of your computer! Unless you're really sure what you're doing, you could damage your computer's components (through static discharge, for example) or yourself. If you have any doubts at all about what you should do to install your new disk correctly and safely, you should have the task done by an authorized party (such as a Certified Apple Reseller, or an Apple Store).

External drives are much easier to connect; they involve little more than plugging them in and turning them on. You can install external drives while the Mac is running.

2 Open Disk Utility

Open the Finder and navigate to the **Applications** folder, then to the **Utilities** subfolder. Launch the **Disk Utility** program by double-clicking its icon.

3 Open the Erase Pane

If you want to make the entire new disk available as one large volume, you will want to "erase" the disk. This process is what most other operating systems refer to as "formatting" the disk—preparing it to hold data within your operating system.

21

▶ **TIP**

You can instead *partition* your disk into several smaller volumes, if you prefer. See **22 Partition a Hard Disk** for further details on partitioning.

All available disks are shown in the left pane of the **Disk Utility** window. Select the new disk (in this example, it's listed as **233.8 GB Maxtor 6Y250M0**), and then click the **Erase** tab. The **Erase** pane is where your disk will be initialized and made available for you to store your additional data.

▶ **TIP**

You can erase either the entire disk, or just a single volume. The sidebar of the **Disk Utility** window shows you whole disks (listed by their model name, such as **233.8 GB Maxtor 6Y250M0**), and volumes within each disk (listed by the volume names you've assigned them, such as **Macintosh HD** or **Secondary Disk**). Before you erase a disk, make sure that you've selected the correct disk or volume. When you erase an entire disk, you create one large volume on it, with the volume name that you specify in the **Name** field.

4 Specify a Volume Name and Format

Select a format for the volume; **Mac OS Extended (Journaled)** is the default and is the best choice for Mac OS X. Don't select any of the other format options unless you intend to use this disk with Windows or Unix machines as well.

Enter a descriptive name for the volume that will be created. You can change this name later if you want; simply click the volume name in a Finder window or on the Desktop, and type a new name (as when renaming any other item).

5 Erase the Disk

Click the **Erase** button to erase the disk. This process might take several minutes; after it is done, the new hard disk volume will be mounted in the Finder and ready for use.

---

22 Partition a Hard Disk

✔ **BEFORE YOU BEGIN**

> 21 Add a Newly Installed Hard Disk to the System
> 143 Back Up Your Information

If you've just added a new disk but you don't want it all to be represented as single large volume—rather you want to slice it up into several smaller volumes—you can *partition* the disk.

21

▶ KEY TERM

Partition—A disk can be used as a single large volume, or it can be divided into several smaller volumes. This can be done for a variety of reasons, from security to performance to simple organizational preference. Each smaller volume is a *partition*, and to *partition* the disk is to divide it into volumes.

Partitioning provides a number of practical and psychological advantages; you can designate one volume for video editing, another for your digital music library, another for random junk, and a fourth for an alternative installation of Mac OS X. Each of these volumes is mounted as a different disk in the Finder and can be navigated separately, with each volume comprising its own unique organizational structure. This arrangement can be much easier to manage than having a single large volume with folders for different uses.

If your disk has multiple volumes, you can put a different custom icon on each one—and let's face it, custom icons are fun. The more, the merrier!

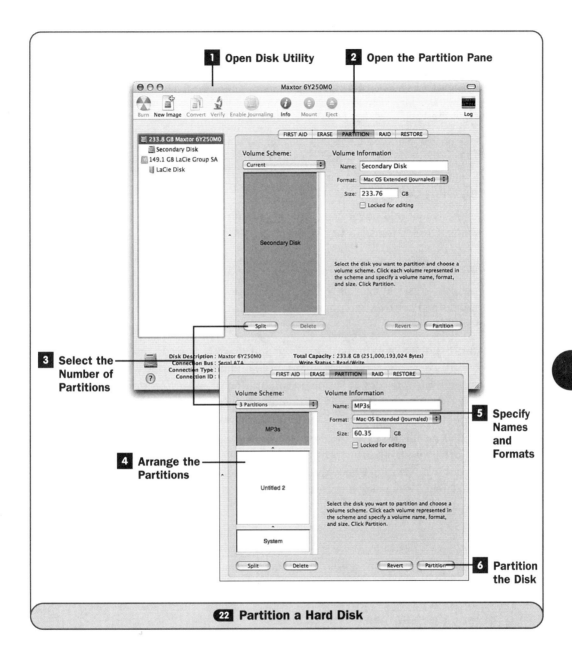

1 Open Disk Utility

2 Open the Partition Pane

3 Select the Number of Partitions

4 Arrange the Partitions

5 Specify Names and Formats

6 Partition the Disk

22 Partition a Hard Disk

▶ **NOTE**

Practically speaking, you can't partition a disk without losing all the data that's already on it. If you want to divide an existing disk, or change the sizes of existing partitions on a disk, you'll have to resign yourself to the idea that your data will be erased in the process. Some third-party commercial software allows partitions to be resized without data loss, but most such packages don't support Mac OS X.

Always back up your hard disk before partitioning anything! The process is straightforward, but that's no consolation if a disk is inadvertently erased.

1 Open Disk Utility

Open the Finder and navigate to the **Applications** folder, then to the **Utilities** subfolder. Launch the **Disk Utility** program by double-clicking its icon.

2 Open the Partition Pane

All available disks appear in the listing on the left. Click the disk you want to partition; the **Partition** tab appears. Click on this tab. The **Partition** pane appears.

Be aware that you cannot partition your startup disk; you can only make such intrusive changes on a secondary disk, and not on the one where your operating system resides. If you want to partition or erase your primary startup disk (which you should only do if you intend to lose all your data and reinstall the operating system from scratch), you will need to do it by booting from your installation CD, an external disk with Mac OS X installed on it, or a network boot server, or by running **Disk Utility** from a second Macintosh, with your own computer booted into FireWire target disk mode. See **141** **Boot from Different Disks Using Keystrokes** for details on booting the computer in different modes.

▶ **NOTE**

You can't partition a volume—you have to select an entire disk from the Sidebar. Each volume is, in fact, a partition.

3 Select the Number of Partitions

The displayed disk is most likely represented as a single large, gray pool of storage space. Divide this space in two by clicking the **Split** button; the pool of space is divided in half. Click **Split** again to create a third partition, dividing one of the first two areas in half again.

Alternatively, you can directly select how many partitions you want from the **Volume Scheme** menu above the visual representation of the partitions. You can have as many as sixteen partitions on a single disk.

4 Arrange the Partitions

Here's the fun part: to specify how large each partition should be, simply drag the horizontal dividing bar between two areas and move it up or down. The **Size** field in the upper-right portion of the window reflects the size of the selected partition; select another partition to see its size.

To specify a size explicitly, click a partition to select it and type the desired size for that partition into the **Size** field. You can prevent a partition's size from changing as you fiddle with the other partitions' sizes by selecting the **Locked for Editing** check box.

5 Specify Names and Formats

Select each partition in turn and type a name for each one in the **Name** field; the name you specify here is the name for the volume that's created when you partition the disk. You can specify different formats for each partition, too, in case you want to ensure compatibility with other operating systems; for best results, however, stick with **Mac OS Extended** (journaled) format option.

6 Partition the Disk

When all the partitions are arranged to your satisfaction, click the **Partition** button. The disk will be erased, formatted, and divided into volumes; after the process is finished, each of the new volumes is mounted in the Finder, ready for you to start using them however you like.

22

---

23 Assign a Folder Action

✔ BEFORE YOU BEGIN	→ SEE ALSO
13 Create a New Folder	**36** Allow Others to Share Your Files
	11 Automate a Recurring Task

AppleScript, the built-in application-aware programming language included in Mac OS X, can be harnessed in order to extend the functionality of the Finder. AppleScript gives you the ability to assign folder actions to individual folders in the system. A folder action is a script (a simple human-readable program) that you attach to a folder; triggered by certain events, such as when you open or close the folder or add an item into it, the folder action script will perform some function. What the script can do is limited only by your imagination.

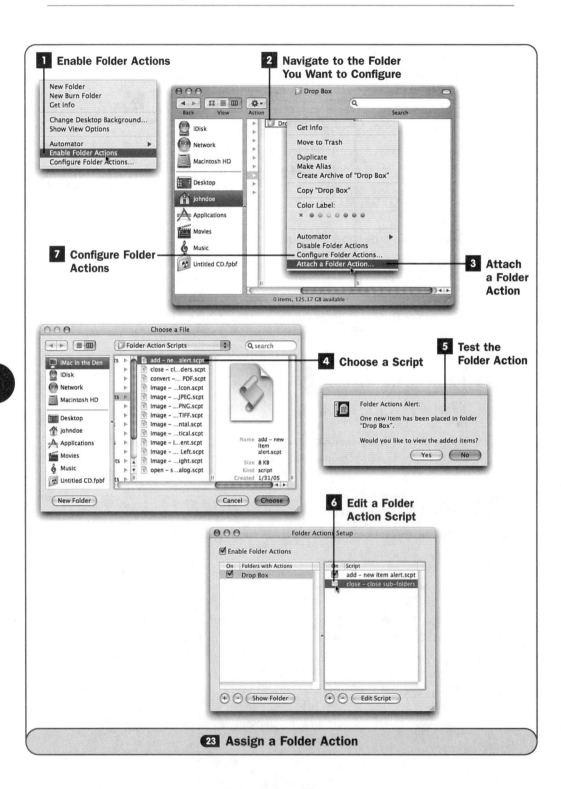

1 Enable Folder Actions

2 Navigate to the Folder You Want to Configure

7 Configure Folder Actions

3 Attach a Folder Action

4 Choose a Script

5 Test the Folder Action

Folder Actions Alert:

One new item has been placed in folder "Drop Box".

Would you like to view the added items?

6 Edit a Folder Action Script

23 Assign a Folder Action

Apple provides a few sample folder action scripts in the **Scripts** folder inside the main system **Library**. These include a script that will display the folder's comments in a dialog box when you open the folder in the Finder (useful for making sure other users are told some useful piece of information if they wander into the folder); one that pops up a dialog box informing you when any new items are added to the folder; and one that, when you close the folder, closes any windows showing subfolders of that folder. If you like, you can modify these scripts or use them as examples for new scripts that you write.

1 Enable Folder Actions

Folder actions are controlled from the contextual menu, which you can open by **Control**+clicking on or inside any Finder window or on the Desktop, or by right-clicking if you have a two-button mouse.

Open the contextual menu; select **Enable Folder Actions**. This turns on **Folder Actions** globally and allows you to assign them anywhere in the system.

2 Navigate to the Folder You Want to Configure

Open a **Finder** window and navigate to the folder to which you want to assign an action script. You can set up folder actions either from within the folder in question, or in the folder above it in the hierarchy.

3 Attach a Folder Action

Control+click or right-click the selected folder and select **Attach a Folder Action** from the contextual menu. A file selector window opens, by default starting in the global **Folder Action Scripts** folder in **/Library/Scripts**.

4 Choose a Script

You can choose from one of the many sample scripts in this folder, or any other script that you have written or downloaded. Choose the script file and click **Choose** to assign the script to the selected folder.

▶ **NOTE**
You can assign multiple scripts to the same folder, if you like.

Inside the **AppleScript** folder in the **Applications** folder, you'll find another collection of folder action scripts that you can attach to folders. Use the built-in navigator to locate these scripts and attach them.

23

5 Test the Folder Action

Depending on what the script does, it will be triggered by different actions—adding an item to the folder, opening or closing the folder, and so on. Make sure that the folder reacts properly when you trigger it. For instance, if you selected the **open - show comments in dialog.scpt** script, first use the **Get Info** panel to add a comment to the folder. Then open the folder and make sure a dialog box pops up showing you the comments you entered. In the example shown here, the **add - new item alert.scpt**, attached to your **Drop Box** folder, pops up a notification to tell you whenever anybody puts a new item into your **Drop Box** folder.

6 Edit a Folder Action Script

After a script has been attached to a folder, you can edit the script directly to modify its behavior. **Control**+click the folder to view the contextual menu, open the **Edit a Folder Action** submenu, and select the script that you want to edit.

After making your changes, click **Save** and test the folder action again.

7 Configure Folder Actions

23

You can manage all the folders in the system that have folder actions attached at once. **Control**+click or right-click on or inside any Finder window or the Desktop to display the contextual menu and select **Configure Folder Actions**. A panel opens up that lists all configured folders and all the scripts assigned to each one. You can turn the individual scripts on and off, add or remove configured folders, and add or remove scripts from folders.

Select any script and click the **Edit Script** button to modify the script so that it does exactly what you want. If you have a lot of folder actions to manage, this is the most direct way to control them all.

24 Add a Second Display

→ SEE ALSO

103 Change Your Desktop Picture

Doubling your Desktop's real estate has always been one of the best things about the Mac; ever since the first expandable Macs, it's been possible to attach a second monitor (or *display*) and instantly be able to use it to the fullest capacity that it would support. For instance, you could hook up a small grayscale monitor in addition to your big color one, and the two monitors would act as one large, oddly-shaped screen, and you could drag your icons and windows seamlessly from one monitor to the other (watching them change from color to black-and-white and back).

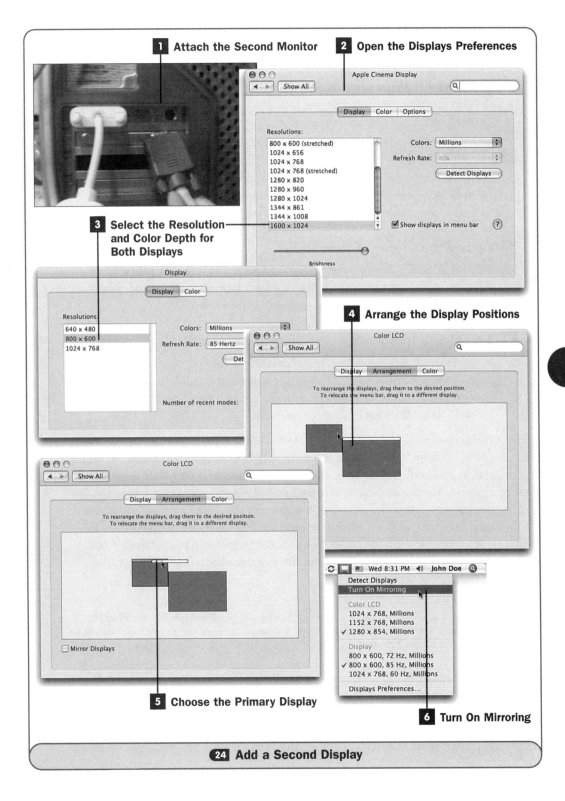

1 Attach the Second Monitor

2 Open the Displays Preferences

Apple Cinema Display

Show All

Display Color Options

Resolutions:
800 x 600 (stretched)
1024 x 656
1024 x 768
1024 x 768 (stretched)
1280 x 820
1280 x 960
1280 x 1024
1344 x 861
1344 x 1008
1600 x 1024

Colors: Millions
Refresh Rate: n/a
Detect Displays

☑ Show displays in menu bar ?

Brightness

3 Select the Resolution and Color Depth for Both Displays

Display

Display Color

Resolutions:
640 x 480
800 x 600
1024 x 768

Colors: Millions
Refresh Rate: 85 Hertz
Det

Number of recent modes:

4 Arrange the Display Positions

Color LCD

Show All

Display Arrangement Color

To rearrange the displays, drag them to the desired position.
To relocate the menu bar, drag it to a different display.

Color LCD

Show All

Display Arrangement Color

To rearrange the displays, drag them to the desired position.
To relocate the menu bar, drag it to a different display.

☐ Mirror Displays

C 🖳 🔲 Wed 8:31 PM ◀) John Doe 🔍
Detect Displays
Turn On Mirroring

Color LCD
1024 x 768, Millions
1152 x 768, Millions
✓ 1280 x 854, Millions

Display
800 x 600, 72 Hz, Millions
✓ 800 x 600, 85 Hz, Millions
1024 x 768, 60 Hz, Millions

Displays Preferences...

5 Choose the Primary Display

6 Turn On Mirroring

24 Add a Second Display

24

It's the same today. All Power Mac models come with video cards that support two monitors, and all PowerBooks have video ports for additional monitors as well. You can even add more video cards if you want to plug in more monitors. Mac OS X lets you define where each monitor is in relation to the others, specify which is the primary monitor (the one that gets the menu bar and the Dock), and control each monitor's resolution and color depth.

1   Attach the Second Monitor

Plug in the new monitor's power cord, and connect the VGA or DVI cable to the available port on your Mac's video card. Mac OS X immediately recognizes the new monitor and repaints the screen.

2   Open the Displays Preferences

Open the **System Preferences**; click **Displays** to open the **Displays Preferences**. You'll notice that there is now a **Displays** window open on both monitors; each one controls the display that it's shown on.

3   Select the Resolution and Color Depth for Both Displays

In the **Display** tab, select the desired resolution (size of the screen, in pixels) from the **Resolutions** box. The display changes immediately to the selected resolution. Similarly, choose how many colors you want displayed on the new monitor, using the **Colors** drop-down menu.

Flat-panel monitors, such as the displays Apple sells, typically have a single "natural" resolution because it is built with a fixed grid of pixels at a certain size. Traditional CRT-based monitors can operate at a variety of resolutions because they are analog devices that can place an arbitrary number of lines on the screen. If you select a resolution other than the "natural" resolution on a flat-panel display, the image may appear blurry as Mac OS X has to interpolate between the pixels to simulate the specified resolution. Consult the manual for your flat-panel display to determine its natural resolution.

▶ TIP

Click the **Show displays in menu bar** check box to put the **Displays** System Menu in your menu bar; this menu lets you immediately select the resolution and color depth for any of your connected monitors.

Every display reproduces colors in a slightly different way; this can wreak havoc on a picture file that you're trying to get to look right on displays other than just your own. When you connect a new display, you should calibrate its colors using the **Calibrate** button found in the **Color** tab of the **Displays Preferences** window. When you do this, you create a *profile* using ColorSync,

24

Apple's industry-standard color-calibration technology. With ColorSync, every picture that you create on your computer (using Adobe Photoshop or any other application that utilizes ColorSync) is embedded with the profile that corresponds to your display's unique color characteristics. Then, when you send the file to another Mac user, that user's ColorSync-calibrated display is able to adjust itself to match what it knows about your display. The result is that the other user gets to see the picture exactly as you see it on your display, even if that monitor's colors are calibrated far differently. Printers, scanners, and other display and output devices can all be ColorSync-calibrated as well.

▶ **NOTE**

Even today, ColorSync doesn't really have an equivalent in the Windows world; this is why the Macintosh is still so popular in the graphics and publishing industry.

4 Arrange the Display Positions

On your primary display, click the **Arrangement** tab. This screen lets you visually select exactly where you want your two monitors to be positioned relative to each other. The primary display is shown in the center of the screen; click and drag the second display, shown adjacent to it, anywhere around the primary display that you want. You can place the second display to the right or left of the primary, or above or below it.

Wherever you drag the rectangle representing the second monitor, that's the position that Mac OS X stores, allowing the monitors to assemble themselves into a virtual "display" of the shape that you have defined here. For instance, in this example, you can drag a window from the primary display to the secondary by moving it to the top left of the screen; keep moving the mouse up and to the left, and the window moves onto the second display.

5 Choose the Primary Display

You can make the second display into your primary display if you want. Your primary display is the one on which your menu bar, Dock, Desktop icons, and any dialog boxes or messages appear. To select which display is the primary one, click and drag the white bar at the top of the rectangle representing the current primary display onto the other display. When you release the mouse button, the displays rearrange themselves accordingly.

24

6 Turn On Mirroring

Mirroring allows you to display the same screen contents to two different displays at once. This is useful in presentations, where you have your laptop hooked up to a projector; any actions that you perform on your laptop's screen are reflected on the projector.

Click the **Mirror displays** check box on the **Arrangement** tab to turn on mirroring. (You can also select **Turn On Mirroring** from the **Displays** System Menu.) Both displays must have the same resolution for mirroring to work; if you mirror the displays, the second display's resolution is changed to match that of the primary display.

---

25 | Set the Time and Date

→ **SEE ALSO**

26 **Enable Automatic Time Synchronization (NTP)**
107 **Adjust the Format of Numbers and Other Notations**

24

It's important for your Mac to be able to keep accurate track of the time. Lots of system functions depend on carefully scheduled execution; for instance, if you have **Software Update** set to check for new updates every week, or iSync set to synchronize your data every hour, your Mac must be able to kick off those processes at the correct time. These are just two of the functions you can see at the user level; Mac OS X, as a Unix system, runs a number of self-cleaning and bookkeeping tasks every day—late at night, when you're most likely asleep, so that those tasks don't interfere with your work. You don't want to have the disk grinding away mysteriously at noon just because you have your system's time set incorrectly.

▶ **TIP**

The Network Time Protocol (NTP) allows your computer to keep its date and time in sync with a central server. (See 26 **Enable Automatic Time Synchronization (NTP)** for more on NTP.) If you don't have a network connection, however, you must check periodically to make sure that your Mac's time is still accurate. Computers' clocks can drift over time, losing or gaining seconds or even minutes each week. NTP corrects this for you, but if you aren't networked, you have to keep an check for drift manually.

If you don't have a network connection, you'll have to set the date and time for your computer manually. You use the **Date & Time Preferences** dialog box to do this.

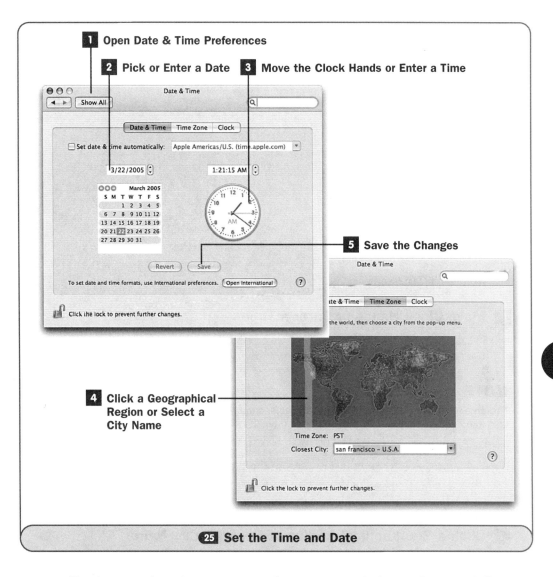

1 Open Date & Time Preferences

2 Pick or Enter a Date   **3** Move the Clock Hands or Enter a Time

5 Save the Changes

4 Click a Geographical Region or Select a City Name

25 Set the Time and Date

The time zone is an important part of your computer's time setting, especially when it comes to communicating with other computers around the world. If you send an email to someone on the other side of the country, for example, the email headers must be able to convey what time zone you're in, so that when the recipient gets the message, his email program can tell him when, *by his clock*, you wrote the message.

Apple provides a graphical method for choosing your time zone, and also allows you to select a nearby city to use its time zone information.

1 Open the Date & Time Preferences

Open the **System Preferences** from the **Apple** menu. Alternatively, you can select **Open Date & Time** from the menu that appears when you click the time display at the far right of the system's menu bar.

Click the **Date & Time** tab, if it isn't already selected. This brings up the manual configuration pane.

2 Pick or Enter a Date

Click a date in the graphical calendar to select another date within the current month.

If the date you want is in another month, use the text field above the calendar to numerically specify a month. Click each of the date fields and either type a number or click a date field. You can increment the field using the **Up** and **Down** arrows.

3 Move Clock Hands or Enter a Time

On the graphical clock, click any of the clock hands and drag it to the position you want. Click the **AM** or **PM** display to toggle between them.

25

▶ **NOTE**

The analog clock remains in motion, with the second hand going around, until you start to make changes; if you move any of the hands, the second hand stops so that you can put it in an accurate position and apply it at exactly the right time by clicking **Save**.

If you prefer, you can enter the time manually. Click any of the time fields above the graphical clock and type a number or use the **Up** and **Down** buttons to increment the values.

4 Click a Geographical Region or Select a City Name

Click the **Time Zone** tab to bring up the time zone configuration pane.

On the graphical map, click as close to your geographical location as possible; the time zone for the location you click lights up. The map also shows the location of a city close to where you clicked (from which the system is actually deriving the time zone information).

If you can't click your location on the map (for instance, if your time zone is really small), you can select a city in your time zone, and the system will adopt it. Use the **Closest City** drop-down menu to locate a nearby city; if you can't find a city in the list, it might be because the list shows cities only in the currently selected time zone. Select the text in the input box and begin typing the name of a major city in your region; the box auto-completes your input to show the nearest match, allowing you to type only as much of the city name as you have to before the system knows where you are.

▶ **NOTE**

Don't worry about Daylight Saving Time or other such localized adjustment systems. If your calendar date is set properly, Mac OS X will know what the correct time zone mode is for whatever location you select. When your area "springs forward" or "falls back" for Daylight Saving Time, your Mac will automatically adjust the system time for you.

Press **Return** to accept a city name that has been automatically completed; your time zone will change to match that city.

5 Save the Changes

As soon as you make any changes, the **Revert** and **Save** buttons on the **Date & Time** pane become active. If you're not already on the **Date & Time** pane, click the **Date & Time** tab to open that pane. Click **Revert** if you don't want to keep your changes; click **Save** to apply the changes.

▶ **NOTE**

You are prompted to either **Revert** or **Save** your changes if you quit the **System Preferences** application or try to move to another preference pane before you click **Save**.

25

26 Enable Automatic Time Synchronization (NTP)

✔ BEFORE YOU BEGIN	→ SEE ALSO
25 Set the Time and Date	**97** Create an iCal Event
28 Dial Up to the Internet with a Modem (PPP)	**107** Adjust the Format of Numbers and Other Notations
30 Configure Networking Manually	**139** Schedule Automatic Software Updates

The *Network Time Protocol (NTP)* allows your computer to keep its date and time in sync with a central server. If you have a network connection—even an intermittent one, as you might with a laptop—it's absolutely better all around to use *network time* rather than manually setting the system's time and date. Network time synchronizes your computer's clock (both the date and the time) with a public NTP server. Whenever your computer's network or Internet connection is active, it communicates with the NTP server to ensure that its clock is accurate; if there is any discrepancy, Mac OS X makes the adjustments automatically. Because this checking takes place in the background, the adjustments to be made are never large enough for you to notice—unless it's been a long time since your connection was active and your system clock has drifted a lot.

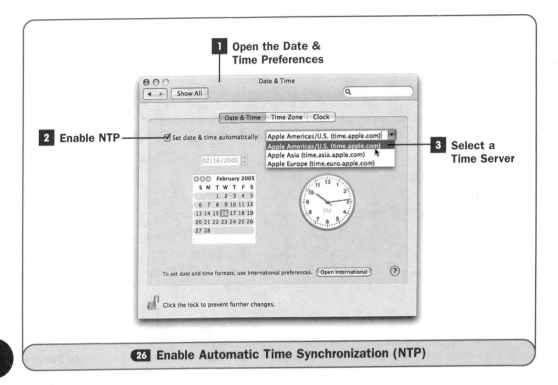

1 Open the Date & Time Preferences

2 Enable NTP

3 Select a Time Server

26 **Enable Automatic Time Synchronization (NTP)**

26

▶ **NOTE**

Some computers' clocks have severe drift problems. If you find that you have to manually set your clock more than once every couple of months—in other words, if your Mac's clock drifts by more than a couple of minutes a month—you should consider having it serviced and getting the clock chip or CMOS/PRAM battery replaced.

▶ **KEY TERM**

Network Time Protocol (NTP)—A technology in which a computer (such as a Mac) can periodically check with any of a number of central, public servers and receive an accurate reading of the current time. The computer can then calibrate its clock to match the central server, which is often of military precision.

A lot of NTP servers are active on the Internet, run by organizations such as the U.S. Naval Observatory and various universities. However, Apple runs its own NTP servers as well, in various places around the world, one of which is bound to be close to your location.

1 **Open the Date & Time Preferences**

Open the **System Preferences** from the **Apple** menu; click **Date & Time** to open the **Date & Time Preferences**. Alternatively, select **Open Date & Time** from the menu that appears when you click the time display at the far right of the system's menu bar.

▶ **NOTE**

The **Clock** tab is used to customize the menu bar clock display, including whether the clock should be shown in the menu bar or in a floating window, and what format the time display should take. You can even set Mac OS X to announce the time in a voice of your choosing.

For more options on how the system should display the time, such as whether to use a leading zero for the hour or how noon and midnight should be represented (as variously used in different countries), click **Open International** at the bottom of the screen. See **107** **Adjust the Format of Numbers and Other Notations** for more.

2 Enable NTP

Select the **Set Date & Time Automatically** check box to enable network time synchronization.

3 Select a Time Server

The default time server is **time.apple.com**, located at the Apple campus in Cupertino, California. There are other choices available— **time.asia.apple.com** for Asia, and **time.euro.apple.com** for Europe—that you might want to choose instead if you're not in the Americas. Because NTP operates by a carefully timed exchange of data packets, it's important to choose a time server that's geographically near to you to minimize network latency during the sync process.

26

If you want to use a different time server (such as **tick.usno.navy.mil**, the United States Naval Observatory's public NTP server), enter its hostname in the input box.

As soon as you select a time server, the time is synchronized; you can then close the window, because no further configuration is needed, and no changes need to be saved.

PART II

Networking and The Internet

IN THIS PART:

4

Networking Your Mac

IN THIS CHAPTER:

No Mac is an island. Computing in the modern world is almost synonymous with Internet connectivity and the ability for one computer to communicate with others, whether down the hall or across the globe. Mac OS X is a thoroughly modern operating system, with professional-grade support for *TCP/IP* (the communication mechanism that runs the Internet) and a suite of full-featured applications that give you the tools you need to make the most of the Internet—use email, browse the Web, and much more. Whether your Mac is connected to the global network using a dial-up modem, or whether you have several computers in your household or office that are connected to each other in a LAN, Mac OS X can handle it all.

▶ KEY TERMS

TCP/IP—Transport Control Protocol and Internet Protocol. This is the general term for the software communication protocols that underlie all networking on the Internet.

LAN—Local Area Network. A group of computers directly connected to each other with cables and devices such as hubs or switches. If you have to connect using a long-distance method such as a dial-up modem or DSL connection, it's a Wide Area Network, or WAN.

Sure, you can do a ton of things with just a single computer—process words, listen to music, edit video, organize photos—but when you plug in an Internet connection, you open up the horizons of a much wider computing world. What's more, when you make the move from a single Mac to several Macs, or add some Windows machines to the household or office, you begin to reap the benefits of Mac OS X's ability to integrate all your machines together seamlessly. You can share files between Macs, or between Macs and Windows machines. You can run programs hosted on other computers. With *.Mac*, you can synchronize your computers' Address Books and web bookmarks so that they're all the same, no matter whether you're using your desktop Mac or your PowerBook on the road. And thanks to *Bonjour*, Apple's configuration-free network-service discovery protocol, you can connect immediately with chat partners and shared music on any computer on your *LAN* (local area network).

▶ KEY TERMS

.Mac—Apple's centralized network service, available for a yearly fee, that allows you to publish the products of your creativity online and make all your Macs operate as one. See **45** Sign Up for .Mac for more information.

Bonjour—A technology built in to Mac OS X (formerly known as Rendezvous) that allows applications on your Mac to automatically find network services that are provided by other computers on the same network, such as shared music, chat partners, and file servers.

To take advantage of all this technology, however, Mac OS X must be set up to connect properly to your network environment. Whether you connect using *Ethernet* cables, *AirPort*, or a modem dial-up over a phone line, there is a fair amount of configuration involved before you'll be able to communicate with the outside world. This chapter covers the basic procedures to get you up and running on the Internet. Furthermore, it covers what you need to know in joining your computer to a home or office network so that it can take part as a member of an interlinked community of computers.

For more information about TCP/IP and networking, refer to *Sams Teach Yourself TCP/IP in 24 Hours* or *Sams Teach Yourself Networking in 24 Hours*, both published by Sams Publishing.

---

27 | Set Your Network Device Preference Order

→ SEE ALSO

30 Configure Networking Manually

43 Create and Configure a Location

Mac OS X allows you to configure multiple different networking devices, such as modems, Ethernet connections, and AirPort cards, and to place them in the order of your preference. With this arrangement, if the primary device is not plugged in or available, Mac OS X tries the next most preferred device.

For instance, you might have an iBook with an *AirPort* card, an *Ethernet* cable you sometimes plug into, and a phone line. However, you don't always have the Ethernet cable plugged in, and the AirPort signal might sometimes be unavailable as well. You want to be able to set up Ethernet as your most preferred connection method, but if you don't have Ethernet plugged into your iBook, you want the computer to use AirPort instead. As a last resort, if neither of the other methods are available, you want to be able to use the modem and phone line to dial up. Mac OS X makes this configuration easy to set up.

▶ KEY TERMS

AirPort—Apple's brand of wireless Internet connectivity devices. Operating over the industry-standard 802.11 protocol (also called Wi-Fi), AirPort and its faster successor AirPort Extreme allow you to connect to the Internet without wires, as long as a *base station* (a device connected physically to the Internet, which broadcasts the 802.11 signal that allows computers within range to access the network) is within range.

Ethernet—A physical connection to a LAN is done using Ethernet, a low-level communication protocol that involves cables that end in RJ-45 jacks, which resemble large phone jacks. All modern Macs have an Ethernet port, which runs at 10, 100, or (on top-end models) 1000 megabits per second.

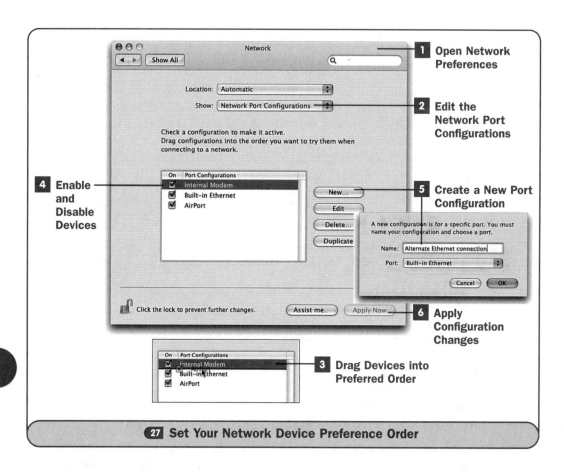

27 Set Your Network Device Preference Order

1 Open Network Preferences

Open the **System Preferences** from the **Apple** menu; click the **Network** icon to open the **Network Preferences** pane.

2 Edit the Network Port Configurations

From the **Show** drop-down menu, which contains entries for each of the network devices in your computer (which you can select to configure those devices directly, as you will see in **30** **Configure Networking Manually**), select **Network Port Configurations**. A screen appears that contains an editable list of network devices. Each one of these devices is actually a *port configuration*, a combination of a network device (port) and a TCP/IP configuration. This allows you to define more than one configuration for a single port—one set of TCP/IP settings for home, and another set for work, but both assigned to your Ethernet port.

▶ **NOTE**

Every physical network has a different series of settings that you must apply in order to connect your computer to it. Your network at the office, for instance, might provide an Ethernet connection and broadcast its settings to your computer automatically, whereas at home, you might have to configure your TCP/IP settings manually, using a fixed address assigned by your service provider, in order to connect to a DSL modem. *Locations* allow you to save these configurations and switch back and forth between them with a single command.

▣ Drag Devices into Preferred Order

To set up your iBook as described earlier, click and drag the port configurations into the following order:

1. Built-in Ethernet

2. AirPort

3. Internal Modem

This organization means that your iBook will first try to connect to the network over the Ethernet connection, using the TCP/IP settings you have defined for it. If your Ethernet cable isn't plugged in, the iBook skips that configuration and tries to connect using the wireless AirPort connection. If AirPort isn't available (for instance, if you're out of range of the base station), the computer will fall back to the internal modem dial-up, although even that connection won't be available unless you manually tell the computer to dial the modem.

▶ **TIP**

If you're using a less-preferred connection method (for instance, AirPort) and a more-preferred one becomes available (for instance, if you plug in the Ethernet cable), Mac OS X will automatically switch to the Ethernet connection.

▣ Enable and Disable Devices

Your Mac might have network devices you know you'll never use. For instance, you might have a computer without an AirPort card, so you know the AirPort configuration will never be used. You can remove it entirely from the preference list, saving time when your computer tries to connect to the Internet. To remove a device, deselect its **On** check box in the configuration list. Turning off a port configuration removes that configuration from the **Show** menu.

⑤ Create a New Port Configuration

Suppose that you have two different sets of Ethernet settings—one for your home network and another one for your office. Depending on whether you're at home or at work, you want to be able to swap one set of TCP/IP settings for the other, with as little effort as possible.

▶ **NOTE**

The TCP/IP settings that allow each of your network devices to connect to the Internet can be obtained from whoever provides your Internet connectivity service. At work or on campus, this would be the network administrator. At home, consult your Internet service provider to find out what settings you need for your Ethernet (or other) connection.

Click the **New** button. A sheet appears that lets you define what kind of port configuration you want to create. Specify a name for the configuration and select the network device you want to use. You can select from the modem, Ethernet, or FireWire ports.

If you want to make a copy of an existing configuration and make changes to the copy, select the configuration and click **Duplicate**. The **Duplicate** option isn't available for the AirPort device.

After the new configuration has been created, you can then select it by name from the **Show** menu and apply the appropriate TCP/IP settings that allow it to connect to the network. See ㉙ **Configure Networking Automatically with DHCP or BootP** to configure the device to connect automatically to a network, or ㉚ **Configure Networking Manually** to configure the device's TCP/IP settings yourself.

⑥ Apply Your Configuration Changes

After all your configuration changes are complete, click the **Apply Now** button. None of your changes are made active until you click this button.

▶ **NOTE**

If you attempt to switch to a different Preferences pane or close the **System Preferences** window, a confirmation dialog box appears prompting you to apply your configuration changes.

28 **Dial Up to the Internet with a Modem (PPP)**

✔ **BEFORE YOU BEGIN**

27 Set Your Network Device
Preference Order

→ **SEE ALSO**

33 Share Your Internet Connection
34 Configure a Secure Tunnel (VPN)

The commonest and most inexpensive form of connecting to the Internet is to use the internal modem that's built in to every Mac. A dial-up PPP (Point-to-Point Protocol) connection can transfer data at up to 56 kilobits per second. A dial-up connection uses a phone line that can't be used for other purposes (such as telephone calls) while the modem is connected, so most modem users connect to the Internet only on an as-needed basis. Modems have their inconveniences, but they're still the most popular way for home computer users to get their Internet connectivity.

To set up a dial-up account, you must have subscribed to a dial-up service with an Internet service provider (ISP). The provider will have given you some information to use in setting up your computer, such as an account name and password, a dial-up phone number, and other pieces of important data. Make sure that you have this information handy.

28

1 Select the Internal Modem Configuration

On the **Network Preferences** pane of the **System Preferences** application, double-click the **Internal Modem** option in the configuration list on the **Network Status** page, or select **Internal Modem** from the **Show** drop-down list. The setup panels for the internal modem configuration appear. Because this is the first time you've set up the modem, the fields in the first **PPP** tab are blank.

2 Enter a Service Provider Name

In the **Service Provider** field, type the name of your ISP (for example, **EarthLink**). This name is simply an identifier so that you can tell which dial-up configuration you're using when you connect.

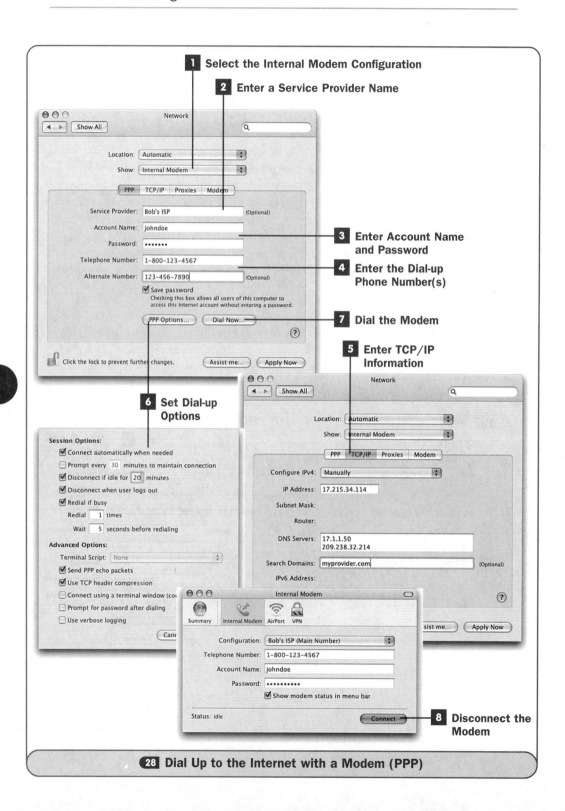

1 Select the Internal Modem Configuration

2 Enter a Service Provider Name

3 Enter Account Name and Password

4 Enter the Dial-up Phone Number(s)

7 Dial the Modem

5 Enter TCP/IP Information

6 Set Dial-up Options

8 Disconnect the Modem

28 Dial Up to the Internet with a Modem (PPP)

28

3 Enter Your Account Name and Password

Type in your account name, which is part of the information that came with your dial-up account from your Internet service provider (for example, **john-doe**), and the password for your account. As you type the password, each letter is hidden for security.

▶ TIP

Your account password is always saved with your dial-up configuration and is automatically passed to the ISP when your modem dials up. If you enable the **Save Password** check box, and there are multiple users set up on your Mac, all the users will be able to dial up using this modem configuration without having to type in your password. If you deselect the **Save Password** check box, each user must have her own dial-up account and configure it in her own login sessions.

4 Enter the Dial-up Phone Number(s)

Your ISP should have given you an access phone number, and possibly an alternate number as well. Enter these numbers in the appropriate fields. If the modem attempts to dial and finds that the primary number is busy, it will automatically attempt the alternate number.

5 Enter TCP/IP Information

Click the **TCP/IP** tab. Most modern ISPs don't require you to enter any TCP/IP information manually; however, if your ISP gave you such information to enter, such as an **IP Address** or **Domain Name Service (DNS) Servers**, select **Manually** from the **Configure IPv4** drop-down menu and enter that information in the appropriate fields.

6 Set Dial-up Options

Return to the **PPP** tab and click the **PPP Options** button. A sheet appears that contains many options you can enable, disable, or tweak according to your needs. For instance, you can select the **Connect automatically when needed** check box to set up your PPP configuration so that you don't ever have to manually connect to the Internet; if any application has to access the Internet, Mac OS X will automatically dial your modem for you. You can also set various options for whether and when Mac OS X should automatically disconnect the modem when it's not being used.

Click the **Modem** tab to configure a few extra connection options. You can set up Mac OS X to pop up a notification if you get an incoming phone call while you're connected to the Internet, or to show the modem status in the menu bar. If you choose this latter option, the **Modem Status** System Menu

28

will appear in the right half of the system's global menu bar (at the top of the screen) and give you the ability to connect the modem with a single click, select between multiple modem configurations (if you have them), or open the Internet Connect application, which lets you manage your modem configurations, dial the modem, and monitor your connection.

7 Dial the Modem

From the **PPP** tab, click the **Dial Now** button to launch the **Internet Connect** application; select your **Configuration** from the drop-down list at the top of the dialog box if needed, and click **Connect** to dial the modem. You can keep the **Internet Connect** window open to show you your connection status while you're online.

▶ TIP

You can also launch **Internet Connect** from the **Network Status** page of the **Network Preferences** pane; simply click the **Connect** button on that page to bring up the **Internet Connect** window.

If you've enabled the **Modem Status** System Menu (in the upper right of the screen), simply select **Connect** from the menu to dial the modem.

8 Disconnect the Modem

When you're done using your Internet connection, click **Disconnect** in the **Internet Connect** window (the **Connect** button changes to **Disconnect** when the connection is established) or select **Disconnect** from the **Modem Status** System Menu.

---

29 | **Configure Networking Automatically with DHCP or BootP**

✔ BEFORE YOU BEGIN	→ SEE ALSO
27 Set Your Network Device Preference Order	**30** Configure Networking Manually **40** Connect to the Internet Wirelessly

---

If you connect to the Internet using Ethernet or AirPort, chances are that your Mac is part of a business or home network that is configured to automatically set each computer's *TCP/IP* settings as soon as it connects. If this is the case, you don't have to do any difficult configuration to get online; you just have to set up your Mac to use the *Dynamic Host Configuration Protocol (DHCP)*—the most popular protocol whereby the computer is automatically assigned an IP address and routing information by a server somewhere on the LAN.

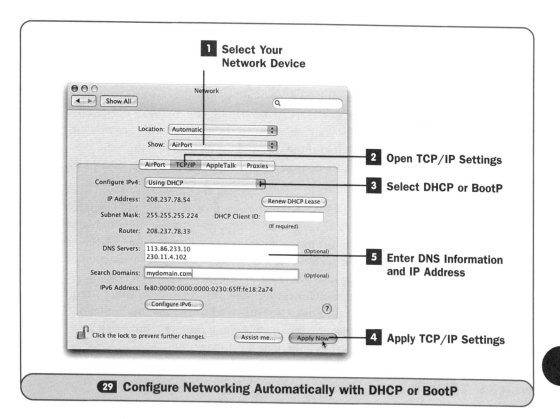

1 Select Your Network Device

2 Open TCP/IP Settings

3 Select DHCP or BootP

5 Enter DNS Information and IP Address

4 Apply TCP/IP Settings

29 Configure Networking Automatically with DHCP or BootP

29

▶ KEY TERM

Dynamic Host Configuration Protocol (DHCP)—A mechanism whereby you can plug a computer into a network and have it automatically receive TCP/IP configuration settings from a server somewhere on the network, freeing you from having to type in those settings yourself.

In DHCP (BootP, another similar protocol, is sometimes used instead), as soon as you plug in an Ethernet cable, join an AirPort network, or power-on a computer that's already plugged in, the computer sends out a broadcast message asking for a computer on the network to tell it what to use as an *IP address*, as well as other critical TCP/IP information, such as the *subnet mask*, the *router*, the *DNS server*, and the *search domain*. If a DHCP server is present on the LAN, it sends a reply directly back to your computer with the TCP/IP information it needs. Your computer applies that information to its own configuration, and it can then communicate on the network and with the Internet.

In the *IPv4* protocol, your IP address uniquely identifies your computer on the Internet. This address is a string of four numbers from 0 to 255, separated by dots (periods). Another string of four numbers, the subnet mask, defines how large your network's address space is. Common subnet masks are 255.0.0.0, 255.255.0.0, and 255.255.255.0; they correspond to networks with 16.7 million, 65 thousand, and 256 IP addresses, respectively. Finally, the router, a device on your local network that enables your computer to communicate with computers on far-flung remote networks around the world, must be present within the address space of the local network defined by the combination of your IP address and your subnet mask.

A further bit of magic is done by DNS servers, which provide a mapping between numeric IP addresses and textual hostnames; this mapping is the Domain Name Service, or DNS. When you connect to the hostname **www.apple.com**, a DNS server must supply the IP address associated with that hostname before your computer can connect to it. If you specify a search domain, the hostnames you type can be shortened; for instance, if your search domain were **apple.com**, you could simply type **info** to connect to **info.apple.com**. Generally you would use this option on a business network, and set it to your company's domain name so that you can connect to internal servers by using only their machine names.

29

▶ KEY TERMS

IP address—A unique numeric address that identifies your computer on the Internet. An IP address is of the form A.B.C.D, where each letter is any number from 0 to 255—for example, **17.112.152.32**.

Subnet mask—Another set of four numbers, each from 0 to 255, the subnet mask is a numeric string that defines how large the address space is on your local network.

Router—A device on your local network that enables your computer to communicate with computers on other networks across the Internet.

DNS servers—Computers on the network that provide a mapping between numeric IP addresses and textual hostnames; this mapping is the Domain Name Service, or DNS.

Search domain—Allows you to type shortened versions of hostnames on the Internet. For instance, if you worked at Apple, your search domain would be **apple.com**, and you could simply type **info** to connect to **info.apple.com**.

IPv4—The current and ubiquitous version of IP, the Internet Protocol, is 4. IPv6 is the next-generation version of IP, and you can configure your Mac to use IPv6 if you're on a network that uses it (click the **Configure IPv6** button)—but most networks don't use IPv6 yet.

1 Select Your Network Device

On the **Network Preferences** pane of the **System Preferences** application, select **Network Status** from the **Show** menu. Double-click the network device you want to configure. Alternately, select the device from the **Show** drop-down menu.

Make sure your network device is turned on and physically connected to the network. For instance, if you're configuring an AirPort card, make sure you're within range of the AirPort base station. If you're configuring an Ethernet connection, make sure the Ethernet cable is plugged in.

2 Open TCP/IP Settings

Click the **TCP/IP** tab to open the screen where you can configure the selected device's TCP/IP settings.

3 Select DHCP or BootP

From the **Configure IPv4** drop-down menu, select **Using DHCP** or **Using BootP**, depending on what protocol your network uses. If you don't know which one to pick, select **Using DHCP** because that protocol is much more common.

29

4 Apply TCP/IP Settings

Click **Apply Now** to commit the configuration. The Mac sends out a DHCP request; in a few seconds, you should see the information fields become filled in with numeric data. You should now be able to connect to the network using your favorite applications.

▶ **NOTE**

If the IP address that the Mac reports has a subtitle of **Self-assigned**, it means that it got no response to its DHCP or BootP request, and therefore wasn't able to obtain a valid configuration. This could be because the DHCP server is not working properly, or it could mean that your Mac is not connected properly to the network. Check your cabling; if it looks correct, contact your network administrator for assistance, or consult the documentation for the device providing DHCP service (such as your AirPort Base Station).

5 Enter DNS Information and IP Address

Normally, you don't have to enter any additional TCP/IP information. However, there are some circumstances under which you might need to enter an IP address or additional DNS information. For instance, you might have a computer that must use a fixed and predetermined IP address, and you must be assured that that IP address will never change, but you still want to be able to get other information, such as the subnet mask and router, automatically through DHCP.

If your DHCP server does not provide DNS information, enter the IP addresses of the network's DNS servers into the **DNS Servers** box—enter the addresses one per line or separate them with commas. (Ask your network administrator or your Internet service provider for the addresses.) If you want, you can enter your company's domain name in the **Search Domains** field to access local servers more quickly.

If you must specify a fixed IP address, use the **Using DHCP with manual address** option in the **Configure IPv4** drop-down menu.

30	**Configure Networking Manually**	
✔ **BEFORE YOU BEGIN**	→ **SEE ALSO**	
27 Set Your Network Device Preference Order	**29** Configure Networking Automatically (with DHCP or BootP)	
	40 Connect to the Internet Wirelessly	

29

On many home and corporate networks, you will not be able to get your TCP/IP information automatically from a DHCP server; instead, you will have to enter all the important pieces of networking data yourself, using fixed addresses that won't change unless you change them yourself.

You should have received all the relevant TCP/IP information to set up your Internet connection when you signed up with an Internet service provider. If you don't have it, ask your network administrator or ISP for the *IP address*, *subnet mask*, gateway *router*, and *DNS servers* that you will have to enter; be sure to have this information ready as you set up your Mac's networking.

1 Select Network Device

On the **Network Preferences** pane of the **System Preferences** application, select **Network Status** from the **Show** menu. Double-click the network device you want to configure. Alternately, select the device from the **Show** drop-down menu.

2 Open TCP/IP Settings

Click the **TCP/IP** tab to open the screen where you can configure the device's TCP/IP settings.

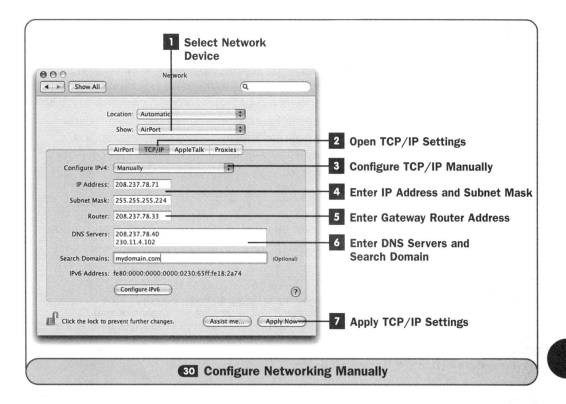

1 Select Network Device

2 Open TCP/IP Settings

3 Configure TCP/IP Manually

4 Enter IP Address and Subnet Mask

5 Enter Gateway Router Address

6 Enter DNS Servers and Search Domain

7 Apply TCP/IP Settings

30 Configure Networking Manually

30

3 Configure TCP/IP Manually

Select **Manually** from the **Configure IPv4** drop-down menu. All the configuration fields become editable.

4 Enter IP Address and Subnet Mask

In the **IP Address** field, replace the default **0.0.0.0** by typing the IP address given to you by your network administrator or ISP. Make sure that you enter the address in the form of four numbers between 0 and 255, separated by periods—for example, **17.112.152.32**.

Enter the **Subnet Mask** as well; depending on your network's architecture, the subnet mask will probably be **255.0.0.0**, **255.255.0.0**, or **255.255.255.0**. You should have this information from your network administrator or ISP.

5 Enter Gateway Router Address

Enter the address of your network's gateway router, as provided by your network administrator or ISP. This address must be on the same network as your IP address, as defined by the subnet mask.

6 Enter DNS Servers and Search Domain

You should have the addresses of one or more DNS servers; these servers might be on your local network, but they don't have to be. Enter them in the **DNS Servers** box, one per line. You can also enter your company's domain name in the **Search Domains** field, if you're on a corporate network, if you want to shorten the hostnames you have to type in for local servers. You can enter multiple search domain names if you use a Virtual Private Network (VPN) to connect to two local networks at once; separate the domains with commas or spaces (Mac OS X adds commas for you if omitted).

7 Apply TCP/IP Settings

Click the **Apply Now** button to apply your settings. You should immediately be able to communicate with the network and the Internet using your favorite applications.

▶ TIP

An easy way to check whether your networking is set up correctly is to open up a **Terminal** window (inside **Applications, Utilities**) and enter **ping www.yahoo.com** at the command line (press **Return** at the end). If you get repeated lines of statistics back at a rate of one per second, you're successfully set up for the Internet. If you get no repeating output (or an error, such as **No route to host**), there is a misconfiguration somewhere. Press **Control+C** to quit the **ping** command.

30

---

31 Configure Proxy Server Settings

✔ BEFORE YOU BEGIN	→ SEE ALSO
30 Configure Networking Manually	**33** Share Your Internet Connection
	34 Configure a Secure Tunnel (VPN)

In some network configurations, you might have to set up *proxies*, which are intermediary computers that sit between your computer and the outside network.

▶ KEY TERM

Proxy—An "intermediary" computer that sits between your computer and the outside network, usually in order to increase access speed to common sites.

Proxies can serve many purposes, but the most common is to speed up access to commonly used data. A proxy does this by posing as the server to which you need to connect, and then sending your request on to the remote server itself. The proxy then saves the information that comes back in a cache, as well as passing it on to you. If you (or another computer) tries to access that same information again, the proxy can simply send back the information it already has, rather than sending out another request for the same data from the remote server. This arrangement saves time and bandwidth, particularly on slow Internet connections.

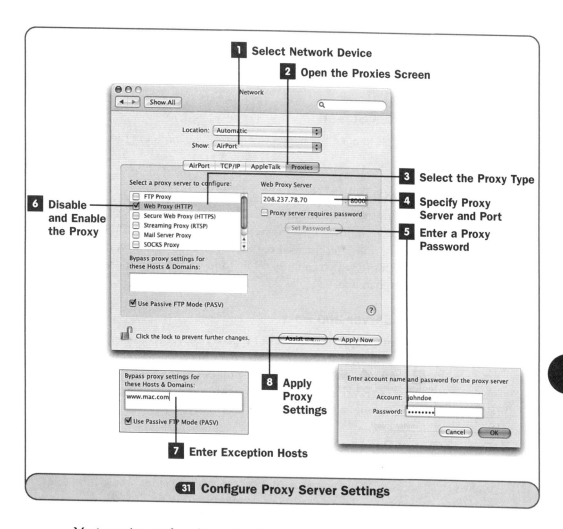

1 Select Network Device

2 Open the Proxies Screen

3 Select the Proxy Type

4 Specify Proxy Server and Port

5 Enter a Proxy Password

6 Disable and Enable the Proxy

7 Enter Exception Hosts

8 Apply Proxy Settings

31 Configure Proxy Server Settings

Most proxies are found in university or corporate networks, for the benefit of the students or employees. If your network administrator provides the addresses of proxy servers, you will need to set up your Mac to use them. You can configure proxies for many different network services, including HTTP, FTP, and email. Each kind of proxy is configured by simply specifying an IP address (and, optionally, a port number), as well as a password if the proxy is password-protected.

1 Select Network Device

On the **Network Preferences** pane of the **System Preferences**, select **Network Status** from the **Show** menu. Double-click the network device you want to configure. Alternately, select the device from the **Show** drop-down menu.

▶ **NOTE**

You can configure any of your available network devices to use proxies; however, you will need to configure the proxies for each such device separately.

2 Open the Proxies Screen

Click the **Proxies** tab to open the screen where you can configure the device's proxy settings.

3 Select the Proxy Type

The **Select a proxy server to configure** box lists the many proxies you can configure. The most commonly used proxies are **Web Proxy (HTTP)**, **FTP Proxy** (file transfer), and **Mail Server Proxy** (email); ask your network administrator which proxies you should set up, and what proxy addresses you should use for each one.

4 Specify Proxy Server and Port

After selecting a proxy type from the **Select a proxy server to configure** box, enter the IP address of the proxy in the **Web Proxy Server** field to the right. If the proxy uses a numeric port, enter the port number in the field after the colon. (Your office's network administrator or your Internet service provider has this information.)

5 Enter a Proxy Password

If your proxy server requires a password, select the **Proxy server requires password** check box; a sheet appears that prompts you to enter an account name and password for the server. Enter this information and click **OK**.

If you ever have to change the account name and password after you've configured the proxy, click the **Set Password** button to retrieve the password sheet.

6 Disable and Enable the Proxy

After you have configured a proxy, you can disable and enable it without losing its configuration (if, for instance, you need to do some task that doesn't work through a proxy). In the **Select a proxy server to configure** box, select or deselect the check box next to the proxy you want to use or bypass.

7 Enter Exception Hosts

Some hosts on the network might be incompatible with proxies, or you might want to exempt them from using the proxy. This is a common practice for telling your Mac what machines are on your home network, so it can connect to them directly rather than going through the proxy. You can do this by listing the hostnames in the **Bypass proxy settings for these Hosts & Domains** box at the lower left. List the hostnames one per line or separate them with commas.

8 Apply Proxy Settings

Click the **Apply Now** button to apply the proxy settings; the settings do not take effect until you click this button.

From now on, each time you connect to any of the services for which you have configured proxies (the Web, an FTP site, email, and so on), the computer will connect to the proxy instead of directly to the specified site. On subsequent times that you access the same site, access to the data should be much faster and more reliable than without the proxy.

32 Activate AppleTalk

✔ BEFORE YOU BEGIN	→ SEE ALSO
29 Configure Networking Automatically (with DHCP or BootP)	**35** Share Another Mac's Files **37** Allow Others to Share Your Files

31

AppleTalk is Apple's own networking protocol, designed for file-sharing and printing over local-area networks before TCP/IP became popular for home or business computing. Most TCP/IP networks in use today no longer explicitly support AppleTalk, which means AppleTalk generally can't be routed from one network (or "zone") to another. Within a LAN, however, AppleTalk operates over just about any networking protocol, and you can still use it to connect to other Macs. Some Mac-based networks are still in use in various places, such as universities, where you can browse different zones and connect to computers across the network using nothing but AppleTalk.

▶ KEY TERM

AppleTalk—Apple's own networking protocol. AppleTalk allows Macs and printers on a LAN to connect directly to one another without any configuration beyond simply turning on the protocol.

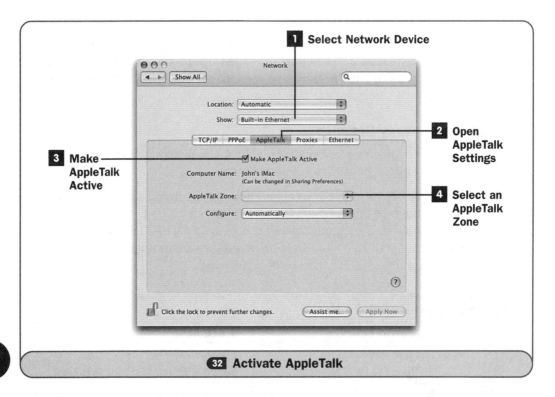

1 Select Network Device

2 Open AppleTalk Settings

3 Make AppleTalk Active

4 Select an AppleTalk Zone

32 Activate AppleTalk

32

AppleTalk is not active by default; you can easily turn it on, but it can be active for only a single network device at a time. Turning on AppleTalk enables your Mac to access disks on other Macs and for other Macs to access your disks; it also means unwanted visitors might end up browsing your computer, so it's generally a good idea not to activate AppleTalk—or any other sharing mechanism, such as Windows Sharing (**38** **Allow Windows Users to Share Your Files**)—unless you really have to.

1 Select Network Device

On the **Network Preferences** pane of the **System Preferences** application, select **Network Status** from the **Show** menu. Double-click the network device you want to configure. Alternatively, select the device from the **Show** drop-down menu.

2 Open AppleTalk Settings

Click the **AppleTalk** tab to open the screen where you can configure the device's AppleTalk settings.

▶ **NOTE**

Not all devices support AppleTalk, and therefore the **AppleTalk** tab might not be present for some devices (such as the Internal Modem).

3 ▌ Make AppleTalk Active

Select the check box to activate AppleTalk. Note that AppleTalk can be active for only one network device at a time; if AppleTalk is already active on another port, a sheet appears informing you of this and asking whether you want to switch AppleTalk to the current device. Click **OK** if you want to do this.

Click **Apply Now** to activate AppleTalk.

4 ▌ Select an AppleTalk Zone

If Mac OS X detects any AppleTalk zones on the network, a list of them appears in the **AppleTalk Zone** drop-down menu. Select which zone you want your Mac to appear in. If there aren't any zones on the network, the **AppleTalk Zone** menu remains disabled.

---

33 ▐ Share Your Internet Connection

✔ BEFORE YOU BEGIN	→ SEE ALSO
27 Set Your Network Device Preference Order	**42** Create a Computer-to-Computer Network
30 Configure Networking Manually	

32

Suppose that you have only a single dial-up Internet connection but several computers that all have to be online at once. Normally, you can hook up only one computer at a time, through its own modem connection. But thanks to Internet Sharing, all the computers can be online at once, sharing the same connection.

In this arrangement, one Mac is the central server that shares its connection with all the other computers. That Mac must have a working Internet connection such as the internal modem, Ethernet, or any other network port. That central Mac must also be hooked up to the other computers using an infrastructure such as AirPort or Ethernet. For instance, you might have a Mac with an Ethernet connection to a DSL modem, and an AirPort card with which it can share its connection with other AirPort-equipped computers; or your Mac might have a dial-up modem connection and be plugged in using Ethernet to a hub, with all the other computers likewise plugged into the same hub.

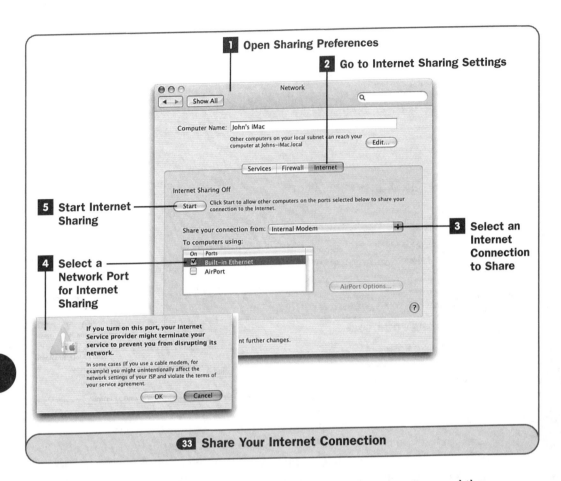

1 Open Sharing Preferences

2 Go to Internet Sharing Settings

5 Start Internet Sharing

3 Select an Internet Connection to Share

4 Select a Network Port for Internet Sharing

33 Share Your Internet Connection

One network port on the central Mac is the active Internet connection, and the other port is the one you use to share the connection. All the other computers on the network need only be configured to use DHCP to obtain their TCP/IP information, and to use the same network device for their Internet connections that you're using to share it. For instance, if you are sharing your connection over AirPort, all the other computers must be using AirPort or compatible *802.11 devices* as well.

▶ KEY TERMS

802.11—A protocol for wireless network connections. Apple's implementation is called AirPort; the same technology is also referred to in the rest of the industry as Wi-Fi. 802.11b, the earlier standard version, runs at 11 megabits per second; 802.11g, the more modern version, runs at up to 54 megabits per second and is called AirPort Extreme by Apple. AirPort is an optional add-on for most Macs.

Network Address Translation (NAT)—A scheme that allows computers on one side of the router to have different IP addresses in a special range—usually **192.168.2.0** to **192.168.2.255**—and for those computers to all share a single true IP address on the other side of the router.

When your Mac has **Internet Sharing** enabled, the computer is actually acting as a DHCP server and *NAT*-enabled router. This means that external computers can't connect directly to any of the computers sharing their Internet connection from your Mac, because all they can see is the single real IP address that all the computers on your network are sharing.

▶ **NOTE**

Computers sharing their Internet connections from your Mac don't all have to be Macs. Windows and Unix machines can all share your Internet connection; all they have to do is get their TCP/IP information through DHCP and use the network device you're using to share your Mac's Internet connection.

■ Open Sharing Preferences

Open the **System Preferences** application and click the **Sharing** icon to open the **Sharing Preferences** pane.

■ Go to the Internet Sharing Settings

Click the **Internet** tab to open the **Internet Sharing** configuration panel.

■ Select an Internet Connection to Share

All your active network ports are shown in the **Share your connection from** drop-down menu. To share your Internet connection, select the connection you want to share. For instance, if your connection to the outside Internet comes from a dial-up modem, select **Internal Modem**.

■ Select a Network Port for Internet Sharing

In step 2, you selected the network device (or port) that represents *your* main Internet connection. Now, you need to select the port that *other* computers will use to connect to your Mac, in order to share its main connection.

Depending on which network port you have selected as your active connection, the list of available devices in the **To computers using** box at the lower left changes to show only the devices available for Internet sharing. For instance, the **Internal Modem** option never appears in this box because a modem can't be used to connect a local-area network of other computers to the Internet. AirPort can be used for connecting to the Internet or for sharing the connection to other computers, but not both. Ethernet, however, can be used both to connect to the Internet and to share the connection with other computers.

Select the check box next to each network port to select the ports you want to use for Internet sharing. You can select more than one network port at once, if (for instance) you want other computers to be able to connect to your Mac via both Ethernet and AirPort and share your Mac's modem connection.

A dialog sheet appears, warning you that many ISPs do not allow you to "sublet" your Internet connection to other users; for most home networks, this should not be a concern, and you can simply click **OK** to dismiss the warning. However, if you have any doubts about your ISP's policy regarding sharing your Internet connection, you should check with the ISP before enabling this feature.

▶ NOTES

Ethernet can be used both as your main connection method, and as the shared port for other computers.

If you select **AirPort** for Internet Sharing, you will want to set up your AirPort options (click the **AirPort Options** button). The sheet that appears allows you to define a name for your network, select an 802.11 channel, or enable WEP encryption (Wired Equivalent Privacy, wherein your AirPort traffic is scrambled so other wireless users can't intercept it) and set the password required for computers to join your AirPort network.

5 Start Internet Sharing

When you have selected at least one network port to use for sharing your connection, you can click **Start** to create the network and begin sharing the connection. You can then connect all the other computers to the network using the same type of device that you're using to share the connection.

---

34 Configure a Secure Tunnel (VPN)

✔ BEFORE YOU BEGIN	→ SEE ALSO
30 Configure Networking Manually	**35** Share Another Mac's Files
33 Share Your Internet Connection	

One major problem with using the Internet for mission-critical business is that data transmitted over the Internet is subject to being intercepted by malicious eavesdroppers. A confidential document being sent from San Francisco to New York might be captured in transit by someone in Chicago or China; clearly this isn't something that will fill stockholders with confidence.

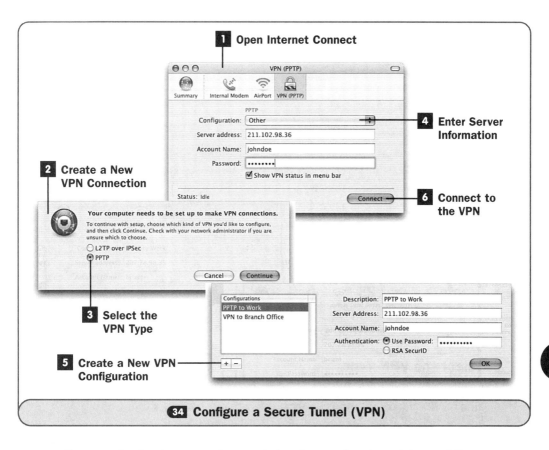

1 Open Internet Connect

4 Enter Server Information

2 Create a New VPN Connection

3 Select the VPN Type

5 Create a New VPN Configuration

6 Connect to the VPN

34 Configure a Secure Tunnel (VPN)

Fortunately, there's a way of transmitting data so that it can't be usefully intercepted: a *Virtual Private Network (VPN)*. A VPN is a kind of "tunnel" on the Internet, a method for encrypting (scrambling) your transmitted data and sending it to a server at the other end of the tunnel that descrambles it so that it can be read by the intended recipients. If your computer is part of a VPN, it uses a different set of TCP/IP settings from the ones it normally uses on the open, "cleartext" Internet. Other computers in the VPN are also configured as though part of the same virtual network, hence the name.

▶ KEY TERMS

Virtual Private Network (VPN)—A virtual "tunnel" that allows you to send and receive scrambled (private) traffic to a secure remote location, such as to your corporate network from home.

PPTP protocol—Point-to-Point Tunnel Protocol, a popular type of VPN architecture.

L2TP/IPSec protocol—Secure IP, a newer and more versatile form of VPN architecture.

Many companies use VPNs to connect one office to another, or for employees to gain access to the private internal network protected by a *NAT* gateway. Your Mac can use the *PPTP* or *L2TP/IPSec* protocols to create a VPN tunnel to an appropriate server and join its virtual network, provided that you have a valid username and password for the VPN.

1 Open Internet Connect

To create a VPN, you must use the **Internet Connect** application. This utility can be launched a number of ways, the simplest of which is to simply navigate to the **Applications** folder and double-click its icon. You can also open **Internet Connect** from the **AirPort** or **Modem** System Menus (if you have enabled them, these menus appear at the far right of the Mac's menu bar), or by clicking the **Connect** button on the **Network Status** page of the **Network Preferences** pane.

2 Create a New VPN Connection

Choose **File, New VPN Connection**. A sheet appears that prompts you for the type of VPN connection to make.

3 Select the VPN Type

Enable the radio button for either **L2TP/IPSec** or **PPTP**, depending on the kind of VPN you're using to connect. Consult your network administrator if you're not sure which kind of VPN it is. Click **Continue**.

4 Enter Server Information

The menu bar at the top of the **Internet Connect** window now has an icon for the new VPN connection, named either **VPN (L2TP/IPSec)** or **VPN (PPTP)** depending on the type you chose.

Enter the VPN server's IP address, and your username and password for the account on the remote network in the fields provided.

5 Create a New VPN Configuration

You can create more than one VPN configuration and switch from one to another each time you connect. Having multiple VPNs can be useful if you regularly use more than one VPN.

Select **Edit Configurations** from the **Configuration** drop-down menu. Click the + icon to create a new configuration and fill in the server details. Click **OK** when you're done; this newly defined configuration now appears as the active configuration. From now on, if you open **Internet Connect** and click the **VPN** icon in the toolbar, this configuration will automatically appear.

34

▶ **TIP**

You can always manually define a new VPN configuration without saving it by selecting **Other** from the **Configuration** menu and filling in the server information yourself.

6 Connect to the VPN

Click the **Connect** button. Mac OS X connects to the VPN server, exchanges account information, and sets up the tunnel. You can then communicate directly with the hosts on the other side of the tunnel until you click the **Disconnect** button.

▶ **TIP**

Select the **Show VPN status in menu bar** check box to have the VPN status appear among the System Menu icons, in the right side of the Mac's global menu bar; this icon shows you how long you've been connected, as well as allowing you to select between multiple VPN tunnels and to open **Internet Connect**.

---

35 Share Another Mac's Files

✔ BEFORE YOU BEGIN	→ SEE ALSO
30 Configure Networking Manually	36 Allow Others to Share Your Files
	37 Share Files from a Windows PC
	40 Connect to the Internet Wirelessly

34

When your Macs are networked, you no longer have to keep copies of all your files and applications on each individual machine; you can store them all in one central location, and connect to that machine (the server) whenever you need to access those items. You can even create aliases to items hosted on remote servers, and when you try to open them, Mac OS X will mount the remote server automatically and open the item for you.

You can even connect to Macs that aren't on your local network; you can mount a shared resource from a computer in Boston onto your Desktop in San Francisco, as long as you know the remote computer's hostname or IP address.

1 Open Finder Window

Create a new window by clicking the **Finder** icon in the Dock or by pressing ⌘N.

2 Browse the Local Network

Click on the **Network** icon in the Sidebar of the Finder window. This icon leads you to all the browseable resources available on the local network.

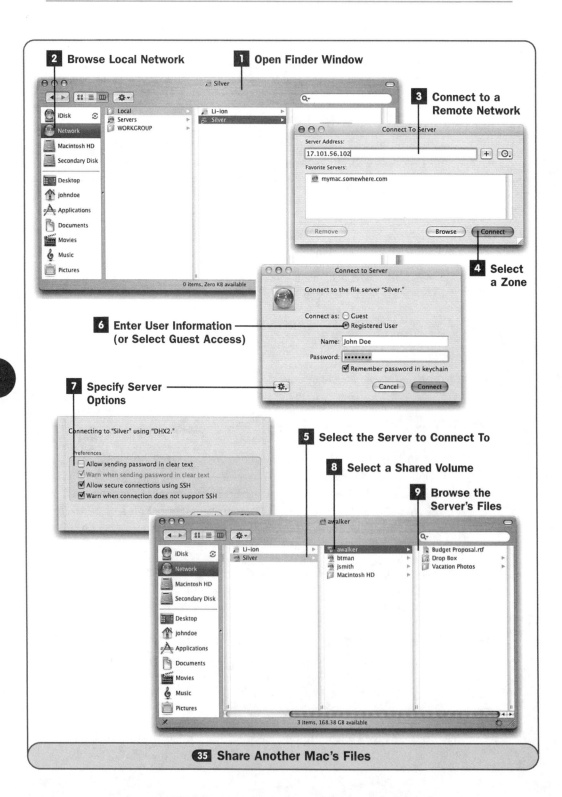

2 Browse Local Network

1 Open Finder Window

3 Connect to a Remote Network

4 Select a Zone

6 Enter User Information (or Select Guest Access)

7 Specify Server Options

5 Select the Server to Connect To

8 Select a Shared Volume

9 Browse the Server's Files

35 Share Another Mac's Files

35

The Finder can show you only those servers on the local network (LAN). To connect to a server in a remote location on the Internet, or to go directly to a server whose name you know without having to browse, you can enter its network name, Internet hostname, or IP address manually, using the following method.

3 Connect to a Remote Network

Press ⌘K or select **Connect to Server** from the Finder's **Go** menu. Type the hostname or IP address of the server you want to connect to into the **Server Address** box, and then click **Connect**. You will then be presented with a similar authentication dialog box to the one you would get if you had browsed to the server on your local network.

Use the + button next to the **Server Address** box to add the server to your **Favorite Servers** list, and use the **History** button next to it to select from recently used server addresses.

4 Select a Zone

Most Macs today operate without *zones* (logical groupings of computers under descriptive names). Existing Mac-based networks that have always used *AppleTalk* for their in-house networking might have multiple named zones to choose from; click the name of the zone you want. If your network has only newer Macs, however, they will all be found in the **Local** zone. Double-click the zone (or single-click in column view) to open the zone's server listing.

5 Select the Server to Connect To

Each of the available servers appears in the Finder window. Double-click the one to which you want to connect; in column view, click the **Connect** button that appears in the preview pane. A dialog box appears that prompts you for your name and password, or to opt for guest access.

6 Enter User Information (or Select Guest Access)

If you have a registered user account on the Mac you're connecting to, enter your name (either your full name or your short name, as you specified when you first set up Mac OS X—see **118 Add a New User** for more on users' full names and short names) and password and click **Connect**. If you don't have an account on that machine, click **Guest**; this will give you limited access to the publicly shared resources on the server to which you're connecting.

If you connect to a server directly, by typing in a machine name or IP address in the **Connect to Server** dialog box instead of by browsing, you can specify some extra options in the connection screen.

7 Specify Server Options

Before connecting, choose **Options** from the gear button to bring up a dialog box that permits you to set certain default behaviors for when you connect to a Mac server. For privacy and security, you will probably want to deselect the **Allow sending password in clear text** option, and select **Allow secure connections using SSH.** Click OK to save these settings for future connections to this Mac server.

Select the **Remember password in keychain** check box to save the password so that you don't have to remember it the next time you connect.

8 Select a Shared Volume

All the server's shared resources (which are thought of as *volumes* in the context of file sharing) are accessible as soon as Mac OS X connects to the server. All these volumes are listed beneath the selected server in the Finder's hierarchy. If you've connected as a **Guest**, each user account appears as a volume; if you have authenticated with a user account instead, you can select from the physical disk volumes attached to the remote Mac as well as from your own **Home** folder.

35

▶ NOTE

If you connect as a **Guest**, and you select any user's **Home** folder as the volume to mount, you are connected directly into that user's **Public** folder. You cannot browse any of the user's other files or folders.

9 Browse the Server's Files

If you've connected to the server directly, Mac OS X connects to the server and mounts the selected volume as a new data source in the Finder. The volume appears on the Desktop if you have configured it to do so; the volume also appears in the Sidebar of any Finder window that is open. Click the icon for the volume and browse its contents as you would any other mounted volume.

If you've connected by browsing using the **Network** icon in the Finder, the server resources can be browsed using that icon's hierarchy. The server volumes do not appear on the Desktop, nor will they be listed in the Sidebar of the Finder window.

▶ NOTE

The Finder responds more slowly when you're browsing remote files than locally mounted files. All the information about the remote resources must be transferred to your computer as you browse, and if you open any document, the entire document must be transferred to your computer as well. The circular "progress" icon in the lower-right corner of a Finder window indicates that the system is transferring data.

▶ **TIP**

You can send files to individual users on remote servers, privately, using the **Drop Box** folder inside each user's **Public** folder. To do this, connect as a **Guest** and navigate into the volume corresponding to the user's short name. Open the volume; then drag any items you wish to the user's **Drop Box** folder. Just as with a physical drop box, you won't be able to see what's inside this folder; but you can add items to it, and the owner of the folder can then open the folder and retrieve the items.

36	**Allow Other Mac Users to Share Your Files**
✔ **BEFORE YOU BEGIN**	→ **SEE ALSO**
33 Share Your Internet Connection **35** Share Another Mac's Files	**37** Share Files from a Windows PC

Although it is definitely useful to share files stored on any Mac on the network, privacy concerns dictate that each Mac be set up by default to share nothing. You must enable **Personal File Sharing** before other computers can access your data.

Additionally, your Mac can act as a web server, hosting web pages and other items that other people can download as they would from any Web site. Mac OS X provides a feature called **Personal Web Sharing** to accomplish this.

35

1 Open Sharing Preferences

Open the **System Preferences** by selecting **System Preferences** from the **Apple** menu. Click **Sharing** to open the **Sharing Preferences** pane. Click the **Services** tab if it's not already selected.

2 Set Your Computer's Name

The **Computer Name** text box contains an automatically chosen name for your computer, based on your full name (for instance, **John Doe's Computer**). Enter a more appropriate or more creative name for your computer if you want; this name is what remote users browsing your network for file-sharing servers will see.

3 Enable Personal File Sharing

Select the **Personal File Sharing** check box in the **Select a service to change its settings** list box. Click the **Start** button or the corresponding check box in the **On** column to start up Personal File Sharing.

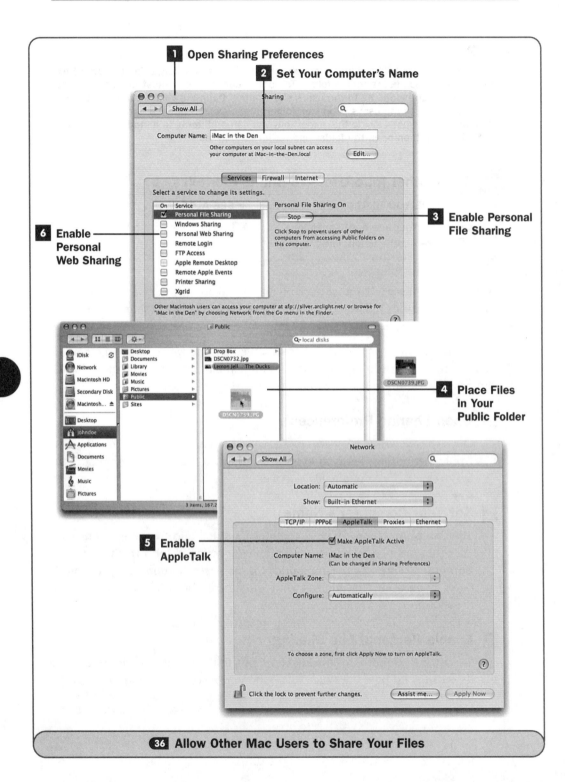

36 Allow Other Mac Users to Share Your Files

4 Place Files in Your Public Folder

With Personal File Sharing enabled, anybody in the world can connect to your computer—they can browse to it by name if they're on the local network or, if they know your IP address or hostname, they can connect to it directly without browsing, from anywhere on the Internet. If the remote user doesn't have an account on your Mac, he can only connect using Guest access; but with that level of access, he can mount your **Public** folder (or any other user's **Public** folder) and browse its contents.

Place files in the **Public** folder inside your **Home** to make them publicly accessible. Be sure to avoid placing anything in that folder that you wouldn't want the whole world to see!

5 Enable AppleTalk

Modern Personal File Sharing on the Mac uses AppleShare/IP, a protocol based on the older proprietary *AppleTalk* that is designed to operate over TCP/IP (meaning that it can be used over standard routed networks such as the Internet).

▶ **NOTE**

The older AppleTalk protocol is more elegant and streamlined than AppleShare/IP, but it is generally useful only in all-Mac networks or networks specifically designed to be compatible with AppleTalk. If you have such a network, you might find it to your advantage to enable AppleTalk, which gives you the ability to define a zone for your computer and to browse multiple levels of Macs in other zones.

To enable AppleTalk, open the **Network Preferences** pane (click the **Network** icon in the **System Preferences**). Double-click the network interface you want to use (you can enable AppleTalk on only a single interface at a time), then click the **AppleTalk** tab. Use the options in that screen to make AppleTalk active, select an existing zone, or create your own zone. See **32 Activate AppleTalk** for details.

6 Enable Personal Web Sharing

Personal Web Sharing allows you to share files with anybody who has a web browser. To enable Personal Web Sharing, open the **Sharing Preferences** pane (click the **Sharing** icon in the **System Preferences** application), and click the **Services** tab. Select **Personal Web Sharing** in the list of services, and click the **Start** button (or enable the **On** check box). When Personal Web Sharing starts up, text appears at the bottom of the window informing you of two URLs that others can use to access your Mac: one for accessing the global page for the computer, and one for accessing your own Personal Web Sharing folder, called **Sites**. Click either of the URLs to view the pages to which they

36

refer, or right-click (or **Control**+click) one of the URLs and select **Copy** from the contextual menu to copy the URL to the Clipboard so that you can paste it into an email message or a text document in another application.

Place files into your **Sites** folder to share them with the world. If you name a file **index.html** and place that file in your **Sites** folder, that file becomes the "default" page for the URL that is reported in the **Sharing Preferences** window for your Personal Web Sharing site; it appears if no filename is specified at the end of the URL. (If no **index.html** file is present, a user can browse the list of files in the folder.) Similarly, place files in the **Library**, **WebServer**, **Documents** folder under the top level of your hard disk to make them accessible to a user who accesses your computer using the URL reported for your computer's global website.

---

37   Share Files from a Windows PC

✔ BEFORE YOU BEGIN	→ SEE ALSO
35 Share Another Mac's Files	**38** Allow Windows Users to Share Your Files
36 Allow Others to Share Your Files	

36

Mac OS X can share files with Windows machines just as easily as it can with other Macs; in fact, it can be more straightforward to network a Mac and a Windows PC together than to network two PCs.

Sharing files with Windows machines is a two-way process: First you must mount a remote Windows machine as a volume on your Mac, and then you have to set up your Mac to share its own files with Windows users.

■ Browse the Network in the Finder

Open a **Finder** window; click the **Network** icon in the Sidebar. The available Windows domains and workgroups appear in the column view listing along with any Mac *zones*.

2 Select a Domain or Workgroup

Click the name of the *domain* or *workgroup* containing the Windows machine you want to use.

A Windows domain is managed by a *domain controller*, a Windows computer whose administrator controls all the computers in the domain. User accounts on Windows machines that are part of a domain authenticate their passwords with the domain controller, not the client Windows machine itself.

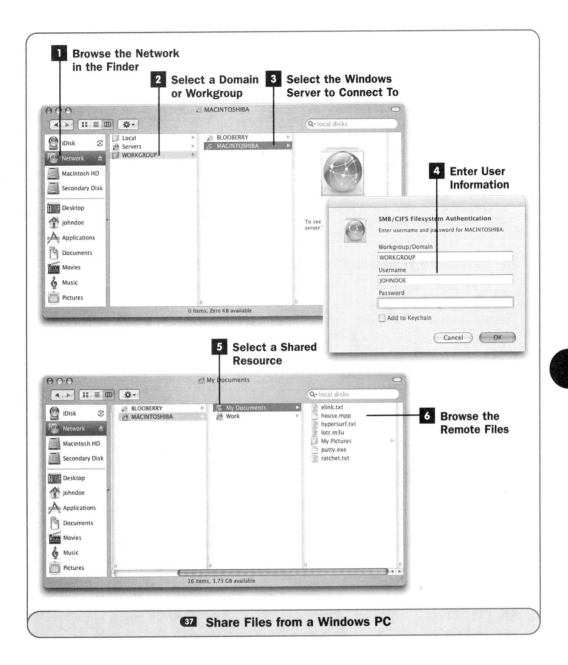

1 Browse the Network in the Finder

2 Select a Domain or Workgroup

3 Select the Windows Server to Connect To

4 Enter User Information

5 Select a Shared Resource

6 Browse the Remote Files

SMB/CIFS Filesystem Authentication

Enter username and password for MACINTOSHIBA:

Workgroup/Domain
WORKGROUP

Username
JOHNDOE

Password

☐ Add to Keychain

Cancel   OK

37 Share Files from a Windows PC

From the Mac standpoint, there is really no practical difference between a workgroup and a domain; both operate the same way to the Mac.

▶ KEY TERMS

Zone—A named collection of Macs in an AppleTalk network. AppleTalk zones have no built-in authentication; they're just logical groupings for more convenient access.

Workgroup—In Windows, a workgroup is very similar to an AppleTalk zone—it's simply a name used to group Windows computers together so that they can be browsed more meaningfully.

Domain—Centrally managed groups of Windows computers with centralized password management and administration.

3 Select the Windows Server to Connect To

The name of each available Windows server appears in all capital letters. Double-click the one you want to connect to; if you're in column view, select the server and click the **Connect** button in the preview pane. The server's **SMB/CIFS Authentication** dialog box appears.

4 Enter User Information

To connect to a Windows machine, you must have a username and password for that machine. Enter that information in the dialog box and select the **Add to Keychain** check box if you want to save the password for future connections. Click **OK** to connect.

5 Select a Shared Resource

After your user information is authenticated, the Windows server is mounted in the Finder and shown in the Sidebar. You can navigate into it to choose a shared resource (also called a *share*). Shares are individual folders configured on the Windows machine for sharing. All shared folders configured under the account you used for authentication are available for you to mount.

6 Browse the Remote Files

Navigate into any available share; you can then browse it as you would any other volume.

37

38   Allow Windows Users to Share Your Files

✔ BEFORE YOU BEGIN

36 Allow Others to Share Your Files
37 Share Files from a Windows PC

Setting up your Mac OS X machine to allow Windows users to access it is very similar to configuring it for Mac-based access. The only difference is that because Windows file sharing requires you to authenticate with a real user account and not with Guest access, each Windows user who wants to access your Mac must have a user account on your Mac. See **118** **Add a New User** for how to add a new user on your Mac.

The steps in this task describe a network environment with a fairly simple Windows network structure. Some environments, such as what might be in place at a large company, can introduce complexities that prevent these basic procedures from working. To deal with complex Windows networking problems, consider a book dedicated to the topic such as *Sams Teach Yourself Windows Networking in 24 Hours* (Sams Publishing).

38

▶ TIP

By default, your Mac is a member of the workgroup called **WORKGROUP**. You may wish to change this name, so you can browse an existing workgroup of a different name, or so others can connect to your Mac using an existing domain. To do this, open the **Directory Access** application, found in the **Utilities** folder inside **Applications**.

Authenticate as an administrator by clicking the lock icon at the bottom. Then double-click **SMB**, and type the desired workgroup or domain name in the sheet that appears. You can specify a WINS server as well, if necessary. Click **OK**, and then quit **Directory Access**.

1 Open Sharing Preferences

Open the **System Preferences** from the **Apple** menu. Click the **Sharing** icon to open the **Sharing Preferences**. Click the **Services** tab if it's not already selected.

2 Enable Windows Sharing

Select the **Windows Sharing** option in the **Select a service to change its settings** box and click the **Start** button or the corresponding check box in the **On** column to start up Windows Sharing.

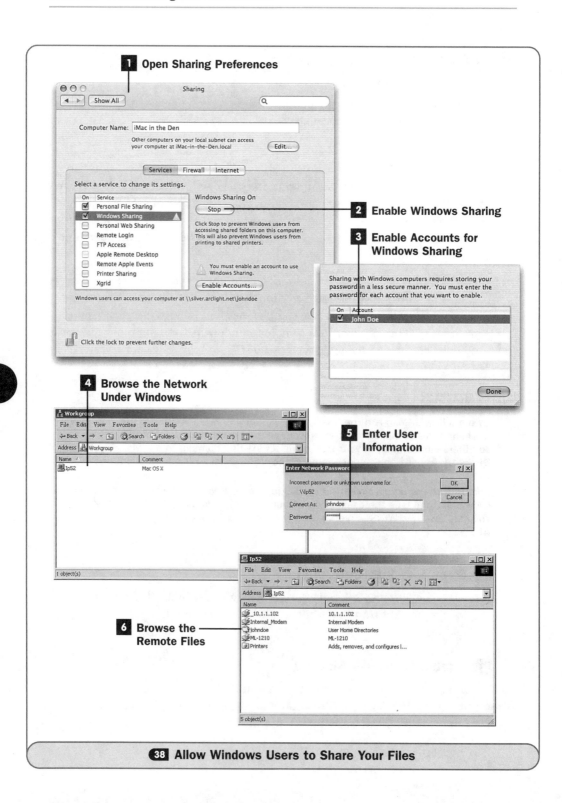

1 Open Sharing Preferences

2 Enable Windows Sharing

3 Enable Accounts for Windows Sharing

4 Browse the Network Under Windows

5 Enter User Information

6 Browse the Remote Files

38 Allow Windows Users to Share Your Files

If your Mac has been running Mac OS X since version 10.0 or 10.1, you might have difficulty connecting to it from a Windows machine; this is because Windows Sharing requires a separate encrypted password database to be stored on your Mac, and that database did not exist in earlier versions of Mac OS X. If your user accounts were created before that password database existed, Windows users won't be able to connect to your Mac using those accounts.

To solve this problem, open the **Accounts Preferences** and change each user's password. You can change each password to the same string as the current password, if you want. When you do this, Mac OS X creates the necessary entry in the Windows File Sharing password database, enabling Windows users to connect properly.

▶ **NOTE**

If your Mac started life with Mac OS X 10.2 (Jaguar) or later, or if your user accounts were all created using these recent versions, Windows users should be able to access your Mac without difficulty.

3 Enable Accounts for Windows Sharing

When you enable Windows Sharing, Mac OS X notifies you that in order to share files with Windows computers, your Mac's account passwords must be stored in a less secure manner than usual. You have to individually enable each account you wish to make visible to Windows computers. Click **Enable Accounts** to see the list of users.

Enable users by clicking the **On** check box next to their names. As you enable each user, you are prompted to enter the user's password.

Click **Done** when you're finished enabling users.

4 Browse the Network Under Windows

On a Windows machine on the same network as your Mac, open the **My Network Places** window; navigate to **Entire Network**, then **Microsoft Windows Network**. Open the workgroup called **Workgroup**. You should then see the hostnames for your Mac and any other Samba-based machines on your network.

38

▶ **NOTE**

Your Mac will appear in the Windows network by its hostname as determined by a reverse network lookup (in this example, the hostname is **lp52**). Make sure that the proper hostname is associated with your machine's IP address in order for it to show up correctly in the listing! If it is not, depending on the version of Windows you're using, you might see only a string representing the version of Samba your Mac is using (for instance, "Samba" followed by a version number). Contact your network administrator for assistance if this happens.

5 Enter User Information

Double-click the entry representing your Mac. A dialog box pops up, prompting you for a username and password. Depending on the version of Windows, this dialog box may report an **Incorrect password or unknown username** error; this is normal. Enter the requested information, matching the account information on the Mac, and click **OK**.

Windows 2000 and later allow you to specify both a username and a password when connecting to a remote server. However, the Windows 95/98 series allows you to enter only a password; the username is derived from your Windows profile name. If you're using one of these older versions of Windows, you must be using a Windows profile with the same name as the short name of the account you're connecting to on the Mac. Consult your network administrator for assistance in finding out or changing your Windows profile name.

If one is present (not all versions of Windows have one), click the **Remember my password** check box to save the password for future connections.

6 Browse the Remote Files

After authenticating successfully, the available shares on the Mac appear in the window; these include the **Home** folder for the account you've authenticated for, the Mac's built-in modem, and any connected printers. You can navigate these items, create shortcuts to them, and access them as though they were local or served from another Windows machine.

After you have authenticated once, you won't have to do so again for your current Windows session. However, if you log out or reboot the Windows machine, you must authenticate again.

38

39 Discover Nearby Websites

✔ BEFORE YOU BEGIN	→ SEE ALSO
36 Allow Others to Share Your Files	**61** Keep Track of Websites with Bookmarks
	63 Access Your Bookmarks Using .Mac

Mac OS X allows any Mac to be a web server, hosting files that can be accessed from anywhere in the world using only a browser. However, if you don't know the IP address or hostname for each Mac, the usefulness of this feature is limited.

It's common, though, for individuals in a household or office network to use Personal Web Sharing to make certain files available just to the other members of the household or office. *Bonjour* makes this possible without requiring anybody to know the hostnames or IP addresses of the Macs that are sharing the files. In **Safari**, Apple's built-in web browser, you only have to go to the **Bonjour** section of your bookmarks to see all the websites hosted by Macs on the local network along with the status pages for all Bonjour-enabled printers.

1 Open Safari

Open a **Finder** window and navigate to the **Applications** folder; double-click the **Safari** icon. You can also click the **Safari** icon in the Dock to launch the application.

2 Open the Bookmarks Pane

Click the **Bookmarks** icon (at the far left of the Bookmarks Bar). If the Bookmarks Bar is hidden, choose **Show All Bookmarks** from the **Bookmarks** menu (or press ⌘+**Option+B**). The **Bookmarks** pane opens, showing all your bookmarks in their various collections.

3 View Bonjour Locations

Click the **Bonjour** entry in the **Collections** list. All the websites served by Macs (or Bonjour-enabled printers) on the local network appear in the list, named according to the full name of the owner of the account hosting each site.

39

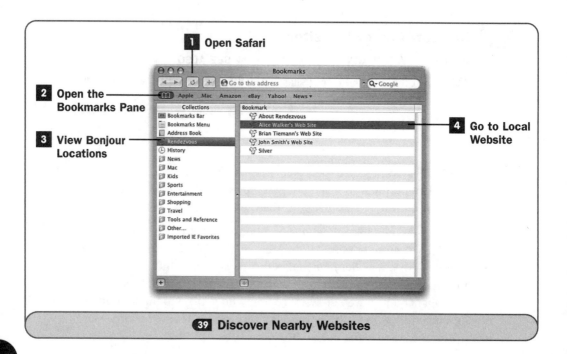

1 Open Safari

2 Open the Bookmarks Pane

3 View Bonjour Locations

4 Go to Local Website

39 Discover Nearby Websites

39

▶ **TIP**

Personal Web Sharing uses your **Sites** folder as its web root; in other words, the URL **http://your.host.name/~johndoe** will show you the contents of John Doe's **Sites** folder, or (if one exists) the **index.html** file inside that folder. The default settings for the built-in Apache web server, which is what powers Personal Web Sharing, are such that if you don't have an **index.html** file in your **Sites** folder, you will be able to see a file listing of that folder and access every file in your browser. Make sure to put an **index.html** file in your **Sites** folder if you want to hide its contents from other users!

4 **Go to Local Website**

Double-click any listed site to open it in the same Safari window.

5

Going Mobile

IN THIS CHAPTER:

Networking takes on a whole new dimension when you unplug the Ethernet cable or phone line and go wireless. Apple's AirPort technology introduced the computing world to the freedom of 802.11 wireless networking back in 1999, and it's become one of the great hits of our time. Wireless-enabled coffee shops, restaurants, bookstores, and other public locales are springing up daily, giving patrons the ability to shed the chains of a stationary, hard-coded Internet configuration. It's all dynamic and automatic now, and the future will only be more so, as sales of laptops (both in the Windows world and among Macs) continue to outstrip sales of even the most powerful desktop computers. Mobility is a much-prized commodity these days.

Wireless networking involves two basic pieces of equipment you have to know about: the AirPort or AirPort Extreme card, and the AirPort Base Station.

Apple's AirPort Base Station ($200) and AirPort Express ($129) are devices that broadcast the wireless network signal to your computer. There might be one (or a compatible device, often referred to as an "access point") installed already at your workplace, or you might choose to buy one in order to set up a home wireless network. It's a fairly complex piece of networking equipment, acting as a wireless hub, media bridge, NAT router, and DHCP server; the details of its operation are beyond the scope of this book and will not be addressed here.

The AirPort card, AirPort Extreme card, and AirPort Extreme or AirPort Express Base Stations make it possible for your Mac to connect to other users without a hard-wired Internet connection.

▶ **NOTE**

AirPort is Apple's term for 802.11b, currently the most common form of wireless networking. 802.11b can transmit data at up to 11 megabits per second, at a signal range of 50 feet. *AirPort Extreme* is Apple's implementation of 802.11g, the next-generation standard for wireless networking. 802.11g is backward-compatible with 802.11b (devices using both can share the same network), but it transmits at up to 54 megabits per second. The signal range is the same as that of 802.11b.

Many Mac models come with the AirPort card built-in, but you can install such a card in any Mac, whether a desktop or a laptop. Portable computers (PowerBooks and iBooks) are clearly the ones most likely to benefit from the mobility of AirPort, but stationary desktop computers can reap the rewards too—you can wire an entire household for Internet access without stringing any Ethernet cables under carpets or over doors.

True, AirPort is somewhat slower than Ethernet, and there's always the issue of signal strength, especially in larger houses; but because most Internet connections—even broadband—are nowhere near as fast as AirPort is, in real-world terms you're not going to see the disadvantage. Downloading a web page over AirPort will be just as fast as over Ethernet because the speed bottleneck is in the Internet link itself, not in the LAN. The freedom afforded to you and your computer by AirPort, and the ability to roam freely from home to work to the coffee shop, more than make up for the slight speed penalty wireless networking incurs.

If you have a portable Mac that you frequently take with you from one place to another, chances are that you will often have to switch back and forth between the network configurations that are compatible with each place you go. You might have one set of TCP/IP settings at home, another one at work, and another one at your favorite wireless-enabled coffee shop. It's no fun to have to constantly open up the **Network Preferences** pane and enter a new set of TCP/IP settings. Mac OS X makes configuring TCP/IP much more direct than Windows does, but it's still not the best use of several minutes of your time when you've just opened up your PowerBook to show someone a cool website.

Fortunately, there's a way to avoid all that tedious configuration: *locations*. All the TCP/IP configuration that you now know how to do is all part of a "location," which is a configuration profile that applies to a certain network environment. If you have other network environments, each of those can have its own location and its own associated TCP/IP settings. Then, whenever you go from one place to another, you have simply to select which networking location you want to use, and the associated configuration will automatically go into effect.

▶ **KEY TERM**

Location—A set of network configuration settings that you define in association with a certain networking environment, such as your home or work network. Switching from one location to another immediately changes your networking settings.

A location can contain not just TCP/IP settings, but also a profile of which network ports are active. For instance, you might have an Ethernet network at the office, but only AirPort at home; switching from your **Work** location to your **Home** location can disable the Ethernet port and enable AirPort. A location can also include *VPN* settings, as well as a unique preference list for what network devices you do have available.

Of crucial importance to mobile computing is power management. You need to be able to configure your iBook or PowerBook to use its precious battery power efficiently on long airline flights, and yet be able to take advantage of continuous power through a wall adapter if it's plugged in; for example, decreasing the processor speed and letting the display go dim are ways to save power while keeping the computer active. Because configuring your Mac's power-saving behavior is applicable to all Macs, and not just laptops, power management is covered in **125 Choose a Power-Saving Profile**.

---

40 Connect to the Internet Wirelessly

40

→ **SEE ALSO**

41 Set Up AirPort to Automatically Reconnect
43 Create and Configure a Location

You're walking down the street, and you see one of those telltale chalk marks on a building that means "open wireless network." Or you wander into a store in the mall that advertises free wireless Internet access, or you're sitting in the airport terminal with nothing to do but wait for your flight. You see other people with laptops typing happily away. How do you, your Mac, and AirPort join in?

1 Check for AirPort Networks

Click the AirPort Status System menu icon, in the right side of the Mac's menu bar. The resulting menu lists all the public AirPort networks that are within range, displayed by their network names. If no networks are present, a message saying **No AirPort networks within range** appears instead.

▶ TIP

You can't tell from the menu which networks have the strongest signal, but there's a way to check. Click to open and close the **AirPort Status** System Menu several times. If some of the networks in the list have a very weak signal, they might disappear and reappear from the list. Try to select a network that stays steadily in the list, or try to discover the location of the base station (if you know who owns it, ask him or her) and move closer to it.

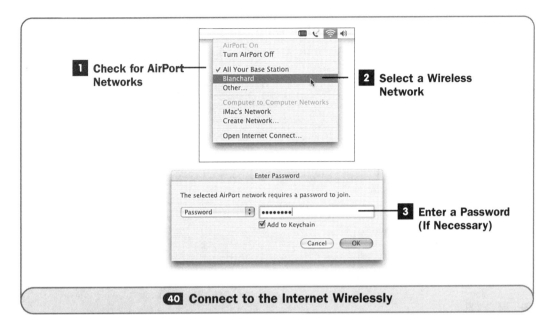

1 Check for AirPort Networks

2 Select a Wireless Network

3 Enter a Password (If Necessary)

40 Connect to the Internet Wirelessly

▶ **NOTE**

If the **AirPort Status** System Menu doesn't show on your Mac, turn it on in the **Internet Connect** application, found in the **Applications** folder. Open **Internet Connect**, click the **AirPort** toolbar icon, and select the **Show AirPort status in menu bar** check box.

▶ **TIP**

You can turn your AirPort card on and off from the **AirPort Status** System menu. If you turn AirPort off, you can save a fair amount of battery power. It's a good idea to turn off AirPort if you know you're not going to be near a wireless network anytime soon.

2 **Select a Wireless Network**

Choose a network to join, and click its name in the **AirPort Status** System Menu. Mac OS X attempts to connect to the network.

"Private" (or "closed") networks do not appear in the **AirPort Status** System Menu. You can still connect to them, however. To do this, select **Other** from the menu; a dialog box appears, asking for the name of the network you want to join, and a password (along with several encryption methods if the network uses WEP encryption) if one is required. The network name is case sensitive, so make sure that you know it exactly.

3 Enter a Password (If Necessary)

The owner of the wireless network you've chosen might have configured it to require a password. If so, it might be in one of several different forms. Depending on the manufacturer of the base station and whether WEP encryption is enabled, you might have to enter an encrypted string of alphabetical or hexadecimal characters as your password. Other networks might accept a plain-text password. The administrator of the network will be able to tell you both the format and the password; if it's a network in a public area, where you don't know the administrator, then it's a private network that you won't be able to join.

Select the format for the password, and type the password into the field. Click **OK** to join the network.

Allow 5 to 10 seconds for Mac OS X to apply the network settings and for the network to become usable.

▶ NOTE

40

Some public networks (such as in airport terminals) allow you to connect without a password to the wireless network, but then ask you for credit card information as soon as you try to go anywhere on the Web. Once you enter this information and purchase some time on the wireless network, your computer will be allowed to access any Internet resource you want.

41 Set Up AirPort to Automatically Reconnect	
✔ **BEFORE YOU BEGIN**	→ **SEE ALSO**
40 Connect to the Internet Wirelessly	**43** Create and Configure a Location

If you frequently go to a certain place with a wireless network that you have to join manually each time you open your laptop, you might find it useful to configure Mac OS X to automatically reconnect to that network. This way, you'll be able to be online as soon as you activate the computer.

1 Open Network Preferences

Open the **System Preferences** application by choosing **System Preferences** from the **Apple** menu. Click the **Network** icon to go to the **Network Preferences** pane.

If you've set up a location for the place where you use the wireless network, select it from the **Location** drop-down menu.

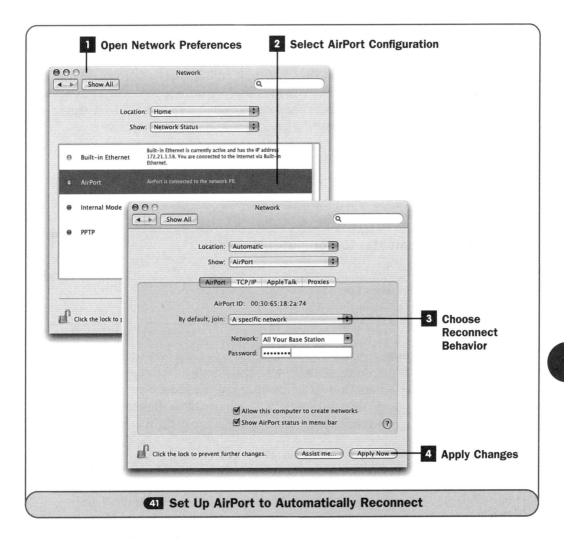

41 Set Up AirPort to Automatically Reconnect

2 Select AirPort Configuration

Double-click the AirPort configuration in the **Network Status** pane, or click to select it and then click **Configure**. Then click the **AirPort** tab to configure the AirPort-specific options.

3 Choose Reconnect Behavior

The **By default, join** drop-down list has two options you can choose from for what your Mac should do when you restart or wake from sleep.

Select **Automatic** if you will be using the Mac in a wide-area wireless network with many base stations, such as a university campus or a convention hall. This option causes Mac OS X to connect automatically to the AirPort network with the best signal, giving preference to the most recently used network (if it's available).

Select **A specific network** if there are multiple base stations where you want to be online, but only one of the networks is appropriate for you. This option is useful if you have a home wireless network and so do your neighbors. Enter the network name and the password, typing the name manually if it's a private network.

4 Apply Changes

Click **Apply Now** to commit the AirPort behavior settings.

---

42 Create a Computer-to-Computer Network

→ SEE ALSO

35 Share Another Mac's Files
36 Allow Others to Share Your Files

41

AirPort isn't just for connecting a mobile computer to a fixed base station—although that's certainly the most useful application for it. You can also connect two AirPort-equipped computers together, so that you can share files or iTunes music, without a base station anywhere in the vicinity. This is what's known as a computer-to-computer network, and you can create many of them at once—up to 11.

Any computer-to-computer network can support connections to as many other computers as you wish; essentially what you're doing is making your computer into a base station, except without the *NAT* (Network Address Translation) and *DHCP* (automatic TCP/IP configuration) that characterize a full-featured base station. Non-routed protocols that operate on a LAN—such as *AppleTalk*—work just fine over a computer-to-computer network.

1 Choose Create Network Command

From the **AirPort Status** System Menu at the top of the screen, select **Create Network**. A dialog box appears that prompts you for a name and (optionally) a channel for the new network.

2 Enter a Name for the Network

Enter a descriptive name for your network. The name can be at most 32 characters long. This is the name that will show up on other people's computers when they scan for available wireless networks.

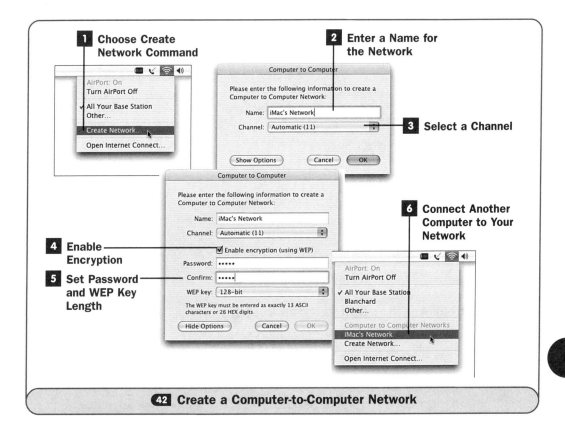

1 Choose Create Network Command

2 Enter a Name for the Network

3 Select a Channel

4 Enable Encryption

5 Set Password and WEP Key Length

6 Connect Another Computer to Your Network

42 Create a Computer-to-Computer Network

3 Select a Channel

AirPort automatically selects a channel from the 11 available. Normally, you don't need to change this, but if you have to select a specific channel to avoid colliding with another 802.11 device in the neighborhood, you can do so.

4 Enable Encryption

Click the **Show Options** button to reveal the advanced options for the network.

Encryption keeps your communications private. *WEP*, or *Wired Equivalent Privacy*, is an encryption scheme designed to make a wireless network as impermeable by unauthorized users as a wired Ethernet network is. That is, the wireless network can be freely joined by anybody who has permission to do so, but is unavailable to those who don't have permission. WEP isn't the most secure encryption protocol in the world (a 40-bit key can be cracked by tools that are readily available), but you can specify a 128-bit key if you're concerned about security and your partners' computers can support it. (All AirPort cards produced after mid-2001 can support 128-bit keys.)

▶ KEY TERM

Wired Equivalent Privacy (WEP)—An encryption scheme that prevents unauthorized parties from eavesdropping on the wireless Internet traffic that is present anywhere within range of the base station.

Encryption is optional, but it's a good idea if you want to keep your communications secure from eavesdroppers with their own 802.11 cards. To turn on encryption for the network you are creating, check the **Enable encryption (using WEP)** check box.

5 Set a Password and WEP Key Length

If you enable encryption, you must set a password. Enter it twice to ensure that it's what you want. Select the WEP key length that's right for your situation (40-bit or 128-bit key lengths are available).

Click **OK** to create the network.

6 Connect Another Computer to Your Network

On the second computer, open the **AirPort Status** System Menu on the right side of the global menu bar and look for available wireless networks. Your newly created network should appear by name in the list. Connect to it just as you would a base station. You can now use one computer to browse the other for file sharing or printing via AppleTalk, or use any Bonjour-enabled services between the two computers, such as iTunes music sharing.

To disconnect the computer-to-computer network, switch your AirPort card back to a different wireless network (using the **AirPort Status** System Menu), or turn AirPort off.

---

43 Create and Configure a Location

✔ BEFORE YOU BEGIN	→ SEE ALSO
27 Set Your Network Device Preference Order	44 Switch to a New Location
40 Connect to the Internet Wirelessly	

Your Mac starts out with a single *location*: **Automatic**. This location is set up to use the most automatic TCP/IP setup methods possible for all available network devices, such as DHCP and automatic connection to the nearest AirPort network. If your Mac is a stationary desktop machine, you can safely change the settings on the default **Automatic** location to match your local network; however, it's best—especially if your Mac is a portable, but even if it isn't—to create a new location and use it to hold your specific connection configuration.

42

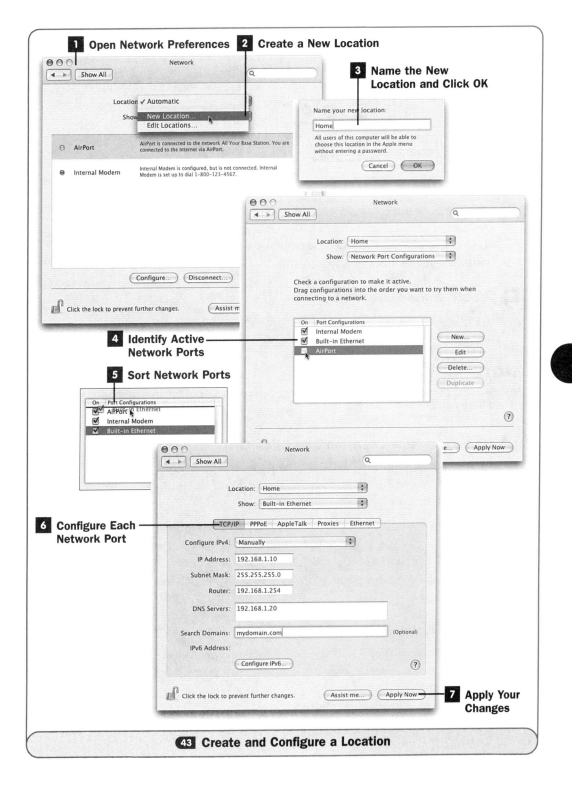

1 Open Network Preferences   **2** Create a New Location

3 Name the New Location and Click OK

4 Identify Active Network Ports

5 Sort Network Ports

6 Configure Each Network Port

7 Apply Your Changes

43 Create and Configure a Location

After you've created a new location, you have to set up the networking configuration associated with it. The networking configuration depends on what types of network connectivity are available, what kinds of manual options you want to have available, and what role your computer plays in the network. Your laptop might just be an AirPort-connected web-surfing device while you're at home, but at work it might have to connect to two or three different *Ethernet* networks and a *VPN*. Any number of configurations is possible—each location can have an entirely different style of networking from the next.

❶ Open Network Preferences

Open the **System Preferences** application (using the **Apple** menu or the **Applications** folder) and click the **Network** icon to open the **Network Preferences**. Alternatively, open the **Network Preferences** directly from the **Location** submenu of the **Apple** menu.

❷ Create a New Location

From the **Location** drop-down menu, choose **New Location**. A sheet appears that asks for a name for the new location.

▶ NOTE

As the sheet points out, your new location is accessible by any of the users on your Mac, if you have multiple users set up.

❸ Name the New Location and Click OK

Enter a name for the new location. The name can contain any special characters you like, and can be as long as you want. Use a short, descriptive name such as **Home** or **Joe's Coffee**.

Click **OK** to create the new location. The **Network Preferences** now shows the configuration for this location, but it isn't active until you click **Apply Now** to make your changes take effect. Before you click that button, though, you should adjust the networking settings for your various devices to match the network the location represents.

❹ Identify Active Network Ports

From the **Show** menu, select **Network Port Configurations**. On the configurations screen, you can disable any network devices you don't use, duplicate configurations for devices you want to use in different circumstances, or rename your device configurations.

Determine which network devices will be useful in the location you're configuring. If you won't ever have access to an AirPort network in this location, for example, deselect the check box next to the **AirPort** entry.

▶ TIP

To add a *VPN* configuration to your active network ports, open **Internet Connect** (from the **Applications** menu) and create a new VPN connection, as described in **34 Configure a Secure Tunnel (VPN)**. After the VPN configuration is complete, the new configuration appears in the **Show** drop-down menu in the **Network Preferences** pane.

5 Sort Network Ports

Click and drag the network devices in the port configuration list into your preferred order. Sort the devices so that the fastest, most flexible devices are at the top of the list, followed by devices that are more reliable and likely to be available. For instance, Ethernet is faster than AirPort, but you might not always have Ethernet plugged in; if you put Ethernet at the top of the list and AirPort below it, Mac OS X will use Ethernet if it's connected, but otherwise will fall back on AirPort (assuming that you're within range of a base station).

6 Configure Each Network Port

Select each network device in turn from the **Show** drop-down menu. Using the **TCP/IP** tab for each device, configure the TCP/IP settings according to the environment in the location you're configuring. For instance, configure the device to use DHCP if automatic configuration is available (usually the case in AirPort and corporate Ethernet networks—see **29 Configure Networking Automatically with DHCP or BootP**), or configure the settings manually if necessary (see **30 Configure Networking Manually**).

7 Apply Your Changes

When your configuration is complete, click the **Apply Now** button. The TCP/IP configuration for the network device that's highest in your preference order and that is connected will be applied immediately.

43

44 Switch to a New Location

✔ BEFORE YOU BEGIN

43 Create and Configure a Location

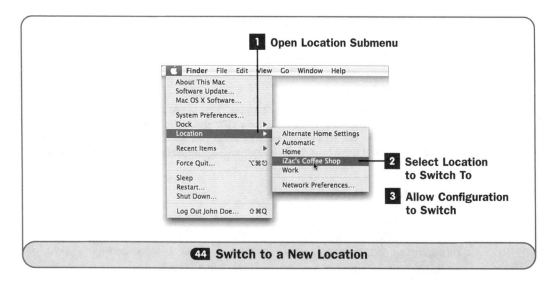

1 Open Location Submenu

2 Select Location to Switch To

3 Allow Configuration to Switch

44 Switch to a New Location

After your *locations* are set up, switching from one to another is a straightforward matter. As soon as you turn on or wake up the computer in a new location, simply select the new location from the global **Apple** menu; the most preferred access method for your new location is automatically activated.

1 Open Location Submenu

Open the **Apple** menu and hover the mouse over the **Location** option; a submenu appears, listing all the currently configured locations.

2 Select Location to Switch To

Find the location whose configuration matches the place where you are; click the location entry to switch to that location.

3 Allow Configuration to Switch

Depending on the kind of network devices that are configured as part of the selected location, Mac OS X may take several seconds to apply the configuration and activate the most preferred device in your list. Allow 5 to 10 seconds before attempting to connect to the network with your favorite applications.

6

.Mac Services
and iDisk

IN THIS CHAPTER:

In the modern computing world, more and more of what we think of as "computing" involves the exchange of data over the Internet. Not only that, but this digital exchange is no longer just the impersonal web-surfing of the Internet's first explosive years; nowadays, the way we interact with our computers and the Internet is increasingly personalized. Online commerce has reached the level where a great many people are as comfortable shopping on the Web as they are using a catalog or going to a store. An even more infectious phenomenon, though, is the proliferation of personalized services that take advantage of the new digital devices we use in our daily lives. Personal web publishing, file sharing, photo albums, network storage—these things all have come about only recently as a result both of the ever-decreasing price of data storage and the explosion of digital lifestyle devices on the market—the so-called "Digital Hub" that Steve Jobs announced as Apple's strategy in the year 2000. It was only with the maturation of Mac OS X and its core technologies, and the introduction of .Mac, that the digital hub strategy truly became a reality.

Digital cameras don't just take pictures; they remove a dozen tedious steps from what once was a laborious and technically demanding process standing in the way of anybody who wanted to share those pictures with the world. The same is true of digital camcorders, MP3 players, personal organizers, and Internet applications such as web browsers and email programs—each one is fun on its own, but its appeal is enhanced by the availability of easy-to-use data management applications supported by centralized data services such as .Mac and Microsoft's .NET.

By signing up for .Mac and configuring your computer to use your .Mac account, you raise its capabilities to a whole new level. When you start up your .Mac-enabled Mac, you automatically log in to your *.Mac* account at Apple's servers. A whole host of personalized services becomes available: network disk storage (iDisk), one-click purchasing of photo prints and music downloads, iChat instant messaging, email service, and a lot more. Apple keeps bringing out new features for .Mac users every time we turn around—virus-protection software, data backup tools, synchronization of Address Book contacts and Safari bookmarks, and so on. Some people might find it disconcerting to have their personal information stored at a remote site, and information privacy is certainly not a trivial thing to worry about, but Apple's .Mac services are becoming so rich and so compelling that their benefits outweigh the risks inherent in centralized data management. After a few months on .Mac, it's hard to imagine computing without it. See **100 Synchronize Your Information Using .Mac** for more information.

▶ **KEY TERM**

.Mac—An architecture in which Mac users all over the Internet can store their personal data and preferences on central servers at Apple.

.Mac costs $99 per year. Apple offers a free 60-day trial account, which you can sign up for directly from Mac OS X. At the end of the trial period, you can either stop using .Mac or pay the yearly fee and upgrade to a full .Mac account.

iDisk is a central feature of .Mac; it's a network disk system that allows you to store data on Apple's central servers. Whenever you use .Mac to host a web page, synchronize your contacts, or read your email, you're using the disk space on the iDisk system. Every .Mac account comes with 250 combined megabytes of iDisk space (you can divide that total however you like between .Mac mail and iDisk storage), and you can buy more—up to a gigabyte—for $50 extra per year.

Your iDisk is a mountable network drive that acts like a remote version of your **Home** folder—it has a **Pictures** folder, a **Movies** folder, and **Documents**, **Sites**, and **Music** folders, just like your local Mac does. Items you put in these folders can be shared with others using applications such as iPhoto, or with the .Mac services that store data in those folders according to their type. But the foremost purpose of iDisk is to let you share your data among multiple Macs; if you put your documents into the **Documents** folder on your iDisk, for instance, you can connect to your iDisk from any Mac and access those documents no matter where you are.

▶ **TIP**

A full description of each of the folders in your iDisk and what they're used for can be found in the document called **About your iDisk**, found in the top level of your iDisk.

As an additional convenience, iDisk features automatic synchronization: As long as you have an active network connection, your Mac will keep a local copy of your iDisk so that you can access all the items in it quickly. If you make any changes to the items in the local iDisk, the changes are automatically propagated to the central server and then to your other Macs as well, so they all always have the most current copies of your important files.

▶ **TIP**

In your iDisk, you'll also find a **Software** folder, which contains copies of many download-able applications provided by Apple. Browse these pieces of software by category, find one you like, and drag it to your Desktop to download it.

Through .Mac and iDisk you'll have the opportunity to download a variety of free software provided at the .Mac website: games, utilities, and the virus protection software Virex. As a Mac user, *viruses* won't be nearly as much of a problem for you as they would be on Windows, simply because most viruses are written for Windows, but Virex is a worthwhile tool to install nonetheless, just in case. You don't want to be one of the unlucky few who fall prey to a rare Mac virus!

▶ NOTE

Software such as Virex, which scans for both Mac and Windows viruses, is a benefit not just to you as a Mac user, but to any Windows users on your network. A Windows virus might not hurt your Mac, but if a Windows user connects to it over the network, the virus can spread to it and wreak havoc. In other words, your Mac might be immune to most viruses, but it *can* be a carrier.

▶ KEY TERM

Virus—A malicious pieces of software that gets surreptitiously installed on your computer with the intent of causing digital harm or mischief.

In addition to the services that .Mac provides in its own right, it also enhances other applications by allowing you to keep their information in sync across multiple Macs. See **100 Synchronize Your Information Using .Mac** for more information on synchronizing your Safari bookmarks, your Address Book contacts, your iCal appointments, and your Mail settings. Only a few of the myriad features of .Mac are covered in the tasks in this chapter, but they should be sufficient to get you started and pointed in the right direction.

45

45 Sign Up for .Mac	
✔ **BEFORE YOU BEGIN**	→ **SEE ALSO**
28 Dial Up to the Internet with a Modem (PPP)	**47** Create a .Mac Web Page
30 Configure Networking Manually	**50** Connect to Your iDisk

To use the .Mac services, you must have a .Mac account. The username (also called a "member name") and password associated with this account are specified in your .Mac Preferences. After your account is set up, whenever you want to use any of the .Mac services that tie into any of the applications you use, the account information comes straight out of your computer's preferences; you don't have to type them in.

If you're concerned about your credit card information being stored in a central server where it might be subject to theft or hacking, don't worry. .Mac does not ask for a credit card when you sign up.

1 Open .Mac Preferences

11 Enter Your .Mac Information

3 Enter Your Personal Information

4 Choose a Member Name and Password

5 Enter Verification Information

6 Accept Terms and Conditions

2 Go to the .Mac Sign-up Site

8 Add Addresses to the Recipient List

45

7 Announce Your New Email Address

10 Continue to the .Mac Website

9 Send the Announcement iCard

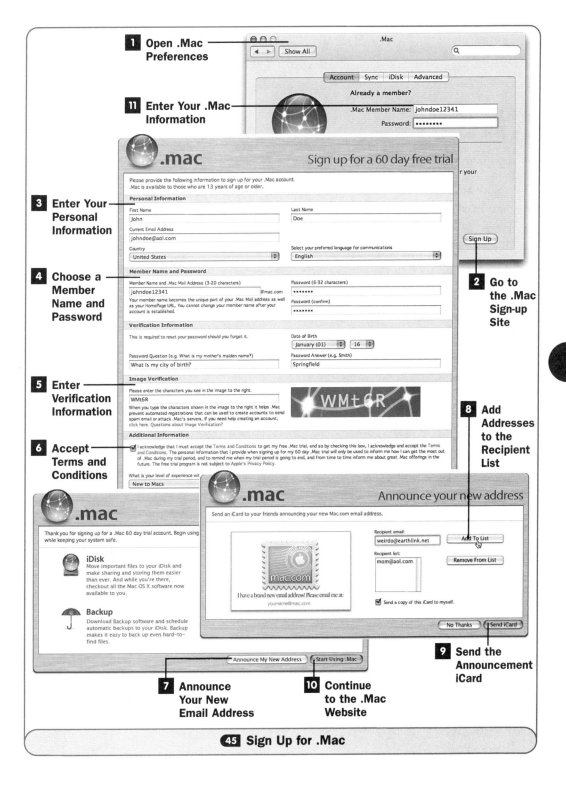

45 Sign Up for .Mac

For certain online purchasing functions, you can enable *1-Click ordering*, which does store your credit card information in a central server. However, for your .Mac account itself, a credit card is not necessary. You must be at least 13 years old to get a .Mac account.

▶ KEY TERM

1-Click ordering—A technology pioneered by Amazon.com that allows you to predefine your credit card information at the server, so that you can later purchase items (on websites or in .Mac-enabled applications) with a single click.

When you first install Mac OS X, or when you first turn on a brand-new Mac, you are guided through an optional procedure to set up a new .Mac account. If you didn't sign up at the time of installation, you can easily sign up for your .Mac account at any time by starting from the **System Preferences**.

▶ NOTE

You must have a working Internet connection before you sign up for .Mac.

45

1 Open .Mac Preferences

Open the **System Preferences** application from the **Apple** menu. Click the .Mac icon to go to the .Mac Preferences pane.

2 Go to the .Mac Sign-up Site

Assuming that you don't already have a .Mac account, begin the sign-up procedure by clicking the **Sign Up** button at the bottom of the window. Your web browser (usually Safari) launches and takes you to the sign-up page for .Mac.

Alternatively, go to **http://www.mac.com** in your browser and click the **Free Trial** button to sign up for a free 60-day trial .Mac account.

3 Enter Your Personal Information

In the first section of the form, enter your first and last name, your current email address, your country of residence, and your preferred language for using the .Mac services. As of this writing, English and Japanese are the only supported languages.

4 Choose a Member Name and Password

Select a member name. This name can be as short as three letters long or as long as twenty, but it can only contain alphanumeric characters (letters and numbers).The password must be between 6 and 32 characters; for maximum security, use a password that's at least 8 characters long, and use non-alphanumeric symbols (!@#%) instead of a word that can be found in the dictionary.

▶ **TIP**

When selecting a member name for your .Mac account, try using your Mac OS X "short name" (**jsmith**, for example); it's always good to keep things simple, and if your .Mac account name can be the same as your account name on your own Mac, that's one fewer name to remember. In case this name is taken, however, make sure that you have a few alternative names in mind.

5 Enter Verification Information

Apple requires that you provide a personalized question and answer, and your birth date, for verification purposes. If you forget your password, you will be asked this question, and you must be able to answer it correctly to be reissued your password.

6 Accept Terms and Conditions

If you know a friend with a .Mac account, enter her **@mac.com** email address in the field provided; this referral entitles your friend to a discount on her .Mac services.

Follow the links to read the .Mac Terms and Conditions and Privacy Policy. Fight the temptation to skip this step; reading these agreements is tedious, but it's an excellent habit to be in, just in case. Click the check box when you're done reading.

An image at the bottom of the page contains several random letters against a hard-to-read background; type the letters you see into the box provided. This is a security measure designed to foil automated software that signs up for fraudulent accounts.

From the drop-down menu, select your level of experience with Macs. You can choose **New to computers**, **New to Macs**, or **Experienced Mac user**. If you select either of the first two options, you are given a quick .Mac tour and the opportunity to announce your new email address to a list of your friends. If you selected the third option, you'll skip directly to the .Mac website, at step 10.

Finally, click the **Continue** button.

45

7 **Announce Your New Email Address**

If you selected either **New to computers** or **New to Macs** when asked about your Mac expertise, you are first shown a screen with your account information, to print or write down for future reference. After you have recorded this information, click **Continue**. Next appears a page with links to further information about .Mac services, as well as a button labeled **Announce My New Address**. Click this button to set up the announcement postcard.

8 **Add Addresses to the Recipient List**

You are shown a preview of the announcement iCard, an electronic postcard. There is a list of addresses, initially empty, that you can fill with the email addresses of as many friends as you like. Enter their addresses one by one in the **Recipient email** field and click **Add to List** to put each address into the recipient list.

9 **Send the Announcement iCard**

When you've added all the addresses to the list that you want, click the **Send iCard** button. The postcard is sent to all the recipients, and you will be taken back to the .Mac welcome screen.

You can click the various icons on the .Mac welcome screen to view information about certain key .Mac services, or click **Start Using .Mac** to go on to the .Mac website.

10 **Continue to the .Mac Website**

The .Mac website contains all the services that you'll find useful for your .Mac account, including downloadable premiums, news and tutorials, technical support, and links to external .Mac community sites.

▶ **WEB RESOURCE**
http://www.mac.com
The .Mac website is where you start to access your email and your iDisk space, which come with your .Mac membership.

▶ **TIP**
Consider setting the .Mac site as your browser's home page, so that it's the first page that opens each time you launch your browser.

You'll most likely be automatically logged in at the .Mac site using your new .Mac member name and password; if not, click the **Log in** link to log in.

As you navigate the .Mac website in the future, you will be periodically asked for your member name and password. This is another security measure to ensure your account's privacy. The Safari web browser helps you out by offering to save your login information (member name and password) for you and fill it in automatically; go ahead and allow it to do this, unless you're using a shared computer in a public space (such as a library), in which case you should not allow the browser to save your login information.

🔟 Enter Your .Mac Information

Return to the **System Preferences**. In the same **.Mac Preferences** pane you started from, enter your new .Mac member name and password. The settings are immediately saved, and all your .Mac-aware applications can now use your .Mac account.

46 Share a Slideshow Screensaver

✔ BEFORE YOU BEGIN	→ SEE ALSO
45 Sign Up for .Mac	**87** About iPhoto and Digital Photography
	104 Select a Screensaver

One of the easiest and most fun ways to get into the spirit of .Mac is to create a public slideshow screensaver. Anybody with a Mac can subscribe to your public screensaver and watch your published pictures fade and pan across their screens. Apple provides the infrastructure; you provide the pictures. All you have to do is publish them using a free downloadable application provided as part of your .Mac account.

1 Download the .Mac Slides Publisher

Using your web browser, go to the .Mac website (**http://www.mac.com**). Click the **Member Central** link at left, then click the down-arrow link to the **.Mac Slides Publisher** installation file (**Mac_Slides_Publisher.dmg**). The file downloads to your computer, and the disk image mounts automatically in the Finder.

▶ **TIP**

If the disk image did not automatically mount after downloading, simply go to your Desktop (or wherever you downloaded the file) and double-click its icon to mount it.

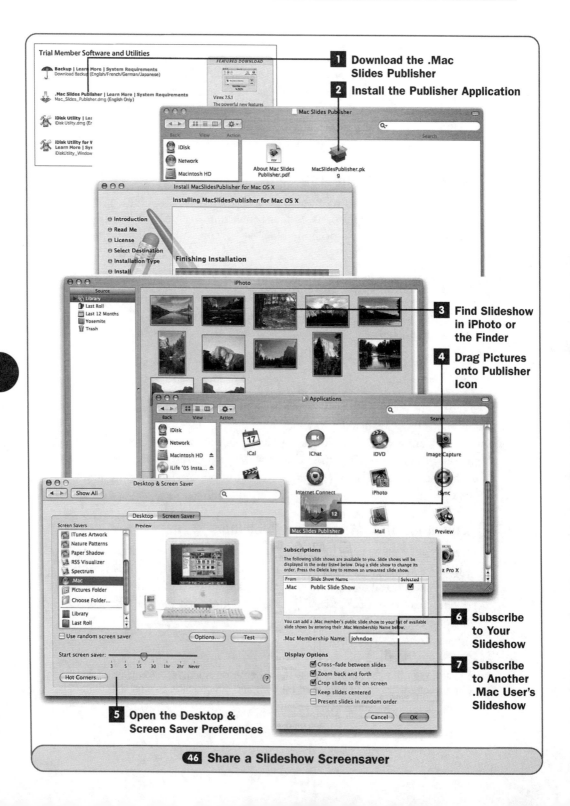

Trial Member Software and Utilities

Backup | Learn More | System Requirements
Download Backup (English/French/German/Japanese)

.Mac Slides Publisher | Learn More | System Requirements
Mac_Slides_Publisher.dmg (English Only)

iDisk Utility | Lea
iDisk Utility.dmg (En

iDisk Utility for V
Learn More | Sys
iDiskUtility_Window

FEATURED DOWNLOAD

Virex 7.5.1
The powerful new features

1 Download the .Mac Slides Publisher

2 Install the Publisher Application

Mac Slides Publisher

iDisk
Network
Macintosh HD

About Mac Slides Publisher.pdf

MacSlidesPublisher.pkg

Install MacSlidesPublisher for Mac OS X

Installing MacSlidesPublisher for Mac OS X

⊖ Introduction
⊖ Read Me
⊖ License
⊖ Select Destination
⊖ Installation Type
⊖ Install

Finishing Installation

iPhoto

Source
Library
Last Roll
Last 12 Months
Yosemite
Trash

3 Find Slideshow in iPhoto or the Finder

4 Drag Pictures onto Publisher Icon

Applications

iDisk
Network
Macintosh HD
iLife '05 Insta...

iCal   iChat   iDVD   Image Capture

Internet Connect   iPhoto   iSync

Mac Slides Publisher   Mail   Preview

z Pro X

Desktop & Screen Saver

Show All

Desktop   Screen Saver

Screen Savers   Preview
iTunes Artwork
Nature Patterns
Paper Shadow
RSS Visualizer
Spectrum
.Mac
Pictures Folder
Choose Folder...
Library
Last Roll

☐ Use random screen saver   (Options...)   (Test)

Start screen saver: ————————————
                    3   5   15   30 1hr 2hr Never

(Hot Corners...)   ?

Subscriptions
The following slide shows are available to you. Slide shows will be displayed in the order listed below. Drag a slide show to change its order. Press the Delete key to remove an unwanted slide show.

From	Slide Show Name	Selected
.Mac	Public Slide Show	☑

You can add a .Mac member's public slide show to your list of available slide shows by entering their .Mac Membership Name below.

.Mac Membership Name johndoe

Display Options
☑ Cross-fade between slides
☑ Zoom back and forth
☑ Crop slides to fit on screen
☐ Keep slides centered
☐ Present slides in random order

(Cancel)   (OK)

6 Subscribe to Your Slideshow

7 Subscribe to Another .Mac User's Slideshow

5 Open the Desktop & Screen Saver Preferences

46 Share a Slideshow Screensaver

46

2 Install the Publisher Application

Open the newly mounted disk image, if a window for it is not already open. Double-click the installer package, **MacSlidesPublisher.pkg**. The installation program begins; follow the on-screen instructions to install the application.

3 Find Slideshow in iPhoto or the Finder

To make a slideshow, you need a collection of pictures. To make things easy, collect all the pictures you want to use in your slideshow in a single folder so that you can select them all at once. Alternatively, select a group of pictures from within iPhoto.

▶ NOTE

The pictures you choose must be in JPEG format. JPEG image files can have up to 16.7 million colors, but are compressed to achieve a small file size; this compression can result in degraded image quality. Because the compression/quality tradeoff is so flexible, JPEG is by far the most widely used image format on the Internet.

4 Drag Pictures onto Publisher Icon

After selecting the pictures, drag them into the Finder window containing the **.Mac Slides Publisher** application, and release them on top of the icon. You'll know your mouse is positioned properly when the application icon darkens to show that it is capable of opening those files.

46

The **Slides Publisher** launches. Using your stored .Mac account information, the application connects to the .Mac server, processes the picture files one by one, and uploads them to the server. You will see a progress meter and thumbnail versions of each picture as it is processed. After the pictures have all been uploaded, the application quits.

5 Open Desktop & Screen Saver Preferences

Now you must do what any other user must do to view your slideshow: subscribe to your .Mac screensaver. To do this, open the **System Preferences** (under the **Apple** menu); click the **Desktop & Screen Saver** icon, and then on the **Screen Saver** tab to open the screensaver setup page. Click the **.Mac** option in the **Screen Savers** list; the **Preview** window shows the default .Mac slideshow screensaver, which is a series of promotional product photos.

6 Subscribe to Your Slideshow

Click the **Options** button. A sheet appears that lets you subscribe to any .Mac member's slideshow. Type your own .Mac member name into the **.Mac Membership Name** field and select or deselect the check boxes next to the various display options to suit your taste. (You can always reopen this sheet later to tweak the options.) Then click **OK**.

▶ **NOTE**

Your computer downloads all the pictures in the slideshow in the background; if you have a slow connection, it might take several minutes before all the pictures in the slideshow appear.

Your slideshow appears in the **Preview** pane in the **Desktop & Screen Saver Preferences** window. To see the slideshow full-screen, click the **Test** button; the screensaver displays until you move your mouse again. The next time your screensaver activates as a result of your configured settings, it will use your slideshow pictures.

7 Subscribe to Another .Mac Member's Slideshow

You can subscribe to another person's slideshow just as easily as you can your own—if you know his .Mac member name. In the **Desktop & Screen Saver Preferences** pane, click **Options** again to reopen the **Subscriptions** sheet, and enter the other person's .Mac member name in the **.Mac Membership Name** field. (Notice that your own .Mac member name now appears in the list at the top of the sheet, as another available slideshow from which you can choose.) Click **OK**; your active screensaver is now your friend's .Mac slideshow.

46

▶ **NOTE**

To delete a slideshow, you must delete the pictures from where they are stored on your iDisk. See **50** Connect to Your iDisk for more information about using your iDisk; simply drag the **Public** folder out of the **Slide Shows** folder inside **Pictures** on your iDisk, and put it in the Trash to remove your slideshow.

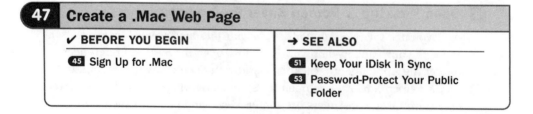

**47	Create a .Mac Web Page**	
✔ **BEFORE YOU BEGIN**	➔ **SEE ALSO**
45 Sign Up for .Mac	**51** Keep Your iDisk in Sync
	53 Password-Protect Your Public Folder

.Mac is all about personal publishing. Whether you want to display a photo album, write a personal journal or newsletter, share files with other web users, or post a résumé, .Mac provides ready-made templates you can use to create your online presence quickly, easily, and attractively.

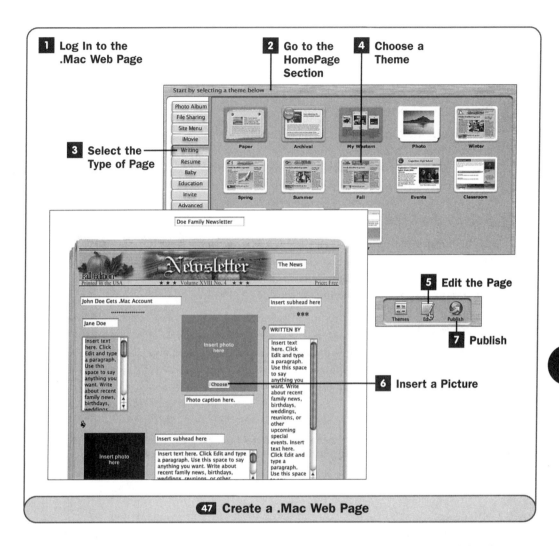

1 Log In to the .Mac Web Page

2 Go to the HomePage Section

4 Choose a Theme

3 Select the Type of Page

5 Edit the Page

7 Publish

6 Insert a Picture

47 Create a .Mac Web Page

This procedure explains how to create a home page using Apple's predefined themes and page structures. If you're an experienced web designer, though, you can publish your pages in a much more streamlined way: by adding files to the **Sites** folder in your iDisk. Copy an **index.html** file and other pieces of web-page content to upload them to the .Mac server, and they will be immediately available at **http://homepage.mac.com/<*membername*>**.

If you use a locally cached copy of your iDisk (see **51** **Keep Your iDisk in Sync** for details on how to do this), publishing is even quicker: Items that you move into the **Sites** folder are immediately copied to the local cache, and are then automatically synchronized to the server in the background, so you don't have to wait for the network's latency in transferring files.

1 Log in to the .Mac Web Page

Using your web browser, go to **http://www.mac.com** and log in using your .Mac account information if you aren't already logged in.

2 Go to the HomePage Section

Click the **HomePage** icon in the menu on the left side of the screen. You are taken to the main screen for your HomePage, where you can create new pages, manage existing pages, view news about the HomePage service, and add special features such as password protection.

3 Select the Type of Page

At the bottom of the screen is a vertical row of tabs, each corresponding to a style of web page. Click the tab that best matches the kind of web page you want to create. For this example, click the **Writing** tab to create a page on which you can publish personal writings.

4 Choose a Theme

47

Each page style comes with a palette full of ready-made themes designed by Apple; they range from the basic and austere to the flashy and downright gaudy. Click the icon for the page style you like best.

▶ NOTE

You can always change the theme for your web page later, even after you've entered all the content, by clicking the **Theme** button at the top of the **Preview** page.

5 Edit the Page

After selecting your theme, you are taken to the **Preview** page, where you can view the layout of the page with dummy text and pictures. Click the **Edit** button at the top of the page. All the changeable fields become editable; you can click any of them and type text to your heart's content.

▶ TIP

You can return to the HomePage start page at any time by clicking the **HomePage** title at the top of any page during the editing process. Doing so cancels editing or creating your in-progress page.

6 Insert a Picture

Some types of pages let you place pictures of your choice—selected from the **Pictures** folder on your iDisk, not your Mac hard disk—in certain positions in the layout. (See **50** **Connect to Your iDisk** and **51** **Keep Your iDisk in Sync** for more information on accessing the contents of your iDisk and placing pictures into its **Pictures** folder.) In places where you can put a picture, there is always a **Choose** button; click this button to be taken to the iDisk file browser page. This screen looks similar to the Column view of the Finder, and gives you access to the **Pictures** and **Movies** folders in your iDisk, as well as to the .Mac **Image Library**. You can browse any subfolders that might exist inside these folders to locate a file. The only difference between this screen and a Finder window is that instead of double-clicking a picture file, you must click to select it and then click **Choose**. It is, after all, a web page, and double-clicking doesn't do anything.

7 Publish

When you're done editing the page, click **Preview** to return to the **Preview** screen and see the page with all your modifications. From there (or directly from the **Edit** page), when you're ready to publish the page and make it available to web surfers, click the **Publish** button. You are given a link in large letters that goes to the newly created page; you can copy the URL (address) and send it to friends, or click the handy **iCard** button to send the link in an electronic postcard.

47

▶ TIP

After you've created a page or two, experiment with the options at the **HomePage** start page. You can edit or delete existing pages, add password protection, or even click and drag pages in the list to change the order in which their links are listed (the first page, shown in bold, is the main page that users see when they go to your home page's URL: **http://homepage.mac.com/<membername>**, where **<membername>** is your .Mac member name).

48 Use .Mac Webmail

✔ BEFORE YOU BEGIN	→ SEE ALSO
45 Sign Up for .Mac	54 Configure a New Mail Account

Every .Mac account comes with a free email address: *<membername>*@mac.com, where *<membername>* is your .Mac member name. This means you have a .Mac mail account that you can access either using your desktop **Mail** application in Mac OS X, or the **Webmail** service provided by .Mac.

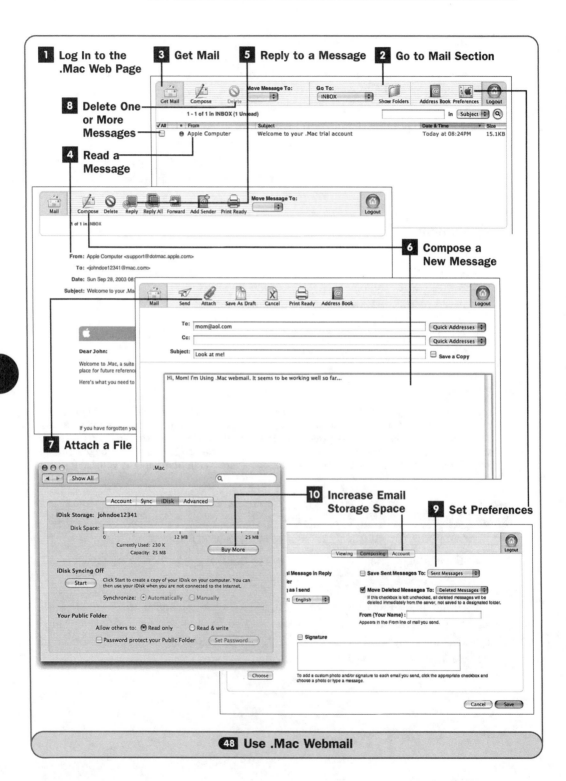

1 Log In to the .Mac Web Page

3 Get Mail

5 Reply to a Message

2 Go to Mail Section

8 Delete One or More Messages

4 Read a Message

6 Compose a New Message

7 Attach a File

10 Increase Email Storage Space

9 Set Preferences

48 Use .Mac Webmail

.Mac email accounts use *IMAP, the Internet Message Access Protocol*. IMAP allows you to store your messages on a central mail server, organize them into server-side folders, and access them using any mail program from any computer. The chief rival to IMAP, the *Post Office Protocol (POP)*, operates by downloading new mail to your desktop computer. POP means faster access to your messages (because they're stored on your own computer rather than over the network), but you can use POP with only one computer, the one to which you download all your messages.

▶ KEY TERMS

Internet Message Access Protocol (IMAP)—An email delivery method that allows you to read messages that are stored and managed on the server.

Post Office Protocol (POP)—An email delivery method in which your email application downloads all your messages to store on the local computer.

Webmail is a way for you to access your email using a web browser. After logging in to the .Mac website, you simply go to the **Mail** section to view your **Inbox**; click any message to display it as a web page. You can write messages, organize your mail into folders, and do just about everything in Webmail that you can on your desktop—with the bonus that you can access your mail from any computer in the world instead of just your own. The only downside is that it's a bit slower and has a less sophisticated interface than a dedicated email program. The trade-off, for many people, is more than fair.

48

1 Log In to the .Mac Web Page

Using your web browser, go to **http://www.mac.com** and log in using your .Mac account information if you aren't already logged in.

2 Go to the Mail Section

Click the **Mail** icon in the menu on the left side of the screen. You are immediately taken to a view of your mail account's **Inbox**, the folder to which all new mail automatically comes.

3 Get Mail

Click the **Get Mail** button at the top left of the screen to refresh the message listing and display any newly arrived messages. New messages, by default, are shown at the top of the list.

▶ TIP

As you can with many other applications, you can sort the messages in your **Inbox** by clicking the column headers. Click a column header a second time to reverse its sorting direction (indicated by the triangular arrow in the header).

4 Read a Message

Click any listed message to read it. If the message has an attachment, a paperclip icon appears next to it in the message listing; when you view the message, all attachments are shown as links at the top of the message. Clicking on the links downloads the attachments as files to your computer.

5 Reply to a Message

When viewing a message, click the **Reply** icon in the toolbar at the top of the screen. If the message was sent to you and several other recipients, you can send your reply to all the original recipients by clicking **Reply All**. The original message appears "quoted"—indented in front of a column of > characters—in a large text-input field; you can add your reply text either above or below the quoted text, and delete any of the quoted material. Quoting is good Internet etiquette; it reminds your correspondent of what she was talking about and makes communication much easier.

▶ **TIP**

You can turn off quoting in the **Webmail Preferences**, accessible by clicking **Preferences** in the toolbar of the Webmail page that lists your messages; deselect the **Include Original Message in Reply** check box.

48

6 Compose a New Message

To create a new message, click the **Compose** toolbar icon when viewing the message list. You can select contacts (people to whom you want to send the email message) from your Address Book by clicking the **Address Book** icon in the toolbar; select the contacts you want, select a destination (the **To:**, **Cc:**, or **Bcc:** fields), and click **Apply**.

The **Quick Addresses** drop-down lists to the right of the **To:** and **Cc:** fields contain names from your .Mac Address Book that you have selected to be included in your **Quick Addresses** list. Simply select a name from one of the lists, and it will be copied into the appropriate input field.

When you're done typing your message, click **Send** in the toolbar or at the bottom of the screen to send it.

7 Attach a File

To attach a file, click **Attach** in the toolbar or at the bottom of the screen. You are taken to a page where you can select a document from your computer, click **Attach**, and repeat for as many documents as you want to attach; when you're done, click **Apply** to attach the files to the message.

8 Delete One or More Messages

When viewing the message list, select the check boxes to the left of the **From** column to select the messages you want to delete. The **Delete** icon in the toolbar becomes active; click it to delete the selected messages.

9 Set Preferences

.Mac Webmail has a number of settings you can adjust to suit your taste; access these options by clicking the **Preferences** icon in the main toolbar (in the message list view). You can choose whether or not to include the original message in a reply, choose whether and where to save copies of your sent mail, add a photo and custom signature to all your messages, and many more behavior options. Be sure to click the **Save** button (located at the bottom of the page) when you're done changing your preferences.

48

10 Increase Email Storage Space

A standard .Mac account comes with 250MB of combined storage space for your **@mac.com** email and your iDisk storage, by default divided evenly so that you have 125MB of space for your email. You can see how much of that allotted space you are currently using by opening the **.Mac Webmail Preferences** pane (by clicking **Preferences** on the toolbar on the message list page) and looking at the usage bar at the top. If you need to reallocate how much storage space is earmarked for email and how much for iDisk, you can do so by clicking the **Account** icon on the .Mac web page (**http://www.mac.com**).

If you find that you need more space altogether, you can purchase more by clicking the **Buy More** button on the **.Mac Webmail Preferences** pane or in the **iDisk** page of the **.Mac Preferences** pane of **System Preferences**. Your .Mac storage can be upgraded to a full gigabyte in total, for an extra $50 annual fee.

49   Reset a Lost .Mac Password

✔ **BEFORE YOU BEGIN**

45 Sign Up for .Mac

Everyone forgets passwords. Even with the help of *Keychain* (Apple's password-management system, which is described in **135** **Extract a Password from the Keychain**), passwords can get lost—and your .Mac password, because it holds the key to all your .Mac services on which you might come to rely, is an especially bad one to lose.

▶ **KEY TERM**

Keychain—A technology built into Mac OS X that keeps track of all your passwords for you, whether in web pages, applications, or other parts of the system. A single master Keychain password unlocks all your other passwords to be used automatically on request.

Fortunately, the procedure for recovering access to your .Mac account isn't difficult. Apple provides two methods for obtaining a new password, which you can choose between depending on your circumstances.

1 Go to the .Mac Login Screen

Using your web browser, go to the .Mac website at **http://www.mac.com** and click the **Log in** link to attempt to log in. You are presented with the main .Mac login screen.

2 Click the Forgot Your Password? Link

If you can't remember your password, click the **Forgot Your Password?** link below the password field to begin the password recovery process.

3 Enter Your Apple ID (.Mac Email Address)

Your Apple ID is the same as your .Mac email address, *<membername>*@mac.com. Enter that into the **Apple ID** field and click **Continue**.

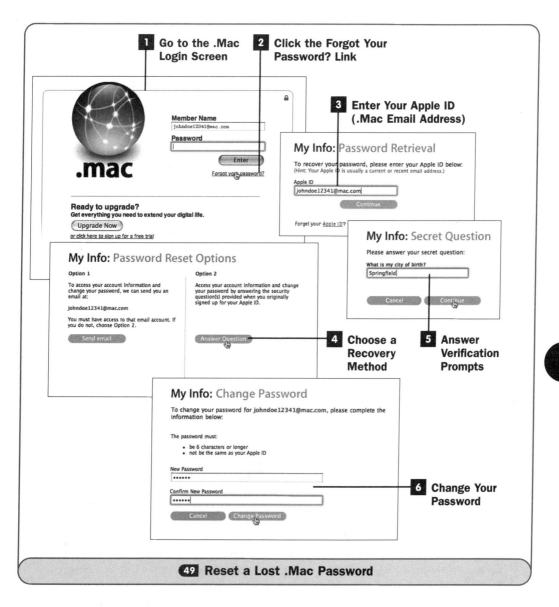

1 Go to the .Mac Login Screen

2 Click the Forgot Your Password? Link

3 Enter Your Apple ID (.Mac Email Address)

Member Name
johndoe12341@mac.com

Password

Enter

Forgot your password?

Ready to upgrade?
Get everything you need to extend your digital life.

Upgrade Now
or click here to sign up for a free trial

My Info: Password Retrieval

To recover your password, please enter your Apple ID below:
(Hint: Your Apple ID is usually a current or recent email address.)

Apple ID
johndoe12341@mac.com

Continue

Forget your Apple ID?

My Info: Password Reset Options

Option 1

To access your account information and change your password, we can send you an email at:

johndoe12341@mac.com

You must have access to that email account. If you do not, choose Option 2.

Send email

Option 2

Access your account information and change your password by answering the security question(s) provided when you originally signed up for your Apple ID.

Answer Question

My Info: Secret Question

Please answer your secret question:

What is my city of birth?
Springfield

Cancel   Continue

4 Choose a Recovery Method

5 Answer Verification Prompts

My Info: Change Password

To change your password for johndoe12341@mac.com, please complete the information below:

The password must:
• be 6 characters or longer
• not be the same as your Apple ID

New Password
••••••

Confirm New Password
••••••

Cancel   Change Password

6 Change Your Password

49 Reset a Lost .Mac Password

4 **Choose a Recovery Method**

You are given two options for how to reset your password. If you can access your **@mac.com** email (and are therefore only trying to change your password, rather than recover a lost one), use **Option 1**, in which Apple sends you an activation code in an email message to that account. If, however, you don't have access to that account (which is likely the case if you don't know your .Mac password), choose **Option 2**, which asks you for your verification question's answer.

5 Answer Verification Prompts

Apple first asks for your birthday. Provide this date and click **Continue.** You are then asked your verification question. You must provide the exact answer that you specified in your account information. If you do, you will be taken to the screen where you can enter a new password.

6 Change Your Password

Apple has a fairly lax policy regarding password "strength," or the alphanumeric complexity of the password string. (A strong password contains mixed uppercase and lowercase letters, numbers, and special characters, and cannot be found in any dictionary.) All Apple requires is that the password be at least six characters long, and that it not be exactly the same as your Apple ID (your .Mac email address). You can use your old password, too, if you have found your way into this procedure accidentally—so don't worry about having to come up with a new and unused password if you only have one password in mind. (.Mac does not tell you what your old password is, as a security measure.)

After changing your password, you are given a set of links to lead you back to the .Mac login page or to various other destinations at Apple's site.

49

50   Connect to Your iDisk

✔ **BEFORE YOU BEGIN**	→ **SEE ALSO**
45 Sign Up for .Mac	51 Keep Your iDisk in Sync
	52 Share Your iDisk Public Folder with Others

iDisk is like any other network server—you must connect to it before you can access what's inside it. Fortunately, iDisk is integrated into .Mac, so you don't have to waste time logging in and entering passwords when you want to connect. To connect to your iDisk—after your .Mac member information is entered into the **.Mac Preferences** pane of the **System Preferences**—click the **iDisk** icon in the Finder sidebar.

1 Open .Mac Preferences

Open the **System Preferences** application using the **Apple** menu. Click the .Mac icon to open the **.Mac Preferences** pane. Click the **.Mac** tab if it's not already selected.

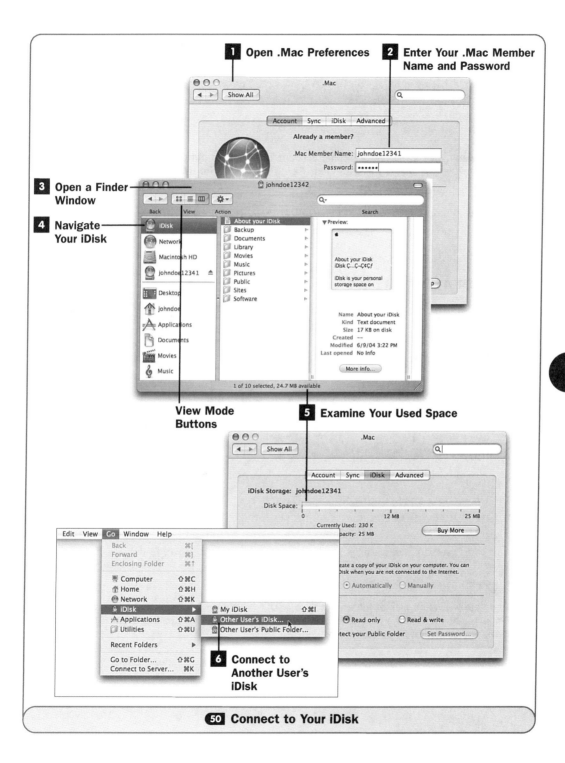

1 Open .Mac Preferences   **2** Enter Your .Mac Member Name and Password

3 Open a Finder Window

4 Navigate Your iDisk

View Mode Buttons

5 Examine Your Used Space

6 Connect to Another User's iDisk

50 Connect to Your iDisk

2 Enter Your .Mac Member Name and Password

You might have entered your .Mac information already, during the initial setup of the system. If you haven't, however, enter your member name and password into the boxes provided.

▶ NOTE

If you haven't yet signed up for a .Mac account, the **Sign Up** button provides a convenient link to the site where you can do so. See **45** **Sign Up for .Mac** for more information.

Close the **System Preferences** window when you're done entering your .Mac name and password. This action saves the account information you've entered.

3 Open a Finder Window

After you enter your .Mac information, the next time you open a Finder window, you'll see an **iDisk** icon at the top of the Finder's Sidebar.

4 Navigate Your iDisk

Click the **iDisk** icon to open its contents in the right pane of the Finder window. Switch to the view mode you like and navigate the various folders that are available.

You can add documents, folders, and other items to any of the folders in your iDisk by simply dragging them from the Desktop or from another Finder window into the window showing your iDisk contents.

Dragging items to your iDisk copies the items to the remote iDisk space (just as with any network server) and makes the files available for use in your .Mac web pages and slideshows. If you want to make files available for other .Mac users to access, drop those files into your iDisk **Public** folder.

▶ NOTE

To delete individual files or folders from your iDisk, navigate into the iDisk (using the Finder) until you find the files you want to delete; then drag them to the Trash. The items are immediately deleted from the iDisk server.

You can access your iDisk from as many different Macs as you wish, or even from non-Mac computers. If you want certain documents, applications, or other files to be available to you no matter what computer you're using, iDisk is the perfect solution—it's like having a copy of the same disk attached to every one of your computers. (This is especially true if you turn on local .Mac synchronization, as discussed in **51** **Keep Your iDisk in Sync**.)

50

5 Examine Your Used Space

There are two ways to see how much of your allotted iDisk space is used up. The quickest is to simply click the **iDisk** icon in the Finder, or navigate to any folder in your iDisk; the readout at the bottom of the Finder window shows how much space is available.

To see a more detailed readout—one that shows you how much space is allocated to your .Mac account, as well as how much space has been used—open the **.Mac Preferences** pane of the **System Preferences** application and click the **iDisk** tab. Your iDisk storage is displayed graphically, showing you the overall capacity and how much is currently used. If you decide you need more iDisk space, click the **Buy More** button. You can increase the amount of iDisk space you have from the basic 250MB (at no extra cost) to as much as 1GB for $350 per year. You can also adjust how much of your 250MB is allocated to email and to your iDisk, using the **Account** section of the .Mac web page (**http://www.mac.com**).

6 Connect to Another User's iDisk

If you have another .Mac user's member name and password, you can connect to her iDisk—her own personal storage space on Apple's central servers, not her own Mac—and browse its files just as you would your own. To do this, open the **Go** menu in the Finder and choose the **iDisk** option. From the submenu that opens, select **Other User's iDisk**. A **Connect To iDisk** dialog box appears; enter the .Mac user's member name and password, and click **Connect**. The user's iDisk appears in the Sidebar of the Finder window as well as on your Desktop, labeled with the user's .Mac member name.

50

▶ **NOTE**

Sharing your entire iDisk is advisable only if you completely trust the other person and her ability to control her own computing security—after all, you're giving away your .Mac password, which means giving away access to your entire .Mac account. Generally this feature is intended for people who have more than one .Mac account, or manage more than one .Mac account in a household or business.

The best way to share files using iDisk is to put them in your iDisk's **Public** folder, and then allow others to access that folder (which does not require an access password unless you set one). See **52 Share Your iDisk Public Folder with Others**.

You can connect to your iDisk using any of several different operating systems, including Windows, by using the downloadable **iDisk Utility** (if you're using Windows XP or Mac OS X 10.1 or 10.2). See **52 Share Your iDisk Public Folder with Others** for details on how to do this. To access your entire iDisk (or that of any other .Mac member) from another operating system, use the URL

http://idisk.mac.com/<*membername*> (where <*membername*> is the user's
.Mac member name) when specifying the server location.

Many applications that are aware of .Mac accounts—such
as **Address Book**—allow you to connect directly to a .Mac
user's iDisk. In the user's Address Book card, click the identifier (such as **work** or **home**) next to the **@mac.com** email
address and select **Open iDisk** from the menu that pops up.

---

51 Keep Your iDisk in Sync

✔ BEFORE YOU BEGIN	→ SEE ALSO
45 Sign Up for .Mac	**100** Synchronize Your Information
50 Connect to Your iDisk	Using .Mac

---

iDisk is at its best when you use it to keep all your Macs—if you're fortunate
enough to have more than one—in sync with each other. Using this feature of
Mac OS X, you can keep a copy of your iDisk on your own computer at all times,
making access to it as fast as accessing your own hard disk. Any changes you
make to your local iDisk are published to your remote iDisk on the .Mac server in
the background, without requiring any effort from you. From your remote iDisk,
the changes are propagated automatically to any other Macs that are logged in
to your .Mac account. No matter which Mac you use, the files, folders, and applications you've placed into your iDisk are immediately available.

You can elect to synchronize your iDisk manually, if you choose. For instance,
while you're trying to get work done online, you might not want your Mac to
take up precious bandwidth synchronizing with the remote iDisk server. But if
you let your Mac synchronize automatically, you can use your iDisk as your primary disk for important files that you need to access a lot—and those files will
always be at your fingertips, regardless of which of your Mac computers you're
using.

1 Open the .Mac Preferences

Open the **System Preferences** using the Apple menu. Click the **.Mac** icon to
open the **.Mac Preferences** pane. Click the **iDisk** tab to view the iDisk
options.

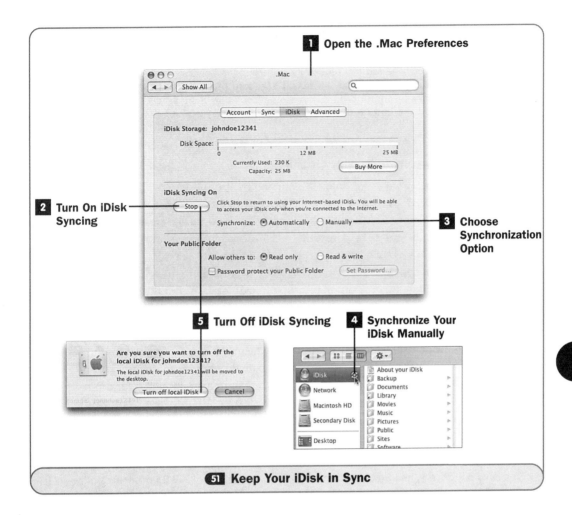

1 Open the .Mac Preferences

2 Turn On iDisk Syncing

3 Choose Synchronization Option

5 Turn Off iDisk Syncing

4 Synchronize Your iDisk Manually

51

51 Keep Your iDisk in Sync

2 Turn On iDisk Syncing

Click the **Start** button under the **iDisk Syncing Off** heading. This action enables iDisk synchronization and kicks off the first synchronization process, which might take a long time, depending on how much data is in your remote iDisk and how fast your Internet connection is. The iDisk status text updates to reflect that the local iDisk is now starting up, and the rotating "sync" icon appears next to the iDisk icon in the Finder's Sidebar until the first sync is complete. (The **Start** button changes to read **Stop** when iDisk syncing is on.)

▶ **TIP**

Click the **?** button in the dialog box for further information about how automatic and manual syncing work.

▶ **NOTE**

After the initial sync process is complete, the local iDisk also appears on your Desktop, as a separate volume that you can use as you would any other disk. (You can hide the iDisk on your Desktop by turning off the **CDs, DVDs, and iPods** option in the **Finder Preferences**, under the **General** tab.) Whenever your iDisk is being synchronized, its progress is shown at the bottom of the Finder window when you're looking at the iDisk's contents.

3 Choose Synchronization Option

The default behavior is for your iDisk to be synchronized automatically, whenever Mac OS X detects that your local or remote iDisk has been changed. The synchronization process can be bandwidth-intensive; if you don't want your Mac to be constantly exchanging information with the .Mac server as you use your local iDisk, select the **Manually** option. However, it's recommended that you keep your iDisk synchronization set to **Automatically** at all times, unless you're on a very constricted network connection or an older Mac with limited processor power.

Some special iDisk folders from the .Mac server are not copied to your local computer: **Backup**, which holds archives written by Apple's Backup application; **Library**, which keeps application-specific data for .Mac services; and **Software**, which has copies of many pieces of shareware provided for download by Apple. You don't need these folders or their files on your local hard disk, and you wouldn't want to download all those files at once!

▶ **NOTE**

The **Backup, Library**, and **Software** folders you can see on your local iDisk become aliases to their counterparts on the remote iDisk on the .Mac server so that you can still connect and view them. While you are disconnected from the remote .Mac iDisk, however, the local aliases might appear with the wrong icon. If you double-click the icons, the remote .Mac iDisk mounts and the correct aliases are restored.

4 Synchronize Your iDisk Manually

Wait until Mac OS X has completed synchronizing your local iDisk for the first time; the status message at the bottom of a Finder window showing your iDisk's contents tells you when the process is done.

If you have selected to synchronize your iDisk manually, you can start a new sync process at any time by clicking the circular **Sync** button next to the **iDisk** icon in the left pane of the Finder window. Alternatively, right-click (or **Control**+click) the **iDisk** icon on your Desktop and select **Sync Now** from the contextual menu that appears.

Repeat steps 1 through 4 for all your Macs; when all of them have been synchronized for the first time, automatic synchronization will operate efficiently in the background, keeping all your computers up to date.

5 Turn Off iDisk Syncing

If you choose, you can turn off the local synchronized iDisk; simply go back to the **iDisk** page of the .**Mac Preferences** pane of the **System Preferences** application and click the **Stop** button under the **iDisk Syncing On** heading. If you do this, your local iDisk will be converted into a *disk image* and placed on your Desktop. You can keep it in a safe place (double-click it to mount it so you can access its contents) or dispose of it in the Trash, as you prefer.

---

52 Share Your iDisk Public Folder with Others

✔ BEFORE YOU BEGIN	→ SEE ALSO
45 Sign Up for .Mac	53 Password-Protect Your Public Folder
50 Connect to Your iDisk	

51

Although iDisk is most useful in keeping your Macs' files synchronized, that is not by a long shot its only function. Your iDisk can also be used as a quick way to share files with other users—even if they're not using Macs.

The **Public** folder in your iDisk, like the **Public** folder in your **Home** folder on your local Mac, is accessible to anybody on the Internet. Anything you place into that folder can be accessed by Mac OS X users, Windows XP users (using the free **iDisk Utility** for Windows), Mac OS 9 users, or anybody with a web browser; all they have to know is your .Mac member name.

1 Place Files in Your Public Folder

Open your **iDisk** (whether accessed remotely or using the local copy) in the Finder; drag files or folders into the **Public** folder inside your iDisk. If you're using a locally synchronized copy of your iDisk, this will be an almost instantaneous process (you will need to click the **Sync** button next to **iDisk** in the Finder's Sidebar to publish the files to the server, if you have chosen to sync your iDisk manually); if you're connecting to your iDisk remotely, it will take a few moments to copy the files to the server.

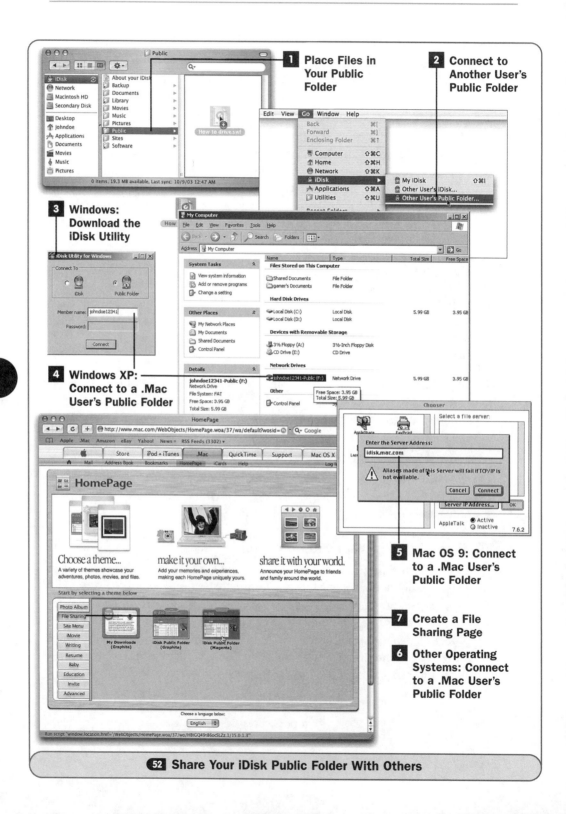

1 Place Files in Your Public Folder

2 Connect to Another User's Public Folder

3 Windows: Download the iDisk Utility

4 Windows XP: Connect to a .Mac User's Public Folder

5 Mac OS 9: Connect to a .Mac User's Public Folder

7 Create a File Sharing Page

6 Other Operating Systems: Connect to a .Mac User's Public Folder

52 Share Your iDisk Public Folder With Others

2 Connect to Another User's Public Folder

If you know another .Mac user who has placed files in his iDisk's **Public** folder, you can access that folder directly knowing only the user's member name. Open the **Go** menu in the Finder; in the **iDisk** submenu, then select the **Other User's Public Folder** option. Enter the other user's .Mac member name in the dialog box that appears and click **Connect.** The other user's iDisk **Public** folder will appear in the left pane of your Finder window, as well as on your Desktop under the name *<membername>*-**Public** (where *<membername>* is the other user's .Mac member name).

▶ NOTE

If the other user has protected his **Public** folder with a password, another dialog box appears, prompting you for that password. Enter it and click **OK**.

Depending on the other user's iDisk settings, you might be able to copy files into his **Public** folder by dragging them or delete files by ⌘+dragging them; if the user has allowed **Read only** access to the Public folder, however, you will not be able to make any changes to the files in that user's **Public** folder.

3 Windows: Download the iDisk Utility

If you have a PC running Windows XP, you can access the files in a .Mac user's **Public** folder using the free **iDisk Utility**, available at the .Mac website. Go to **http://www.mac.com** using your Windows web browser, and log in using your .Mac account information; click the **iDisk** icon, and follow the links to the **iDisk Utility**. Download the ZIP archive for Windows and install the program.

▶ TIP

If you're using Mac OS X version 10.1 or 10.2, you also must download the **iDisk Utility** before you can access other users' iDisks or **Public** folders. This functionality is built into Mac OS X Panther (version 10.3) and later, but earlier versions don't have it as part of the system. Download the **Mac OS X** version of the **iDisk Utility** if you have one of these older releases of Mac OS X.

4 Windows XP: Connect to a .Mac User's Public Folder

Open the **iDisk Utility** and click the radio button next to the **Public Folder** icon. Type the .Mac user's member name whose **Public** folder you want to connect to in the **Member Name** box.

Click the **Connect** button; if a password is required to open the folder, enter it in the dialog box that appears and click **OK**.

52

The user's **Public** folder will be mounted as a network drive within Windows, accessible via the **Windows Explorer** or **My Computer**; you can browse its contents and place files into it (if the owner has granted **Read & Write** access to others).

5 Mac OS 9: Connect to a .Mac User's Public Folder

To connect to another user's iDisk **Public** folder from a Mac OS 9 machine, open the **Chooser** (using the **Apple** menu) and click the **AppleShare** icon on the left. Click the **Server IP Address** button and then type **idisk.mac.com** in the **Enter the Server Address** field. Click **Connect**.

You are prompted to enter the person's .Mac member name; if the **Public** folder requires a password, type it in the **Password** field. If the folder doesn't require a password, type the word **public** instead. Click **Connect** to continue.

In the next dialog box, select the shared resource whose name matches the user's .Mac member name (it should be the only one available); when you click **OK**, the iDisk share will appear on your Desktop.

6 Other Operating Systems: Connect to a .Mac User's Public Folder

52

You can connect to a .Mac user's iDisk with other operating systems, too. In Windows 2000, select **Map Network Drive** from the **Tools** menu, then click **Web folder or FTP site** and enter the URL **http://idisk.mac.com/ <membername>-Public/** (where **<membername>** is the user's .Mac member name).

In Windows 98, open **My Computer** and double-click the **Web Folders** option. Then double-click **Add Web Folder** and enter the URL **http://idisk.mac.com/<membername>-Public/**.

You can even connect to a user's **Public** folder using Linux or Unix if you have a WebDAV client (iDisk operates using WebDAV). Enter this URL when you are prompted for the server location by the client: **http://idisk.mac.com/<membername>-Public/**.

7 Create a File Sharing Page

You can create a .Mac web page to share the contents of your iDisk **Public** folder with anybody who has a web browser. To do this, go to the .Mac website at **http://www.mac.com** and log in using your .Mac account information. Then click the **HomePage** icon. Create a new page using the **File**

Sharing theme tab in the lower portion of the screen (see **47** **Create a .Mac Web Page**). Customize the page as you would any other .Mac web page, giving it a proper descriptive name; then click **Publish**. The .Mac service will then give you the URL for your new File Sharing page.

Use this URL to open a web page that shows a listing of all the files and folders in your **Public** folder; give the URL to your friends so that they can access those same files. However, people don't even have to know the URL of your File Sharing page, as long as they know your .Mac member name: People can go directly to **http://homepage.mac.com/<*membername*>** (where <*membername*> is your .Mac member name). There will be a link at the top of the page to your File Sharing page, listed by the name that you gave it when you created it.

53   Password-Protect Your Public Folder

✔ **BEFORE YOU BEGIN**

45 Sign Up for .Mac
52 Share Your iDisk Public Folder with Others

52

Anybody, anywhere, can access whatever is in the **Public** folder on your iDisk—and that includes not just the people whom you *want* to allow access, but also a lot of people you might *not* want to see your files. As a rule of thumb, don't put anything in your **Public** folder that you wouldn't want to show up in the newspaper.

Sometimes it's necessary (or just too convenient) to use your **Public** folder to exchange files of a sensitive nature that ought to be password-protected, or you might want to provide your **Public** folder with a measure of privacy out of principle. Fortunately, iDisk provides that capability.

1   Open the .Mac Preferences

Open the **System Preferences** using the **Apple** menu. Click the .**Mac** icon to open the .**Mac Preferences** pane and click the **iDisk** tab.

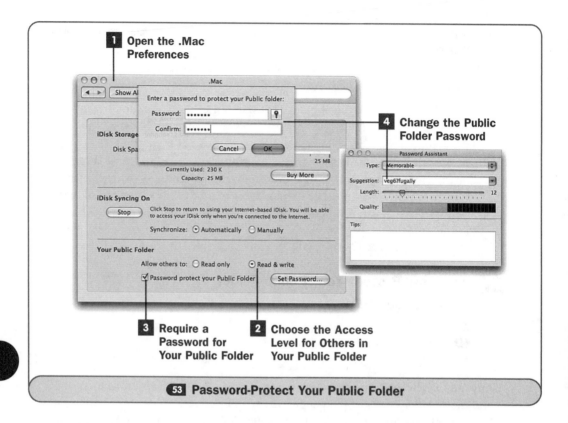

1 Open the .Mac Preferences

4 Change the Public Folder Password

3 Require a Password for Your Public Folder

2 Choose the Access Level for Others in Your Public Folder

53 Password-Protect Your Public Folder

2 Choose the Access Level for Others in Your Public Folder

You can choose what kind of capabilities other users can have within your iDisk's **Public** folder. You can make it so that other users can put files into your **Public** folder (**Read & Write** access), but this level of access also enables users to delete or change files that are already in the folder. On the other hand, you can give your **Public** folder **Read only** access, which allows others to access existing files but not to alter them or add any of their own; this forgoes the convenience of allowing others to put files into your iDisk's **Public** folder, but it's much safer.

▶ NOTE

It's important to stress the difference between your iDisk **Public** folder and the **Public** folder inside your **Home** folder on your local Mac. Your local **Public** folder is accessible from other Macs only; it has a **Drop Box** subfolder, which other users can use to send files to you while maintaining your privacy. The **Public** folder in your iDisk, however, doesn't have a **Drop Box** subfolder; you can only choose between **Read only** and **Read & Write** privileges for the iDisk **Public** folder.

3 Require a Password for Your Public Folder

Select the **Password protect your Public Folder** check box to set a password on your iDisk **Public** folder. A sheet appears that prompts you to enter a password (twice); click **OK** when you've done so.

If you need help coming up with a good password to use, click the "key" button to open the **Password Assistant** panel. This is a tool that suggests appropriate passwords for you to use according to several different schemes, including **Memorable** (for passwords composed of English words cleverly strung together), **Letters and Numbers**, and **Manual**. Use the **Length** slider to select how long you want the suggested password to be; longer passwords are better and more secure, as indicated by the **Quality** meter below the slider. In **Manual** mode, type a password of your choice into the **Suggestion** box, and the **Quality** meter shows how good the password is; the **Tips** box offers pointers on how to improve your entered password, such as pointing out whether it's derived from dictionary words, too short, or otherwise too easy to guess.

▶ **NOTE**

The Password Assistant utility automatically fills in its suggested password into the **Password** field of the sheet in the **.Mac Preferences** pane; however, it doesn't fill it into the **Confirm** field. You have to type that yourself, to make sure you've memorized the password.

53

▶ **TIP**

As with many panes of the **System Preferences** application, you might have to close the **System Preferences** window (or click the **.Mac** tab and then click the **iDisk** tab again) to force the changes to take effect. To remove the password protection, just deselect the **Password Protect your Public Folder** check box.

4 Change the Public Folder Password

If you want to change the password on your iDisk **Public** folder, click the **Set Password** button on the **iDisk** tab of the **.Mac Preferences** pane. Enter the new password (twice, as prompted) in the sheet that appears. When you click **OK** and close the **System Preferences** application, the password for your iDisk **Public** folder will be changed.

7

Email

IN THIS CHAPTER:

Arguably the most revolutionary and pervasive part of the Internet (rivaled only by browsing the Web), email is an application whose use has joined the world's lexicon as firmly as television did—and much more quickly. It's easy to understand why: Now, effectively for free, a person anywhere on Earth can communicate nearly instantaneously with someone else no matter where she is on the planet. Email has become the *lingua franca* of the Information Age; people use it to send each other everything from brief one-line messages to whole picture albums or business documents. Email can get you in touch with everybody from a family member down the hall to your congressman or favorite author. For all that, email is still conceptually one of the simplest of applications: You type in some text, and off it goes into the cloud of flowing bits that is the Internet.

Anybody who has ever used email before, though, will know that there's actually a lot more to it than that. Everybody has their own style for how they use email, from what "signatures" they attach to the ends of messages to how they prefer incoming messages to be listed. Email applications in recent years have become increasingly complex, adding more and more convenience and flexibility so that the user has complete control over the entire experience of interacting with their virtual mailboxes. Applications such as Microsoft Outlook, in particular, have set a new standard for just how complex a concept as simple as email can be made.

Apple's **Mail** application, built in to Mac OS X, provides all the flexibility of programs such as Outlook, coupled with the intuitiveness and elegance typical of Apple software. While .Mac Webmail (covered in **48** **Use .Mac Webmail**) offers you convenient but rudimentary access to your .Mac mail account, it can be vastly more intuitive, fast, and flexible to use **Mail** to read the email in that account (and any other email accounts you might have) on your own computer rather than on the Web. All the advanced features of modern email programs are incorporated into Mail—automatic junk-mail filtering, color-based message flagging, automated message organization with user-definable rules, *LDAP* directory integration, and support for *POP* and *IMAP* mail access protocols. Starting in Mac OS X Tiger, Mail incorporates the searching technology of Spotlight (see **12** **Find an Item**) to allow you to search and organize your incoming email messages like a master conductor directing a symphony orchestra. Mail's **Preferences** window contains innumerable ways to configure the application to match your work style; this chapter will concentrate on the most important core features of Mail, while pointing out areas where you can customize it to your taste.

Working in tandem with your Address Book (a small application that keeps track of all your "contacts," the people you correspond with via email, phone, instant-message chat, or any other means) and synchronizing all your information using iSync and .Mac, Mail is able to turn a formerly austere and potentially confusing form of communication into one that anticipates what you want to say and who you want to say it to. Refer to **95** **Add a Person to Your Address Book** to start making the most of your Address Book, and **100** **Synchronize Your Information Using .Mac** for more about synchronizing your contacts across all your Macs.

▶ KEY TERMS

Lightweight Directory Access Protocol (LDAP)—The standard "directory service" mechanism, allowing email applications to obtain names, phone numbers, and email addresses automatically with a query to a corporate server.

54	**Configure a New Mail Account**

✔ **BEFORE YOU BEGIN**	→ **SEE ALSO**
30 Configure Networking Manually **45** Sign Up for .Mac	**55** Find and Read Messages and Attachments

If you have a .Mac account, using the **@mac.com** email address that comes with it is the easiest way to use the **Mail** application. .Mac email accounts use ***IMAP***, the ***Internet Mail Access Protocol***; so do accounts hosted on a Microsoft Exchange server, as is often the case in corporate networks. You can set up many kinds of email accounts to use IMAP, from free hosting services to your own ISP's email service (consult with the provider of your email service to see if it is capable of using IMAP). If you specify that your email account is a .Mac account, however, **Mail** uses certain default settings to allow you to interact with the .Mac mail servers without any further configuration.

54

Mail can support many kinds of email accounts, but each account must be configured in the application before you can use it. When you configure the Mail program to use your email account, you'll have to enter a fair amount of information. Be sure that you have all the information you need from your Internet service provider (ISP) or network administrator: the type of email account, your email address, the incoming and outgoing mail servers, and your account name and password.

IMAP operates by keeping all your messages and mailboxes on the mail server at the Internet service provider. When you use Mail to check for new messages, it accesses those messages on the server and downloads copies to your Mac so that you can peruse them at your leisure (even when you're offline). The messages are not deleted from the server until you delete them using Mail; when you do that, messages are moved into the **Trash** folder on your computer's hard drive. The local message cache means you can always access your messages quickly; however, a downside of IMAP accounts is that when you navigate your mail folders that are stored on the server, there is some lag time as Mail synchronizes its information with the state of the mailboxes on the server.

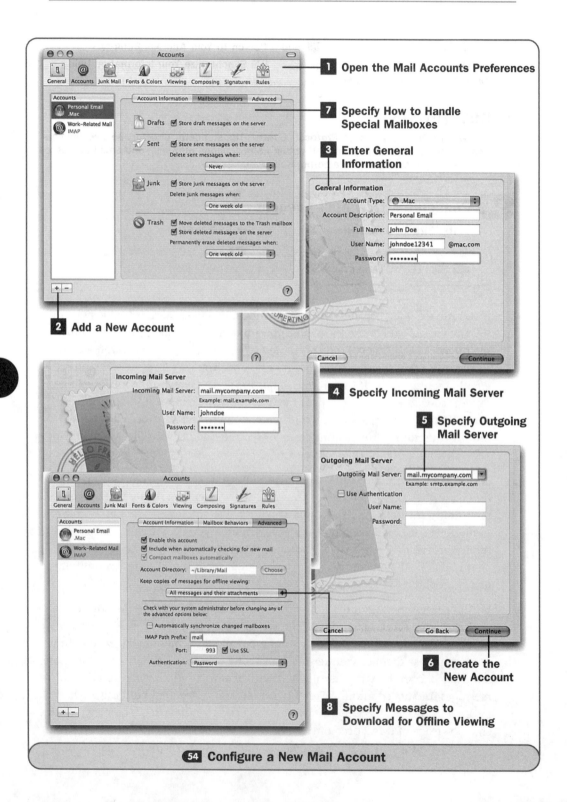

54

1 Open the Mail Accounts Preferences

7 Specify How to Handle Special Mailboxes

3 Enter General Information

2 Add a New Account

4 Specify Incoming Mail Server

5 Specify Outgoing Mail Server

6 Create the New Account

8 Specify Messages to Download for Offline Viewing

54 Configure a New Mail Account

This behavior is distinct from *Post Office Protocol (POP)* mail accounts, in which Mail downloads all new messages to your computer and removes them from the server. With IMAP, you can always access your mail from any computer; with POP, you can properly read your mail only from a single computer. Furthermore, IMAP frees you from having to worry about what happens if your Mac crashes and you lose your data; you can simply connect again with a new or freshly rebuilt computer, and your messages are all still there. With POP, unless you've diligently backed up your data, your old mail messages are gone forever if your hard drive crashes. (See **143** **Back Up Your Information** for more on backing up your important data!)

▶ **NOTE**

POP accounts are easier for many ISPs to administer. Because the ISP doesn't have to store everybody's mail in POP accounts, they don't require as much server disk space or processing time.

POP is traditionally the most popular type of email account, although more and more Internet service providers are switching to *IMAP* because of its flexibility. POP accounts are still quite common; if your Internet service provider has set you up with one, it means that whenever you get new mail, the **Mail** application downloads it to your Mac and removes it from the server. You can configure Mail to leave messages on the server for a certain period of time, but after that period expires, the messages on the server will be deleted and you won't be able to access your mail from any computer but the one that downloaded the messages. The upside of this arrangement is that your own Mac will always be able to access the messages and their attachments quickly, whether online or offline, because the messages have already been downloaded completely; the messages will also never disappear from that Mac, as long as you make sure your Mac's data is backed-up.

54

1 **Open the Mail Accounts Preferences**

Launch the **Mail** application by clicking its icon in the Dock or by double-clicking its icon in the **Applications** folder. Mail consists of a single window with a column of mailboxes on the left, a listing of messages in the selected mailbox at the top, and the text of the selected message in the large pane below that. Until you set up your first email account, though, no messages will appear.

If you had previously set up a .Mac account (see **45** **Sign Up for .Mac**), your @mac.com account is already set up, and you can skip the rest of this task and proceed to **55** **Find and Read Messages and Attachments**.

To set up a new .Mac, POP, IMAP, or Exchange mail account, select **Preferences** from the **Mail** menu and click the **Accounts** icon in the toolbar to open the **Accounts** pane, if it isn't already open.

2 Add a New Account

At the bottom of the list of accounts on the left, click the + icon to create a new mail account. A sheet appears that contains a series of configuration screens that will guide you through the creation of the new account.

3 Enter General Information

Select .**Mac**, **POP**, **Exchange**, or **IMAP** from the **Account Type** drop-down menu, depending on the kind of email account your Internet service provider or network administrator has assigned for you.

▶ TIP

Consult your ISP if you're not sure whether you have an IMAP or POP account; if you're configuring your .Mac mail account (*<membername>*@**mac.com**), select .**Mac**.

54

Type a descriptive name for the account in the **Account Description** field. This name is what will appear in the **Mailboxes** drawer in Mail; choose a name that adequately describes what the account is for, such as **Work-Related Email** or **My .Mac Account**.

In the fields provided, type your full name and your email address (or, if this is a .Mac account, the .Mac member name and password); these are used in constructing the return address on the messages you send out, so make sure they're accurate!

Click **Continue** to move to the next step.

4 Specify Incoming Mail Server

If you're setting up a .Mac account, the incoming and outgoing mail servers are set to the .Mac defaults; you are shown an **Account Summary** screen reflecting your settings, and you can click Continue to complete the account creation process; skip to step 6 to fine-tune advanced mailbox behaviors.

For POP, IMAP, and Exchange accounts, you must now specify the incoming mail server. Type the hostname of the incoming mail server provided by your ISP or network administrator. This server name is usually of a form similar to **mail.somecompany.com** (where **somecompany.com** is your company's or ISP's domain name).

▶ **TIP**

You can specify either a hostname or an IP address for your incoming mail server. Using a hostname (such as **mail.somecompany.com**) is easier to type and to remember, but because it is dependent on an extra layer of networking architecture (DNS, the Domain Name System), there is a risk that your email service may be interrupted if DNS service is not available due to a network problem. If you specify an IP address (for instance, **112.113.114.115**), your email service will be a little more fault-tolerant, as it no longer depends on DNS.

In the fields provided, specify your account username and password. The user/account name is typically the same as the first part of your email address, before the @ symbol. For instance, if your address is **johndoe@mac.com**, the account name is **johndoe**.

If you're creating an Exchange account, and your network administrator has given you the name of a server for Outlook Web Access (or an Internet Information Services server, or IIS), enter it in the **Outlook Web Access Server** field. This server may be the same as your incoming mail server. If you specify an Outlook Web Access server name, the Mail application will filter incoming mail to prevent special Exchange messages, such as meeting notifications, from appearing in your Inbox.

54

▶ **TIP**

If you have an Exchange account, you might actually want Exchange messages such as meeting notifications to appear in your Inbox; such messages contain attachments that you can double-click to open them in iCal and add them to your personal calendar (see **97 Create an iCal Event**). To do this, simply set up the account as an **IMAP** account rather than an **Exchange** account.

Click **Continue** to move to the next step. Your incoming mail server is checked for validity; if you have entered incorrect information in any of the fields, an error message will appear and you'll have to stay on this screen until you've corrected the information.

5 Specify Outgoing Mail Server

The next step is specifying the outgoing mail server (or SMTP server—meaning the Simple Mail Transfer Protocol, the delivery mechanism for handling messages that you send). Your ISP or company should have given you a server name to use; it might, in fact, be the same as your incoming mail server.

If you have an outgoing mail server from your provider, enter the server name in the **Outgoing Mail Server** field. If the SMTP server requires authentication for sending mail, select the **Use Authentication** check box and specify a user name and password in the fields provided.

▶ **NOTE**

If the provider's SMTP server supports secure SMTP (using *Secure Sockets Layer*, or *SSL*), or if it uses a different IP port than the default 25, visit the **Account Information** tab of the **Accounts** pane in the **Mail Preferences** after setting up the account completely, and click the **Server Settings** button at the bottom; these advanced settings can be specified there.

▶ **KEY TERM**

Spam—Unsolicited commercial email.

Some kinds of email accounts, notably accounts from free web hosting services, don't provide SMTP server access. This is a measure intended to fight *spam*, or unsolicited email broadcast through mail servers on the Internet. To defend against spam, many hosting services do not permit remote users to send mail through their SMTP servers at all. This means that even if you are setting up an account to fetch mail from a remote service on the Internet, you might have to set the account to use an SMTP server provided by your Internet service provider. Your ISP will almost certainly make a usable SMTP server available to you as a customer on its local network.

54

If your ISP has not given you an outgoing mail server, you can use your .Mac account to gain access to the **smtp.mac.com** server, provided that you have set up your **@mac.com** account already in Mail; click the down arrow to show previously specified SMTP servers, and choose **smtp.mac.com:<*membername*>**, which uses your .Mac account information for authentication, from the list. The fields under **Use Authentication** are automatically filled in.

Click **Continue** to move to the next step. Your outgoing mail server is checked for validity; if you have entered incorrect information in any of the fields, an error message will appear and you'll have to stay on this screen until you've corrected the information.

6 Create the New Account

An **Account Summary** screen appears, showing you the settings you've specified so far. If they all look correct, click **Continue** to create the new account. (To make any changes, click **Go Back** to return to previous screens.) The account's mailboxes immediately appear in the Mailboxes pane of Mail, and you are given a button to **Create Another Account** if you wish, or to click **Done** to exit the account creation process.

7 Specify How to Handle Special Mailboxes

Now, back in the **Accounts** pane of the **Mail Preferences** window, you can adjust the more detailed settings of your account. Click the **Account**

Information tab if it's not already selected, and select your newly created account from the **Accounts** list. Click the **Server Settings** button to specify advanced options for the outgoing mail server, such as SSL encryption or an alternate server port.

Click the **Mailbox Behaviors** tab. This brings up the page where you can fine-tune the behavior of mail that is automatically sorted into your **Drafts**, **Sent**, **Junk**, and **Trash** folders. For any of these mailboxes, you can elect to have their contents stored on the server rather than downloaded permanently to your computer. You can also specify when Mail should automatically delete messages in those folders—after a day, a week, a month, whenever you quit Mail, or never.

▶ **NOTE**

By default, Mail downloads messages in these special mailboxes and removes them from the server to save disk space. However, if you stick with this default behavior, you can't access the contents of those mailboxes from other computers. If you elect to keep the messages on the server, they will take up more space on the server (as well as being slower to access), but you can browse them from any computer. For instance, if you keep your **Drafts** mailbox on the server, you can begin a message with one computer, save it, and resume working on it in another computer before sending it.

54

8 **Specify Messages to Download for Offline Viewing**

Click the **Advanced** tab. The **Advanced** page allows you to configure several additional options, including whether the account is *enabled* (appears in the **Mailboxes** drawer), whether your connections to the incoming mail server are secure (using SSL), and whether Mail should download copies of all your messages automatically so that you can read them even when you're not online. Use the **Keep copies of messages for offline viewing** drop-down menu to select whether Mail should keep all messages or just the ones you've read, and whether it should download attachments or not.

▶ **TIP**

If you're setting up an IMAP account to access mail on a Unix shell system, you will probably have to specify the **IMAP Path Prefix**. On most servers, this prefix is typically **mail**. If you don't set this path, every file in your home directory on the server will appear as a mailbox in Mail!

55 | Find and Read Messages and Attachments

✔ BEFORE YOU BEGIN	→ SEE ALSO
54 Configure a New Mail Account	56 Send a Message
	57 Filter Junk Mail

It won't be long before you have received your first few email messages. Indeed, chances are that before you know it, you'll be getting more than you can handle (particularly in the form of junk mail or *spam*, which the Mail program can filter for you—as you see in 57 **Filter Junk Mail**). The first function of the **Mail** application is to allow you to read these messages, as well as to open any attached files that might come with the messages.

Within your email account (and each additional account, if you happen to have more than one), you have a number of mailboxes—which can be thought of as "folders" within your email account. The primary mailbox—which each account has—is the **Inbox**. The rest of the mailboxes depend on the types of accounts you have; but the most common important mailboxes are **Sent**, **Trash**, and **Junk**, as well as the **Drafts** mailbox. The **Sent** mailbox holds every message you send; the **Trash** mailbox contains all the messages you delete; and **Junk** has the messages that the Mail application deems junk mail. The **Drafts** mailbox is used to hold partially completed messages while you're composing them, and Sent turns into Sending and receives a copy or each outgoing message while Mail is attempting to deliver it. Additionally, you can create as many other mailboxes as you want—either stored locally on your Mac or remotely on the server (for IMAP accounts).

New messages always appear in your Inbox, unless they are moved elsewhere by an automated rule, as you will see in 58 **Create a Mailbox.**

1 Open the Mailbox You Want to Read

All your available email accounts and all their associated mailboxes appear in the **Mailboxes** pane of the Mail application, the column at left. (If this pane is not visible, choose **Show Mailboxes** from the **View** menu.) Depending on the types of accounts you have and what options for the special mailboxes you have already specified, the mailboxes are sorted according to their importance and how likely you are to need access to them. Your Inboxes appear at the top of the list, all grouped together into a single unified **In** box; you can either expand the **In** mailbox (using the triangle control to its left) to view each individual account's Inbox, or you can click the **In** mailbox itself to see all the messages in all your Inboxes at once.

55

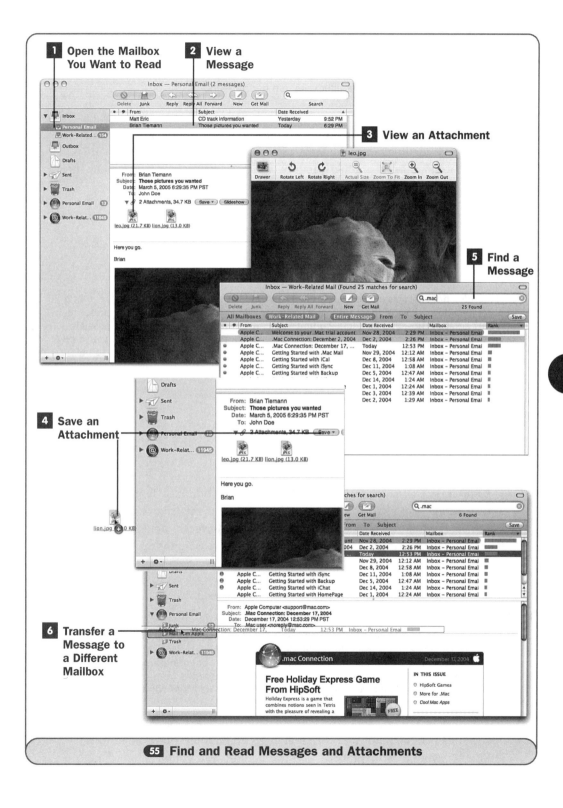

1 Open the Mailbox You Want to Read

2 View a Message

3 View an Attachment

5 Find a Message

4 Save an Attachment

6 Transfer a Message to a Different Mailbox

55

55 Find and Read Messages and Attachments

▶ **NOTE**

Each mailbox indicates how many unread messages are in it. If there are any unread messages, the number of them appears in an oval next to the mailbox name. If there are no unread messages in the mailbox, no number appears.

Click the mailbox you want to view; the messages in that mailbox appear listed in the Message List pane. The number of total messages in the mailbox appears in the title bar of the Mail application; in this example, there are eight messages in the mailbox, four of which are unread (as indicated by the blue dot next to each unread message).

2 View a Message

Click a message's subject to view that message in the Message pane below.

▶ **TIP**

If you prefer, double-click a message in the Message List pane to open the message in a separate window. Viewing messages in a separate window can be useful if you prefer to see only a list of message subjects, so that you can see as many messages as possible, or so that you can control messages without downloading them (for instance, if you're on a very slow network link). Double-click the horizontal divider between the panes to hide the Message pane and create a larger Message List pane.

55

The top part of the message consists of the *headers*, which are several lines of information describing who sent the message, to whom it was addressed, when it was sent, and the subject (shown in bold), as well as a variety of other optional pieces of data. Then, below a horizontal dividing line, the body of the message itself appears.

Email messages can come in two styles: Plain Text and Rich Text. Rich Text, a designation that includes HTML and inline attachments, allows a message to have text in custom colors and fonts and styles; however, these messages are also larger and take longer to download. For this reason, many messages—such as informational messages from web-based services—are sent as Plain Text.

▶ **TIP**

Not all available columns are shown in the message list pane. You can enable more columns by choosing them from the **View**, **Columns** submenu, or by right-clicking (or **Control**+clicking) the column header bar, and selecting new column names. For example, in a grouped mailbox or Smart Mailbox that shows messages from many mailboxes, you might turn on the **Mailbox** column to see where each message comes from.

Often, Plain Text messages are laid out to organize text into tabular format, such as in billing reports that list line-items and a total. However, for this kind of layout to work properly, you must tell the Mail application to use a monospaced font for Plain Text messages. Otherwise, the letters will all be different widths and won't line up properly. To do this, open the **Mail Preferences** window, click the **Fonts & Colors** icon, and select the **Use fixed-width font for plain text messages** check box.

3 View an Attachment

In addition to Plain Text or Rich Text content, an email message can also contain one or more *attachments*—files, folders, or applications that are sent along with the message for you to open and save on your own computer. Email attachments have become the *de facto* standard method for transferring pictures, Word and Excel documents, and ZIP archives around the office or across the Internet.

▶ **NOTE**

Rich Text messages can have pictures and other types of data embedded directly into the body of the message; to view or save these items, double-click them or drag them from their position in the message to your Desktop or a **Finder** window (or even straight into another application, such as **Preview**). However, for both Plain Text and Rich Text messages, all attachments are listed in the header portion of the message, so that you can examine the filename and type of each attachment.

55

If an email message has an attachment, you will see a line in the headers area noting how many attachments there are, as well as a **Save** button menu, and (if the attachments are pictures) a **Slideshow** button as well. Click the triangle to the left of this line to expand the attachments summary; double-click any listed attachment to open it in its default application. You can also right-click (or **Control**+click) the attachment icon to choose which application to open it in, just as you would in the Finder.

If the message contains a series of attached pictures, click the **Slideshow** button to begin an automatic full-screen slideshow of the pictures. A translucent toolbar at the bottom of the screen gives you the option to play or pause the slideshow, skip forward or back one picture at a time, show all pictures in an index sheet (similar to the "All Windows" mode of Exposé), import the pictures one at a time into iPhoto, and more.

4 Save an Attachment

If you simply view an attachment by double-clicking it, it will open in its associated application; but if you want to save the attachment permanently on your hard disk, move it from the Mail application into the Finder. Click and drag any attachment icon from the expanded header area onto the Desktop or into a Finder window; the green + symbol next to the mouse pointer as you drag indicates that a copy of the item will be saved wherever you drop it.

▶ **TIP**

Choose **Save All** from the **Save** button menu to choose a location and have the Mail application save all the message's attachments to that location at once.

Any attachments that are pictures are listed by their thumbnail icons and filenames in the **Save** button menu. Select an individual picture file to save it in a selected location, or choose **Add to iPhoto** to send all the message's picture attachments into your iPhoto Library. (See 87 **About iPhoto and Digital Photography** for more about using iPhoto to manage your photographs.)

5 Find a Message

You can quickly locate a message if you know any text that appears in its **Subject** line or contents, or if you know to or from whom it was sent. Just type the desired text into the **Search** bar (the white oval in the upper right), and the mailbox you're currently viewing is immediately filtered to show only the messages that match what you've typed, sorted by a "rank" that reflects how closely the messages' contents matched your search text.

55

▶ **TIP**

Click the gray circled **X** at the right end of the **Search** bar to clear the contents of the field and go back to viewing your mailbox normally.

The results of the search are displayed in the same manner as a Finder search, with control buttons at the top of the window allowing you to specify whether the search terms should apply to the **From**, **To**, or **Subject** fields, or the entire message's text, and a menu to select the mailbox or hierarchy in which to search. You can even save a message grouping resulting from a search as a Smart Mailbox, using the **Save** button (see 59 **Create a Smart Mailbox That Automatically Contains Certain Types of Messages** for more details on this process).

Click the magnifying glass icon at the left end of the Search bar to select what part of the message to search. By default, Mail searches the entire contents of all your messages; if you want to narrow the results down still further, you can select **From**, **To**, or **Subject** from the magnifying-glass list to limit the searching to one of those header fields. You can also tell Mail to search messages in all your mailboxes instead of just the mailbox you're currently viewing.

6 Transfer a Message to a Different Mailbox

To help you organize your communications more efficiently, you can create new mailboxes in any of your accounts, either those on your local hard disk or those on the remote server (for .Mac, IMAP, or Exchange accounts); see **65 Create a Mailbox** for instructions. Mail lets you sort your messages into your various mailboxes by simply dragging and dropping. Click any message and drag it to the mailbox you want to move it to. You can move messages from any mailbox to any other mailbox (except for Smart Mailboxes), including mailboxes in other accounts.

▶ TIP

The Mail application supports a form of the "spring-loaded folders" feature used by the Finder: To move a message into a mailbox that's deeply nested within other mailboxes, drag the message to the top mailbox and hold the mouse pointer there until the mailbox expands. Repeat for a mailbox inside that one, if necessary, until the target mailbox is visible. Then drop the message into the mailbox where you want it to go.

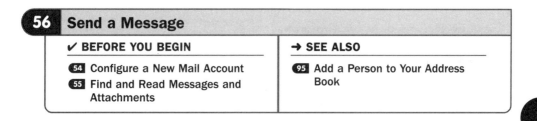

56	**Send a Message**
✔ **BEFORE YOU BEGIN**	→ **SEE ALSO**
54 Configure a New Mail Account **55** Find and Read Messages and Attachments	**95** Add a Person to Your Address Book

55

Naturally, email isn't just for receiving messages; you'll also want to send messages of your own. You can send email to anybody whose email address you know, whether they're in your Address Book or not. Note, however, that the more people you add to your Address Book, the easier it is to communicate with the important people in your life.

To reply to a message that someone else has sent to you, simply click the **Reply** or **Reply All** button while viewing the message; you can then type whatever you want to say in response.

Internet etiquette ("netiquette") dictates that you should always *quote* the message you're replying to—that is, you should include the other person's text in your message, so that she knows what she said that you're talking about. The Mail application automatically quotes the entire message for you when you click **Reply**. You can add your own reply at the top of the quoted text, at the bottom of the quoted text, or interspersed between the paragraphs in question.

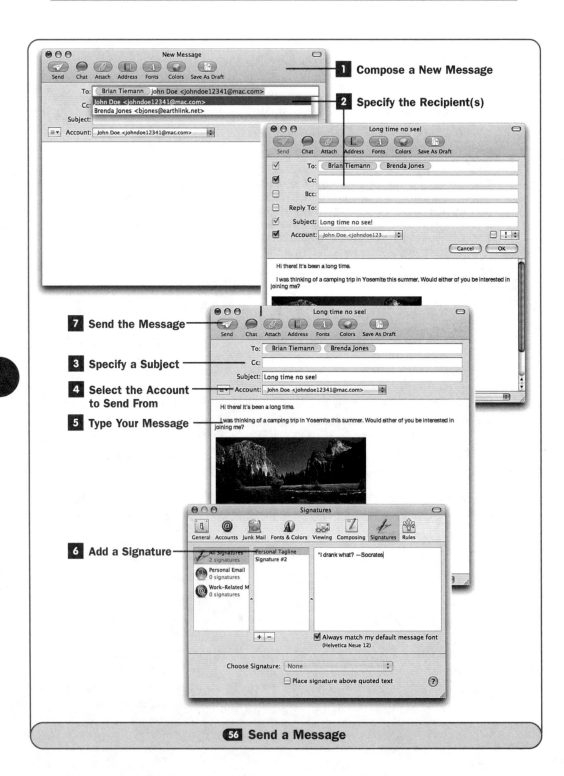

1 Compose a New Message

2 Specify the Recipient(s)

7 Send the Message

3 Specify a Subject

4 Select the Account to Send From

5 Type Your Message

6 Add a Signature

56

56 Send a Message

▶ **NOTE**

If you don't want Mail to quote the other person's message for you, you can turn off this feature by deselecting the **Quote the text of the original message** check box in the **Composing** pane of the **Mail Preferences**. It's probably best to leave this option enabled, however!

The Mail application's default behavior is that if you have selected a portion of the other person's message when you click **Reply**, only the selected text is quoted. You can turn this feature off as well in the **Composing** pane of the **Mail Preferences**.

Rather than writing a new message or replying to a message that was sent to you, you have a couple of further options. You can forward a message to another recipient—just click the **Forward** button, and then specify the new recipient's email address in the composition window that appears. Add some message text of your own, if you like, above or below the quoted body of the message. Then click **Send**.

Similarly, you can use the **Redirect** command (found in the **Message** menu) to resend the message to a different email address without quoting the body or changing any of the headers; this is useful if you mistakenly receive a piece of misdirected mail and want to pass it on to the proper recipient. Finally, the **Bounce** command (in the **Message** menu) sends a simulated error message back to the sender, making it appear that your email address no longer works (useful if you're trying to shake off a secret admirer or get off a mailing list).

56

To compose a new message of your own, without replying to or forwarding an existing message that someone sent you, follow these instructions.

▶ **TIP**

Mail comes with a default set of control buttons in its toolbar, but like the Finder, it allows you to choose a different set of controls that you might find more to your liking. Choose **View**, **Customize Toolbar** to see a sheet containing all possible toolbar icons, some of which are grouped into conceptual clusters; drag an icon to the toolbar to add it as a permanent control. Drag an icon off the toolbar to remove it. Click **Done** to save your toolbar configuration.

1 Compose a New Message

Click the **New** button in the toolbar of the main Mail window to begin a new email message.

2 Specify the Recipient(s)

In the **To** field of the new email message, enter the name or email address of the person to whom you want to send the message. If the recipient is someone you've emailed before, or if the person is in your Address Book, the Mail application will automatically complete the name or address as you type it; press **Tab** or **Return** to accept the first name that matches, or use the arrow keys or the mouse to scroll through the drop-down menu to select from all the names that match.

▶ **TIP**

Mail automatically matches a name no matter which part of it you type: the first name, the last name, or the email address. When you finish specifying a recipient's name and address, the address changes to a colored oval showing the person's full name, which you can then drag from one place to another—from the **To** field to the **Cc** field, for instance, or to any other application that accepts text. When dragged into another application, the recipient's name and address is copied in the form **John Doe <johndoe12341@mac.com>**.

Specify more than one recipient by typing a new name as soon as the first one is accepted, or by separating the addresses with commas.

▶ **TIPS**

If you don't want Mail to hide the email addresses in recipients that you specify, select **Show Name and Address** (rather than **Use Smart Addresses**) in the **Addresses** sub-menu of the **View** menu.

56

Select the **Mark addresses not in this domain** option in the **Composing** pane of the **Mail Preferences** window, and specify your company's Internet domain, to have Mail use a red colored oval instead of a blue one on recipients who are not within that domain. This is intended to help you distinguish between intra-office correspondence and mail that travels outside the company.

The **To** field can accept more than one address, if you want to send the message to multiple people. However, it can often be useful to use the **Cc** (Carbon Copy) field to specify other recipients, instead of listing them all in the **To** field. Typically, **Cc** recipients are included for informational purposes only; if it's a business correspondence, only the recipients in the **To** line are expected to respond. This, however, is all just netiquette, and nothing really compels people to behave according to these rules.

Everybody who receives the message can see all the other recipients in the **To** and **Cc** fields. If you want to send a private copy of the message to another recipient, so that the primary recipients don't know you've sent this person a copy, you can use the **Bcc** (Blind Carbon Copy) field. This field is normally not shown in a **Compose** window; choose **View, Bcc Address Field** to create a **Bcc** field. If you use the **Bcc:** header or other special headers a lot, choose **Customize** from the **Action** menu (labeled with a gear icon) above the message input area to add those header fields permanently to all your future message composition windows.

3 Specify a Subject

Type a descriptive subject for the message. Keep the subject brief and informative; when coming up with a subject, imagine what it would be like to receive a message with the subject you specify. Nobody likes receiving messages with empty or cryptic subject lines—or subject lines that are as long as the message itself!

▶ NOTE

If you're replying to a message instead of composing a new one, the text in the **Subject** field begins with **Re:** to indicate that this reply is "regarding" the original message. A long string of email exchanges can generally take place with a single subject line, with every message after the very first one starting with the **Re:** prefix. Most email applications, including Mail, don't add another **Re:** prefix if there's one there already.

The Mail application can view messages in *threads*, or groupings of related messages. Mail can also group relevant messages into threads even if the subject line is different, based on other identifiers in the headers. To view your messages in threads, choose **Organize by Thread** from the **View** menu.

When viewing messages in threads, click a collapsed thread to see a list of all the messages in the thread. Click one of the listed messages in the message pane to view that message (and expand the thread).

▶ KEY TERM

Thread—A single string of correspondence, between any number of people, in which all the messages share the same subject line (barring the **Re:** prefix in all subsequent messages to the first one).

4 Select the Account to Send From

If you have configured more than one email account, there will be an **Account** drop-down menu above the message input area. Use this menu to select which identity you want to send the message as. Always check this menu to make sure that you're using the right address!

▶ TIP

The Mail application will automatically use the account associated with the mailbox you're currently viewing. To make sure that you always send using the correct identity, it can be a good idea to be in the habit of selecting the **In** mailbox for the account you want to use before composing a new message. Doing so ensures that you use the right account even if you don't check what's shown in the **Account** menu.

56

5 Type Your Message

Compose your message. You can use whatever style you like—you can make your message massively long, or just a few words; you can style your text with bold and italics and special fonts, or you can make it plain text; you can even add pictures by dragging image files into the message window from the Finder.

Select **Plain Text** from the **Format** menu in the **Composing** pane of the **Mail Preferences** window if you want to compose your messages using plain, unstyled text. A Plain Text message cannot be formatted with text styles, but if you have selected the **Use fixed-width font for plain text messages** check box in the **Fonts & Colors** tab, the text you type will be laid out using a monospaced font. Using a fixed-width font can be helpful if you want to create a message that contains tabular information, such as a column of numbers.

Any picture or other file that you drag into the message window becomes an attachment; the recipient can view the attachment along with the message, or (if he is using a sufficiently capable email application) he can view the picture inline, right where you placed it in the message. As you compose your message, use the **Image Size** menu at the bottom of the window to adjust how large your included pictures will appear to the recipient, and use the **Message Size** readout to gauge the overall message's size in bytes, which corresponds to how long it will take the recipient to download it. For example, if you include several photos that make the message add up to more than one megabyte (1024KB, or kilobytes), try setting the **Image Size** selection to **Small**, to reduce the message's overall size.

56

▶ NOTE

Be aware that many email servers place a limit on the size of messages that they will accept; this limit is often 2 or 4 megabytes. If your message's total size—including the total size of all attachments, which you should multiply by 1.3 to account for encoding overhead—exceeds about 2 megabytes, consider sending several messages with smaller attachments instead of one big message, to make sure it will get through. Otherwise the mail server may return the message to you as an error.

6 Add a Signature

The Mail application allows you to define *signatures*, or predetermined bits of text that it can insert at the end of a message with a quick command. You can define as many signatures as you like; when you compose a new message, you can select the signature you want or allow Mail to automatically insert a certain signature into every message (useful if, for instance, you have to include your business contact information at the end of every message you send). Mail can even choose a signature for you at random from the ones you've defined.

▶ **TIP**

If you use Mail from more than one Mac, you can synchronize your signatures using .Mac, ensuring that your defined signatures are always available no matter which computer you use. See **100** **Synchronize Your Information Using .Mac** for more.

Define your signatures in the **Signatures** pane of the **Mail Preferences** window. First select **Signatures** in the first column to create a global signature, or select one of your account names to create a signature that applies only to that account. Next click the + button to create a new signature; type a description (which is what will appear in the **Signature** menu in the Compose window) into the middle column and the signature text into the right column. Repeat to create as many different signatures as you need. The signatures are saved when you close the **Preferences** window or switch to another pane.

Back in the message composition window, select **Customize** from the **Action** menu above the message input area; select the check box next to the Signature menu, and then click **OK**. Now, for this message and any messages you compose in the future, you can select a signature from the **Signature** menu above the message input area.

7 **Send the Message**

Double-check your message and proofread it if you want. When you're satisfied with how it looks, click the **Send** button in the toolbar at the top of the Compose window to deliver it to the mail server, and from there to the recipient.

While you are composing your message, it is saved in the **Drafts** mailbox. This arrangement allows you to quit the Mail application and come back to it right where you left off. Also, if you are using a server-based email account and have configured your account to keep the **Drafts** mailbox on the server, you can come back to your half-composed messages and finish them using a different computer.

When you click **Send**, Mail copies the message to your **Out** mailbox while it tries to deliver it. If the delivery attempt is successful, the message moves to your **Sent** mailbox. If delivery fails, however, the message remains in your **Out** mailbox while Mail keeps trying to send it. Mail will prompt you for a

56

different mail server to try. You can select any properly configured SMTP server from the list Mail gives you, or you can elect to try again later (or edit the message if you made an error in addressing).

▶ **TIP**

If you want to cancel sending a message, select **Try Again Later** from the sheet that Mail presents, and then go to the **Out** mailbox and delete the pending message.

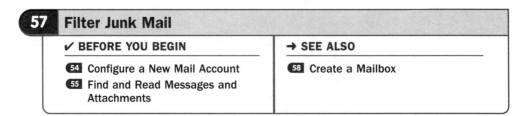

57 **Filter Junk Mail**

✔ BEFORE YOU BEGIN	→ SEE ALSO
54 Configure a New Mail Account	**58** Create a Mailbox
55 Find and Read Messages and Attachments	

If there is a downside to email, it would have to be what is commonly known as *spam*, or junk mail. Anybody who has ever used email has been plagued with junk messages—unsolicited business propositions, pornographic advertisements, get-rich-quick schemes, and even viruses and Trojan Horses (malicious programs that sneak onto your computer via innocuous means, such as in an email attachment). Some people get so much junk mail that their real, legitimate email is lost in the shuffle. What's really infuriating is that there's usually no good way to defend against this kind of onslaught. Sure, you could set up a rule to delete messages from a certain sender or with a certain subject, but junk mail always comes from different sender addresses and has constantly changing subject lines and content. What's an email user to do?

Fortunately, Apple's **Mail** application helps you fight back. Mail contains a heuristics-based junk-mail filtering system that learns with time what kinds of messages you consider to be "junk" and which ones you don't.

When you turn on junk mail filtering, Mail can operate in either of two modes: It can delete messages it determines to be junk, moving them into a special **Junk** folder, or it can simply mark junk messages with a certain color, allowing you to review them later. This latter mode, **Training** mode, is what you can use while Mail is "learning" how to spot junk messages. When the Mail program has gotten good enough at recognizing junk mail, you can put it into **Automatic** mode, keeping junk mail out of your face for good.

1 **Enable Junk Mail Filtering**

Open the **Mail Preferences** dialog box and click the **Junk Mail** icon in the toolbar at the top. If it is not already checked, select the **Enable Junk Mail filtering** check box.

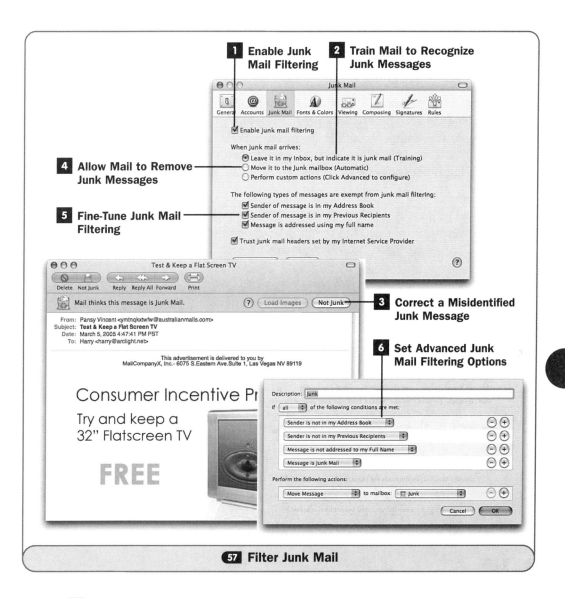

1 Enable Junk Mail Filtering

2 Train Mail to Recognize Junk Messages

4 Allow Mail to Remove Junk Messages

5 Fine-Tune Junk Mail Filtering

3 Correct a Misidentified Junk Message

6 Set Advanced Junk Mail Filtering Options

57

57 Filter Junk Mail

2 Train Mail to Recognize Junk Messages

Mail begins in **Training** mode, in which it leaves junk messages in your **In** mailbox, but doesn't do anything but mark the messages with a certain color (light brown) and a special symbol in the **Flags** column. This way, you can check which messages it has identified as junk mail, and make sure that the program has made the right decision before deleting those messages yourself.

3 Correct a Misidentified Junk Message

While Mail is in **Training** mode, you need to help it correctly identify junk mail and ignore messages that it mistakenly flags as junk.

For a message that Mail incorrectly identifies as Junk Mail but that you actually want to receive, select or open the message and then click the **Not Junk** button, which appears both in the brown header area of the message and in Mail's toolbar. This action adds an entry into Mail's heuristics database, so that future messages that share the characteristics of this message will have a higher likelihood of being allowed through.

For an unwanted message that didn't get marked as junk mail, select or open the message, and then click the **Junk** button in the toolbar to tell Mail that this kind of message is something it should catch.

4 Allow Mail to Remove Junk Messages

The Mail application should spend at least a couple of weeks in **Training** mode, learning to identify junk mail properly. Judge for yourself when you're ready to let Mail start automatically deleting junk messages on its own instead of just turning them brown for your review.

57

▶ **TIP**

After a couple of weeks in **Training** mode, Mail gives you an informative message that reminds you that it might be time to switch to **Automatic** mode.

When you deem Mail to be ready to go into **Automatic** mode, open the **Mail Preferences** window and click the **Junk Mail** icon; select the **Move it to the Junk mailbox (Automatic)** radio button. From that point on, all messages that Mail determines to be junk are automatically moved into the **Junk** mailbox for that account.

▶ **TIP**

You might still see unwanted messages in your Inbox, even when Mail is in Automatic mode; these are messages that Mail is still not identifying as junk messages. You can continue to train Mail to trap these messages by selecting them and using the **Junk** button, which now moves the messages to the **Junk** folder as well as adding their contents to Mail's heuristics database.

Mail is designed to err on the side of caution—it will sooner leave a junk message in your Inbox than send a legitimate message to the **Junk** mailbox. Just the same, it's a good idea to open up your **Junk** mailbox occasionally and look for "false positives," messages that Mail has incorrectly identified as junk mail. Use the **Not Junk** button to reprimand Mail for these transgressions and, with time, they won't happen any more.

5 Fine-Tune Junk Mail Filtering

Mail's junk filtering depends on several exception conditions, which you can control using the check boxes in the **Junk Mail** tab of the **Mail Preferences** window. Mail's default behavior is to ignore messages that come from addresses in your **Address Book** or **Previous Recipients** list, or if the address contains your full name (something that spammers seldom do, because usually all they have are lists of email addresses). Deselect these check boxes if you want Mail to be stricter with these kinds of messages.

6 Set Advanced Junk Mail Filtering Options

Select the **Perform custom actions (Click Advanced... to configure)** radio button and then click the **Advanced** button to gain access to even finer detail regarding how Mail deals with junk mail. In the sheet that appears, you can define an arbitrary number of criteria for what causes a message to be flagged as Junk. For instance, **Message is junk mail** means that Mail's heuristics database determines that the message is likely junk. **Sender is not in my Address Book** ensures that if the message is sent to you by someone you know (who is listed in your **Address Book**, as discussed in **95 Add a Person to Your Address Book**), Mail's filters will never trap the message.

Use the – button next to any of these criteria to remove them from Mail's junk filtering scheme, or click + in any line to add a new criterion (which you can then specify using the extensively populated drop-down list). Finally, you can choose between whether **all** or **any** of the criteria have to be met for messages to be marked as Junk, using the drop-down menu at the top of the sheet; if you change the sense to **any**, Mail will mark far more messages as Junk than otherwise.

57

58 Create a Mailbox

✔ BEFORE YOU BEGIN

54 Configure a New Mail Account
55 Find and Read Messages and Attachments

→ SEE ALSO

59 Create a Smart Mailbox for Certain Types of Messages
60 Import Mailboxes from Another Email Application

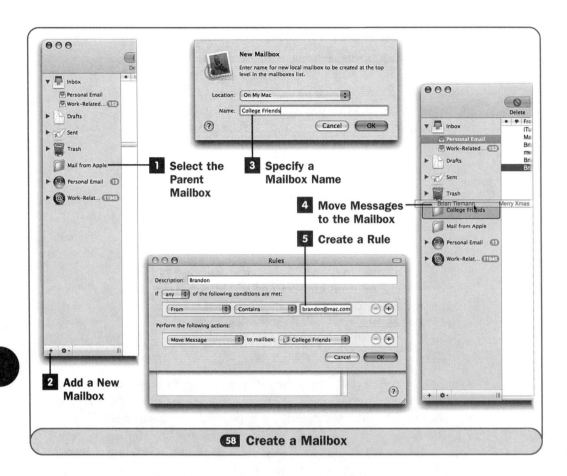

58 Create a Mailbox

Central to a modern email application is the ability to define custom mailboxes, which you can think of as "folders," to hold categorized messages. The **Mail** application already uses special mailboxes for incoming mail, sent messages, junk mail, and deleted messages, but you can also define your own mailboxes to hold messages related to a certain project, for instance, or for correspondence with a certain person over the years. Mail even lets you define rules that automatically direct new messages into special mailboxes, depending on certain criteria that you can define.

New in Mac OS X Tiger is another kind of mailbox, the Smart Mailbox; this is a specialized grouping construct that shows any messages that match certain criteria that you define. See **59** **Create a Smart Mailbox for Certain Types of Messages** for more information.

1 Select the Parent Mailbox

In the **Mailboxes** pane at the left side of the Mail window, select the mailbox inside which you want to create the new mailbox. For instance, to create a mailbox at the top level in an account, select the icon for that account in the mailbox listing; to create a mailbox inside an existing mailbox in that account, expand the account (using the triangle) and select the mailbox you want to use.

You can also create mailboxes on your local computer, independent of any account; select the **On My Mac** icon, or any mailbox underneath it, to create a local mailbox. If you don't see the **On My Mac** icon (which only appears if you have server-based mail accounts, such as .Mac or IMAP, instead of POP), don't select any mailbox icon.

▶ **NOTE**

Different kinds of email accounts support different kinds of mailboxes. For instance, .Mac or Exchange email accounts allow you to create *nested* mailboxes, or mailboxes within mailboxes. IMAP accounts permit you to create only a single layer of mailboxes, just underneath the top level. POP accounts don't let you create mailboxes on the server at all; if you're using a POP account, you have to create all new mailboxes under the **On My Mac** icon, or (if you only have POP accounts) as folders in the **Mailboxes** list.

58

2 Add a New Mailbox

Click the + icon at the bottom of the **Mailboxes** pane. Carefully read the dialog box that pops up; it tells you where exactly the new mailbox will be created. If it doesn't report the correct location, click **Cancel** and select the correct parent mailbox.

3 Specify a Mailbox Name

Type a short name for the new mailbox.

Mailbox names can't contain slashes (/). If you put a slash in the name of the new mailbox, Mail will actually create a subfolder within the parent mailbox, and put the new mailbox inside the subfolder; the slash separates the name of the subfolder from the name of the mailbox. This can be quite useful, depending on what you want to do. For instance, if you specify **Vacations/2003** as the name of the new mailbox, Mail will create a subfolder called **Vacations**, and a mailbox called **2003** inside it. You can then create further mailboxes inside the **Vacations** folder—even if you're using an IMAP account.

▶ **NOTE**

The only downside to using the slash to create subfolders is that you can't place messages directly into the **Vacations** subfolder (which shows up with a white folder icon instead of a blue one); you can only put messages into the blue **2003** mailbox folder inside the **Vacations** folder.

4 Move Messages to the Mailbox

Click and drag any message or group of selected messages to the mailbox you want to move them to. You can automatically expand a hierarchical structure of mailboxes by dragging the messages onto the top mailbox and holding them there without releasing the button; as with spring-loaded folders in the Finder, the mailboxes expand so that you can drill down to the mailbox you want.

5 Create a Rule

Open the **Mail Preferences** window and click the **Rules** icon at the top. Click **Add Rule** to create a new rule. Give the rule a descriptive name so that you can find it later.

Use the + and – buttons to add conditions for new messages to match. For instance, if you want Mail to identify all messages from a certain mailing list, all such messages might come from a particular address, or they might all have a certain string in the **Subject** line (such as [**Motor-List**]). The Mail application provides many different kinds of criteria you can define, from substrings of various header fields to complex conditions, such as whether the sender is in your Address Book. You can specify as many of these conditions as you want, and you can require that new messages match **all** of these conditions or **any** single one of them.

In the **Perform the following actions** area of the **Rules** dialog box, select **Move Message** from the first drop-down list and then select the target mailbox from the **to mailbox** drop-down list. Click **OK**.

From this point on, all messages that match the criteria you specified in your rule are moved into the specified mailbox so that you can peruse them at your leisure.

58

59   Create a Smart Mailbox for Certain Types of Messages

✔ BEFORE YOU BEGIN	→ SEE ALSO
54 Configure a New Mail Account	**58** Create a Mailbox
56 Send a Message	**14** Create a Smart Folder That Contains Certain Types of Items

A new feature in the **Mail** application included in Mac OS X Tiger is called **Smart Mailboxes**. If you're already familiar with **Smart Folders** in the Finder, or with **Smart Playlists** in iTunes, you already know the idea: a Smart Mailbox is essentially a canned database query, presenting an up-to-date grouping of messages in your existing mailboxes filtered according to certain criteria that you define in advance. You don't place messages into a Smart Mailbox yourself, nor do you set a rule to do so automatically. A Smart Mailbox gives you a dynamic list of messages that match your criteria, no matter where they are within your mailbox hierarchy.

The uses of Smart Mailboxes are legion, limited only by your needs. Mail comes preloaded with a variety of useful and demonstrative Smart Mailboxes, such as **Viewed Today** (which shows you all messages you've read in the current day), **90's Mail** (all messages you received during the 1990s), and **Images** (all messages with picture attachments). You can set up Smart Mailboxes to catch all messages to or from a particular person, to show all messages with high priority that are sent to your work account, or to collect just the messages from people in your Address Book. Let your imagination run wild—Mail armed with Smart Mailboxes gives you a whole new way to think about organizing your digital correspondence.

59

1 Add a New Smart Mailbox

Click the "gear" button at the bottom of the Mailboxes pane. From the menu that appears, choose **New Smart Mailbox**. A sheet appears that allows you to specify the details of the new Smart Mailbox.

2 Specify a Smart Mailbox Name

Choose a name for the new Smart Mailbox that's descriptive of its function. For example, if you want to create a Smart Mailbox that collects all messages you sent to your business partner that contain image attachments, call it **Pictures To Bob**.

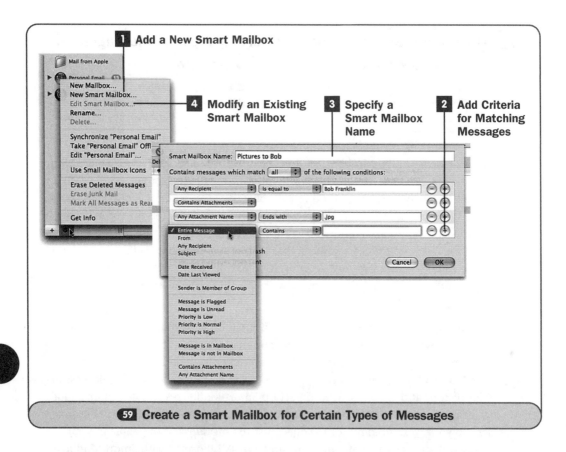

59 Create a Smart Mailbox for Certain Types of Messages

3 Add Criteria for Matching Messages

Use the + button to add a new criterion. The drop-down menus and text entry fields in each criterion line, which vary in format depending on the criterion you select, allow you to define a new filter for matching messages. For example, select **Any Attachment Name** from the first menu, then **Ends with** from the second menu, and enter **.jpg** in the third to create a criterion that all matching messages should contain JPEG image attachments. After you've defined at least two criteria, use the drop-down menu to choose whether messages must match **any** or **all** of the criteria you have defined.

Use the – button on any existing criterion to delete that criterion. Use **Include messages from Trash** to allow the Smart Mailbox to show messages that are in the **Trash** mailbox; if not selected, messages in the Trash (waiting to be automatically deleted) are not shown in the Smart Mailbox.

When you're done defining your Smart Mailbox, click **OK**. The Smart Mailbox is created and now appears in the list of mailboxes, with a "gear" icon indicating that it's a Smart Mailbox. From now on, simply click the Smart Mailbox icon to see a list of all the messages that match its criteria.

▶ **NOTE**

If you delete a message from the listing while viewing a Smart Mailbox, the message is deleted from its original folder.

4 Modify an Existing Smart Mailbox

You can modify an existing Smart Mailbox's criteria at any time, if the listing it presents isn't quite what you need. First, select the mailbox by clicking its folder icon. Then, from the "gear" button at the bottom of the Mailboxes pane, choose **Edit Smart Mailbox**. The same sheet you used to create the Smart Mailbox appears again, allowing you to make changes to its name or criteria. Alternatively, double-click the Smart Mailbox's icon to open the editing sheet, or click its name to rename the Smart Mailbox directly.

60 Import Mailboxes from Another Email Application

✔ BEFORE YOU BEGIN

54 Configure a New Mail Account

59

Mail isn't the only email application out there for Mac OS X. True, it's one of the best, and it's certainly the one that's best integrated into the operating system and the one that's most enthusiastically under development. More and more Mac users—even the old-time experts—are discovering Mail and falling in love with its straightforward approach to configuration and its intuitive integration of advanced features. However, nearly every new Mac user has used some email program before in her life, and that means there's a lot of mail built up inside whatever email application the person previously used.

The Mail application provides the capability to import mailboxes from any of a number of different popular email applications: Microsoft Entourage or Outlook Express, Eudora, Netscape, Claris Emailer, or even bare Unix-style "mbox" files. All you have to do is tell Mail where to find these mailbox files, and it will reformat them into its own **Mailboxes** list so that you can continue using all your archived mail.

▶ **NOTE**

Sadly, Mail does not support importing mailboxes from America Online accounts.

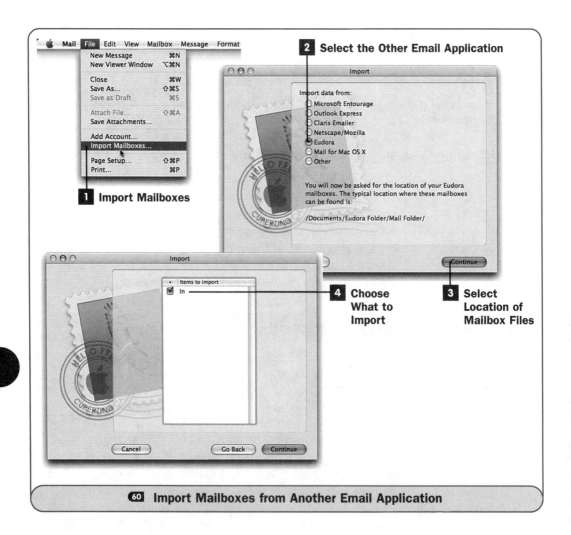

60

60   Import Mailboxes from Another Email Application

1 Import Mailboxes

Select **File, Import Mailboxes** from the main **Mail** menu. The first page of the **Import** dialog box sequence appears.

2 Select the Other Mail Application

Select the email application you used before switching to **Mail**. This is the email application that contains the mailboxes you want to salvage. After you select the appropriate radio button, explanatory text appears telling you what the next step in importing the mailboxes will be. For some email applications, Mail will launch the other application to drive the mailbox conversion itself; for others, you are simply told where the mailbox files for that application are probably located. Open a Finder window and navigate to that location to check whether the mailbox files are there, and then click the **Continue** button in the lower right of the **Import** dialog box to begin the import process.

▶ **NOTE**

Some email applications, such as Netscape, exist on multiple platforms. If you are coming from Windows and want to import your Windows Netscape mailboxes into Mail, you might find that your mailboxes are corrupted after they are imported. This can be the result of the line-break characters in text files being different in Windows and Mac OS X. To solve this problem, a text formatting utility such as Linebreak Converter X by Josh Aas might be useful (go to **http://maccrafters.com/lbc/**). Use this program to convert the mailbox files from Windows to Unix format before you import them into Mail.

3 Select the Location of the Mailbox Files

In the navigation sheet that appears, go to the location of the mailbox files you want to import; select the folder that contains the mailbox files and click **Choose**. If Mail launched the other email application instead of giving you the navigation sheet, follow the instructions on-screen for importing the mailboxes from the given application.

4 Choose What to Import

Mail's importer script can import items such as contacts, calendar items, and other pieces of information as well as simply mailboxes (if the other mail application supports these features). However, in most cases, all you will be able to import are mailboxes, which appear in the **Items to Import** list in the next screen. Select the check boxes on the mailboxes you wish to import, and then click **Continue**.

Mail then imports the mailboxes, and they appear under the **On My Mac** icon in the **Mailboxes** pane. You can now reorganize the mailboxes according to your taste, moving your old messages into your new mailbox hierarchy, or leaving them where they are.

60

8

Surfing the Web

IN THIS CHAPTER:

It's hard to deny that the principal function of a computer in this day and age is to run a web browser. Surfing the World Wide Web—be it for shopping, banking, business, research, or plain old personal fun—is what has driven the Internet's explosive growth in recent years. Surfing the Web is easy, it's useful, and it's indelibly entered our common consciousness. The Web has changed a lot since its inception, and we can't predict what it will eventually become; however, we're all certainly enjoying the ride.

▶ **NOTE**

The terms "Web" and "Internet" are often used synonymously; however, correctly, the *World Wide Web* is a term specifically meant for the network of hyperlinked graphical and textual pages "surfed" using browsers such as Safari or Internet Explorer. The *Internet* is a much broader term, composed of not just the Web, but also email, instant messaging, and every other online activity.

There are some tricks to Web surfing, though. Mac OS X includes Apple's own browser, *Safari.* Although Safari is a very intuitive and simple application to run, for a user whose only experience has been with Microsoft Internet Explorer on Windows, there are some subtle details about Safari that you might find surprising, as well as some features that might be new to you. The tasks in this chapter focus on using Safari to navigate the Web.

▶ **KEY TERM**

Safari—Apple's web browser. Released in January 2003, Safari has largely supplanted Microsoft Internet Explorer (which is no longer being actively developed) as the default means for Mac users to surf the World Wide Web.

61	Keep Track of Websites with Bookmarks	
✔ **BEFORE YOU BEGIN**	→ **SEE ALSO**	
30 Configure Networking Manually	100 Synchronize Your Information Using .Mac	
	63 Access Your Bookmarks Using .Mac	

Saving a reference to a favorite website so that you can quickly access it again later is known as *creating a bookmark* for that site, or *bookmarking the site.* (Internet Explorer uses the term *Favorites* instead of *bookmarks,* but they're effectively the same thing.) Safari allows better bookmark organization than most other browsers, giving you a full-screen bookmark manager page (the **Bookmark Library**) in which you can organize bookmarks into folders and edit them visually. You can also use bookmarks that are stored in the *Bookmarks bar,* shown just below the toolbar; folders of bookmarks in the Bookmarks bar (below the main toolbar) are indicated with a triangle, and expand into drop-down menus from which you can select websites with a single click.

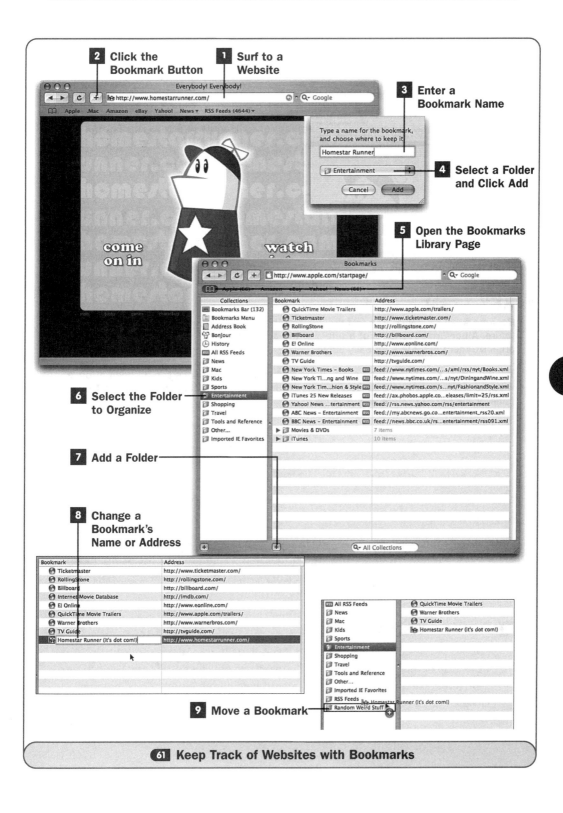

2 Click the Bookmark Button

1 Surf to a Website

3 Enter a Bookmark Name

4 Select a Folder and Click Add

5 Open the Bookmarks Library Page

6 Select the Folder to Organize

7 Add a Folder

8 Change a Bookmark's Name or Address

9 Move a Bookmark

61 Keep Track of Websites with Bookmarks

If you enable *tabbed browsing*, a feature that allows you to open several web pages at once within a single Safari window (each one behind its own labeled tab under the Bookmarks bar), bookmark folders have an additional perk: When you open a bookmark folder as a menu, from the Bookmarks bar or the **Bookmarks** menu, an additional menu option appears—Open in Tabs. If you select this option, every bookmark in the folder opens at the same time, each in its own tab. This feature can become unwieldy with large numbers of pages opening at once, so for best results, make sure your folders are organized as small collections of 10 bookmarks or less.

▶ **TIP**

With tabbed browsing enabled, a new column called **Auto-Click** appears in the **Bookmark Library** page. If you select the check box in this column for a folder, that folder's behavior changes so that if you click its title in the Bookmarks bar, the menu does not open, but rather the bookmarks inside it all open in tabs automatically in unison. An Auto-Click–enabled folder in the Bookmarks bar has a square next to its name instead of a triangle.

▶ **KEY TERM**

Bookmark—A reference to a favorite website that you would like to return to in the future. A bookmark consists of a title and the address of the site, and Safari lets you organize them in folders for easy access.

Tabbed browsing—A browsing method in which several web pages can be open at once within a single Safari window, each one in its own labeled tab. Enable this in the **Tabs** pane of the **Safari Preferences** window.

Safari also provides another advantage over other browsers in bookmark management: It lets you specify a descriptive name for each bookmark at the time you create it. Most browsers automatically use the web page's title as the name of the bookmark, but this isn't always what you want. Although other programs allow you to edit bookmark names after you create them, that can be tedious. Safari lets you enter an appropriate name right when you create the bookmark.

Safari's bookmark management function, unlike that of many other browsers, is both a full-featured editing utility and a hierarchical catalog for accessing bookmarks directly. From the **Bookmarks Library** page, you can go to any bookmark's address by double-clicking the bookmark in the list.

1 Surf to a Website

Launch Safari and enter a URL (website address) in the Address bar (the text box) at the top of the screen; then press **Return** to go directly to that site. You can also search for a website that suits your interest by entering search terms into the *Google* search box in the upper-right corner of the screen and pressing **Return**.

61

▶ KEY TERM

Google—The most popular "search engine" on the Web. Located at **http://www. google.com**, Google is faster and more accurate than most other search engines available. Safari allows you to perform a Google search without having to go to Google's site first.

2 Click the Bookmark Button

Click the + button to the left of the Address bar. This action brings up a sheet that prompts you for the bookmark name and location.

3 Enter a Bookmark Name

The default name for the bookmark is the web page's title; that name is selected, though, so if you don't like it, simply type a name that's more to your liking.

4 Select a Folder and Click Add

Click the drop-down menu to show all your bookmark folders. Select the folder where you want to save your new bookmark.

61

▶ TIP

Safari, in its default configuration, comes with a few folders with some bookmarks already defined for you: **News**, **Mac**, **Kids**, **Sports**, and so on. As you add more folders for your bookmarks, as explained later in this task, those folders will appear in a hierarchical list (all folders are shown, even folders inside other folders) when you add a new bookmark.

Click the **Add** button to add the new bookmark to your list. You can now access the bookmark by clicking the **Bookmarks** icon at the left end of the Bookmarks bar (the icon looks like an open book) to open the **Bookmarks Library** page, and then opening the correct folder. When you find it, double-click the newly added bookmark to go to the site it marks.

▶ TIP

To delete a bookmark from the **Bookmarks Library**, select the bookmark and press **Delete**. You can undo a deletion by selecting **Undo** from the **Edit** menu.

5 Open the Bookmarks Library Page

Any bookmark-organizing efforts you might want to make begin on the **Bookmarks Library** page. Open the **Bookmarks Library** page by clicking the book icon at the far left end of the Bookmarks bar.

6 Select the Folder to Organize

Click any folder in the **Collections** list on the left side of the **Bookmarks Library** page. The contents of that folder appear in the pane on the right.

▶ TIP

Bookmark folders can contain other folders. In the right pane of the **Bookmarks Library** page, you can open and browse folders the same as you can in List view in the Finder. Note the triangles that indicate whether the folder is expanded or collapsed.

7 Add a Folder

Click the + icon at the bottom of the right pane to create a new folder inside the currently selected folder. Click the + icon at the bottom of the **Collections** pane to create a new top-level folder to appear in that list. The default folder name appears as **untitled folder**; it is selected as soon as the folder is created, so that you can immediately type a new name for the folder.

8 Change a Bookmark's Name or Address

Click to select a bookmark in the right pane of the **Bookmarks Library** page, pause briefly, and then click the name or address field again to select that field's contents for editing. Alternatively, right-click or **Control**+click the bookmark and choose **Edit Name** or **Edit Address** from the contextual menu. Type the new name or the new URL and press **Return**.

9 Move a Bookmark

To move a bookmark, drag it from one folder to another or to another position within the same folder. To navigate down into a subfolder, hover the mouse (while still dragging the bookmark) over the folder you want to expand; after a moment, it will open automatically.

You can move (or copy, by holding down ⌘ as you drag) bookmarks into the special **Bookmarks Menu** collection by dragging them from where they're listed in the right pane into the collection at left. Bookmarks that you add to the **Bookmarks Menu** collection appear as items under the **Bookmarks** menu; this is a quick way to access important bookmarks that aren't quite frequently enough used for you to put them in your Bookmarks bar.

61

▶ **TIP**

The Bookmarks bar is special. You can drag bookmarks into it and off it from the **Bookmarks Library** page, or you can drag an address into it straight from the Address bar. The Bookmarks bar is represented as its own collection/folder in the **Bookmarks Library** page; you can move bookmarks into it as you would into any other folder. Click and drag to change how bookmarks are positioned in the Bookmarks bar; you can also delete a bookmark from the bar by dragging it off the bar and dropping it away from the browser window.

---

62   Browse and Organize RSS Feeds

✔ BEFORE YOU BEGIN	→ SEE ALSO
61 Keep Track of Websites with Bookmarks	**63** Access Your Bookmarks Using .Mac **100** Synchronize Your Information Using .Mac

---

New in Mac OS X Tiger is a feature called **Safari RSS**; built in to Safari is the ability to subscribe to *RSS feeds*, which are simplified summaries of articles on web pages such as news sites and web logs (*blogs*). When viewing an RSS feed, instead of seeing a complete website with all its embedded graphics and ads, all you see are the headlines and the first few dozen words of each article, in a long and unadorned list. A link at the end of each article excerpt leads to the full article in its original form that you can view normally in the browser, if it interests you enough for you to click the link. RSS feeds help you more efficiently keep track of frequently updated news pages, personal blogs, and specialized websites such as **iTunes 25 New Releases**, a selection of new songs at the iTunes Music Store that is updated every week. Safari RSS comes preloaded with a large number of useful RSS feeds for you to use.

Safari RSS allows you to sort articles on an RSS-enabled page by date, title, or the name of the items' sources; you can also use the handy links in the sidebar to see only the items posted within well-defined time frames such as **Today** and **This Month**. A slider control allows you to select the length of the article summaries that appear on the page, from large excerpts all the way down to bare headlines. A search bar even allows you to perform topic-based instant searches in the current page, or you can load several RSS feeds at once and perform the same filtering search on all the articles on all the RSS pages you're viewing at once, creating a "personal clipping service" on a certain subject. Perhaps most importantly of all, Safari RSS keeps track of which items on a given RSS-enabled page you've already seen, and which ones are new; the number of new items shows up next to the RSS feed's name in the bookmarks, so you know when there are new items to read on your favorite frequently updated sites. Using these features, you can get the up-to-date gist of all the items appearing on your favorite news sites, with a fraction of the time and effort needed to go to the sites and read them in place.

61

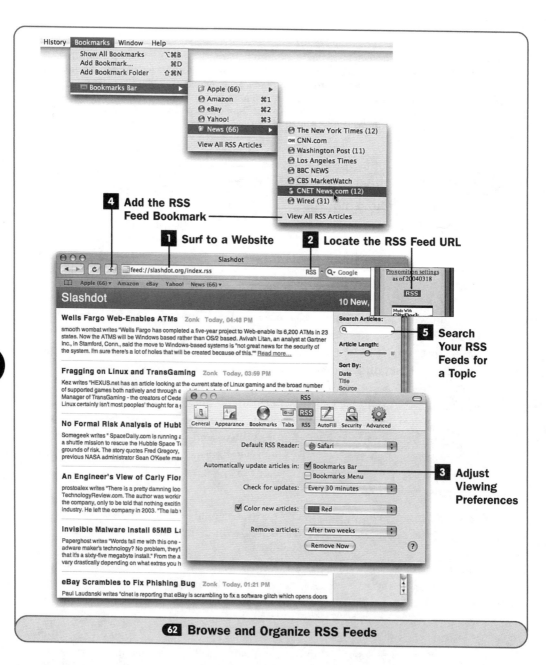

62 Browse and Organize RSS Feeds

► **NOTE**

The number of unread articles in all your RSS feeds organized inside the **RSS Feeds** bookmark folder in your Bookmarks bar appears in parentheses after **RSS Feeds** in the bar.

Several preferences that you can set in Safari allow you to customize your RSS viewing experience to suit your needs. You can adjust how frequently Safari checks for new articles on your RSS feeds, and which feeds to check; you can have new articles tinted with a color of your choice; and you can indicate that Safari should not display old RSS articles, and choose how far back in time the cutoff should be.

▶ KEY TERMS

Really Simple Syndication (RSS) feed—A simplified formatting of a news site or web log, in which all the articles on the site appear as headlines followed by the first few dozen words of each article.

Blog—A shortening of "web log"; a serial news site or journal, usually maintained by one or more individuals and often dedicated to a certain special interest, in which the author posts new entries on an ongoing basis.

1 Surf to a Website

Launch Safari and enter the URL (website address) of a desired website in the Address bar (the text box) at the top of the screen; then press **Return** to go directly to that site. You may also reach the desired site from your own bookmarks, or by following links on other sites on the Web.

2 Locate the RSS Feed URL

Many news sites and blogs feature an RSS feed, although not all do. Such sites that do have RSS feeds will display a link or button somewhere on the page, indicating **RSS, RDF, XML, Syndicate**, or some similar label—all of them are forms of RSS feeds that Safari can display.

Click the link or label graphic to load the RSS feed in Safari.

▶ TIP

An alternative way to have your Mac track a favorite RSS feed is using the **RSS Visualizer** screen saver. This feature rushes headlines and article summaries across your screen in a rotating 3D environment that's so cool that you might find your co-workers gathered around your computer staring at it when you get back from lunch.

3 Adjust Viewing Preferences

An RSS feed displayed in Safari always has a standardized format: a blue bar at the top indicating the feed's title, how many items are in the feed, and how many of those are new. In the main pane at left is the article listing; at right is a navigation column with several links and controls that let you customize the feed's behavior. Use the **Article Length** slider to select how long each article summary should be; move it all the way to the right to see long excerpts of articles, or move it all the way to the left to see the headlines only.

Several more behaviors of Safari RSS can be controlled from the **Safari Preferences**. Choose **Preferences** from the **Safari** menu; click the **RSS** icon to open the **RSS** pane. Here you can select an alternate RSS reader (if you have a better RSS application than Safari). You can also choose the behavior of Safari in looking for new articles: Select the check boxes for **Bookmarks Bar** and for **Bookmarks Menu** according to your preferences. Selecting one of these check boxes for a specific collection in your bookmarks means that Safari will automatically check for and display the count of new articles for RSS feeds that are inside that collection. For example, only if you organize an RSS feed into your **Bookmarks Menu** collection will Safari update its count of new articles for that feed, if you've selected the **Bookmarks Menu** check box.

► **TIP**

Use the **Check for updates** drop-down list to choose how frequently Safari should look for new articles. Be aware that each time Safari checks these sites can involve significant sudden network traffic and disk activity, so don't set the interval too short if you have a slow connection or a slow computer!

62

Select the **Color new articles** check box and select a color to turn the headlines of new articles that color, to help you see which ones are new. Finally, the **Remove articles** drop-down list lets you specify a maximum "age" for articles displayed in Safari; if you set it to **After two weeks**, articles older than two weeks will be deleted from Safari's local cache. Click **Remove Now** to immediately delete all expired articles; alternatively, wait until Safari automatically checks for new articles, at which time it also removes old ones.

► **TIP**

If you accidentally remove the articles in an RSS feed that you wanted to keep, delete the RSS feed from your bookmarks and then add it again—this resets the feed to default conditions and restores all its articles as "new."

4 Add the RSS Feed Bookmark

RSS feeds can be organized just like any other bookmarks. While viewing an RSS feed, simply click the + button and choose an appropriate bookmark title and a convenient location anywhere in your bookmark hierarchy, as described in **61** Keep Track of Websites with Bookmarks.

You can open a group of RSS feeds all at the same time. To do this, group the feeds into a bookmark folder, and put that folder into the **Bookmarks Bar** or **Bookmarks Menu** collection. Now, when you open that folder from the

Bookmarks bar or the **Bookmarks** menu, you can choose the **View All RSS Articles** menu option, and all the feeds in that folder are opened simultaneously, with all their aggregate articles appearing in the same list. This works for nested folders as well as parent folders; if you open all the feeds in a parent folder, all feeds in nested folders will also open. Be careful not to overwhelm your computer with too many feeds at once!

5 Search Your RSS Feeds for a Topic

With one or several feeds open in your browser window, enter search text into the **Search Articles** input field. All the articles in the loaded RSS feeds are filtered to match your search text. This way, you can create what Apple calls a "personal clipping service," gathering all the articles on a given topic from across all the RSS feeds in your bookmark collection for maximum browsing convenience.

Click the **X** in the **Search Articles** field to clear the search text and restore all your feeds' loaded articles.

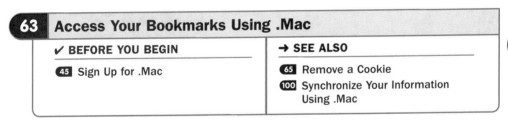

63 Access Your Bookmarks Using .Mac

✔ BEFORE YOU BEGIN	→ SEE ALSO
45 Sign Up for .Mac	65 Remove a Cookie
	100 Synchronize Your Information Using .Mac

62

A handy feature for users of Apple's .Mac service is the ability to access your Safari bookmarks from any computer at any location, even a Windows PC. All you need to do is synchronize your computer with the .Mac server so that the bookmarks are stored at the central, network-accessible location and kept up-to-date with the ones on your Mac.

This feature is particularly useful if you frequently need access to your bookmarks when you're accessing the Internet from coffee shops or libraries, where you might not have access to your own Mac and instead have to use a public computer. The .Mac service allows you to be productive even if you have to use Windows!

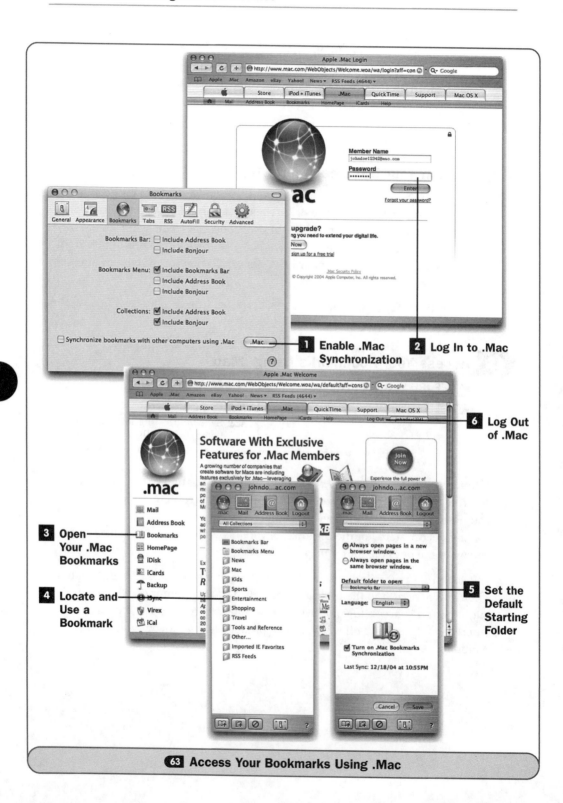

1 Enable .Mac Synchronization

2 Log In to .Mac

6 Log Out of .Mac

3 Open Your .Mac Bookmarks

4 Locate and Use a Bookmark

5 Set the Default Starting Folder

63 Access Your Bookmarks Using .Mac

When accessing your bookmarks on a public computer, you should be very careful about what kind of data you are exposing to the public. Some web addresses, for instance, can contain encoded passwords to services that you access. Similarly, public computers might have surreptitious web cams or keyboard sniffers installed to spy on you in case you enter sensitive information such as credit card numbers. Always assume the worst about the security of a public computer: Would you feel safe about the prospect of the next person sitting down at that same computer from which you have just accessed your bank account online?

If you have any doubts at all about the security of the computer from which you're accessing the Web, don't go to any sites in your bookmarks that might reveal sensitive information. This doesn't just apply to your .Mac Bookmarks, either—any time you use a public computer for anything, you should always clean up after yourself: Empty the Trash (or Recycle Bin), clear the browser's cookies and caches, and close down all browser windows before you leave the computer.

1 Enable .Mac Synchronization

You must ensure that Mac OS X is logged in to your .Mac account before beginning this task; be sure to set it up at the .Mac pane of the System Preferences application as detailed in **45 Sign Up for .Mac**.

Choose **Preferences** from the **Safari** menu; click the **Bookmarks** tab. At the bottom of this pane, select the **Synchronize bookmarks with other computers using .Mac** check box. Close the **Preferences** window; now, from the **Sync** System Menu in the upper right of the menu bar, choose **Sync Now** to publish your Safari bookmarks to the .Mac server. (If the **Sync** System Menu does not appear in your title bar, you can enable it as described in **100 Synchronize Your Information Using .Mac**. Another way to synchronize your bookmarks manually is to use the **Sync Now** button on the **Sync** page of the **.Mac Preferences** pane.)

▶ **NOTE**

Bookmarks are just one of the kinds of data that can be synchronized to .Mac and thus across all your Macs. See **100 Synchronize Your Information Using .Mac** for more information on taking full advantage of this feature, such as configuring the time interval for automated synchronization of all your data with .Mac.

2 Log In to .Mac

On your Mac, another Mac, or even a Windows PC, surf to the .Mac website at **http://www.mac.com**. If you are not already logged in, click the **Log in** link and enter your .Mac member name and password when prompted.

63

3 Open Your .Mac Bookmarks

Click the **Bookmarks** icon in the left pane. If this is the first time you've synchronized your .Mac bookmarks, a notification screen appears that tells you that your .Mac bookmarks will be synchronized. Click **Sync Now** to continue. .Mac then shows a progress screen while your bookmarks are synchronized at the .Mac server. This process takes about thirty seconds.

Now, and every subsequent time you open the **Bookmarks** section of .Mac, you see a **Welcome** window to inform you that your bookmarks are available; click the **Open Bookmarks** button to pop them up in a small, palette-sized external window.

4 Locate and Use a Bookmark

The floating **Bookmarks** window lists all your bookmark folders, the same as in the sidebar of the **Bookmarks Library** page in Safari. Click any of the listed folders to move into that folder, and use the drop-down menu above the folder list to select a folder to jump to.

When you find the bookmark for the site you want to visit, click it. The site will open in a new browser window.

5 Set the Default Starting Folder

Because the Bookmarks window starts with a top-level listing of all your bookmark collections, you will always have to navigate down into one or more of the collections before you find the folder with the bookmark you want. If you always browse from a certain collection, such as your **Bookmarks** bar, you can set that collection as the default location that your .Mac **Bookmarks** window always starts with.

To set this and other options, click the **Preferences** icon (a light switch) at the bottom of the palette-sized Bookmarks window and choose the desired collection from the **Default folder to open** menu. Click **Save** to preserve your changes.

▶ NOTE

If the computer you're using is a public terminal (such as a computer in a public library), don't have .Mac automatically save your password for that computer! Remember, anybody in the world could be next to sit down at that computer; if you've enabled this option from that computer, that person would have complete access to your bookmarks.

6 Log Out of .Mac

When you're done using any public computer, always be sure to log out of any services that might provide access to your personal information—including .Mac. Don't forget to end your session by clicking the **Logout** link at the top of the floating **Bookmarks** window.

64 SnapBack to the First Page of a Site	
✔ **BEFORE YOU BEGIN**	→ **SEE ALSO**
61 Keep Track of Websites with Bookmarks	**65** Remove a Cookie

Safari has a feature that is absent from other browsers: *SnapBack*. This feature allows you to navigate websites more efficiently by letting you jump instantly to the entry point of any site, lifting you out of the site's inner pages.

▶ KEY TERM

SnapBack—A Safari feature that returns the user to the entry point of a website, regardless of how far into the site—or subsequently linked sites—the user has wandered.

63

When you visit a bookmark or enter a web address manually, Safari "marks for SnapBack" the page where you arrive at the site. This means that no matter how many subsequent pages you visit by clicking links found on the site—even if those links take you to entirely different sites—you can always find your way immediately back to the first page where you were taken by the bookmark or the manually entered address, simply by clicking the orange **SnapBack** icon in the Address bar.

The *Google* search box in the upper-right corner of the Safari screen makes use of the SnapBack feature as well. If you use the box to do a Google search, you can prowl through the sites that Google returns, looking for what you want. When you decide that the site you've been looking in doesn't have what you're after, simply click the **SnapBack** icon to return to the page of Google results.

1 Enter a Web Address or Click a Bookmark

Type a web address (URL) into the **Address** bar and press **Return**; alternatively, select any bookmark to travel directly to a favorite site.

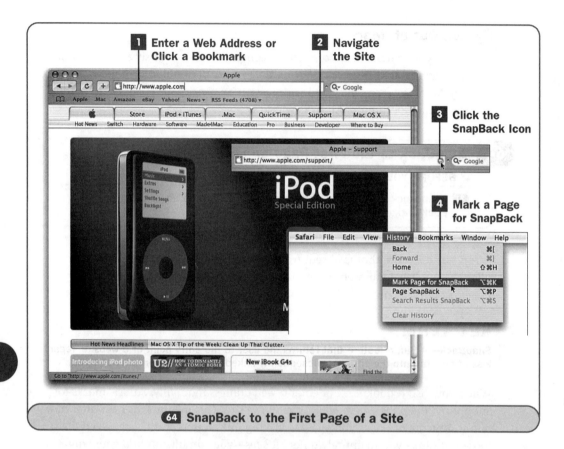

64 SnapBack to the First Page of a Site

2 Navigate the Site

Click links within the site to move from page to page. As soon as you browse to a new page, the orange **SnapBack** icon appears in the Address bar to signify that you can now use the SnapBack feature to return to the original page.

3 Click the SnapBack Icon

Click the orange SnapBack icon in the Address bar, and you are taken back to the first page you visited.

▶ NOTE

Safari immediately jumps back to the entry point as cached in its own history; you can then navigate either forward or backward through the pages in the browser's history.

4 **Mark a Page for SnapBack**

You can manually define any page as the destination point for when you click the **SnapBack** icon. If you find yourself at a site that you know you want to return to, choose **Mark Page for SnapBack** from the Safari **History** menu. You can then surf the links in the site and return immediately to the starting page using the **SnapBack** icon.

When you mark a new page for SnapBack, the orange **SnapBack** icon disappears, meaning that the page you're currently on is where you will SnapBack to. Click on a link, and the icon will again appear.

65 **Remove a Cookie**

✔ **BEFORE YOU BEGIN**

61 Keep Track of Websites with Bookmarks
63 Access Your Bookmarks Using .Mac

Cookies are small pieces of information that some websites store on your computer. A cookie is generally nothing to worry about; it's usually used for convenience, storing your preferences for how to view a given site, for instance. There is seldom anything more sensitive in a cookie than a username or password for a certain site, and that information can only be exchanged with the website that put it there.

▶ **KEY TERM**

Cookie—A piece of information that a website may store on your computer to keep track of your preferences for the site or your username and password.

However, cookies can also be used in nefarious ways—to track web users' surfing habits, to try to capture your passwords, and so on. There have even been documented cases of malicious sites using "cross-site scripting" tactics to harvest credit card information or other personal data that you had submitted to another, legitimate site. Regardless of how seldom or frequently you use the Web, it's a good idea to know how to remove a cookie (or all your browser's accumulated cookies) and thereby "clean" your computer of sensitive information on a regular basis.

Although it might be tempting to simply remove all your cookies at once, be careful—doing so can mean the loss of good cookies, the ones that store your personalized profile information for sites that you use frequently. It's a good idea to look carefully at the domain or hostname for each of your cookies, and only remove the ones you don't recognize, rather than simply deleting all your cookies in one fell swoop.

64

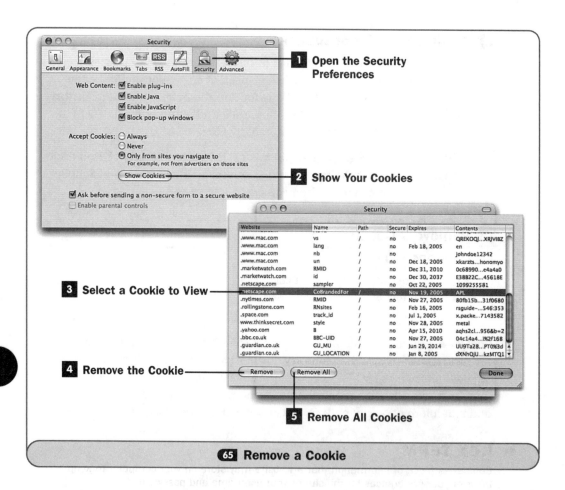

1 Open the Security Preferences

2 Show Your Cookies

3 Select a Cookie to View

4 Remove the Cookie

5 Remove All Cookies

65 Remove a Cookie

Removing all your cookies, however, can be exactly the feature you need if you're trying to clean up the computer so you can give it to someone else.

1 Open the Security Preferences

Select **Preferences** from the **Safari** menu. Click the **Security** icon to bring up the security options.

2 Show Your Cookies

Click the **Show Cookies** button to display a sheet listing all the cookies currently stored on your computer, what sites created them, when they're set to expire, and what information is stored in them.

Don't worry if the **Contents** column shows what seems to be incomprehensible garbage. Cookies aren't meant to be read by people, but rather by computers; sometimes you'll be able to tell what information a cookie is storing, but just as often the contents will be a mystery. You never know when seeing your cookies' ingredients might come in handy, however....

③ Select a Cookie to View

Click any cookie to select it.

▶ TIP

You can select multiple cookies by holding down ⌘ or **Shift** as you click. You might want to select several cookies if you want to remove all the cookies for a given site.

④ Remove the Cookie

Click **Remove** to delete the selected cookie or cookies from your browser.

⑤ Remove All Cookies

To completely clean your browser of all cookies and return it to its original, pristine condition, click **Remove All**. Be aware, however, that any preferences you might have stored for certain websites are also reset, and you'll have to set them up again if you return to those sites.

Safari keeps records of your browsing history—all the sites you've visited—for up to a week. This can be very convenient because it enables you to go back immediately to any site you've been to in the last seven days, using either the **History** menu or the **History** collection in the **Bookmarks** page.

However, if you're using Safari on a computer that's shared among multiple users (and particularly if you're using a public machine), it might not be a good idea to leave your browsing history where just anybody can come in and rummage through it. When you're done browsing on a shared computer, use the **Reset Safari** option under the **Safari** menu. This option not only clears out your complete browsing and Google-searching history, it also deletes all your cookies, clears out the browser's cache (local copies of web files the browser stores for quicker access), and removes sensitive information such as names and passwords from AutoFill form fields.

On the **Reset Safari** dialog box that appears, be sure to click the **Reset** button instead of the **Cancel** button—for safety, **Cancel** is the default action button in the dialog box.

65

66 Connect to an FTP Server

✔ BEFORE YOU BEGIN	→ SEE ALSO
30 Configure Networking Manually	**31** Configure Proxy Server Settings

The *File Transfer Protocol (FTP)* is a venerable form of Internet communication still widely used today. When you download a piece of software from its publisher's website, you might well be downloading it from an FTP server. This is because FTP is well suited to transferring large binary files (such as application packages), rather than the many short text transactions that make up navigation on the Web (which typically are done using HTTP, the Hypertext Transfer Protocol).

▶ KEY TERM

File Transfer Protocol (FTP)—A method of transferring files from one computer to another, dating back to the earliest days of the Internet and still in use today for downloading large files (such as software packages).

Another key feature of FTP is that you can upload files as well as download them. If you have a website or Unix shell account on a remote server, you can use FTP to upload your web pages and image files.

Mac OS X integrates FTP into the Finder, and when you encounter an FTP link in Safari, Safari passes the FTP connection into the Finder so that you can navigate the FTP server as you would any network server.

▶ NOTE

Of course, Mac OS X is Unix—so if you're a Unix expert and prefer to use the traditional command-line **ftp** program, just fire up the Unix **Terminal**.

① Enter a Public FTP Server URL

In Safari, enter the URL of the FTP server or click the link to the FTP server if such a link is presented in a web page.

A public FTP URL (as offered, typically, by shareware sites) is of the form **ftp://ftp.hostname.com/path/to/directory**. Optionally, you can add a trailing slash (which does not affect the system's behavior) or a filename. If you specify the filename, Safari downloads the file directly and transparently, using the **Downloads** window. If you specify only the path to a directory, Mac OS X connects to the server and opens that directory as a folder in a Finder window.

② Enter a Private FTP URL

Not all FTP sites are public; some, such as the one you might have as part of a website account with an Internet service provider, are private—meaning that only you can access it, and only after you provide a valid username and password combination (which are also part of your account with the service provider).

A private FTP URL is of the form **ftp://*username<:password>*@ftp.*hostname*. com/*path/to/directory*. The password is optional, as is the path. For instance, if your username on the FTP server **somewhere.com** is **jsmith** and your password is **abc123**, and you want to connect directly into the home directory of your account, use the following URL: **ftp://jsmith:abc123@somewhere.com.**

If you'd rather not specify your password so that it can't be seen over your shoulder, you can leave it out: **ftp://jsmith@somewhere.com.** If you do this, you will be prompted with a dialog box to provide the password for the account.

▶ **NOTE**

Standard FTP does not provide for a secure connection method. This means that whether or not you specify your password as part of the URL, the password is transmitted over the network in clear text. An eavesdropper who is snooping on the network can obtain your password this way. Be aware of this security risk when using private FTP; you might want to look into a more full-featured FTP program, such as Panic's **Transmit**, which provides secure FTP transactions with servers that support them.

66

▶ **WEB RESOURCE**

http://www.panic.com/transmit/

Download Panic's **Transmit** FTP application from this website. Transmit provides a much more user-friendly and feature-rich interface than using FTP in the Finder, and allows secure transfers as well.

3 Open the Server in the Finder

After you type the URL in Safari's Address bar and press **Return** (or click an equivalent FTP link), a dialog box appears showing that Mac OS X is connecting to the FTP server. After the connection is established (which might take a few moments), a Finder window appears showing the contents of the target folder specified in the URL. The FTP server is listed in the Finder's Sidebar as a standard network server.

4 Upload and Download Files by Dragging

Navigate the FTP server as you would any hierarchical folder system, using Icon, List, or Column views as you prefer. When you find a file you want to download, drag it to your Desktop or to another target in the Finder. A dialog box appears to show the progress of the download.

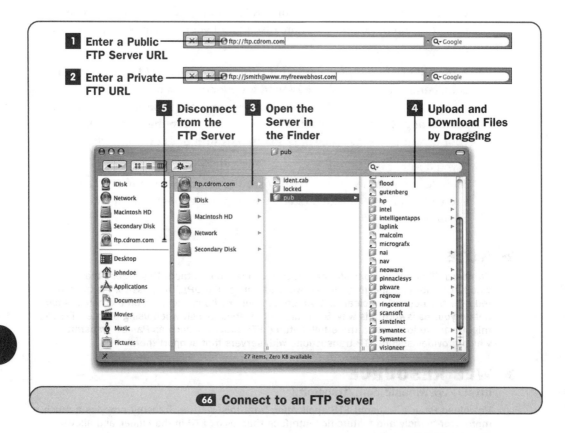

1 Enter a Public FTP Server URL

2 Enter a Private FTP URL

5 Disconnect from the FTP Server

3 Open the Server in the Finder

4 Upload and Download Files by Dragging

66 Connect to an FTP Server

Uploading files—transferring them from your computer to the FTP server—is just as easy: Drag a file or folder from your Desktop or a Finder window into the window showing the FTP server. However, unless it is an authenticated private FTP session, you might not have permission to upload files. An error message appears if you try to upload a file to a server that does not permit it.

▶ **NOTE**

The FTP uploading feature in some versions of Mac OS X is poorly implemented, preventing you from uploading files even if you have properly authenticated and have uploading permission. If you need to upload files, the command-line **ftp** program or Panic's **Transmit** might be a better choice for you.

5 **Disconnect from the FTP Server**

When you're done transferring files, click the **Eject** icon next to the FTP server in the left pane of the Finder window; alternatively, drag the server's icon from the Desktop into the Trash, which becomes an **Eject** icon while you're dragging the icon.

9

Instant Messaging with iChat

IN THIS CHAPTER:

Instant messaging has become one of the most important forms of communication on the Internet in recent years. With even more immediacy than email, and with an even more personal focus, instant messaging—pioneered by applications such as ICQ and AOL Instant Messenger (AIM), and further advanced by offerings from Yahoo! and Microsoft—has become the preferred means of quick, informal communication for millions of people at both the personal and professional levels. Incorporating text, audio, and video chat capabilities as well as multiparty conversations, instant messaging has evolved from a simple means to send a quick note to pop up on someone else's screen to a full-fledged telepresence and information-sharing infrastructure.

iChat is Apple's integrated chat client, compatible with the AOL Instant Messenger network and incorporating all the connectivity and graphics technologies that make Mac OS X itself streamlined and attractive. Paired with a FireWire video camera, such as Apple's iSight, you can chat not only with the traditional instant text messages made so popular with AIM, ICQ, Yahoo! Messenger, and MSN Messenger, but with audio and full-motion video as well, even with multiple partners at once. Because iChat is integrated into Mac OS X itself, finding chat partners, receiving messages, and exchanging files is often as simple as dragging an icon or selecting a globally available menu option.

Apple's iSight video camera with microphone connects over FireWire and mounts to any kind of Mac display.

There are a lot of little details to using iChat, such as sending hyperlinks, setting chat background pictures, configuring your chat text's appearance, tuning your privacy options, and using smileys; this chapter explains some of the features that are most immediately useful, allowing you to explore the rest at your leisure.

67 Set Up Your AIM or .Mac Account

✔ BEFORE YOU BEGIN	→ SEE ALSO
30 Configure Networking Manually	**68** Set Up Your Picture
45 Sign Up for .Mac	**70** Start a Text, Audio, or Video Chat Session
54 Configure a New Mail Account	

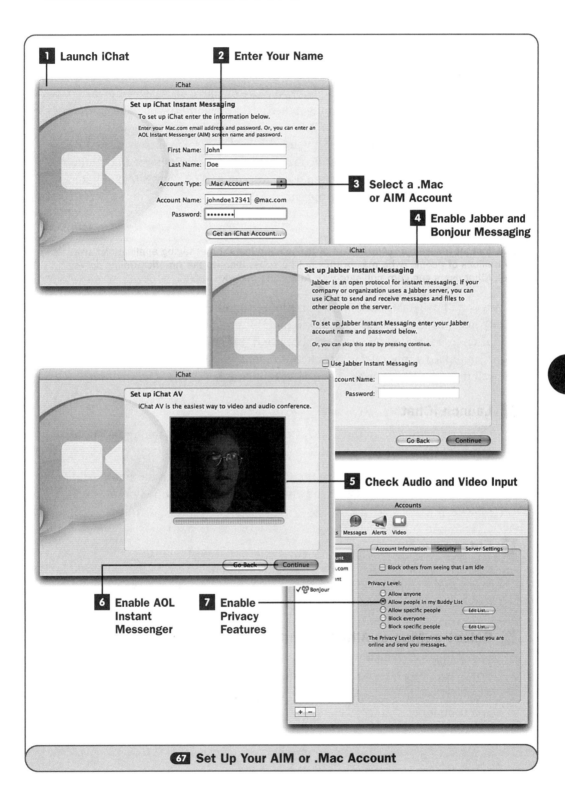

1 Launch iChat

2 Enter Your Name

3 Select a .Mac or AIM Account

4 Enable Jabber and Bonjour Messaging

5 Check Audio and Video Input

6 Enable AOL Instant Messenger

7 Enable Privacy Features

67

67 Set Up Your AIM or .Mac Account

The first step in using iChat is to set up your **iChat account**, an identification that's necessary for you to use iChat. Either your .Mac member name or a pre-existing *AIM* screen name qualifies as an iChat account ID. iChat supports both .Mac accounts and AIM screen names; if you already have an AIM name—for example, if you're an AOL user or if you used AIM previously—you can continue to use that as your identification in iChat, and you won't have to create a new identity when you first start iChat. If you have a .Mac account, however, you might want to use it for your identification in iChat, as it stores more information about you than an AIM identification does. You can add all your AIM buddies to your iChat Buddy List just as they appear in AIM.

▶ KEY TERM

AOL Instant Messenger (AIM)—One of the leading instant-messaging applications, used by millions of people (who may or may not be subscribers to the America Online service). iChat users can communicate with AIM users and vice versa.

If you don't have a .Mac account or an AIM screen name, follow the **Get an iChat Account** link (a button on the account information screen) during iChat's initial setup. Setting up an iChat account using this method is free of charge; it signs you up for a trial 60-day .Mac account, and your iChat ID remains active after that period expires, even if you don't fully activate a paid .Mac account.

67

1 Launch iChat

Click the **iChat** icon in the Dock; alternatively, navigate to the **Applications** folder and double-click the **iChat** icon.

If this is the first time you have run iChat, you will be taken through the initial setup screens. Click **Continue** after reading the information on the first screen.

2 Enter Your Name

In the next screen, enter your account information. Type your first and last name in the boxes provided. You must enter both names before you can proceed.

3 Select a .Mac or AIM Account

Depending on whether you will be using a .Mac or an AIM account with iChat, select the account type from the drop-down menu. Fill in the remaining blanks with your account name and password. Click **Continue** when you're done.

▶ **NOTE**

AOL Instant Messenger (AIM) is a part of the America Online service (AOL), but it can be used by people who aren't AOL subscribers. If you're an AOL customer, the Instant Messenger service is automatically configured for you, just as iChat's setup is stream-lined if you have a .Mac account, but millions of people use the standalone version of AIM who are not AOL subscribers, and iChat can use either a true AOL screen name or a separately created AIM name, if you don't have a .Mac account.

4 Enable Jabber and Bonjour Messaging

iChat primarily operates using the AIM network, in its primary function of communicating with other people across the Internet. However, it also inter-operates with two other types of instant-messaging networks: *Jabber* and *Bonjour*. These two kinds of networks are somewhat different, but both oper-ate similarly from your perspective. Both Jabber and Bonjour are ways for you to communicate instantly with other people on a local network (such as a corporate intranet, a university, or a home network).

Jabber communication requires that a central Jabber server be present on the network; if your organization has such a server, iChat will detect it automati-cally and list all the other users on it. Consult your network administrator to see whether your network supports Jabber.

Bonjour, on the other hand, is a networking technology built into Mac OS X that enables many advanced features having to do with your computer auto-matically "discovering" other computers on the local network, such as other computers running iTunes that can share their music with you, or Macs run-ning iPhoto with shared photos. iChat benefits from this technology by auto-matically finding all other iChat users on your local network and listing them for instant communication, without the need for any central server to be present.

67

▶ **KEY TERM**

Jabber—An instant-messaging protocol that allows communication and file exchange between computers on a local network, such as a corporate intranet or a university, where a central Jabber server is present.

In the next setup screen, choose to enable Jabber instant-messaging by select-ing the check box and entering your Jabber account name and password; or skip Jabber by simply clicking **Continue**.

The next screen lets you select whether you want to enable Bonjour messag-ing. Select the check box if you wish to be able to see and communicate with other iChat users on your local network. Otherwise, skip the check box by clicking **Continue**, and your chatting will be limited to the iChat and AIM partners that you explicitly add and that appear in your **Buddy List** window. You might choose to disable Bonjour messaging if your Mac is the only one on the local predominantly Windows network—Bonjour would be of no use to you in this case.

▶ NOTES

Chatting with Bonjour or Jabber partners is faster than chatting with the AIM/.Mac users in your **Buddy List**, as the text you type appears immediately on the other person's screen letter by letter as you enter it, rather than waiting for you to finish typing and press **Return** before each message is sent.

---

iChat operates using three different lists of chat partners: your **Buddy List** (which shows users with AIM and .Mac accounts, to which you add chat partners manually), and your **Jabber** and **Bonjour** lists (which automatically show all other potential chat partners on your local network). You can choose to show one list, two, or all three, depending on your circumstances and needs. To display or switch to any of the three lists, select **Buddy List**, **Bonjour**, or **Jabber** from the **Window** menu in iChat.

5 Check Audio and Video Input

The next iChat setup screen shows you the current status of your camera, if you have one connected. Be sure to open the camera's shutter (as you have to do with Apple's iSight camera) so that the camera is active. iChat will show you the camera's current image, as well as the audio input level. This lets you ensure that the camera is working properly. When you're satisfied that your camera and microphone are working correctly, click **Continue**.

▶ NOTE

With the exception of the Power Mac G4 and G5 (which have a port for an external microphone), all Macs have a built-in microphone that can be used for audio input. The microphone is a little pinhole next to the screen on most Mac desktop and laptop models.

If your camera has a built-in microphone, you can choose whether to use this microphone or the one that's built into your Mac, using the drop-down menu that appears.

6 Enable AOL Instant Messenger

If you entered information for a .Mac account, you might be prompted to enable AOL Instant Messenger access. Click **Enable** to do this.

You are now set up to use iChat. You can communicate immediately with other iChat users on the local network who appear in the **Jabber** or **Bonjour** windows, or add .Mac or AIM buddies to your **Buddy List** (see **69 Add a Buddy**).

7 Enable Privacy Features

If you're concerned about your privacy, you can take some extra steps to ensure it in iChat. Choose **Preferences** from the **iChat** menu; under the **Accounts** tab are listed all your iChat accounts. Remember that because iChat uses the AIM network but integrates .Mac users into it, you have both a .Mac and an AIM account, but only one may be marked with a check at once, indicating that that's your primary account. You might also have a Jabber account and a Bonjour account, or more than one of each, depending on how you initially set up iChat.

Select your primary .Mac or AIM account (the one with the check mark) and click the **Security** tab. Under the **Privacy Level** heading, choose a privacy profile that describes how you want to use iChat. The option you select, ranging from **Allow anyone** to **Allow specific people** or even **Block everyone** (if you only want to be able to contact others and not be contacted by them), determines who is able to see you in their own Buddy Lists and send you messages. Use the **Edit List** buttons to set up "whitelists" (for **Allow specific people**) or "blacklists" (for **Block specific people**) that define exceptions to the overall rule you choose.

67

68 Set Up Your Picture

✔ BEFORE YOU BEGIN	→ SEE ALSO
67 Set Up Your AIM or .Mac Account	**95** Add a Person to Your Address Book

After you've set up your iChat account, it's time for the most critical part of all: choosing your picture. This picture is what represents you visually in a chat with another person, so you should choose something that accurately depicts your personality, your likes and dislikes, and your usual mood. Or you'll just want to find something nice and silly to use.

iChat starts you out using the picture from your card in Address Book, if you have defined one, or your Mac OS X login picture. You can tell iChat to use a different picture by simply dragging it into iChat from the Finder (or even straight from a web page).

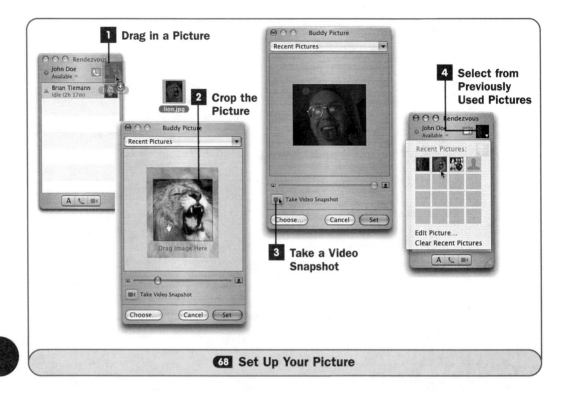

1 Drag in a Picture

2 Crop the Picture

3 Take a Video Snapshot

4 Select from Previously Used Pictures

68 Set Up Your Picture

1 Drag in a Picture

Launch iChat, using the icon in the Dock or in the **Applications** folder. Make sure that one of your iChat windows is visible—either your **Buddy List** or one of the **Bonjour** or **Jabber** lists (select one from the **Window** menu if one is not visible). Either window shows your picture in the upper-right corner of the window.

▶ TIP

Try to choose a picture that's "facing right"—that will look good at the left side of a chat window. Although on your side of a chat, your picture appears on the right side of the window, your chat partners see your picture on the left side of their windows. For aesthetic reasons, the picture you choose to represent you should show you facing right (towards your text) rather than left.

Open the Finder and locate the picture you want to use. Drag it to the square containing your current picture in iChat. You can even drag an image from a Safari window, if you find a picture on the Web that you'd like to use.

2 Crop the Picture

The **Buddy Picture** picture-editing screen appears, showing the picture you've dragged into iChat. Use the slider below the picture to set the "aperture" size, or the size of the square that defines your iChat picture relative to the whole picture you've dragged in. You can scale down the entire picture to fit into the square, or you can select only a small portion if you prefer. Click and drag in the picture window to set where the square is centered, and click **Set** when you're satisfied with how it looks.

3 Take a Video Snapshot

If you have a digital video camera hooked up to your Mac over FireWire, the **Take Video Snapshot** button at the bottom of the **Buddy Picture** widow becomes active. Click the button; the output from your video camera appears in the picture-editing window. A series of beeps sounds, becoming progressively quicker; as the beeps speed up, aim the camera at yourself (or at anything else you want to take a picture of), and in a few seconds iChat will freeze-frame an image, using whatever is on the camera at the time. You can then edit the image using the aperture and drag tools in the **Buddy Picture** window.

Just about any kind of digital video camera will work with the login picture selector; any FireWire camera that iChat recognizes will activate the feature. Apple's iSight and other FireWire webcams are ideal, but you can also use a standard digital camcorder; just connect it to your computer, put it in stand-by mode, and the video signal will automatically be picked up by the system and used in the video snapshot.

68

▶ NOTE

G3-based Macs slower than 600MHz cannot use iChat's video capabilities, and thus the **Take Video Snapshot** option is also unavailable (iChat will say that videoconferencing is not supported on this computer).

▶ TIP

To invoke the picture-cropping window directly without dragging in a new picture, select **Change My Picture** from the **Buddies** menu.

If you don't like your snapshot, you can immediately take another one by clicking the **Take Video Snapshot** button again. Keep trying until you have a picture you like.

4 **Select from Previously Used Pictures**

While you're using iChat, you can change your picture immediately to any picture you've used in the past. Click your current picture in either the **Buddy List**, **Bonjour**, or **Jabber List** window, and a sheet showing all your recently used pictures appears. Click the picture you want to switch to, and it becomes your active picture.

---

69 **Add a Buddy**

✔ BEFORE YOU BEGIN	→ SEE ALSO
67 Set Up Your AIM or .Mac Account	**70** Start a Text, Audio, or Video Chat Session
	72 Set a Custom Status Message
	95 Add a Person to Your Address Book
	100 Synchronize Your Information Using .Mac

68

Bonjour lets you see all the iChat users on your local network immediately, and Jabber shows you all users currently logged into your network's Jabber server, but when it comes to talking with people who are elsewhere on the Internet, these technologies won't help you. In those situations, you have to rely on your **Buddy List** and the .Mac and *AIM* users listed there to connect you with them across large Internet distances.

iChat lets you select "buddies" from your **Address Book** or specify them manually. To add a buddy manually, you must know the .Mac or AIM account name they're using.

You must be connected to the Internet before you can add a buddy to your Buddy List.

1 **Open the Address Book Sheet**

Launch iChat using the icon in the Dock or in the **Applications** folder; open the **Buddy List** window, if it is not already open (choose **Buddy List** from the **Window** menu).

Click the + button in the lower-left corner of the **Buddy List** window. This brings up a sheet that shows a simplified version of your Address Book, with your Groups at the left and the individual addresses on the right.

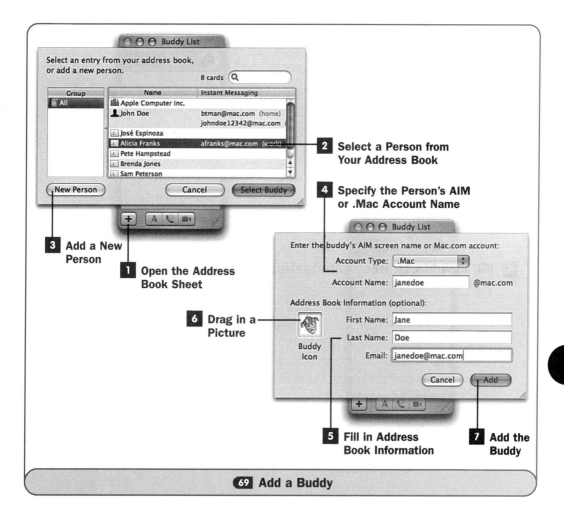

69 Add a Buddy

2 Select a Person from Your Address Book

If the buddy you want to add is in your Address Book already, simply find his or her name in the list and double-click it.

▶ TIP

You can filter the names by typing a partial name into the **Search** box at the top of the Address Book sheet.

3 Add a New Person

To add a buddy manually to your Buddy List, click the **New Person** button at the bottom of the **Address Book** sheet. A new sheet appears, with form fields that allow you to specify the person's name and other information. This information adds the person to your Address Book as well as to your Buddy List in iChat.

You must know beforehand what kind of chat account the other person has—an AIM name or a .Mac account. The account name and type is the minimum information you need to have to add a new person. Contact the person through other means (such as email) to find out his information.

4 Specify the Person's AIM or .Mac Account Name

From the **Account Type** drop-down list, select the type of account the person you want to add to your Buddy List has (.Mac or AIM), and then type the account name for that person.

5 Fill in Address Book Information

If you leave the rest of the fields blank, this buddy will appear in your Buddy List with a generic picture icon and with his account name instead of a full name. To make the person's entry appear a little more streamlined in the Buddy List window, specify a first and last name and an email address here. This information will be added to the person's new address card, which is automatically created in your Address Book, and the full name appears in the Buddy List instead of the .Mac or AIM ID.

6 Drag in a Picture

If this person has already specified a picture in his copy of iChat, that picture will appear next to the person's name in your Buddy List as soon as the person appears online. However, if you want, you can drag any picture into the **Buddy Icon** well to use instead, and this image will override any picture provided by your buddy.

7 Add the Buddy

When you've specified all the pertinent information for the buddy you are adding to your Buddy List, click **Add**. The information sheet closes and your Buddy List updates to reflect the person's online status; if the person is online, his full name and picture will appear if they are specified by the other person. In addition to finding the person in your Buddy List, you will also find this person listed in a new card in your Address Book.

69

70 Start a Text, Audio, or Video Chat Session

✔ BEFORE YOU BEGIN	→ SEE ALSO
67 Set Up Your AIM or .Mac Account	**71** Send a File
69 Add a Buddy	**72** Set a Custom Status Message

You can start a chat session with anybody in your Buddy List or Bonjour or Jabber lists who's available—in other words, anybody who has a green dot next to his or her name in the list. (You cannot send messages to people who are offline.) When you send a message to an online user and the other person replies, a chat has begun.

► **TIP**

The difference between a Direct Message and an Instant Message, either of which you can send to any online user in your Buddy List, is that an Instant Message is relayed through a central server on the Internet, whereas a Direct Message is sent straight from your computer to the other person's computer. Use a Direct Message (choose it from the Buddies menu) if you are concerned about the risk to privacy that comes with sending your messages through the central server.

You can start chatting using plain text (which appears in your iChat window surrounded by glossy balloons), audio (using your Mac's built-in microphone or the microphone in your video camera), or video (using an external FireWire camera, such as a DV camcorder or Apple's iSight camera). You can even chat with multiple partners, regardless of whether you're using text, audio, or video, making iChat a very capable groupware application.

If you choose, you can have your text chats saved as transcripts; each time you chat with another person, the entire session is saved in a file in the **iChats** folder inside the **Documents** folder in your **Home** folder. Simply double-click a chat file to open it for review. Each individual chat transcript is saved at the time that you close a chat window; the transcript files are named according to the person you were chatting with and the date and time when the chat took place, for orderly sorting.

► **TIP**

You must enable chat transcripts for them to be saved automatically; you can do this by selecting the **Automatically save chat transcripts** check box in the **Messages** pane of iChat's **Preferences**, which are accessible through the **iChat** menu.

70

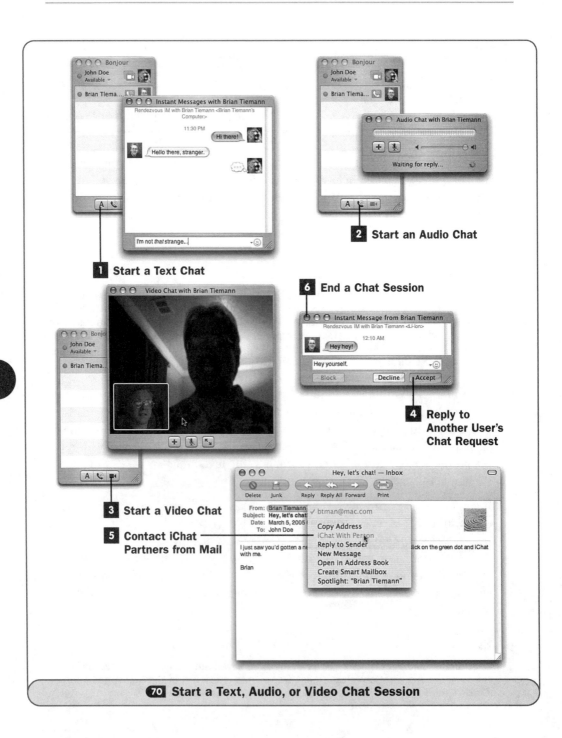

1 Start a Text Chat

2 Start an Audio Chat

6 End a Chat Session

4 Reply to Another User's Chat Request

3 Start a Video Chat

5 Contact iChat Partners from Mail

70 Start a Text, Audio, or Video Chat Session

You can start a chat immediately with any active person on your Buddy List by using the **iChat** System Menu, a cartoon word-balloon in the menu bar; simply select the name of the person under **Available Buddies** to send a message.

You can turn the **iChat System Menu** on and off using the **Show status in menu bar** check box in the **General** pane of the iChat **Preferences** window, which is accessible through the **iChat** menu.

1 Start a Text Chat

The simplest kind of chat, a text chat, can be initiated simply by double-clicking the name of the buddy you want to chat with in either the Buddy List or Bonjour window. (Alternatively, select the buddy from the list and click the **A** button at the bottom of the window.) An **Instant Messages** window appears in which you can type your message; press **Return** to send the text you've typed.

Your message appears on the right side of the chat window. When your chat partner replies, his messages appear on the left side of the window. A cartoon bubble with an ellipsis (...) in it indicates that your partner is typing a response.

70

▶ TIPS

To save your chats for future perusal, open the **iChat Preferences** and go to the Messages tab; select the **Automatically save chat transcripts** check box. The **Open Folder** button opens a Finder window showing the contents of the **iChats** folder inside your **Documents**; this is where a transcript of each chat session is stored, named according to the name of the chat partner.

To review any stored chat session, navigate to this folder and double-click the session you want; it will open in an iChat window.

When chatting with a Bonjour or Jabber partner, the text you type is sent immediately as you type it without waiting for you to press **Return** (your buddy can see all the typos you make and when you backspace over them). If you'd rather iChat wait until you've fully composed your message before sending it, you can turn off this behavior in the **Messages** pane in iChat's **Preferences**.

To insert a carriage-return into your message (that is, to break one line and start typing on the next line) without sending the message, press **Option+Return**.

To begin a chat with multiple partners, choose **New Chat** from the **File** menu; then drag participants from the Buddy list into the **Participants** drawer next to the chat window.

2 Start an Audio Chat

If you have a microphone and the other user is capable of an audio chat, a green "telephone" icon appears next to her picture in your buddy list. Click this icon or select the user from the list and click the **Telephone** button at the bottom of the window.

▶ **NOTE**

If the other user doesn't have a microphone, you can still set up a one-way audio chat, in which she will be able to hear you, but not vice versa. To do this, select the user from the list and then choose **Invite to One-Way Audio Chat** from the **Buddies** menu.

A small window appears, with the name of the buddy you are trying to contact in the title bar. The window displays your audio input gain along with status messages showing whether the audio chat is properly set up yet. When the chat is initiated correctly, the status messages disappear and you should be able to talk and hear the other person.

To monitor the quality of your connection, use the **Connection Doctor** (available in the **Audio** menu). The **Connection Doctor** panel shows you the frame rate and bandwidth (bit rate) used by the connection, as well as a meter showing the connection's quality. This information can be useful in diagnosing network problems that arise.

Add more audio chat partners by clicking the + icon at the bottom of the window; select the person from the window that appears. You can audio-chat simultaneously with as many as nine other people.

3 Start a Video Chat

If you and your chat partner each have a video camera hooked up and turned on, you can start a video chat. Click the green camera icon next to the user's picture, or select the user and click the **Camera** button at the bottom of the window.

▶ **NOTE**

If the other user doesn't have a camera, you can still set up a one-way video chat, in which he will be able to see and hear you, but not vice versa. To do this, select the user and then choose **Invite to One-Way Video Chat** from the **Buddies** menu.

A window appears showing your moving image as your camera sees it, with a connection status bar at the top showing whether the chat is set up or not. When the chat starts, the status bar disappears, and the other user's image takes up the whole window. Your image shrinks to a small "picture-in-picture" view, which you can drag to another position in the window or change its size (by dragging its corner).

70

Add more video chat partners by clicking the + icon at the bottom of the window; select the person from the window that appears. Each new person in the video chat appears in a three-dimensional panel in the video chat window, arranged with other video panels so as to suggest that you're all sitting around a shiny black table facing each other. You can video-chat simultaneously with as many as three other people.

▶ **TIP**

Click the **Full Screen** button at the bottom of the video chat window (it's labeled with arrows pointing to the corners) to expand the video chat to your entire screen, making the conversation seem even more face-to-face.

You might have difficulty starting a chat with other users on your local network using Bonjour if your firewall is enabled. To allow iChat traffic to get through the firewall, open the **Firewall** tab in the **Sharing Preferences** (click **Sharing** in the **System Preferences**), then enable the exception rule for **iChat Bonjour** (ports 5297 and 5298). For more information on working with the firewall, see 🔳 **Add or Remove Firewall Rules.**

4 Reply to Another User's Chat Request

70

If another person invites you to a text, audio, or video chat, you will see a message pop up in the upper-right corner of the screen telling you about the invitation. (A sound effect plays, too; for text chats, it's a soft "pop" sound, whereas for audio and video chats, it's a "ring" sound.)

Click the translucent message to turn it opaque and see its contents; the window also has buttons you can use to accept the chat, refuse it, or block the user from contacting you in the future. If you click **Accept**, the chat session will start.

To end any chat session, simply close the chat window.

To turn off iChat altogether, quit the application. However, iChat still launches to accept incoming messages even if the application isn't running, unless you select the **When I quit iChat, set my status to Offline** check box in the General tab of the iChat Preferences.

▶ **TIP**

To make sure incoming messages can't reach you, choose **Offline** from the **iChat** System Menu (or from the menu under your name within iChat if it's running); you will then appear "offline" to other iChat and AIM users, and they won't be able to send messages to you. Also be sure to explore the more powerful options in the **Privacy** tab of the **Accounts** pane of the **iChat Preferences.**

5 Contact iChat Partners from Mail

Open the **Mail** application (click its icon in the Dock) and view your Inbox. If any messages in it were sent to you from someone in your Address Book who is currently using iChat, a green dot appears next to his or her name in the message listing and in the headers of the message itself. Click the dot to begin a direct iChat session with that person. Alternatively, click the down arrow next to the person's name to access the **iChat With Person** command as well as several other communication options.

▶ TIP

Update your Address Book to make sure that the email address for each of your contacts is the same as the one that he uses for iChat! Remember that you can enter multiple email addresses in Address Book for each person.

6 End a Chat Session

When you're done chatting with the other person, simply click the **Close** button on the chat window to end the session.

Set your status to **Offline** (using the menu under your name) if you wish to stop receiving new messages from other users.

70

---

71 Send a File

✔ BEFORE YOU BEGIN	→ SEE ALSO
67 Set Up Your AIM or .Mac Account	72 Set a Custom Status Message
69 Add a Buddy	35 Share Another Mac's Files
70 Start a Text, Audio, or Video Chat Session	

You can use iChat to transfer files instantly between users. You can send a file directly to anybody in your **Buddy List** or **Bonjour** or **Jabber** lists simply by dragging the file to that person's entry in the list; similarly, anybody can send you a file, which appears as a document or picture embedded in one of their text messages during an iChat.

1 Find the File to Send

Use the Finder to locate the file you want to send to the other person.

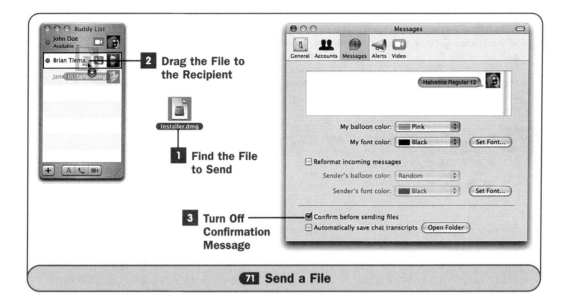

Send a File

2 Drag the File to the Recipient

Make sure that the Buddy List, Bonjour, or Jabber window containing the person' name is open and that the person is online (a green dot appears next to the user's name if he is online). Drag the file to the user's name in the list and drop the file on the recipient's name. A dialog box opens, prompting you to confirm that you want to send the file; click **Send** to send it.

► TIP

If you're already in a chat with a user, a common mistake is to drag the file into the chat window. The result of this action can be surprising, especially if the file you're trying to send is a picture—this is the procedure you'd use to set the background picture for the chat window! Make sure that you drag the file to the user's name in the Buddy List, Bonjour, or Jabber window, not into the chat window. (You can, however, drag a file into the text input area to send it as part of a text message.)

3 Turn Off Confirmation Message

If you don't want iChat to confirm whether you want to send a file before you send it, click the **Don't ask again** check box in the confirmation dialog box. Alternatively, open the iChat **Preferences** dialog box and click the **Messages** icon to display the **Messages** pane. Deselect the **Confirm before sending files** check box.

▶ **NOTE**

When a chat partner sends a file to you, you are prompted to download it with a dialog box, or—if the file is presented within a text chat—an icon that you must click to begin the download. Beware of files that others send you, as always; make sure you trust the file and the person sending it before you open or install the downloaded file. Always be aware of potential viruses and Trojans!

72   Set a Custom Status Message

✔ BEFORE YOU BEGIN	→ SEE ALSO
67 Set Up Your AIM or .Mac Account	**68** Set Up Your Picture
	70 Start a Text, Audio, or Video Chat Session

By default, you can select from only two status messages that iChat displays to other users under your name: **Available** and **Away**. Your status changes to **Idle** if you have been idle (that is, if you have not touched your keyboard or mouse) for 10 minutes. You can set your status to **Away** to let others know that you're not at your computer to answer instant messages, but if you want others to see a more detailed message to explain what you're doing, it's easy to set one.

1 Select a Custom Status Message

Launch iChat using the icon in the Dock or in the **Applications** folder. Make sure the **Buddy List**, **Bonjour**, or **Jabber List** window is open; select one of these from the **Window** menu if none of the windows is present.

In one of the windows, click the down arrow next to your status message to open the menu of selectable status messages. Select the **Custom** option under either **Available** or **Away**; the status message in the window's title bar turns into a text input box.

2 Type a Temporary Custom Message

Type a new message of your choice in the text box and press **Return**. The new message appears under your name in others' Buddy Lists, until you change it or go offline.

▶ **TIP**

To cancel entering a new message, leave the text entry field blank and press **Return**.

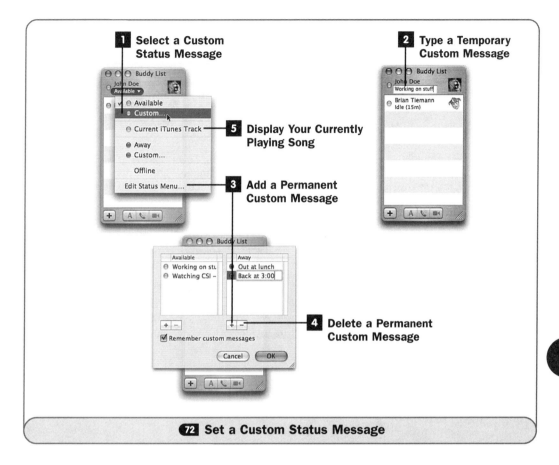

1 Select a Custom
Status Message

2 Type a Temporary
Custom Message

5 Display Your Currently
Playing Song

3 Add a Permanent
Custom Message

4 Delete a Permanent
Custom Message

72 Set a Custom Status Message

72

3 Add a Permanent Custom Message

From the status message menu, select **Edit Status Menu** to bring up the custom message definition sheet. Click the + icon under either the **Available** or **Away** column; a new blank message becomes selected in the appropriate column. Type a message that you want to keep so that you can select it at opportune times. This message, along with any others that you define, appears under either **Available** or **Away** in the status message menu under your name, or in the **iChat** System Menu; click the message you want to set it as your new status message.

You can define as many custom messages as you want, to match the myriad different ways you can be "available" or "away."

4   Delete a Permanent Custom Message

To remove a custom status message from the list, open the custom message definition sheet (select **Edit Status Menu** from the status message menu). Select the message you want to delete and click the – (minus sign) button under the column in which the message is listed.

▶ TIP

You can delete multiple messages at the same time: Holding down **Shift** or ⌘ while clicking the messages you want to delete. Then click the – (minus sign) button to delete all the selected messages. Be careful—there is no "undo" function, and if you delete any custom messages, they're gone for good.

5   Display Your Currently Playing Song

From the status message menu (either under your name in an iChat user list window or in the **iChat** System Menu), choose **Current iTunes Track**. This sets your status message to the title of the song currently playing in iTunes. This way, other iChat users can always see what music you're listening to. This is bound to be a good way to start conversations!

72

PART III

Making It Work
Together

IN THIS PART:

10

The Home Office: Word Processing, Drawing, and Creating Presentations

IN THIS CHAPTER:

When discussing what kinds of things the Mac does well, most people usually mention graphics, video, music, and other such multimedia disciplines. Something that often escapes notice, though, is the Mac's usefulness as a tool for everyday office productivity—word processing, diagrams, presentations, spreadsheets, and other such applications that have come to be thought of as strictly the domain of Windows computers and Microsoft software.

Microsoft Office for Mac OS X, which contains Mac-native versions of Microsoft Word, Excel, and PowerPoint (as well as Entourage, the Mac version of Outlook), is a fine piece of software; it's the best way to achieve complete compatibility with your Windows-using co-workers. However, Microsoft Office is expensive (as much as $300), and you might find that you can get by with the Office compatibility that's built in to Mac OS X applications that are available for much less cost or free. This chapter looks at a few of the built-in capabilities the Mac has for accomplishing the same tasks your co-workers do in Windows. Even without additional software, Mac OS X gives you the tools to create text documents, read and write Microsoft Word files, process your handwriting into text using a graphics tablet and pen, and manage fonts. Adding AppleWorks or iWork—both available as commercial packages for less than $100, or bundled free with new consumer-level Macs—gives you many additional capabilities, including many that Windows users can't match.

AppleWorks is a venerable productivity suite published by Apple and bundled with many new consumer-class Macs. It contains component applications for word processing, spreadsheets, databases, vector-based drawings, pixel paintings, and presentations. However, AppleWorks's age is showing, and most of its components are rather less than adequate in today's world. Yet it will open Word and Excel documents (as well as documents from other word-processing applications, such as WordPerfect) and save them again using those applications' native formats, allowing you to interact with your colleagues using Microsoft Office's most popular component applications. Furthermore, its vector-based drawing tools (drawings created using shapes like circles and rectangles that you can resize and stack and fill with patterns) are quite useful and well-developed, with no analogous consumer-level equivalent on Windows.

At the time of Tiger's introduction, **iWork**—which contains the applications **Pages** and **Keynote**—is a new $79 package sold by Apple and billed as an eventual replacement for AppleWorks. However, iWork does not yet contain replacements for any of AppleWorks's components except for the word processing and presentation modes, and it is not bundled free with new Macs. If your computer does not have iWork, or to create other types of documents (drawing, painting, spreadsheets, and so on), AppleWorks remains the *de facto* standard application on the Mac, although this is expected to change as iWork is further developed in the future.

73 Create a New Text Document

✔ BEFORE YOU BEGIN	→ SEE ALSO
2 Find, Launch, and Quit an Application	**18** Set a Color Label
19 Move, Copy, or Delete a Document or Folder	**94** Access Your Desk Accessories (Dashboard)

Even today, text documents are the bread and butter of computing. Whether you use your computer for video editing, email, gaming, or photography, you've most likely also found indispensable the ability to enter some quick textual notes into a document—a shopping list, a phone number, a description of the dream you had last night—and while there are specialized applications designed to handle each of these situations, nothing is more versatile than the good old-fashioned text file.

Text documents can take two forms: *plain text* and *rich text*. A plain text document has nothing in it but the letters, numbers, and other characters you type— no special formatting, pictures, defined fonts (typefaces), or other complications. A rich text document, however, can have styled text (text in bold, in italics, underlined, or in different fonts), special paragraph formatting, pictures, page layout information, and much more. Most of the features though of as being part of *word processing* are made possible with the support of rich text.

▶ KEY TERM

Plain text—A document containing only letters, numbers, and other typed characters, but no special formatting such as boldface, italics, paragraph styles, or different fonts.

Rich text—A document containing text styled in any number of ways, including different fonts, paragraph styles, boldface, italics, or even pictures and tables. In some applications (such as Mail), HTML formatting is referred to as rich text.

Word processing—A term that generally refers to creating and editing documents with rich text content, formatted for attractive printing; it also includes operational features such as text block editing, spell-checking, and style management.

Mac OS X lets you create documents in either of these two formats, using the built-in **TextEdit** application, a handy little word-processing program with some surprising capabilities. Plain text files are more versatile in many ways—you can transfer them from one platform to another, open them in very simple applications (such as Notepad in Windows), serve them from a web server to be shown natively in a browser, and so on. But rich text documents—which Mac OS X can save in RTF (Rich Text Format), HTML (Hypertext Markup Language), or Microsoft Word format—must be opened in more specialized software, such as Word.

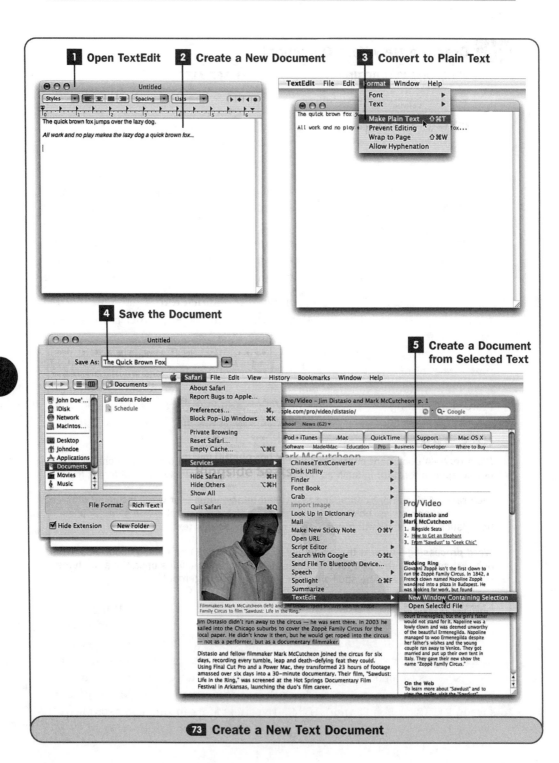

1 Open TextEdit   **2** Create a New Document   **3** Convert to Plain Text

4 Save the Document

5 Create a Document from Selected Text

73

73 Create a New Text Document

1 Open TextEdit

Open a **Finder** window, navigate to the **Applications** folder, and double-click the **TextEdit** icon.

2 Create a New Document

When TextEdit launches, a new blank document window appears, with simple formatting controls and tab markings at the top. (The presence of these controls means that TextEdit is in rich text mode.)

▶ TIP

To create a new document from scratch, choose **New** from the **File** menu.

You can now type text into the window, format it using the displayed controls and the **Format** menu, print the file's contents, and so on.

▶ TIP

Double-click a word in any selectable block of text in any Mac OS X application, and the whole word will become selected. Triple-click and the entire paragraph will be selected.

3 Convert to Plain Text

This step is optional. At any point while the document is open, if you want, you can convert it to plain text mode. You might choose to do this if you want to use the document in a web page, at the Unix Terminal command line, or another such application that can only handle plain text.

To convert the open document to plain text, choose **Format**, **Make Plain Text**.

4 Save the Document

Before you invest too much time in creating a text document, you should save the file to your hard disk. Saving files periodically as you're working on them is an excellent habit to get into.

Select **Save** from the **File** menu. The **Save** dialog box appears. Type a filename, select a location for the document, and (if it's a rich text document) choose which format—RTF, HTML, or Microsoft Word format—to save it in. (If you converted the document to Plain Text mode in step 3, this option is not available.) You can also choose whether or not to hide the filename extension; the **Hide Extension** check box is automatically selected or deselected depending on the filename you type.

73

Whatever you enter in the **Save As** box is how the filename will be displayed. If you don't type the extension, an appropriate one is added automatically to the filename and hidden.

▶ NOTE

The standard extensions are **.txt** for plain text documents, **.rtf** for Rich Text Format documents, **.html** for HTML documents, and **.doc** for Microsoft Word documents.

5 Create a Document from Selected Text

If you already have some text in another application that you want to turn into a text document, there's a quick one-step way of doing it. Select the text you want to save and open the application menu (in the example shown here, I'm saving a chunk of text I found on a web page with Safari). From the **Services** submenu, select **TextEdit**, and then select **New Window Containing Selection**. A new TextEdit window will appear with the selected text in it. You can then save the text as a new file, print it, or do whatever else you want.

73

74 Type §¶éçïå£ ¢hÁràc†érs

✔ **BEFORE YOU BEGIN**	→ **SEE ALSO**
2 Find, Launch, and Quit an Application	**108** Change the System's Language
73 Create a New Text Document	

The Macintosh has a history of being especially adept at handling special characters—accented letters, punctuation marks, mathematical or scientific symbols—in an intuitive and efficient manner. The **Option** key is what makes this possible; pressing **Option** along with any of the regular keys either creates a special symbol (such as the copyright symbol, ©) or a *combining character*, which is an entity that combines with the next character you type. For example, to create an accented e (é), you first press **Option+E** to create the acute accent combining character ('), one of a large variety of such combining characters; then you press **E** again, and the letter combines with the acute accent to create the desired character. After pressing **Option+E**, you can also press **A**, **I**, or any of several other letter keys to get an accented version of that letter.

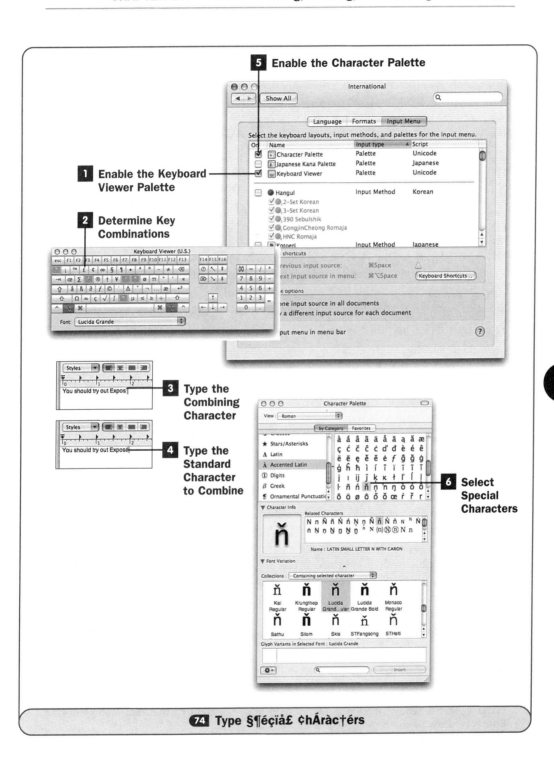

5 Enable the Character Palette

1 Enable the Keyboard Viewer Palette

2 Determine Key Combinations

3 Type the Combining Character

4 Type the Standard Character to Combine

6 Select Special Characters

74

74 Type §¶éçïå£ ¢hÁràc†érs

Every alphanumeric key on the keyboard is bound to a special **Option** key character, including a second special character binding that you get if you hold the **Shift** key as well as the **Option** key. The bindings are laid out in a carefully planned manner. Rather than making you hunt through a table for special characters or remember symbols by their ASCII number, the Mac is designed to let you memorize the intuitive built-in bindings for immediate access to commonly used symbols. Some key combinations are suggested by the shape of the character, for instance the Japanese yen character (¥), which you get by pressing **Option+Y**, or the lowercase delta (∂), which is summoned with **Option+D**. Other bindings are based on the most common usage of a combining diacritic—for instance, the **E** key generates the acute accent because the acute-accented é is so common, and the umlaut (¨) is generated with **Option+U**; the tilde diacritic (~) is generated with **Option+N** because of the common Spanish ñ character, but it can also combine to form the Portuguese ã and õ characters. Still other bindings are suggested, loosely, by the pronunciation of the natural key and the symbol, as with the trademark symbol (™) which is generated with **Option+2** (both "trademark" and "two" start with a similar sound).

It can be interesting to try to figure out the reasoning behind each key binding and to explore what each key does when combined with the **Option** key; fortunately, however, trial and error isn't the only way to figure out what keys you have to press. There are two input palettes at hand that assist in this investigation: **Keyboard Viewer**, which gives you a visual map of what each key does, and the **Character Palette**, which lets you select a character from a comprehensive grid and copy it directly into your document.

1 Enable the Keyboard Viewer Palette

Open the **International Preferences** pane (click **International** in the **System Preferences**, available under the **Apple** menu). Click the **Input Menu** tab and then enable the **Keyboard Viewer** check box. The **Keyboard Viewer** is now available in the **Keyboard Input** System Menu, a flag icon among the System Menus on the right side of the Mac's menu bar that indicates the current keyboard layout mode by its displayed icon (a U.S. flag for the standard U.S layout).

▶ TIP

The **Keyboard Viewer** can show you a lot of the most commonly used special characters, but to access all the character sets that Mac OS X supports, you must use the **Character Palette**. Fortunately, most Mac OS X applications that deal with text (such as TextEdit) have a handy option in the **Edit** menu: click **Special Characters** to pop up the **Character Palette** and browse for just the right character.

2 Determine Key Combinations

Select **Show Keyboard Viewer** from the **Keyboard Input** System Menu. The palette that appears lets you explore **Option**-key bindings visually; you can press and hold **Option** to see what each key's meaning becomes. Press and hold **Shift+Option** to see the second, alternative meanings of characters already modified by the **Shift** key. From the **Font** drop-down list, select a font for the key caps so that you can see exactly what the symbols will look like when you type them.

In the Keyboard Viewer palette, combining character keys are indicated in orange; these are the keys you must press along with **Option** to create a combining character to combine with a regular letter to produce a desired variant on that letter.

3 Type the Combining Character

In a TextEdit window (or in any other application where you can enter text, including changing filenames in the Finder), press the **Option** key combination you want. For instance, to create a capital O with a circumflex (Ô), press **Option+I** to invoke the circumflex combining character (^). The symbol appears in your text, highlighted in yellow, to indicate that the next character you type—if such a combined character exists—will be combined with the circumflex to create an accented character.

▶ **NOTE**

For symbols that don't require a combining character, such as the *c* with cedilla (ç), pressing the correct **Option** key combination creates the character immediately, and you can continue typing without having to press a second key to create the special character.

4 Type the Standard Character to Combine

Press the key that creates the "standard" version of the character to combine with the combining character. For instance, press **O** to enter a lowercase *o*, or press **Shift+O** to enter a capital O. The character combines with the preceding circumflex to form the desired character, Ô. You can now continue typing as usual.

The same procedure can be used to create any common accented character. For example, to create the Â character, press **Option+I**, then **A**. To create Ü, press **Option+U**, then **Shift+U**.

74

5 Enable the Character Palette

If you're having difficulty using the **Keyboard Viewer** (some people have trouble translating the special characters shown there to the correct key on their physical keyboard, and many special characters aren't available as standard key bindings), you can insert special characters into your text by using the **Character Palette**. You might have to do more scrolling in the **Character Palette** window than in the **Keyboard Viewer**, but the **Character Palette** lets you see exactly what you're selecting.

Open the **International Preferences** pane (click **International** in the **System Preferences** application). Click the **Input Menu** tab and then select the **Character Palette** check box to add it to the listing under the **Keyboard Input** System Menu, if it is not already enabled.

6 Select Special Characters

Click the **Keyboard Input** System Menu icon and choose **Show Character Palette**. All characters in the vast Unicode spectrum are available in this palette. From the **View** menu at the top of the palette, select the class of characters you want (such as **Roman**); depending on which class you select, a variety of different organizing categories are available. (For instance, select **Japanese** from the **View** menu if you want to browse characters by radical, by category, or by code table.) Every class lets you browse **by Category** (click that tab near the top of the palette) or by **Favorites**, which are characters that you use often (use the **Add to Favorites** button to add a character to your Favorites list).

Browse until you find the character you want; then either double-click it or select it and click **Insert** to copy the character into your current document.

74

---

75 Use Microsoft Word Documents Without Word

✔ **BEFORE YOU BEGIN**

2 **Find, Launch, and Quit an Application**
7 **Assign an Opener Application to a File**
73 **Create a New Text Document**

Mac OS X has built-in support for Microsoft Word documents; TextEdit, the work-horse text-editing application, can read documents that were created in most versions of Word, and it can write documents that Word users can open.

TextEdit can handle basic rich-text word processing; however, many features of Word documents, such as tables, collaborative editing, web links, and so on require additional software, such as *AppleWorks*, *Pages*, or Microsoft Word itself.

▶ NOTE

Be aware that applications such as TextEdit and Pages don't support all the features of Word, such as advanced table management and revision tracking. If you edit a Word document in these applications, content written using these advanced features (if present) may disappear from the document. Only use the techniques in this task if you don't have Word available!

▶ KEY TERMS

AppleWorks—A commercial application sold by Apple for about $80, or bundled free with many new Macs. AppleWorks is a suite of productivity tools, including a word processor, a spreadsheet program, a drawing program, and more components designed to provide most of the functions of Microsoft Office.

Pages—The word-processing and page layout component application in iWork, Apple's new $80 productivity suite designed to eventually replace AppleWorks.

1 Open a Word Document in TextEdit

75

If you don't have Word installed, TextEdit is the default opener application for Word documents (identified by their **.doc** file extensions). Simply double-click a **.doc** file to open it in TextEdit.

2 Save a TextEdit Document in Word Format

After you've finished typing a text document in TextEdit, you can save the document as a Microsoft Word document. Choose **Save** or **Save As** from the **File** menu; in the **Save** dialog box that opens, choose **Rich Text Format (RTF)** or **Word Format** from the **File Format** drop-down menu. Select **Word Format** to create a **.doc** file that Microsoft Office users can open without ever knowing that it was created on a Mac—and a Mac that didn't even have Office installed, at that.

Microsoft Word can read RTF documents; RTF is, indeed, a Microsoft-developed format. However, if you have included pictures, tables, or other complex items in an RTF document, Mac OS X uses a somewhat unique format for storing the document's contents. An RTF document with pictures and other objects gets the extension **.rtfd**, or Rich Text Format Directory, though the extension is usually not shown. This extension refers to the fact that the file is not a single file at all, but a *bundle* (or *package*)—a folder that masquerades as a file. Inside this folder are all the included pictures and objects, as well as the document's text, in standard RTF. You can right-click or **Control**+click an

.**rtfd** file and select **View Package Contents** to see the various items inside the document. However, Microsoft Word can't read **.rtfd** bundles, and TextEdit cannot save Word documents with included pictures and other items; if you have to create complex files that work with Word, you will need to use AppleWorks or Microsoft Word itself.

▶ **TIP**

You can also save rich text documents in HTML format in TextEdit; this is the format in which web pages are written.

3 Open a Word Document in AppleWorks

AppleWorks is a suite of applications sold or bundled by Apple that incorporates many of the features of Microsoft Office, although by no means all of them. AppleWorks can read many different types of Word documents; if TextEdit can't open a Word file, try opening it in AppleWorks instead.

You can select **File, Open** in AppleWorks, browse to the Word file you want to work with, and click **Open.** Alternatively, in the Finder, right-click or **Control**+click the Word file; from the contextual menu, select **Open With,** and then select **AppleWorks** to open the file directly in AppleWorks.

4 Save an AppleWorks Document in Word Format

You can save an AppleWorks word processing document in any of several different versions of Word format. Select **Save** or **Save As** from the **File** menu; in the **Save** dialog box, use the **File Format** drop-down menu to choose which format you want to use. For best results, use the most recent version of Word that's listed in the menu.

5 Open a Word Document in Pages

iWork is a new suite of applications sold by Apple, designed to gradually replace AppleWorks as new component applications are added to it. One of these components is **Pages,** a word processing and page layout application with many advanced features. You can open a Word document in Pages, make changes to it, and save it again in Word's native format (as well as other formats such as PDF, RTF, and HTML).

When launching AppleWorks, click **Open an Existing File** in the template chooser sheet; this allows you to navigate to the location of a Word document you want to open. Select the document and click **Open.** Alternatively, in the Finder, right-click or **Control**+click the Word file; from the contextual menu, select **Open With,** and then select **Pages** to open the file directly in Pages.

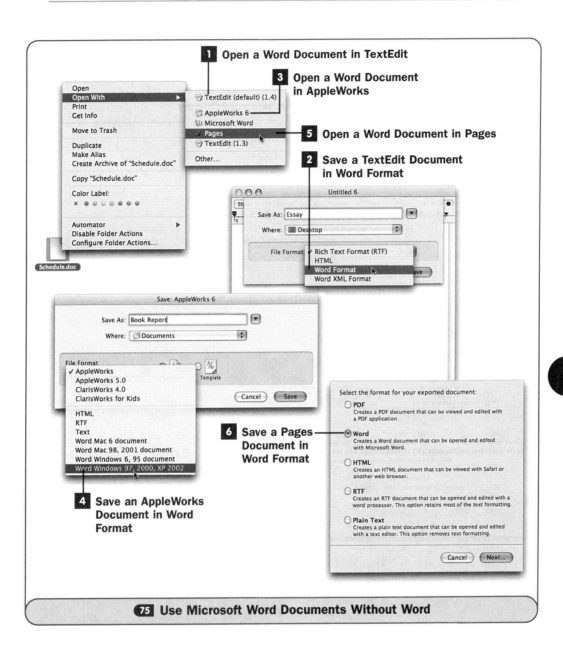

1 Open a Word Document in TextEdit

3 Open a Word Document in AppleWorks

5 Open a Word Document in Pages

2 Save a TextEdit Document in Word Format

6 Save a Pages Document in Word Format

4 Save an AppleWorks Document in Word Format

75

75 Use Microsoft Word Documents Without Word

▶ **TIP**

If you want all your Word documents to open automatically in AppleWorks or Pages, use the **Get Info** panel and the **Open with** heading to specify which application to use. Click **Change All** to apply the new setting to all Word documents. Refer to **7** **Assign an Opener Application to a File** for more information on how to do this.

6 Save a Pages Document in Word Format

You can save a Pages word processing document in five formats other than its own native format: Portable Document Format (PDF), Word, HTML, Rich Text Format (RTF), or Plain Text. Select **Export** from the **File** menu; in the sheet that appears, select the format you want to save in and click **Next**. You are then prompted for a location to save the new Word file. Navigate to the desired location, specify a name, and click **Export**.

▶ **NOTE**

Some export formats, such as Plain Text, remove features from your document that the format cannot support. To keep your Pages documents looking their best, use Pages's native file format to save; only export to another format if you want to share the document with someone who doesn't have Pages.

---

76 | **Install a New Font**

✔ BEFORE YOU BEGIN	→ SEE ALSO
73 Create a New Text Document	**77** Create a Font Collection

75

Mac OS X comes with a large variety of *fonts*, or typefaces, to use in your applications. However, nobody who has used computers for any length of time has ever been satisfied with their system's default font selections. Fortunately, there are hundreds of sites on the Web from which you can download new fonts, and catalogs of commercial fonts from which you can order if you do professional layout work.

Fonts available for download are generally available in either "Windows" or "Mac" format. Both Windows and Mac OS X can use *TrueType* or *PostScript* Type 1 fonts; however, there are subtle differences in formats, such as between the Windows and Mac versions of "TrueType" (originally an Apple technology, but popularized in a reduced format by Windows). Because Mac OS X can read Windows TrueType fonts without trouble, don't worry too much about whether to download the Mac or Windows version, if you have a choice. In fact, it might be easier to simply download the Windows version, as the Mac version is often designed for use in Mac OS 9 and earlier, in which fonts were distributed either as "suitcases" (unified files containing multiple styles) or with multiple files for the "outline" and "bitmap" font definitions. These conventions are largely obsolete with Mac OS X's smooth font technology, so you can save yourself a headache by simply downloading the unified Windows versions of fonts—but if a Mac version is available at the website where you have found a good font, try downloading both versions to see which one is higher-quality and better packaged.

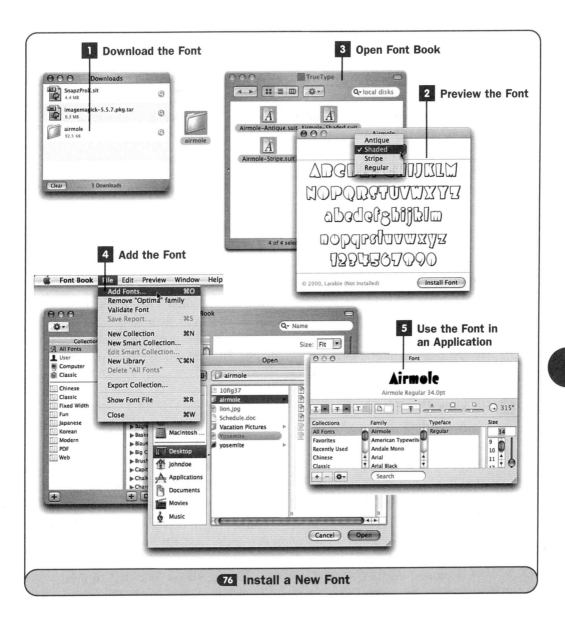

76 Install a New Font

The bottom line when it comes to fonts is that the technology is somewhat in transition, as Mac OS X and its font technologies and standards are still fairly new. Either Windows or Mac fonts ought to work for you, but Windows font packages often contain fewer files and are less confusing to use.

▶ KEY TERMS

TrueType—The most popular font technology today, TrueType was developed jointly by Apple and Microsoft in the early 1990s as a response to the Adobe-owned PostScript. "Mac" and "Windows" versions of TrueType fonts are slightly different.

PostScript—A font technology developed by Adobe in 1984, first popularized on the original Macintosh with PageMaker from Aldus.

Mac OS X lets you install new fonts so that all users of your computer can have access to them, or you can install the font just for your own use. Using the built-in **Font Book** application, you can preview and install fonts directly from the Finder. When a font has been installed using Font Book, any application can immediately use it in its documents. (Some applications may need to be quit and relaunched before they see the newly installed font.)

1 Download the Font

Download the font from the Web, or insert a disc containing new fonts in your CD-ROM drive. Downloaded fonts are usually in an archive, such as a **.zip** or **.sit** file; Safari should automatically expand the archive into a folder on your Desktop after it's done downloading. If it does not, locate the archive file and double-click it to unpack it.

76

2 Preview the Font

Double-click the font file. A panel appears showing you all the letters, numbers, and symbols in the font. Many fonts come in folders that contain several style variants (bold, italic, shadowed, striped, and so on) on the font; if you select more than one font file and then double-click on one of them, all the variants will be available using the drop-down menu in the panel.

 A valid font file is recognizable by its icon, which is of a document with the **Font Book** icon on it, or (for native TrueType fonts) a capital italic letter *A*. The label of the icon can be one of many different types (for instance, TTF, DFONT, LWFN, or FFIL, among others); Mac OS X can use any font file whose icon has the Font Book logo (or a large italic *A*) on it. If you have a choice between TrueType and PostScript (Type 1) fonts, go for TrueType.

3 Open Font Book

With the font preview window open, you're already in the **Font Book** application; select **Font Book** from the **Window** menu to open the main **Font Book** window.

4 Add the Font

Select **File**, **Add Fonts**. A dialog box appears, allowing you to navigate to the location of the new font file. Select the valid font file you were just previewing (files that aren't valid font files or folders are grayed out).

> ▶ **TIP**
>
> You can choose whether to install new fonts by default into your own user-level **Library** folder (so new fonts are available only to you), the global **Library** folder (so new fonts are available to all users of your computer), or the Mac OS 9 system you've selected for use with Classic. Set this in the **Font Book Preferences** (choose **Preferences** from the **Font Book** menu).

In this example, several valid font files for the Airmole font appear in the **TrueType** subfolder inside the newly downloaded **airmole** folder. The different font variants are well labeled by their filenames here, but often this is not the case, as with Windows fonts that are packaged with short filenames. For example, if you had downloaded the Windows version of the "Airmole" font, inside its folder would be files with much more inscrutable filenames than those seen here. However, if you double-click each file in the Finder, the preview panel that appears tells you (in its title bar) the font's full name. For instance, **airmole.ttf** is simply "Airmole"; **airmolea.ttf** is "Airmole Antique"; **airmoleq.ttf** is "Airmole Stripe"; and **airmoles.ttf** is "Airmole Shaded." You can install all of these variations, or just the ones you like.

Every font site packages fonts differently; some archives will be more confusing to navigate than others. The ease with which you can install a free font to your system depends a great deal on the individual font and the site that packaged it. This is one reason why commercially sold fonts are popular: ease of installation.

> ▶ **NOTE**
>
> When you install a font, the font file is *moved* (not copied) to the appropriate **Fonts** folder—the one in your own **Library** if you're installing it just for yourself, or the one in the global **Library** if you're installing it for all users.

> ▶ **TIP**
>
> You can also install a font using the **Install Font** button in the font preview window. This button installs the font into your personal **Library** and makes it available for you only. Another method is to install a lot of fonts at once by dragging them all into the Font Book window from the Finder.

76

5 Use the Font in an Application

In any application that supports multiple fonts, select **Format**, **Font**, **Show Fonts**. This command brings up the **Font** palette, which floats over your application window and lets you choose fonts visually. You can also use the **Font** palette to tune the font's display style, including its foreground and background colors, underlines and strikethroughs, and even drop shadows.

▶ TIPS

Click and drag the control button in the top middle of the **Font** palette to open the **Preview** pane, showing you the font's name in the selected style.

The Font palette changes its format to show more options and information as you make it bigger. Enlarge the palette using the grip in the lower-right corner, and more options and information will appear.

76

77 Create a Font Collection

✔ BEFORE YOU BEGIN

73 Create a New Text Document
76 Install a New Font

Font Book acts as an organizer for your fonts, allowing you to sort your installed fonts into functional groupings according to what you're likely to use them for. Mac OS X comes with predefined font collections such as **Fun**, **Modern**, and **Web**, which appear in the **Font** dialog box and help simplify the process of searching for the right font to use in your application. If you're writing a web page, for instance, you might want to limit yourself to the fonts in the **Web** collection, to make sure that you don't use any fonts that web viewers won't have.

You can also disable font collections or individual fonts; disabling a font collection can help further narrow down the fonts you have to search through in the **Font** panel. You can disable the **Chinese** collection, for example, if you're sure that you won't be using any Chinese text in your word processing application.

1 Open Font Book

Open the **Font Book** application by double-clicking **Font Book** in the **Applications** folder. If you're working in another application, open the **Font** palette by choosing **Format**, **Font**, **Show Fonts**; then click the **Action** button in the lower-left corner of the **Font** palette and choose **Manage Fonts** to open **Font Book**.

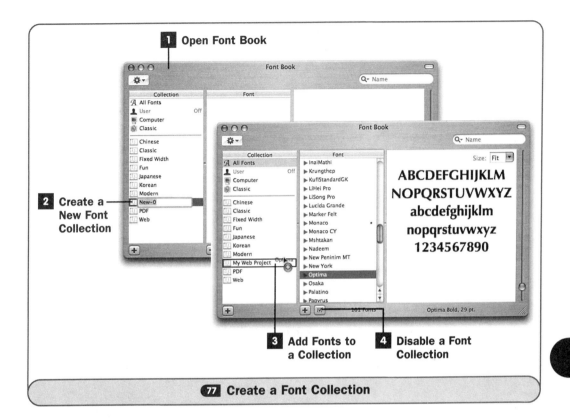

77 Create a Font Collection

▶ **TIP**

You may need to enlarge the **Font** palette (using the grip in the lower-right corner) until the **Action** button appears; the palette changes its format to show more options and information as you make it bigger.

2 Create a New Font Collection

Click the + icon under the **Collection** pane of the **Font Book** window to create a new collection. The name of the collection is selected, so that you can immediately type a new name for the collection. Press **Return** when you're done entering the name.

▶ **TIP**

To rename any font collection, double-click it in the **Collection** pane, type a new name, and press **Return**.

3 Add Fonts to a Collection

Populate your new font collection by dragging fonts from the **Font** column onto the collection's entry. Click the **All Fonts** entry in the **Collection** column to list all the fonts in your system; expand the **All Fonts** entry (using the triangle) to list only globally available fonts or fonts that are available only to you.

4 Disable a Font Collection

Select a collection to disable and then click the **Disable** button (labeled with a check box icon). A sheet appears, warning you that the collection will no longer appear in the **Font** panel; assuming that this is the whole point of what you want to do, click **Disable**. You can also use the check box to tell Font Book not to ask you for confirmation when you disable fonts in the future.

You can disable individual fonts as well; click any font in the **Font** column and then click the **Disable** button underneath that column.

If you ever want to re-enable a disabled font or collection, select it; the **Disable** button at the bottom of the column becomes an **Enable** button (an empty check box). Click it to re-enable the font or collection.

77

11

Printing

IN THIS CHAPTER:

No home office—or real office, for that matter—is complete without the ability to print your documents. It might be an electronic world, but nothing quite beats having a piece of paper in your hand that you can mark up with a red pen.

Mac OS X, with its strong pedigree in the printing and publishing industries, has an advanced printing architecture that allows every application in the system to share a unified printing setup and execution system. Every application you'll use on the Mac has **Page Setup** and **Print** commands in the **File** menu, and each application's command leads to the same dialog boxes and preview screens—and each one takes its settings from the centralized printer queue, in which you can set up as many different printers as you like. Mac OS X supports printers hooked up directly to your computer with a USB connection; network printing using AppleTalk, IP, or Bonjour; and even Windows print queues. What's more, the printing system in Mac OS X can be used to send and receive faxes over your phone line—just as easily as printing documents.

78   Add a New Printer

✔ BEFORE YOU BEGIN	→ SEE ALSO
2 Find, Launch, and Quit an Application	**79** Configure Printer Options from Any Application
73 Create a New Text Document	**80** Print to a PDF File

Before you can print anything, you have to add your printer to the system. You might have an inkjet printer connected to your Mac with a USB cable, a laser office printer that's accessible over the network by its IP address or Windows queue name, or a *Bonjour*-capable network printer that requires no setup. Mac OS X lets you configure any of these printers, add them all to your Mac's printer list, and set one of them as the default printer used by your applications.

Mac OS X comes with drivers for hundreds of popular printers. Many printer models, however, require you to download a driver and install it before it will work in Mac OS X. Most popular printer manufacturers have Mac OS X versions of their printer drivers available on their websites.

1 Connect and Turn On the Printer

Mac OS X automatically detects most printers you connect directly to the computer through USB (the most common method). Plug the printer in and connect its USB cable to your Mac; then turn the printer on and wait for it to finish its self-test cycle, which for most printers is no longer than about 10 seconds.

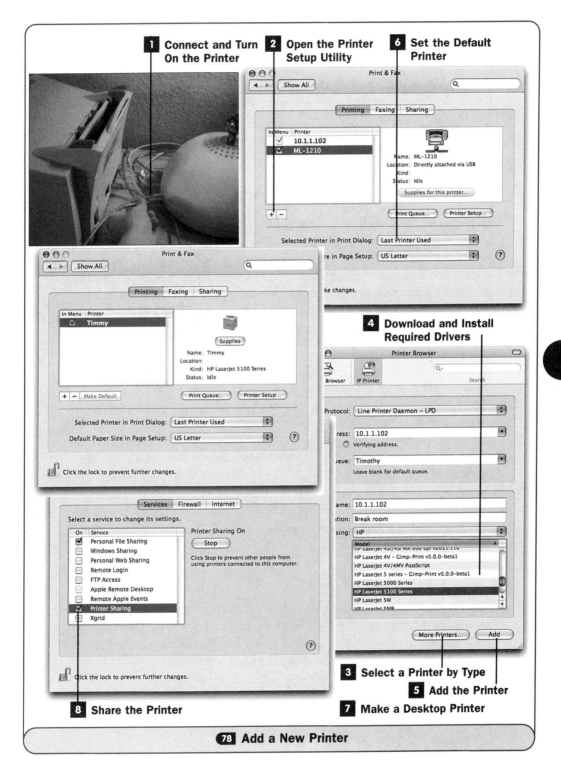

1 Connect and Turn On the Printer

2 Open the Printer Setup Utility

6 Set the Default Printer

Print & Fax

Show All

Printing   Faxing   Sharing

In Menu   Printer
☑   10.1.1.102
☑   ML-1210

Name: ML-1210
Location: Directly attached via USB
Kind:
Status: Idle

Supplies for this printer...

Print Queue...   Printer Setup...

Selected Printer in Print Dialog: Last Printer Used

...ze in Page Setup: US Letter

...ke changes.

4 Download and Install Required Drivers

Print & Fax

Show All

Printing   Faxing   Sharing

In Menu   Printer
☑   Timmy

Supplies

Name: Timmy
Location:
Kind: HP LaserJet 5100 Series
Status: Idle

+ − Make Default   Print Queue...   Printer Setup...

Selected Printer in Print Dialog: Last Printer Used

Default Paper Size in Page Setup: US Letter

Click the lock to prevent further changes.

Printer Browser

Browser   IP Printer   Search

Protocol: Line Printer Daemon – LPD

...ress: 10.1.1.102
    Verifying address.

...ueue: Timothy
    Leave blank for default queue.

...ame: 10.1.1.102

...tion: Break room

...sing: HP

Model
HP LaserJet 4SI/4SI MX 600 dpi v2011.110
HP LaserJet 4V – Gimp-Print v5.0.0-beta1
HP LaserJet 4V/4MV PostScript
HP LaserJet 5 series – Gimp-Print v5.0.0-beta1
HP LaserJet 5000 Series
HP LaserJet 5100 Series
HP LaserJet 5M
HP LaserJet 5MP

More Printers...   Add

Services   Firewall   Internet

Select a service to change its settings.

On   Service
☑   Personal File Sharing
☐   Windows Sharing
☐   Personal Web Sharing
☐   Remote Login
☐   FTP Access
☐   Apple Remote Desktop
☐   Remote Apple Events
☑   Printer Sharing
☐   Xgrid

Printer Sharing On

Stop

Click Stop to prevent other people from using printers connected to this computer.

Click the lock to prevent further changes.

3 Select a Printer by Type

5 Add the Printer

8 Share the Printer

7 Make a Desktop Printer

78 Add a New Printer

► **NOTE**

If you have a network printer, make sure that it is available on the network; Mac OS X won't be able to autodetect it, unless it's a Bonjour, Bluetooth, or AppleTalk printer.

Most networkable printers traditionally support AppleTalk, and many of the newer printers from Epson, Hewlett-Packard, Lexmark, and other manufacturers support Bonjour technology or Bluetooth. Consult the specifications for your printer, or on any printer you're planning to buy, to see whether it supports Bonjour, Bluetooth, or AppleTalk.

2 Open the Printer Setup Utility

Open the **System Preferences** application (under the **Apple** menu); click the **Print & Fax** icon to open the **Print & Fax Preferences** pane. Click the **Printing** tab to view the available printers and the options for setting up new ones. When any printer is set up and selected in the list at left, the right pane shows that printer's status and vital information, including its picture, name, location, and model name, as well as a link for buying printer supplies (ink cartridges and print media) from the online Apple Store. There are also buttons that lead to the printer's **Print Queue** (a window showing you the documents printing and waiting to be printed) and **Printer Setup** (where you can change the printer's settings).

Click the + button to add a new printer. An application called the **Printer Setup Utility** launches, with a single window labeled **Default Browser**. This window displays a list of all printers that your Mac automatically detects (such as directly connected USB printers or auto-detectable network printers), as well as allowing you (through the **More Printers** button) to search for and define new printers of all kinds, including Windows queues and manually defined IP printers.

► **TIP**

You can also launch the Printer Setup Utility manually from the **Utilities** folder, inside **Applications**.

3 Select a Printer by Type

There are many kinds of printers that Mac OS X can use. Each type of printer has its own set of configuration options; some types (such as **Bonjour** printers) are all but self-configuring, while others (particularly **IP** printers) require you to enter a fair amount of information manually.

- **AppleTalk**, **Bonjour**, and **Bluetooth** printers appear automatically by name in the browser list and usually provide their own drivers. You may need to click the **More Printers** button to browse for a printer in a different zone than the one you're in.

78

- **IP Printing** requires that you specify the printer's IP address or hostname, the printing protocol (**LPD/LPR** is most common), the queue name, and the printer model. Consult your network administrator for details on IP printers.

- **USB** printers appear listed by their model number; if a printer is connected to your Mac but a driver is not available, the grayed-out option **Please select a driver or printer model** appears in the **Print Using** menu. You'll have to download and install the appropriate driver before that printer will work.

- **Windows Printing** (available by clicking the **More Printers** button) allows you to select a Windows domain or workgroup and then navigate to a machine to choose from the printers connected to that machine. Use the **Network Neighborhood** menu option in the second drop-down menu in the **More Printers** sheet to see all the available domains.

You have two options in the **Printer Browser** window: You can browse for printers that can be auto-detected, using the **Default Browser** view, or you can specify a network printer by IP address using the **IP Printer** view.

78

If you have a printer that's available through a Windows queue or by a direct IP address, click **IP Printer** in the toolbar. Select the appropriate protocol from the **Protocol** drop-down list (**Line Printer Daemon - LPD** is usually appropriate). In the **Address** field, enter the hostname or IP address of either the printer or the Windows computer to which it is attached (if it's a networked printer on a Windows queue). In the **Queue** field, enter the name of the Windows queue if applicable; if you entered the IP address of the printer itself, leave the **Queue** field blank.

If you have another kind of printer, click **Default Browser**. This shows you a listing of all auto-detected printers, along with their connection types. To add a printer that does not automatically appear in the list, click **More Printers**. This opens a sheet that lets you select a printer from one of several different connection modes: AppleTalk, Bluetooth, Windows Printing, and several vendor-specific networking protocols, each of which has its own method of specifying the printer's network location. Select the protocol appropriate to your printer and specify the requested information if necessary, such as the Windows workgroup or AppleTalk zone; all printers in the specified workgroup or zone appear in the list. Click the desired printer to select it and then click **Add**.

The **Name** and **Location** fields at the bottom of the window are where you can enter helpful nicknames to label the printer; they don't affect the printer's operation, but help you to identify it in lists of printers. The **Name** field is automatically set to the IP address or hostname you entered or to the model name that the printer automatically reports if it was auto-detected, but you can type a new name to override it with something more memorable. If the printer's model was not auto-detected (for instance, if the **Print Using** menu says **Generic PostScript Printer** or another grayed-out option), select the printer's manufacturer from the drop-down menu; a listing appears below it where you can select the printer's specific model, such as **HP LaserJet 5100 Series**.

4 Download and Install Required Drivers

If the Printer Browser indicates that the driver for your printer is not installed (the **Print Using** menu shows **Please select a driver or printer model**), you must install the driver from the printer's installation disc, or download the driver from the company's website. Follow the instructions in the CD or the downloaded installation program to install the driver.

78 ▶ **TIP**

If you have to restart the computer after installing the driver, the Printer Setup Utility might cancel the restart process if its configuration sheet is open. Be sure to quit the Printer Setup Utility before installing the new printer driver, just to be safe.

You might be requested to restart your Mac after installing the printer driver. If you do, reopen the Printer Setup Utility after you've restarted (by repeating steps 1 and 2 in this task) and verify that the printer's manufacturer and driver are reported correctly in the **Print Using** menu. Be aware that many printer drivers have odd names, such as **GDI For Jaguar 1.0** (or something similarly esoteric). In most cases, the correct driver is what is automatically selected when you click the printer in the list.

5 Add the Printer

Click **Add** when you have successfully selected and defined the printer you want to add. The printer appears in the **Printing** page of the **Print & Fax Preferences** pane, showing its model name, location, icon, and status. The printer is also available in the **Print** dialog box in any application from which you can print.

▶ **TIP**

Use the **In Menu** check box on the **Print & Fax Preferences** pane to specify whether the printer should appear in the **Printers** menu of applications' printing dialog boxes.

6 Set the Default Printer

If you have multiple printers configured, use the **Selected Printer in Print Dialog** menu to specify which printer should be the default for your Mac (the default printer is the one that is automatically used when you print a document).

7 Make a Desktop Printer

 A *desktop printer* is an icon of one of your printers that sits on your Desktop (or in your Dock); double-clicking the icon brings up the queue viewer for that printer. Desktop printers make printing a drag-and-drop process: You can print a document simply by dragging it onto the printer icon.

First open the Printer Setup Utility by clicking **Printer Setup** in the **Print & Fax Preferences** pane, or by launching it from the **Utilities** folder. Choose **Show Printer List** from the **View** menu to display a detailed listing of all printers configured for your computer. Click the printer you want to add to the Desktop. From the **Printers** menu, choose **Create Desktop Printer**. Enter a name for the printer icon when prompted and click **Save**. The icon for the printer is added to your Desktop.

▶ TIP

If you'd rather clutter up your Dock than your Desktop, you can add your desktop printer to the Dock. You *could* simply drag the desktop printer icon itself into the Dock, but the desktop printer is itself just an alias to an item in the **Printers** folder inside your **Home** folder's **Library**. Navigate to that folder and drag the printer icon to your Dock from there. You can then throw away the desktop printer icon.

To print a document, drag the document icon directly onto the desktop printer icon.

8 Share the Printer

Open the **System Preferences** application from the **Apple** menu; click the **Sharing** icon to open the **Sharing Preferences** pane. On the **Services** tab, select the **Printer Sharing** check box to allow other people on the network to print using the printers connected to your Mac.

Another way to enable printer sharing is to open the **Print & Fax Preferences** pane (click the **Print & Fax** icon in the **System Preferences** application), click the **Sharing** tab, and then select the check boxes for any of the printers in the list under the **Share these printers with other computers** check box and heading (if the latter check box is not selected, no printers are shared).

78

With printer sharing enabled, other Macs on the network will automatically list your computer's printers in their Printer Setup Utility lists and **Print** dialog boxes. (This is accomplished using the Bonjour technology built into every Mac, which allows each computer to see all the printers—whether they support Bonjour or not—that are attached to any Mac with Printer Sharing enabled.)

---

79 **Configure Printer Options from Any Application**

✔ BEFORE YOU BEGIN	→ SEE ALSO
2 Find, Launch, and Quit an Application	**80** Print to a PDF File
78 Add a New Printer	**90** Print Photos

78

Every Mac OS X application uses the same printing setup screens. There's typically a **Page Setup** dialog box, in which you define how the application should handle fitting your document to a given paper size; and then there's the **Print** dialog box, where you can specify dozens of options specific to your printer before sending the document to be printed. You can configure everything from the number of copies to print to the Quartz and ColorSync post-processing to apply. If you frequently use complex configurations, you can save your configuration as a printing preset.

1 Open Page Setup

From TextEdit, Word, or any other application that can print, choose **File**, **Page Setup**. This command brings up the **Page Setup** dialog box, in which you define the document's layout relative to the style and size of paper that you'll be using.

▶ TIP

The **Page Setup** options often affect how the application itself displays your document, so setting up your page should be one of the first things you do when putting together your document or project.

2 Select the Paper Size and Orientation

Select the size of paper you'll be printing on from the **Paper Size** drop-down menu. Among other things, this option defines how the margins and rulers behave in your application. Then select the **Orientation** you want, using the icons to choose between landscape and portrait configurations.

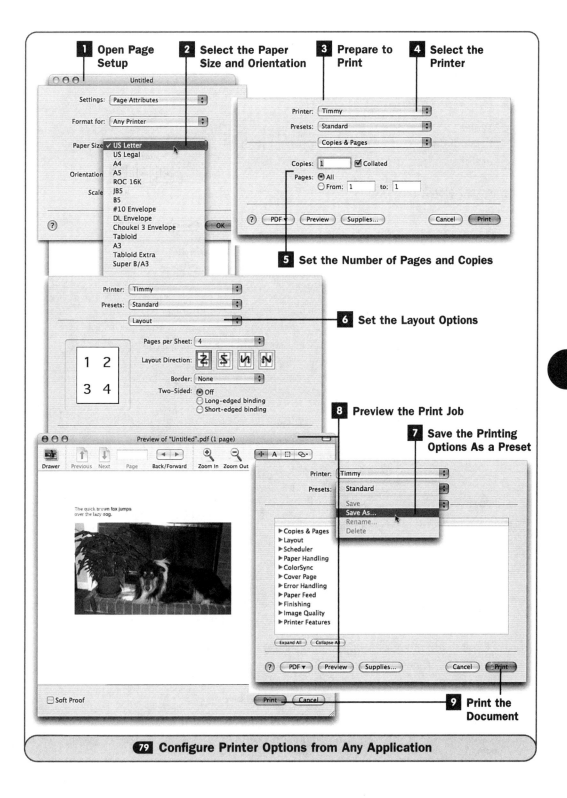

79 Configure Printer Options from Any Application

Many other options are available in the **Page Setup** dialog box; explore the various **Settings** pages to see what other levels of control you have over how your applications' pages are laid out. Click **OK** when you're done.

3 Prepare to Print

When you're ready to print the document, select **File**, **Print** to bring up the **Print** dialog box, in which you can set any of several dozen printer-specific options for how the job should be printed.

4 Select the Printer

Select the printer you'll be using from the **Printer** drop-down list. Many of the other options on the page depend on which printer you select and what it's capable of, so make sure that you select the correct printer.

5 Set the Number of Pages and Copies

Select **Copies & Pages** from the selector menu in the middle of the dialog box, if it's not already selected. Specify how many copies of the document you want, as well as which pages to print; you can print all the pages or specify a range from one page number to another.

79

6 Set the Layout Options

Select **Layout** from the selector menu in the middle of the **Print** dialog box. For multipage documents, you can have Mac OS X print more than one page worth of data on a single sheet. From the **Pages per Sheet** drop-down list, select the number of pages you want to print on a single sheet of paper.

▶ **NOTE**

For quick proofs, you can print "four-up" (meaning four pages of data on a single sheet of paper), or from two to as many as 16 pages per sheet of paper.

Use the visual **Layout Direction** icons to specify the order in which the pages should be printed. You can also separate the printed pages with a single or double outline using the **Border** drop-down list. A preview of the layout on the left shows you what the page output will look like.

Explore the many other option pages using the selector menu; define the options that need to be changed from their default settings.

7 Save the Printing Options As a Preset

After you've finished setting up your printing options, you might want to save them in a "preset" so that you can use them again in the future. Select

Save As from the **Presets** drop-down list at the top of the **Print** dialog box; enter a name for the preset and click **OK**. You can then select this preset from the **Presets** drop-down list in future print jobs, or create other presets and switch easily between them.

8 Preview the Print Job

Click the **Preview** button to see what the final printed output will look like. The preview is generated in PDF format and displayed in the Preview application (which should come as no surprise).

9 Print the Document

Whether you're in **Preview** mode or still viewing the **Print** dialog box, you can click **Cancel** to dismiss the print job or click **Print** to send it directly to the printer.

▶ **TIP**

Some applications, such as Mail and Microsoft Word, have a **Print** icon that appears in the toolbar (or that you can place there using the **Customize Toolbar** command, under the application's **View** menu). Click this icon to send a single copy of the document directly to the default printer.

79

---

80 **Print to a PDF File**

✔ BEFORE YOU BEGIN	→ SEE ALSO
78 Add a New Printer	**56** Send a Message
79 Configure Printer Options from Any Application	

Adobe's *Portable Document Format (PDF)* has become one of the most widely used document formats on the Internet, allowing printer-ready documents to be transmitted and distributed easily over the Web or through email. Mac OS X uses the built-in PDF technology to create its characteristic graphic effects, such as the transparency on menus and the smooth scaling when you magnify the Dock. One of the other nice things about PDF being integrated so tightly into Mac OS X is that it's a trivial matter for the operating system to create PDF files out of anything being sent to the screen or the printing subsystem. The upshot of this is that even if you don't have a printer connected to your computer, you can print your document to a *PDF* file, which is an exact copy of the document as it is sent into the printing queue. It's like freezing a print job for future repeated use; you can email the PDF file to a colleague, for instance, so that she can print it out for you.

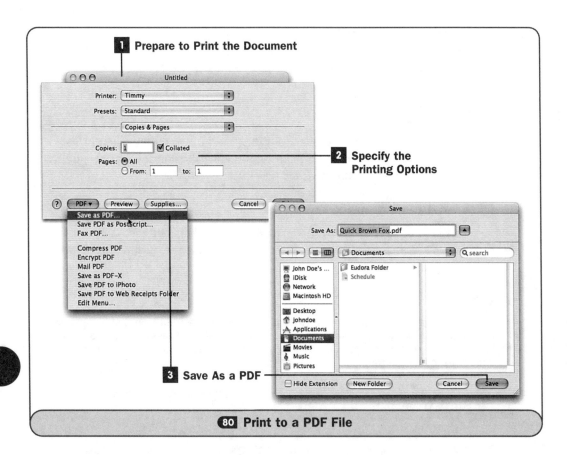

1 **Prepare to Print the Document**

2 **Specify the Printing Options**

3 **Save As a PDF**

80 **Print to a PDF File**

▶ KEY TERM

Portable Document Format (PDF)—A popular printer-ready document format developed by Adobe. PDF documents are totally self-contained and do not depend on any particular application or operating system. Mac OS X uses PDF technology as a key part of its graphics engine.

1 Prepare to Print the Document

From the **File** menu of an application such as TextEdit or Word, select the **Print** option to bring up the **Print** dialog box.

2 Specify the Printing Options

Specify the output options for your print job, using a saved preset or by going to each of the individual configuration screens (using the selector menu) and adjusting the controls to match your needs. For instance, you might want to specify a "four-up" page layout in the **Layout** screen, or define a cover page in the **Cover Page** screen.

▶ **NOTE**

Remember that many of the options in the **Print** dialog box are printer-specific. Not only do some of these options not apply to saving to a PDF file, they might be incompatible with the printer of someone else who tries to print your PDF file. It's best to use the default settings for your printer if you're going to save the print job as a PDF file.

3 Save As a PDF

Click the **PDF** button at the bottom of the **Print** dialog box to reveal a menu of PDF options; choose **Save as PDF**. In the **Save to File** dialog box that appears next, specify a name for the PDF file and a location where it should be saved. Click **Save** to create the PDF file.

▶ **TIP**

You can also choose to print to a PostScript file, using the options in the menu under the **PDF** button (which contains extra printing methods not shown as full buttons). PostScript files are similar to PDFs, and compatible with many older printers and cross-platform viewing applications.

80

12

Using iPhoto and iTunes

IN THIS CHAPTER:

If you're a music lover, a musician, a digital photographer, or a video or movie buff with a Mac, you can already count yourself lucky—you've got a computer that comes preloaded with some of the best software and tools for finding, creating, obtaining, playing, and storing all these kinds of media.

iLife is the name for the packaged collection of Apple's five leading multimedia applications that ship with all new Macs: **iTunes** (for buying and listening to digital music), **GarageBand** (for creating original musical compositions), **iPhoto** (for digital photography), **iMovie** (for digital video editing), and—if you're lucky enough to have a Mac with a DVD-writing drive (a "SuperDrive," in Apple's parlance)—**iDVD**, for writing your digital video and photography projects onto *DVDs (Digital Versatile Discs)* that you can then play on any commercial DVD player. All of these applications work in concert, sharing their digital media with each other; your digital music in iTunes is available for use in the soundtracks of your home movies in iMovie, and iMovie can export its video directly to iDVD, for example. These five applications turn your Mac into what Steve Jobs called the "digital hub": the computer that sits at the center of your digital lifestyle.

▶ KEY TERMS

QuickTime—The multimedia subsystem embedded in Mac OS X that provides for playback of all music, image, and video data.

DVD—Digital Versatile Disc, the increasingly popular CD-sized medium for commercial movies as well as home videos and computer data.

iLife—The packaged combination of iTunes, iMovie, iPhoto, iDVD, and GarageBand.

The first technology for you to understand as part of this topic is *QuickTime*, which is the underlying video playback and multimedia software subsystem embedded throughout Mac OS X and underlying all the applications in iLife. Far from being a simple "video player" application (as it may appear at first, or to Windows users who have had to install the QuickTime Player to watch video files at some time in the past), QuickTime is the basis for all the media you interact with on your Mac, from such simple tasks as handling sound input and output on your Mac to high-level ones such as watching DVD movies on your computer.

Two of the iLife components, iTunes and iPhoto, are applications with wide purpose, allowing you to harness digital music and digital photography, respectively, and perform a wide variety of tasks related to working with those kinds of media.

iTunes and iPhoto each contain a "Library" of digital content: music in iTunes, and photos in iPhoto. The other three components—iMovie, iDVD, and GarageBand—are creative applications, designed to let you start with raw media and edit it into a final presentable form (using available media from your iTunes and iPhoto Libraries) that you can then export into another iLife application or to a recipient on the Internet. These three applications are not covered in this book.

Each of the iLife applications, while designed for simplicity rather than feature richness, makes for a very complex subject; for more in-depth coverage of all of them, pick up a copy of one of the many books available that are dedicated to iLife as a package, or to iTunes, iMovie, iPhoto, iDVD, or GarageBand as an individual topic.

81 About iTunes and Digital Music

One of Apple's most legitimate claims to fame today is the digital music system formed by the jukebox application **iTunes** and the industry-defining family of **iPod** music players. Hardly anybody on the Internet today hasn't yet heard of these products which have, after years of relative quiet, made Apple into a revered household name once again.

81

The iPod, iPod mini, and iPod shuffle.

iTunes and the iPod together form a total music management system that lets you acquire and play new music, organize it into playlists, burn it onto CDs, and (using the iPod) put it in your pocket to take wherever you go. The music in question, and the reason for this revolutionary new kind of listening experience, is *digital audio*. This medium takes the form of either MP3 or AAC audio files that are formed by copying the raw audio data from a digital source (such as a music

CD) and compressing it so that each song takes up much less space on your hard disk—generally between two and six megabytes, as opposed to twenty to sixty megabytes in raw CD form—while retaining most, though not all, of its sound quality.

Digital Audio Formats

The world has accepted *MPEG-1 level 3 (MP3)* as the *de facto* standard format for digital audio; it's versatile, ubiquitous, and mostly free. MP3 files can be played just about anywhere and by anything, from PDAs to cell phones to car stereos. Best of all, they have no *Digital Rights Management (DRM)* technology. Or, perhaps (depending on whom you ask), that's the *worst* aspect of MP3 files. MP3s have been the scourge of the commercial music industry in recent years, enabling music enthusiasts to trade songs freely and amass huge collections of commercial music without paying for it. The large record labels demanded a form of MP3-like digital audio that gave users the flexibility they craved, and yet allowed copyright holders to protect their property by only allowing users to make a limited number of copies of the files; they got it in *Advanced Audio Coding (AAC)*, which is a component of the MPEG-4 standard brought to life in part by Apple.

81 ▶ **KEY TERMS**

MPEG-1 level 3 (MP3)—The most widely used format for digital music, MP3 files sound pretty good but have no copy protection built in.

Digital Rights Management (DRM)—Software algorithms that provide "copy protection" for digital music, usually enforced with digital "keys."

Advanced Audio Coding (AAC)—A new digital audio format co-developed by Apple as part of the MPEG-4 definition; AAC has better quality than MP3, as well as built-in DRM.

Windows Media Audio (WMA)—Microsoft's competitor format to AAC, WMA files are similarly higher-quality than MP3s, but their DRM is more restrictive.

AAC files can be as unfettered as MP3 files; for instance, you can use AAC instead of MP3 to encode tracks from CDs that you own. However, AAC also provides copyright holders the optional capability to control who can play them and where; keyed to a centralized database of users and protected with passwords, AAC files can't be copied from one person's computer to another without the files becoming unusable.

It's because of the DRM-protected flavor of the AAC format that the **iTunes Music Store** has become so popular where other similar ventures without industry-placating safeguards have failed: Built directly into iTunes, the Music Store is an online library of more than a million downloadable tracks in thousands of albums by the most popular commercial artists and obscure cult idols alike. Leading the market by a wide margin, and available in both the Mac and Windows versions of iTunes, the iTunes Music Store lets you buy music through an online account and download it directly into your iTunes Music Library. The purchased music, in AAC format, can be copied and played back on as many as five different computers, whether Windows PCs or Macs. This requires an Internet-based authorization process, however, and without that authorization the files cannot be opened.

Fortunately, AAC brings more to the table than just DRM restrictions; AAC files are smaller and clearer than MP3 files under most circumstances, with true separate stereo tracks and a more efficient codec (encoding and decoding) algorithm. **Windows Media Audio (WMA)** provides similar features and benefits over MP3, although the DRM infrastructure used in WMA files is more restrictive than what is found in AAC.

The downside of AAC files is that they're not as widely used as MP3 or even WMA files. Nearly all digital audio players can play MP3 files, and many can now handle WMA files as well. However, only the iPod can play AAC files. Considering that the iPod is the world's most popular portable digital music player by a huge margin, though, perhaps that is no drawback.

81

iTunes

Available for Windows as well as included with every copy of Mac OS X, iTunes is Apple's superstar application, the best current example of the company's vaunted software design sense. Millions of people have discovered it, whether introduced to it with the purchase of a new iPod, or having downloaded it on their own; indeed, it took only three days for a million copies of the Windows version to be downloaded after its introduction. Integrating intuitive playback controls, organizational lists that sort your music into its natural groupings, drag-and-drop playlist creation, one-button CD importing and burning, and the revolutionary iTunes Music Store, iTunes does everything you can imagine doing with your music—and quite likely a whole lot more.

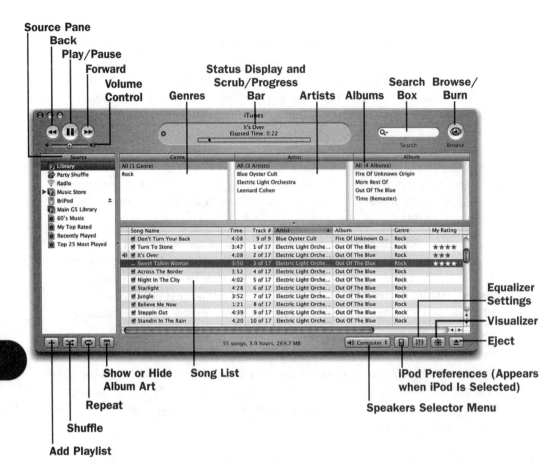

Source Pane
Back
Play/Pause
Forward
Volume Control
Genres
Status Display and Scrub/Progress Bar
Artists
Albums
Search Box
Browse/ Burn

Equalizer Settings
Visualizer
Eject

Show or Hide Album Art
Song List
iPod Preferences (Appears when iPod Is Selected)
Speakers Selector Menu
Repeat
Shuffle
Add Playlist

The main iTunes window provides many features associated with recording and playing back audio files.

Interacting with your music in iTunes is generally a straightforward and intuitive affair. However, a few things about its operation might seem surprising at first. First of all, iTunes should not be thought of merely as a "player" for audio files you keep organized in the Finder; rather, it is a separate, specialized interface for your music. iTunes doesn't use the traditional "documents and folders" computing metaphor for organizing music; instead, it treats each individual audio file as a *song*, and organizes songs on the basis of their *artists*, *albums*, and *genres*, as well as in the custom *playlists* you can define. You don't "open an MP3 file" in iTunes. Rather, you select a song from iTunes' internal **Music Library** and play it. The song you select corresponds to an MP3 or AAC file in a folder on your disk, and the folder it resides in is organized according to the artist and album—but you ideally never have to deal with the files themselves in the Finder in the course of your daily musical enjoyment. iTunes itself keeps track of all that for you.

Playing and controlling music in iTunes is much the same as in the QuickTime Player: The **Play/Pause** button starts and stops the music, the *scrub bar* lets you skip immediately to a specific place in a song by dragging the playhead, and the **Back** and **Forward** buttons skip from song to song in the current listing. Play a song by double-clicking it in the song list or by selecting it and clicking **Play**. There's nothing revolutionary about that. Where iTunes shines is in how it organizes your massive music collection and gets you to exactly the music you want.

▶ **TIP**

If you hold down the **Back** or **Forward** button, it will "fast-forward" or "rewind" the song, the same as with most personal music players.

With **Library** selected in the **Source** pane, you can browse immediately to an artist to see all the songs in that artist's albums, or to an album directly, by using **Browse** view (click the **Browse** button to reveal the navigation lists). The **Genre**, **Artist**, and **Album** lists operate in a manner similar to the Column view of the Finder: Selecting one or more items in one list narrows down which items are shown in the columns to the right (so that if you select **Rock** from the **Genre** list, only Rock artists and albums are listed in the other two columns). You can also zoom straight to a song by typing part of its title into the **Search** box. By sorting the song list by its visible columns of data, you can put all your music in exactly the order you want to play it.

Songs in iTunes' **Library** all have numerous pieces of data associated with them: Aside from the artist and album and genre, each song (potentially) has a track number, a "star" rating that you can assign, a date when it was last played, and many other such fields—all specified in the *info tags* (or *ID3 tags*, for MP3 files) embedded within the file itself. iTunes is really just a big database, managing songs by their info tags, which you can use to sort your songs into automatic ("Smart") playlists, filter them to your preference, and track how often you play them. Through the use of this information, iTunes gradually molds itself to your listening style and preferences.

▶ **KEY TERMS**

Info tags—Data fields built into a digital audio file that contain the song's title, artist, album, track number, album art, and other information. Often called *ID3 tags* in MP3 files.

81

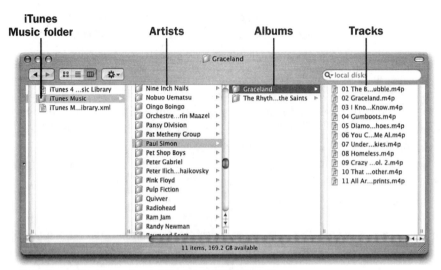

*The hierarchical structure of the **iTunes Music** folder.*

Behind the scenes, iTunes keeps all its music files—MP3, AAC, and other formats it understands—in a special **iTunes Music** folder, inside the **Music** folder in your **Home** folder. Inside the **iTunes Music** folder are folders for every artist in the **Library**, and inside those folders are folders for each album by each artist. MP3 and AAC music files are sorted into those folders, with filenames kept in sync with the info tags you specify for the song name, track number, artist, and album. This way, you can always find your music files quickly using the Finder if you have to. iTunes can also keep track of music files that aren't in its **iTunes Music** folder, but those files won't be automatically organized if you change their ID3 tags.

▶ **NOTE**

Mac OS X uses the HFS+ file system, which assigns a "Unique File ID" to each file in the system. Files can be tracked and addressed directly by applications using this ID, rather than by relying on the path through the folders to a file's location. This means that if you add a file to the iTunes music **Library**, iTunes keeps track of the file by its Unique File ID, not by its path; you can therefore move an MP3 file from one folder to another, as many times as you want, and iTunes won't ever lose track of it. This does not work in Windows.

Chances are that you've used MP3 files at some point in your life—whether you obtained them commercially, or through (*ahem*) other means. Any MP3 files you might have collected can be used in iTunes, and you can fill in any missing ID3 tags right in iTunes's interface to organize the files better. However, before you can do any of that, you must add your MP3 files to the iTunes music **Library**. And before you can add audio files to the **Library**, you must decide how you want iTunes to treat the files. You have two choices:

- iTunes can automatically *copy* any newly added audio file to the managed **iTunes Music** folder; thereafter, the audio file that iTunes uses will be the duplicated one inside its special folder, not your original. If you change the song's info tags in iTunes, iTunes renames the file accordingly and refiles it in the properly named folders. You can do anything you like with the original file; iTunes won't be using it.

- iTunes can use newly added audio files wherever they are in the system. If you change their info tags within iTunes, iTunes still keeps track of the files, but they are not reorganized or renamed.

▶ **TIP**

If you elect to let iTunes use audio files wherever they are in the system, you can later decide to copy all your audio files into the organized **iTunes Music** folder; do this by selecting **Consolidate Library** from the **Advanced** menu. This is a one-way operation; it can't be undone. However, it won't change iTunes's behavior for music files you add in the future.

To select the behavior you want, open iTunes (it's in the **Applications** folder, or click its icon in the Dock), open the iTunes **Preferences** window (choose **Preferences** from the **iTunes** menu), and go to the **Advanced** tab. Select the **Copy files to iTunes Music folder when adding to library** check box if you want iTunes to manage its own copies of your files; deselect the box if you want it to use only your original audio files wherever they happen to be.

MP3 and AAC files, by default, are set to open in iTunes. Locate an MP3 or AAC file in the Finder and double-click it; the file opens and plays in iTunes, and a reference to the file appears in the iTunes **Library**. (Note that if you double-click uncompressed AIFF and WAV audio files in the Finder, the files open in the QuickTime Player rather than iTunes.) If the file's info tags for the song name, artist, and album are set, their contents appear in the song list in the iTunes window, and iTunes can navigate to those songs using the tags.

To add an audio file to the iTunes **Library** without going through the Finder, you can select **File, Add to Library**. A navigator window pops up; use this window to locate and select the file you want to add. Click **Open** to select the file and add it to your iTunes **Library**

▶ **TIP**

Select any song in the iTunes **Library** and choose **File, Show Song File** (or choose the command from the contextual menu you get if you **Control**+click or right-click the song) to open a Finder window showing the folder containing the song file itself. You can then copy or transfer the file, or do anything else that requires you to access the file in the Finder view.

The quickest way to add a file to the iTunes **Library** is to drag it from the Finder into the iTunes application window, or to the **iTunes** icon in the Dock. When you release the mouse button, the file is added to your **Library**.

You can add a whole folder full of MP3 files in this way, too—even a hierarchical folder full of other folders. Provided that the info tags are set correctly, the files immediately become organized by their artists and albums in iTunes, rather than by their folders and filenames, as they are in the Finder. In fact, if you've got a huge collection of MP3 files on your computer already, you can import them all into iTunes in one motion, by dragging the folder they're in from the Finder into the iTunes window. It will take several minutes for iTunes to reorganize and copy all the files, but all you have to do is sit back and watch until it's done.

▶ **NOTE**

iTunes does not create duplicate entries in its database for the same audio files. You can drag a file into iTunes as many times as you want, but it will not create an additional entry or lose track of the file. This means you can safely and cleanly add a whole folder full of MP3s, even if you've already added some of the individual MP3 files to the iTunes **Library**. The **Date Added** field for those files won't even be updated.

81

MP3 files you obtain from random sources on the Internet probably don't have all the ID3 tags filled in properly—and this will prevent you from being able to take full advantage of iTunes' navigation methods to find these songs. While the song is selected or playing, simply click in the blank fields of the song in the song list to type in the proper values. Alternatively, press ⌘I to bring up the **Song Info** dialog box for the current song; in the **Info** tab, you can fill in all the info tags directly. Click **OK** when you're done.

Songs from "compilation" albums—where each track is by a different artist— should have the **Part of a compilation** check box selected in the **Song Info** dialog box. This option allows you to simplify the listing of artists in iTunes; rather than having a dozen new artists added to your Library listing with one song each from a compilation album, you can instead have the entire album show up under the **Compilations** entry in the **Artist** column. (You can disable this behavior by using the **Group compilations when browsing** check box on the **General** tab of the **iTunes Preferences** window.) At the same time, at the Finder level, this option causes the audio files from the album to be placed in a single folder named for the album itself, in a folder called **Compilations** inside **iTunes Music** (rather than each song being listed on its own in a different folder for each artist).

▶ **TIP**

Note that this automatic reorganization in the Finder only takes place if you have selected the **Keep iTunes Music Folder Organized** check box in the **Advanced** pane of the **iTunes Preferences** dialog box.

82   Purchase Music from the iTunes Music Store

✔ BEFORE YOU BEGIN	→ SEE ALSO
30 Configure Networking Manually	**83** Import (or Rip) an Audio CD
45 Sign Up for .Mac	**85** Create (or Burn) a Custom Audio CD
	86 Synchronize with an iPod

In April 2003, Apple opened the iTunes Music Store—the first online music purchasing system that allows customers to buy whole albums or individual tracks, at 99 cents a track or $9.99 an album, with no further obligation or monthly fees. Imitators have come and gone, but Apple's offering has held a commanding lead in the market, and is still the music store that has the best selection and the most consistent and least restrictive terms of use—and it's available in the Windows version of iTunes, too. You can create ("burn") audio CDs from individual songs as often as you like; you can burn unaltered playlists up to 7 times; you can play purchased music on up to five computers; and you can copy the downloaded AAC files to your iPod to take with you wherever you go. The selection of available music is vast (with some notable exceptions, such as the Beatles, under the Apple Records label, which has caused Apple recurring legal troubles), and Apple adds dozens of new albums each Tuesday.

Purchasing music through the iTunes Music Store requires you to have an *Apple ID*—an identification used to lock your purchased music files to yourself and your computer. If you have a paid .Mac account (see **45** **Sign Up for .Mac**), your .Mac email address (for example, **johndoe@mac.com**) is also your Apple ID. If you don't want to buy a .Mac membership, you can create a free Apple ID using iTunes's built-in sign-up process.

You must also be connected to the Internet before you can use the iTunes Music Store.

1   Open the iTunes Music Store

Open iTunes and click **Music Store** in the **Source** pane. iTunes connects to the online Music Store and loads its main page. From there, you can navigate the listed genres or special pages (such as the **Just Added** items), or page through the featured albums listed in the various categories (**New Releases**, **Exclusives**, **Staff Favorites**), or view the most popular downloads listed at the right side of the window.

▶ **NOTE**

Click the **See All** link on the **Just Added** section of the Music Store main page to see lists of music that has been added to the Music Store in each of the last several weekly updates.

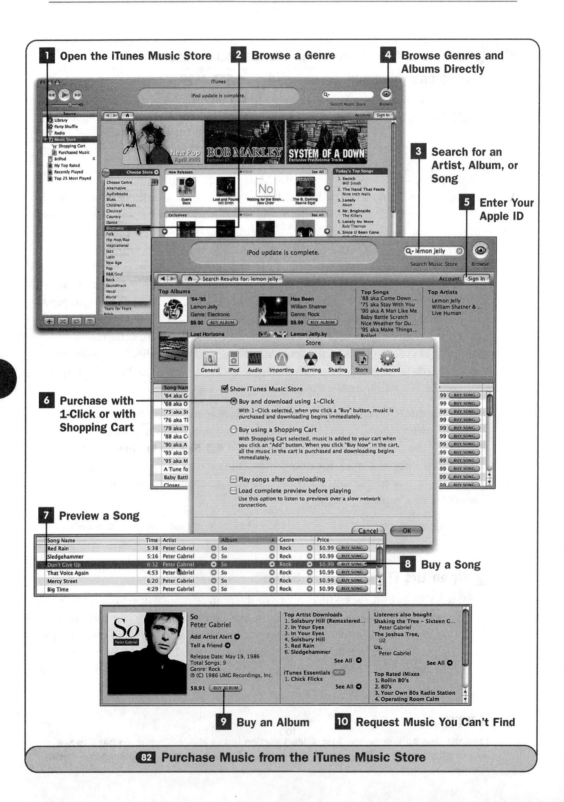

1 Open the iTunes Music Store

2 Browse a Genre

4 Browse Genres and Albums Directly

3 Search for an Artist, Album, or Song

5 Enter Your Apple ID

6 Purchase with 1-Click or with Shopping Cart

7 Preview a Song

8 Buy a Song

9 Buy an Album

10 Request Music You Can't Find

82 Purchase Music from the iTunes Music Store

If this is your first time using the iTunes Music Store, you are prompted to sign in using an Apple ID or .Mac account. If you have a .Mac account, use your .Mac email address (for example, **johndoe@mac.com**); if you don't have a .Mac account, you can create an Apple ID using the **Create Account** button. If you don't want to sign in right away, click **Cancel.** Note that you must sign in before you can buy music.

2 Browse a Genre

Select a genre from the **Choose Genre** drop-down menu at the top left. You can pick from categories such as **Classical, Rock, Electronic, Jazz, Disney,** and several others. Each genre has its own page and its own featured artists; you can scroll through them as you would the main Music Store page. Click an album cover or artist name to go to its download page.

▶ **NOTE**

Some featured artists have their own specially designed pages, with biographical information, iTunes-exclusive tracks, and other special features such as the artists' own musical recommendations from other artists. Such pages also usually have every album the artist ever released, or even special exclusive digital "boxed sets" (as in the case of U2).

82

3 Search for an Artist, Album, or Song

If you have a specific song or artist in mind, you can search for it directly using the **Search Music Store** box. Type the name you're looking for and press **Enter**; a result screen shows you all the matches that iTunes found. Double-click any of the song titles in the list to preview a brief clip of the song, or click the arrow next to the artist or album name in the list to go to its own download page.

▶ **TIP**

Click the magnifying glass in the **Search Music Store** box to narrow your search to match your input only in **Artists, Albums, Composers,** or **Songs.** Alternatively, select **Power Search** to bring up a screen where you can type more specific and customized search terms, such as a specific artist and song name.

4 Browse Genres and Albums Directly

Click the **Browse** button at the top right of iTunes to put it into the direct Browser mode. This mode works like the Finder's Column view. The Browser mode is austere but practical, and allows you to quickly navigate down through the genres to the artists, albums, and songs. Click the arrow next to any artist or album name to go to its download page.

5 Enter Your Apple ID

Unless you are signed in already, a **Sign in** button appears in the upper-right corner of the iTunes window; click it when you're ready to begin buying music. If you've used the Music Store before, simply enter your Apple ID (your .Mac email address, if you have one) and password in the box that appears. If this is the first time you've used the Music Store, however, you are taken to a series of screens where you enter your .Mac information (if you have an account) and set up your purchasing options. Follow the onscreen instructions to enter your credit card information and other data that the system requires.

▶ NOTE

If you are using a shared computer, be sure to sign out of the iTunes Music Store when you're done using it. Sign out by clicking your identity in the **Account** window in the upper right, and clicking **Sign Out** in the dialog box that appears.

6 Purchase with 1-Click or with Shopping Cart

Open the **iTunes Preferences** window (choose **Preferences** from the **iTunes** menu) and click the **Store** icon to open the **Music Store Preferences** pane. A radio button allows you to select whether to use *1-Click*, which means that songs and albums you buy will be downloaded immediately; or with a *shopping cart*, which means that instead of **Buy** buttons you will see **Add** buttons, which place your purchases into a holding area for you to download later at your leisure, piecemeal or all at once. The **Shopping Cart** option is often better if you have a slower Internet connection. Click **OK** when you're done.

7 Preview a Song

In any screen where song files are shown, such as an album page or a search result listing, you can get a 30-second preview of any song by double-clicking the song title (or by selecting the song and clicking iTunes' **Play** button). The preview is selected from the middle of each song so that you get a good idea of the main sound of the song, rather than just its first 30 seconds.

8 Buy a Song

Each song in a listing page has a **Buy Song** (or **Add Song**, if you're using a shopping cart) button next to its price in the listing. Click the **Buy Song** button to buy the track. A dialog box appears in order to confirm whether you want to buy it; the download begins when you click **Buy**.

82

▶ **TIP**

If you're using a shopping cart, songs and albums you add to the cart can be viewed by selecting **Shopping Cart** in the **Source** pane. Buy the songs or albums in the shopping cart individually by clicking the **Buy** buttons next to them, or purchase the cart's entire contents at once using the **BUY NOW** button at the bottom.

9 Buy an Album

On nearly every full album page, there is a **Buy Album** button at the top next to the cover art. Click this button to download the entire album at once. A dialog box appears in order to confirm whether you want to buy it; the download begins when you click **Buy**.

▶ **NOTE**

Not all music in the iTunes Music Store is included under the same licensing terms from the record labels. In some cases, only a partial album is available, which it might or might not be possible to buy with a single click. On some albums, there might be one or more songs that are only available if you purchase the entire album; this is usually the mark of a lopsided album with one hit and eleven tracks of filler. Other songs might be available only on a per-song basis, if they're especially short or long.

10 Request Music You Can't Find

82

Chances are that you'll be looking for some specific song or artist that doesn't seem to be in the iTunes Music Store. You can request it, however, by using the online feedback form on Apple's website.

Choose **Provide iTunes Feedback** from the **iTunes** menu. In the form that appears in your Web browser, enter your name and email address, then select **Music Requests** from the **Feedback Type** drop-down menu. In the **Comments** box, type the name of the song, artist, or album that you're look-ing for. Fill out the rest of the form appropriately. Click **Send Feedback**, and your request is sent to Apple. The Music Store is constantly being updated, with new additions made every Tuesday; if enough people request the music you're looking for, it will likely be added to the Music Store and appear in one of the weekly updates.

▶ **TIP**

Click the **My Account** link or the **Account** button to access your online account options. Among the things you can do in this area are reviewing your purchase history, requesting technical support, and selecting whether or not you want Apple to send you email notifi-cations when the Music Store is updated. Select the weekly notification option to get a message each Tuesday showing you what new music has been added.

83   Import (or "Rip") an Audio CD

✔ BEFORE YOU BEGIN	→ SEE ALSO
30 Configure Networking Manually	**82** Purchase Music from the iTunes Music Store
	85 Create (or Burn) a Custom Audio CD

iTunes exists to help you build your music collection through legitimate purchase of music. Buying it from the iTunes Music Store is rapidly becoming the preferred means of getting more music, but untold numbers of CDs are still sold every year, and you undoubtedly have a lot of CDs that you would like to import into your iTunes music **Library** for use as flexible digital audio. The process of importing digital music from an audio CD is popularly known as *ripping*.

To rip a song from a CD, iTunes must copy the uncompressed *CD Digital Audio (CDDA)* data from the disc, convert the audio stream to the compressed MP3 or AAC format, apply the song names and other data to the new file's info tags, and add them to the iTunes **Library**. Before iTunes, this was usually a process that involved three or four laborious steps; now, however, it's usually a one-button operation.

83

▶ NOTE

Before importing music from a CD, make sure you're connected to the Internet! It's possible to import successfully without an Internet connection; but if you do, the music tracks that you import will not have any titles or other useful organizing information embedded in them, and you will have to enter the track names and artist information manually. If you have an Internet connection, however, iTunes will usually be able to download this information automatically from the central database.

▶ KEY TERMS

Ripping—Creating new MP3 or AAC audio files for use in iTunes by copying them in raw form from a CD and compressing them.

CD Digital Audio (CDDA)—The raw, uncompressed digital audio format in which music is stored on audio CDs.

1 Insert a CD

Find the CD from which you want to import music and insert it into your Mac's CD drive. Wait for it to spin up and mount, a process that could take up to 20 seconds.

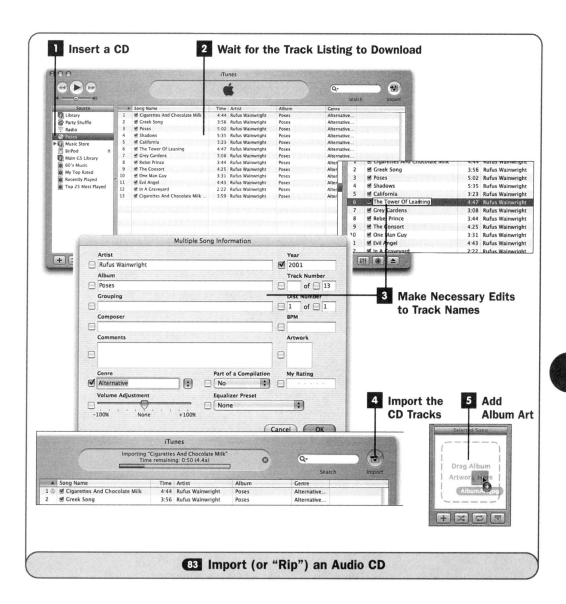

1 Insert a CD   **2** Wait for the Track Listing to Download

3 Make Necessary Edits to Track Names

4 Import the CD Tracks   **5** Add Album Art

83 Import (or "Rip") an Audio CD

83

2 Wait for the Track Listing to Download

If you're connected to the Internet, iTunes will query the centralized CD track database at **http://www.cddb.com**. If the CD is found there, iTunes downloads the track names, album title, artist name, and other information, and applies them to the tracks that appear in the iTunes window when the CD is selected in the **Source** pane.

If you're not connected to the Internet, or if it's a rare CD that isn't in the database, the CD's tracks will appear with generic names (**Track 1**, **Track 2**, and so on). You will have to change these names yourself, either before or after importing, by clicking in the field showing the name and typing the correct title.

▶ **TIP**

After the CD has been mounted and the track information downloaded, the CD appears in the **Source** pane at the left side of the iTunes window. Select the album and click the **Play** button to play audio tracks from the CD directly or double-click the CD to open its track listing in a separate window. This separate track listing can be helpful if you want to work in the main iTunes window and listen to your existing music while you import the CD's songs in the background.

3 **Make Necessary Edits to Track Names**

Although the track information from the central CD database is usually accurate (it contains information for nearly every CD ever produced), there is always the possibility of typos and other errors—after all, the information is provided by millions of volunteers like you, who are only human. Check the track names for spelling errors and inconsistencies; to edit any field, simply click it and edit it as you would a filename in the Finder. You can edit the fields after importing, of course, but it's better to fix the information before importing so that Mac OS X will remember the CD's information as accurately as possible in the future.

▶ **WEB RESOURCE**

http://www.allmusic.com

The All Music Guide website contains comprehensive information on virtually all music albums ever released, including reviews, ratings, and album art images. This site can be an invaluable reference for determining accurate track names, release dates, and songwriting credits.

If you were unable to connect to the Internet, you can manually enter the track names here as well. To enter the artist and album name for all the tracks at once, select them all (press ⌘**A**) and then open the **Info** dialog box with ⌘**I**. Enter as much common information as you want and click **OK**.

Use as many of the info tags as possible in your song files. Click a song and select **Get Info** from the **File** menu to see all the available fields you can set. The more fields you fill in, the better you will be able to organize your music. If you have a multiple-CD set, the query that iTunes makes to the **cddb.com** database might assign album names with suffixes such as (**Disc 1**) or (**1/3**). Consider removing these suffixes (so that all the discs share the exact same album name), and instead use the **Disc Number** field to define which tracks belong to which discs. This will allow iTunes to sort the tracks in the correct order, from the beginning of the first disc to the end of the last, while keeping your album list clean and organized.

4 Import the CD Tracks

When you're satisfied with the appearance of the track data, click the **Import** button at the top-right corner of the iTunes window. The songs begin importing; depending on the speed of your computer, this can take anything from a tiny fraction of the time it would take to play back the CD in real time (1/20th of the time or less) to as much as one-fourth of the time. When the CD has finished importing, the songs appear in your **Library** listing.

If you only want to import certain songs, rather than the entire disc, use the check boxes next to the song names to select the songs you want to import. By default, all the check boxes are selected; deselect check boxes for individual songs to exclude them.

5 Add Album Art

Album art can enhance your music enjoyment in many ways, from providing visual atmosphere when using the iTunes visualizer or listening to your iPod Photo, to letting you print mosaics made up of album art as jewel case inserts for custom mix CDs. iTunes allows you to insert as many pictures as you want into the info headers of your music files, opening the possibility for you to embed scans of complex album booklets full of lyric sheets and band information.

83

▶ NOTE

Since album art pictures are actually embedded into the contents of your music files (and not maintained as separate attachments), the files will grow in size as you add pictures. Very high-resolution pictures (such as scanned lyric books) can increase your files' sizes significantly, though most picture files are only a small fraction of a music file's size.

Music purchased from the iTunes Music Store comes with images of the album art already embedded in every track; but if you rip your music from CDs, there won't be any album art in the song files. You'll have to look up the album art pictures on the Internet and add them yourself. Fortunately, this is not difficult to do.

First locate an image file of the album art you want to add—usually a scan of the CD cover, which can be found at music information archives like the All Music Guide or fan sites for the artist or band in question. Save this file to your Desktop.

Next, make sure the Album Art pane is visible in iTunes. Click the **Show Album Art** button if it is not.

Drag the image file from where it is saved in the Finder into the Album Art pane in iTunes. The image is immediately added to the song and embedded in the file. Click the small "thumbnail" version of the picture to view it full-size in a separate window.

▶ **TIP**

An even quicker way to accomplish this step is to drag a picture directly from your web browser into the Album Art pane of iTunes; this skips having to save the picture to your Desktop at all.

84	**Create a Playlist or Smart Playlist**

✔ BEFORE YOU BEGIN	→ SEE ALSO
82 Purchase Music From the iTunes Music Store	**85** Create (or Burn) a Custom Audio CD
83 Import (or Rip) an Audio CD	

83

Although iTunes makes it easy to locate and play any individual song or album, sometimes you'll want to mix and match your music. It's one thing to be able to select a single artist and simply play through all the songs that artist ever produced; it's quite another to pull together a selection of your personal favorite 30 songs, a choice collection for working out at the gym, a soothing set of songs to fall asleep to, or your most highly rated rock songs from the '70s. These kinds of specialized, personalized groupings are what are known as *playlists*.

▶ **KEY TERMS**

Playlist—A grouping of songs that you create by dragging songs into it in whatever order you please.

Smart Playlist—A playlist that is automatically created according to criteria you specify, updating itself as you add new music that matches those criteria.

iTunes can create two kinds of playlists: standard ones, in which you simply make a new list and then manually add songs to it, and *Smart Playlists*, which are in fact sophisticated saved database queries that automatically select songs that match criteria you specify. (The principle is the same as with a Spotlight search in the Finder, as discussed in **14** **Create a Smart Folder That Contains Certain Types of Items**.) Smart Playlists have near-infinite versatility; how they can be configured is limited only by your imagination.

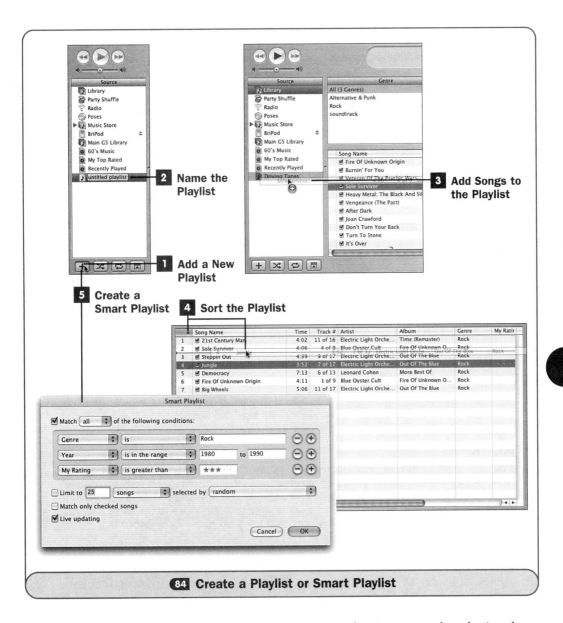

2 Name the Playlist

3 Add Songs to the Playlist

1 Add a New Playlist

5 Create a Smart Playlist

4 Sort the Playlist

84

84 Create a Playlist or Smart Playlist

Whether a playlist is standard or smart, you can play its contents by selecting the playlist from the **Source** pane on the left side of the iTunes window and then clicking **Play**. A playlist can be sorted by its manual sort order or by any of the visible columns, or you can use the **Shuffle** button to stir the playlist into a random order.

▶ **TIP**

The Party Shuffle feature selects a random handful of songs from a specified playlist and shows you your playback history and upcoming songs; you can delete queued songs from the list or add new ones manually as the playlist plays. As the name suggests, this can be great fun when you're arranging the background music for a party.

▪ Add a New Playlist

To create a new playlist, click the + button below the **Source** pane, at the bottom left of the iTunes window. A new playlist appears in the **Source** list, with the name **untitled playlist**.

▪ Name the Playlist

The name of the new playlist is selected so that you can immediately type a new name, such as **Driving Tunes** or **Hair Band Classics**. Press **Return** after typing the perfect title for your collection.

▪ Add Songs to the Playlist

Click the **Library** option in the **Source** pane to view all the songs available in iTunes; navigate to each song you want to add to the playlist and drag it to the playlist in the **Source** pane. Each new song is added to the end of the list. You might find it helpful to double-click the playlist's icon to open the playlist in a separate window as you add songs to it.

▶ **NOTE**

When you drag songs from your **Library** into a playlist, you're not removing them from the **Library**; you're merely creating a list of references to selected songs, and you can always access each song in its original location in the **Library**. You can add the same song to multiple playlists, for example, or add the same song multiple times to the same playlist. If you delete a song from a playlist, the song isn't removed from iTunes altogether.

▪ Sort the Playlist

Click the playlist in the **Source** pane to view its contents in the song list area. Click and drag individual songs to different places in the list to manually sort the list to your taste. You can also click any of the column headers to sort the playlist on that column; click the column header again to reverse the sort order. Click the first column, showing the entry numbers, to return the list to your manual sort order.

5 Create a Smart Playlist

 To create a Smart Playlist, hold down the **Option** key and click the + button; its icon changes from a + sign to a sprocket, indicating the automated mechanism underlying Smart Playlists. Alternatively, select **New Smart Playlist** from the **File** menu.

A **Smart Playlist** dialog box appears in order to give you access to the specifications of the Smart Playlist query. Various check box options are available, such as limiting the list to a certain number of songs. You can add as many organizational criteria as you want by clicking the + button after any shown criterion. You can filter songs using any of the available info tags, as well as comparison operators such as **contains** or **starts with** for textual entries, **is** or **greater than** for numeric entries, or **is after** or **is in the range** for date entries. You can, for instance, create a list composed of all songs in the **Rock** genre that were made in the years **1966–1974**, whose track number was 1. You can even specify that songs in the playlist must also belong to another playlist, such as a Smart Playlist that contains all music by any of several selected artists. The details are all up to you.

Smart Playlists are especially useful in conjunction with the **My Rating** and **Play Count** columns. For instance, you can create a Smart Playlist that consists only of songs you've rated three stars or higher, or to which you've listened at least five times, or both conditions at once. As you listen to your music, rate each song by giving it anything between one and five stars. Do this by **Control**+clicking the song and then picking a rating from the **My Rating** submenu or by selecting a rating from the contextual menu on iTunes' Dock icon. You can also configure iTunes to show the **My Rating** column and then simply click in that column to set the appropriate number of stars. As you rate your songs and listen to the ones you like best, a Smart Playlist that you might have set up to include only highly rated or frequently played songs automatically becomes populated with music.

84

▶ **TIP**

iTunes becomes more and more useful the more you use it; it hones itself to match your listening habits.

85 | Create (or Burn) a Custom Audio CD

✔ BEFORE YOU BEGIN	→ SEE ALSO
20 Burn a CD/DVD **84** Create a Playlist or Smart Playlist **78** Add a New Printer	**86** Synchronize with an iPod

"Rip, Mix, Burn," exhorted Apple's ad when iTunes was released. The whole idea of digital music management is that you can take the music you already own, import it into your computer, organize it according to your own likes and dislikes, and then make your own "mix" CDs of your favorite music arranged just the way you want them.

iTunes makes creating your own mix CDs nearly as simple as importing the music in the first place. Simply create a playlist containing the music you want to burn onto a CD, and then insert a blank writable CD into the CD-ROM drive, and let iTunes do the rest. You can then play the CD in your car, on your portable stereo, at a dance, or wherever your fancy strikes. iTunes even lets you create attractive printed inserts for your CD jewel cases, making custom-burned mix CDs into ideal gifts for music-loving friends or family members.

1 Create a Suitable Playlist

The first step in creating a custom mix CD is to make a playlist containing the songs you want on the disc. (See **84** **Create a Playlist or Smart Playlist** for details on creating a new playlist.) Drag the songs from the **Library** to the playlist, keeping in mind that typical CD-R discs can hold up to either 71 or 74 minutes of music. Don't make the playlist any longer than this! Use the statistics shown at the bottom of the iTunes window to determine how many minutes your playlist will last.

▶ TIP

iTunes can burn playlists that are longer than will fit on a single CD, if you have multiple blank CDs to use. See step 5 for details.

2 Click the Burn Disc Button

When you're viewing the playlist, the **Browse** button in the top-right corner of the iTunes window becomes a **Burn Disc** button; click it to begin the creation of the new disc.

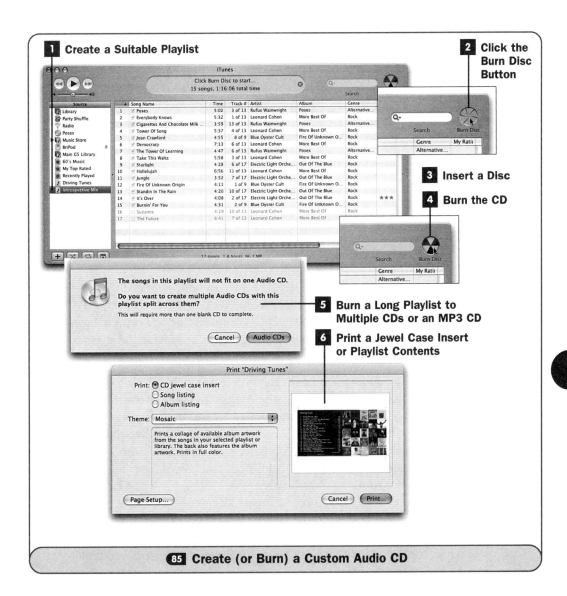

1 Create a Suitable Playlist

2 Click the Burn Disc Button

3 Insert a Disc

4 Burn the CD

5 Burn a Long Playlist to Multiple CDs or an MP3 CD

6 Print a Jewel Case Insert or Playlist Contents

85 Create (or Burn) a Custom Audio CD

3 Insert a Disc

In its display oval, iTunes prompts you to insert a blank disc. If your Mac has a CD tray, it is automatically ejected so that you can insert the disc. When the disc is inserted, iTunes recognizes the blank media and automatically changes the message in the display oval to a prompt telling you to click the **Burn Disc** button again (it is now throbbing gently) to begin burning the playlist to the disc.

If you don't click **Burn Disc** within about 10 seconds, iTunes cancels the operation and ejects the disc.

▶ TIP

4 Burn the CD

Click **Burn Disc** for the second time to begin the burn process. When the process is complete, the CD appears in your **Source** pane to show the tracks you've just burned. Eject the disc to use it in any CD player.

5 Burn a Long Playlist to Multiple CDs or an MP3 CD

If your playlist contains too much music to fit on a CD, iTunes automatically detects this when you click **Burn Disc**. iTunes asks whether you want to burn the entire playlist to multiple CDs, or to cancel the burn process and trim the playlist down to fit on a single disc.

Yet another option you have is to burn the music to an MP3 CD or a data disc, leaving the songs as MP3 or AAC files. Normally, iTunes creates an audio CD, which involves expanding each MP3 or AAC audio track into its uncompressed form and then writing it onto the disc as raw CDDA data—just like a regular music CD. An MP3 CD, on the other hand, is essentially a computer data CD-ROM full of MP3 files, identical to the ones on your hard disk. A CD can hold only 74 minutes of uncompressed CDDA, but it can hold about 12 times that amount of compressed MP3 music. Additionally, an MP3 CD can preserve all your ID3 tags for the benefit of devices that can read them and display them during playback. The downside is that although devices that can read MP3 CDs (including many factory-installed or aftermarket car stereo units) are becoming more common, they are still nowhere near as numerous as standard audio CD players, which can't handle MP3 CDs.

▶ NOTE

▶ **TIP**

You can set iTunes to create audio CDs, MP3 CDs, or data CDs/DVDs by default in the **iTunes Preferences** dialog box on the **Burning** page. You can also use that page to set various options for audio CDs, such as the length of the gap between tracks and the burning speed (cheaper brands of CD-Rs may have to be burned more slowly for reliable results).

6 **Print a Jewel Case Insert or Playlist Contents**

iTunes provides a number of attractive layout formats (or *themes*) for printing paper inserts that can be put into jewel cases for holding your custom mix CDs. You can choose several themes that take advantage of color printers, and several others that are optimized for monochrome printers; you can also select from themes that simply print textual info on solid-color backgrounds, and other themes made automatically from mosaics of the album art embedded into the songs in the playlist. For best results, make sure to add album art to all your songs in the playlist; see **83** **Import (or Rip) an Audio CD** for more information about adding album art to songs that don't have any.

Select the playlist from which you burned the CD, and choose **Print** from the **File** menu. All the options for printing jewel case inserts are provided; browse the options in the **Theme** menu to see a preview of what each layout will look like. Be sure to allow for whether your printer supports color or not; don't pick a color theme if your printer is only capable of black-and-white output.

85

▶ **NOTE**

You can also print a **Song listing** (a sheet containing a simple list of all the songs in the playlist) or an **Album listing** (a sheet with all the songs grouped by album, shown next to the album art for that album) using this dialog box.

When you've found a theme you like, click **Print**. A sheet is printed that has registration marks and full-bleed coverage, allowing you to cut out the jewel case insert with a razor knife. Fold it in half and insert it into the jewel case with your burned CD.

86 **Synchronize with an iPod**

✔ BEFORE YOU BEGIN	→ SEE ALSO
82 Purchase Music From the iTunes Music Store	**101** Synchronize Your Palm PDA and Other Devices
83 Import (or Rip) an Audio CD	
84 Create a Playlist or Smart Playlist	

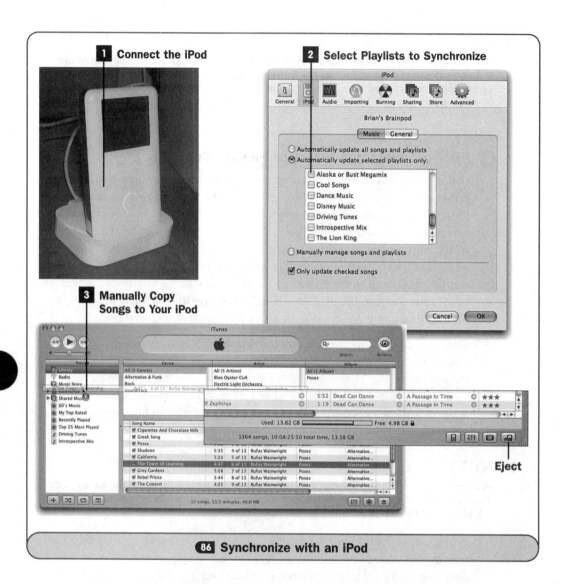

1 **Connect the iPod**

2 **Select Playlists to Synchronize**

3 **Manually Copy Songs to Your iPod**

Eject

86 Synchronize with an iPod

The iPod, iPod mini, and iPod shuffle make up Apple's own family of digital music players and the defining geek toys of our generation. With its capacious internal hard drive (or flash drive, in the case of the iPod shuffle), its small size, and its intuitive button-and-wheel interface, it has defined the field of digital audio players and spawned a horde of imitators. None of these, however, integrates so well with downloaded digital music as the iPod does—which should come as no surprise, as iTunes and the iPod are designed specifically to complement each other.

An iPod is designed to synchronize with your iTunes music **Library** simply through the act of plugging it in. However, a few complicating factors can arise, such as when you have more music in your iTunes **Library** than can fit on your iPod's internal disk. For these situations, a few alternative operating modes are available.

❶ Connect the iPod

If your iPod has a Dock, place the iPod into it. If it has no Dock, plug the FireWire or USB cable directly into the iPod's socket. In a few seconds, Mac OS X recognizes the iPod and iTunes automatically launches. The iPod appears in the **Source** pane, and iTunes automatically synchronizes with it, replacing the iPod's contents with your current iTunes **Library**. If this is the first time connecting an iPod to your computer, and unless it's the flash-based iPod shuffle, all the songs in the **Library** are transferred to the iPod; this process can take 10 or 20 minutes, depending on how large your music collection is.

iPod shuffle owners will notice a feature called **Autofill** at the bottom of the iPod's content display pane; this set of controls works like the **Party Shuffle** feature to choose a random selection of songs from a specified playlist or source to copy to the iPod shuffle. Each time you click the **Autofill** button, a new grab-bag of music selected to match your iPod shuffle's capacity is copied to the device. Autofill is not available for other kinds of iPods.

86

When the iPod's screen returns to its normal menu display and iTunes reports that it is safe to disconnect the iPod, feel free to do so. Do not disconnect the iPod while songs are being transferred—this can result in lost data. It's a good idea to leave the iPod plugged in as long as possible because doing so keeps the battery charged. (The iPod's lithium-polymer battery holds its charge best if you keep it charged as fully as possible, and don't run it until the power runs out before recharging it.)

❷ Select Playlists to Synchronize

If your iPod doesn't have enough capacity to hold all the music in your **Library**, a dialog box tells you so. Open the **iPod Preferences** window (to do this, select the iPod by its name in the **Source** pane and then click the **iPod** button at the bottom right of the iTunes window; alternatively, click the **iPod** icon in the **iTunes Preferences** window). Select the **Automatically update selected playlists only** radio button.

▶ **TIP**

The **Preferences** window does not display the on-disk size of each playlist; you must use trial and error to select a set of playlists that will fit on your iPod. Note that as your playlists change (particularly if you add more songs to your **Library** that are automatically added to a Smart Playlist), the playlists might collectively grow larger than your iPod's capacity. If this happens, you'll have to revisit your playlist selection in the **iPod Preferences** window.

In the scroll box, select the playlists you want to synchronize with your iPod. Every time you connect your iPod to your Mac, these playlists and all their contents are copied to your iPod.

3 Manually Copy Songs to Your iPod

You can configure your iPod so that it doesn't automatically synchronize with your iTunes **Library** at all. If you select the **Manually manage songs and playlists** radio button in the **iPod Preferences** window, you can select and manipulate the songs on your iPod within iTunes as you can any other music source. You can then drag songs and playlists from your iTunes **Library** directly to the iPod's icon in the **Source** list. This way, you can specify exactly which songs to put on it. This method is laborious but exact.

86

▶ **NOTE**

If you set up your iPod to be manually updated, you must eject it (use the **Eject** button at the bottom right of the iTunes window, or click the **Eject** button next to the iPod in the **Source** pane) before you can disconnect it. This is because in manual mode, the iPod is treated as an external hard drive, and iTunes no longer unmounts it automatically when it's done updating its music.

87 About iPhoto and Digital Photography

The graphics and imaging portion of the iLife suite of applications is iPhoto. Apple has focused on digital photography as the primary reason for home users to get into image processing, and they have designed iPhoto accordingly—acting as an organizer for all the photographs you've ever taken with your digital camera. And that's not where its capabilities end.

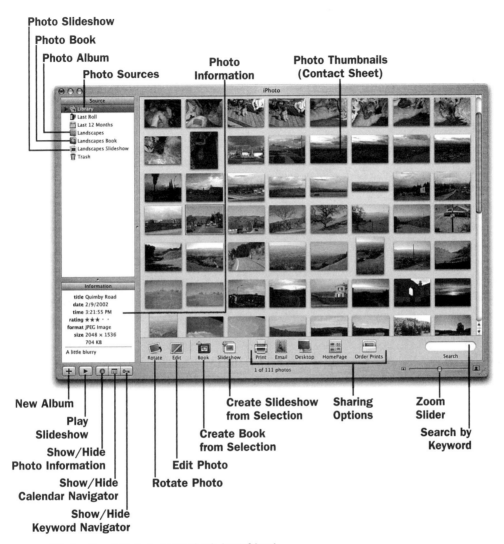

Photo Slideshow
Photo Book
Photo Album
Photo Sources
Photo Information
Photo Thumbnails (Contact Sheet)

New Album
Play Slideshow
Show/Hide Photo Information
Show/Hide Calendar Navigator
Show/Hide Keyword Navigator
Rotate Photo
Edit Photo
Create Book from Selection
Create Slideshow from Selection
Sharing Options
Zoom Slider
Search by Keyword

iPhoto, the digital photographer's best friend.

Digital photography, as anybody who owns a digital camera knows, provides a great many benefits over traditional film photography. Not only do you get to take as many pictures as will fit on your camera's memory card, and delete bad pictures immediately after you take them instead of having to wait until they come back from the developer, but the camera can store all kinds of interesting information about each picture: the date and time when it was taken, the flash and shutter settings, even the model of camera that was used. After the photos have been downloaded to your computer, you can retouch them using your favorite graphics tools, instead of having to rely on the skills of the person at the photo lab. The only thing that digital photography is missing is a way to get the digital photographs onto nice heavy paper so that you can send them to your relatives. That's where iPhoto comes in, providing the "last mile" between your imported digital photos and traditional enjoyment of your photographic efforts.

▶ **NOTE**

It's important to understand that iPhoto is not designed to be a general-purpose image organizer and viewer (like ACDSee on Windows); it's specifically intended as a digital photography tool. If you have a lot of collected image files to browse, it's possible to do so in iPhoto, but you might find another application such as **ViewIt (http://www. hexcat.com/viewit/)** to be more to your liking.

iPhoto revolutionizes the process of organizing your photos. You can scroll through them by *thumbnails* or by name, browse them by "film rolls" (each batch of photos you import from your camera is a "film roll") or by calendar date, assign descriptive names to them, and organize them into "albums" to group them by content or your own artistic pleasure. You can even share your iPhoto albums over your home network so they can be viewed by anyone else in the house with their own copy of iPhoto.

87

When you double-click any photo in iPhoto, the image opens in **Edit** mode so that you can use iPhoto's built-in retouching tools. These allow you to crop the photo, reduce red-eye, reduce blemishes (the **Retouch** tool applies a soft blur effect to what you click), automatically sharpen the contrast and color saturation (the **Enhance** button), or change the color photo to black-and-white or sepia-tone. A floating **Adjust** palette lets you control all aspects of color manipulation visually and with a high level of control; you can adjust the brightness and contrast, color saturation, temperature (red/green/blue balance), tint, sharpness/blurriness, and adjust for the camera's exposure settings to lighten or darken without losing color information. You can even straighten photos with a slider that overlays a grid on the photo and rotates the image until it's aligned with the grid—perfect for photos you've obtained by scanning old photo prints instead of importing from a digital camera. All these effects are achieved using a visual red/green/blue histogram and levels display, which you can watch update visually as you play with the adjustment sliders. A **Reset Sliders** button returns the photo to its original settings, so don't be afraid to experiment!

▶ **TIP**

If you don't like iPhoto's built-in retouching tools, you can assign a different editing program, such as Adobe Photoshop, to launch when you want to retouch a photo. Assign this third-party application by selecting the **Opens photos in** option in the **iPhoto Preferences** window and using the navigation screen that appears to find the retouching application you want to use.

▶ KEY TERMS

Thumbnail—A small version of a picture, useful when you're browsing for the picture you want.

Contact sheet—A group of thumbnail images gathered together onto a single sheet so that you can see them all at a glance.

When you crop, rotate, or edit photos in iPhoto, you aren't actually making any changes to the picture files themselves—iPhoto is merely changing how it displays them to you. If you export or share the photos, iPhoto applies your crops, rotations, and color processing to them in the process of exporting them. This allows you to revert back to the original state of any photo, exactly as it first left your camera, if you want to back out of your changes.

This technique is very similar to how iMovie operates—it keeps the original, unedited digital video clips in their pristine form and merely keeps track of pointers to the edits and rendered transitions you make so that you can always revert to the original media.

▶ TIP

At any time, you can back out of all the changes you've made to a photo or group of photos, by selecting it and then choosing **Photos, Revert to Original**.

When you're satisfied with how your photos look, iPhoto steps up to the plate by giving you a whole bevy of ways you can export or share them. These range from computerized methods for the tech-savvy—such as sending them by email, creating an online photo album on the Web, publishing them to your .Mac account so that others can use them as a slideshow, and burning them onto a CD or DVD—to methods that are much more familiar to traditional photographers: creating *contact sheets*, ordering prints on photographic paper, or creating a hardbound photo book that Apple prints and mails to you as a beautiful keepsake.

The sharing methods that iPhoto provides are all available in the **Share** menu, and (depending on which ones are checked in the **Share, Show in Toolbar** submenu) shown as icons in the toolbar at the bottom of the iPhoto window. The available sharing methods are listed here:

- The **Export** option (only available in the **Share** menu) lets you extract regular image files from iPhoto, which you can then process using whatever external tools you like. This option also lets you create a web page full of thumbnails you can place in your **Sites** folder, or make a QuickTime slideshow of the selected photos.

87

▶ **TIP**

Plug-ins (third-party tools that integrate into iPhoto) are available for the **Export** function, such as a streamlined uploader for the popular Flickr photo-sharing service (**http://www.flickr.com**). Download and install the plug-in to enable this new export functionality.

- The **Print** option lets you print your photos using a color or black-and-white printer, either one per sheet or in contact sheets.

- The **Email** option opens a new email message with the selected photos in it, ready to address to an unsuspecting friend or relation.

- The **Desktop** option creates a selection of photos that are placed in your **Desktop Preferences** pane (under the name **Screen Effects**), which you can then enable as a rotating Desktop background picture.

- The **HomePage** option publishes the selected photos to a web page on the .Mac service's servers, using any of the decorative templates and layouts provided by .Mac.

- The **.Mac Slides** option lets you upload the selected photos as a slideshow that other .Mac users can subscribe to as a screensaver. They must enter your .Mac account name in the .Mac option in their **Desktop & Screen Saver Preferences** pane (see **46 Share a Slideshow Screen Saver** for more information).

- The **Order Prints** option allows you to place an order through Apple for professional photo prints of the selected photos, on whatever size paper you like. You must have a .Mac account (or a free Apple ID) to order prints online with this option.

- The **Send to iDVD** option (if you have a Mac equipped with a DVD-burning SuperDrive) adds the selected photos as a slideshow in your current iDVD project, or creates a new iDVD project containing the slideshow.

- The **Burn Disc** option allows you to burn the selected photos to a CD or DVD.

There are two more options for things you can do with groups of photos: create a printed **Book**, and display them in a **Slideshow**. These options create specialized groupings that appear in the **Source** column for later access when you want to view or tweak them further.

- The **Book** option lets you compose a full-color picture book from your selected photos, printed to your specifications and laid out exactly as you specify. Prices for these linen-bound hardcover or softcover books range from $3.99 to $29.99 (plus extra for additional pages beyond a given number), and many

87

varieties of book formats are available. See **92 Create an iPhoto Book** for more information.

- The **Slideshow** option allows you to create a predefined presentation of a group of photos in sequence with elaborate pan and transition effects, along with any selection of music you choose from your iTunes **Library**.

The full range of iPhoto functionality is covered in *iLife In a Snap* (published by Sams Publishing) or other dedicated books on iLife or iPhoto. The next few tasks look at some of the highlights of iPhoto to get you started using your digital camera to its fullest potential.

---

88 Import Photos from a Digital Camera

→ SEE ALSO

89 Create an iPhoto Album or Slideshow
91 Order Photo Prints Online

When you plug a digital camera into your Mac, iPhoto launches automatically; you don't have to install any drivers. iPhoto goes into Import mode so that it can report how many photos you've taken and are stored on your camera, what kind of camera it is, and other such information. The **Import** button is the only thing you have to click to get your photos from your camera onto your computer and into your iPhoto **Library**.

87

1 Connect Your Camera and Launch iPhoto

Plug your camera into your Mac using the USB cable that came with it. Most cameras connect directly to the computer—all you have to do is plug it in and turn it on, and then wait a few seconds for iPhoto to launch. Some kinds of cameras have a cradle that you rest the camera in and press a button to download the photos; with other cameras, you remove the memory card and put it in a USB card reader to download the photos from it. Consult the instruction manual for your camera to determine the appropriate way to connect your camera to the Mac.

2 Import the Photos

iPhoto launches as soon as it detects that the camera is connected and turned on. The camera appears in the **Source** column at the left; iPhoto switches to Import mode and reports the model of camera (if it can be determined) and how many photos are available to import.

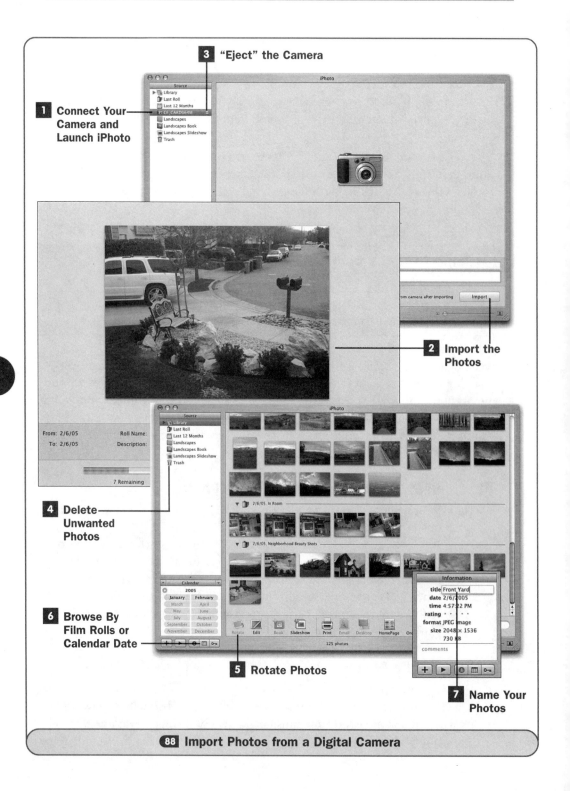

3 "Eject" the Camera

1 Connect Your Camera and Launch iPhoto

2 Import the Photos

4 Delete Unwanted Photos

6 Browse By Film Rolls or Calendar Date

5 Rotate Photos

7 Name Your Photos

88

88 Import Photos from a Digital Camera

▶ **TIP**

If you select the **Delete items from camera after importing** check box, all the photos are erased from your camera after iPhoto has finished importing them. This is the simplest way to keep your camera's memory card clean and ready for you to take more photos. If you want to leave the photos on the camera after importing them into iPhoto, deselect the check box.

Optionally, type in a name for this "film roll" (a single batch of imported photos) and a description; this can help you identify and search for these photos later, for example if this is a batch of photos from a baseball game or a ski trip and you label the film roll accordingly.

Click the **Import** button to copy the photos from your camera into iPhoto.

3 **"Eject" the Camera**

As soon as iPhoto has completed importing the photos (it will beep to let you know it's done), you should eject and disconnect the camera from your Mac. If you forget to do this, your camera's battery can waste away while you edit your pictures!

88

▶ **NOTE**

A key difference between USB (as is used on most digital cameras and the iPod shuffle) and FireWire (as used on external hard disks, camcorders, and the hard-drive-based iPods) is that FireWire is designed to carry enough electricity to power and even charge devices that are connected, as when you plug in an iPod to charge its battery, whereas USB can only provide enough power to run very low-power devices such as mice and keyboards. USB devices that rely on batteries for power will usually not be recharged by a USB connection (though the iPod shuffle will).

Some variants of FireWire (such as Sony's i-Link) do not carry any power at all, and devices (such as camcorders) that use these unpowered FireWire cables can run out of battery power when connected, just as with USB.

Many digital cameras act as mounted disks when connected to the Mac. Thus, before you simply unplug your camera from the USB cable, you should properly "eject" (unmount) the camera from the system to make sure that there is no damage done to the memory card, the camera, or the Mac. Click the **Eject** icon next to the camera's name in the **Source** column and wait for the camera to disappear from the pane. Then you can disconnect the USB cable and turn off the camera.

Some digital cameras do not need to be ejected, and unmount themselves automatically after you have finished importing your pictures. If there is no **Eject** button next to the camera's name in the **Source** column, and if iPhoto is not busy working with it, it is safe to unplug and turn off the camera at any time.

4 Delete Unwanted Photos

Now that your camera is unplugged, you can edit your photos as your leisure. Scroll through the contact sheet in iPhoto's main window to browse your newly imported photos. Use the **Zoom** slider to select a comfortable size for viewing the thumbnails.

▶ TIP

By default, when you double-click a photo in Organize view, that photo appears in iPhoto's Edit view. To save editing changes and return to Organize view, click the **Done** button. You might find it less constraining to have iPhoto open the picture in a separate editing window instead of in **Edit** view in the main iPhoto window. Select **Opens photo in separate window** in the **iPhoto Preferences** window to set this as the default double-click behavior. Editing changes are applied when you close the window or click the **Forward** or **Back** buttons.

88

Not all your photos will be masterpieces; it's best to admit that right away and delete the ones that you aren't likely to show off to all your friends. Click any photo and press **Delete** or drag it to the Trash to delete it.

Select **Empty Trash** from the iPhoto **File** menu to permanently delete all the photos you have moved to the Trash. Until you empty the Trash, all photos in the Trash can be safely moved back into the iPhoto **Library** if you change your mind.

5 Rotate Photos

Chances are that you will have taken some pictures with the camera in a vertical orientation. iPhoto lets you rotate any photo 90 degrees in either direction, repeatedly if necessary. (With some higher-end digital cameras, this is not necessary, as the camera senses when you take a vertical picture and rotates it automatically during import.)

Select any photo and then click the **Rotate** button to rotate the photo 90 degrees counter-clockwise. To rotate the photo clockwise, hold down the **Option** key while you click.

6 Browse by Film Rolls or Calendar Date

Normally, iPhoto keeps every photo that you've ever taken in a single large Photo **Library** that you can scroll through visually. It can be useful for organizational purposes, however, to divide this huge mass of photos—as huge as it will inevitably become—on the basis of "film rolls," which is how iPhoto refers to a single imported batch of photos. Obviously there's no film involved in digital photography, but it does make sense to group your photos as though they *were* part of an actual developed film roll—of which the digital equivalent is a batch of photos downloaded at once from the camera.

Select **View**, **Film Rolls** to allow iPhoto to divide its Photo **Library** by film rolls. When you have done this, each film roll is delineated by a horizontal line and a "film roll" icon along with the roll name you specified (or a generic name, such as **Roll 3**) and the date and time when the batch of photos was imported. Give an unnamed film roll a name by clicking the "film roll" icon, clicking the **Show Photo Information** button (an "i" icon), and then typing a name in the **title** field shown in the information window and pressing **Return**.

▶ **TIP**

You can expand or collapse film rolls in the Photo **Library** view for easier browsing. If you don't want to see all the photos you've ever taken, you can collapse the film rolls you don't want by clicking the triangle icon next to each one.

Film rolls have their drawbacks, though; sometimes they're not the most convenient way to organize your photos, especially if you're in the habit of taking only one or two photos at a time and then importing them immediately. (You could end up with hundreds of very small film rolls this way.) An alternate method, then, is to click the **Show Calendar Navigator** button; this displays a year calendar with month names shown in bold that contain photos. Click any bold entry to show just the photos taken that month. To zoom in further, click the right arrow next to the year; this shows you a month view that lets you select a particular week's photos or just a single day. Click the left arrow to return to the year view, or the **X** icon to unfilter your search and show all photos.

88

▶ **TIP**

Keywords can be an efficient way to organize your photos. Define custom keywords in the **iPhoto Preferences** (under the **Keywords** pane), such as **Dogs**, **House**, or **Hawaii**; assign keywords by selecting photos and choosing **Photos**, **Get Info**, then selecting the **Keywords** tab and checking the appropriate keywords. Then you can browse photos by keyword using the **Show Keyword Navigator** button in the lower left. All photos matching any selected keywords are shown.

7 Name Your Photos

After you import them, each of your photos will have a nondescript, numeric name, such as **DSCN0724** (although this name varies depending on the manufacturer of your camera). Give your photos more descriptive names; this will be very helpful in the future when you order prints or create a photo book.

First make sure the **Information** pane is shown (click the **Show Photo information** button). Click any photo to view its information. Type a title for the selected photo in the **title** field and press **Return** to set a name for the photo.

▶ **TIP**

Although the title for a photo can be just about as long as you want, certain exporting and sharing features—such as HomePage and the Photo Book—limit the **title** field to only 20 or 40 characters. It's best to keep the name of each photo as short as possible while still being descriptive. If you want to add a longer description to a photo, such as notes about when and where it was taken or under what circumstances, enter them into the **comments** field at the bottom. You can do this for an entire film roll if you want.

89 Create an iPhoto Album or Slideshow

✔ BEFORE YOU BEGIN	→ SEE ALSO
45 Sign Up for .Mac	92 Create an iPhoto Book
88 Import Photos From a Digital Camera	93 Create an Online Photo Album

88

iPhoto was designed to operate much in the same way that iTunes does—data sources in the pane on the left, media on the right, organized according to the intrinsic searching and sorting criteria in the media itself. Just as music in iTunes is organized by artist, album, and genre, photos in iPhoto are browsed by their thumbnails, by import date, by keywords, or by film roll. And just as you can create playlists of your favorite songs in iTunes so that you can play them back or burn onto a CD, in iPhoto you can create their equivalent: *photo albums*.

An album is like a playlist of pictures. You can drag as many photos as you want into an album, and you can sort them any way you want. An album can consist of photos from as many different film rolls as you want. This means you can create albums for landscape photography, family friends, holidays, Little League games, baby pictures—anything you fancy. You can even create Smart Albums that automatically contain photos matching certain criteria you specify, such as certain text appearing in any of the descriptive fields, a certain star rating, or a certain import date range. (Hold down **Option** while creating a new album to create a Smart Album.)

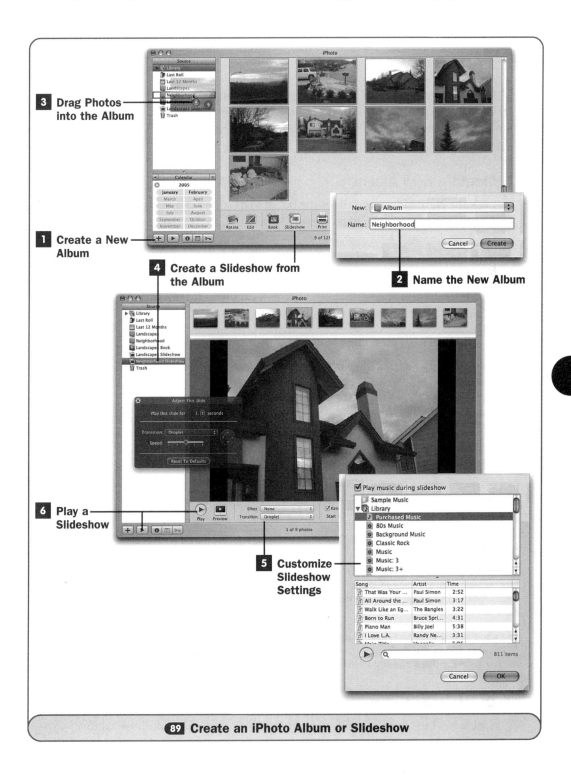

3 Drag Photos into the Album

1 Create a New Album

2 Name the New Album

4 Create a Slideshow from the Album

6 Play a Slideshow

5 Customize Slideshow Settings

89

89 Create an iPhoto Album or Slideshow

A photo album is also a convenient way to group photos for a slideshow. iPhoto allows you to start a slide presentation at any time, using the photos that are selected (if any) or all the photos in the current iPhoto window. You can start a slideshow using your entire Photo **Library** or by manually selecting the photos you want before starting the presentation. But the simplest way is to create a photo album containing just the photos you want to display, and then simply click the **Play Slideshow** button.

1 Create a New Album

Click the **New Album** button at the bottom-left corner of the iPhoto window. This button can also be used to create Smart Albums, books, or slideshows, by choosing from the **New** menu in the sheet that appears.

2 Name the New Album

In the **New Album** sheet that appears, enter a name for the new album. Click **OK** to create the album in the **Source** pane.

89

▶ TIP

You can rename an album at any time by double-clicking its title, typing a new name, and pressing **Return**.

3 Drag Photos into the Album

Populate the album with photos from your Photo **Library**. Drag photos one by one to the album icon in the **Source** pane; you can also select multiple pictures (press **Command** or **Shift** while clicking), and drag them in groups to the album. This is much easier than pasting photos into a book using those little sticky-corner doodads, isn't it?

▶ NOTE

When you add photos to an album, you're not actually moving the photos out of your **Library**—as with playlists in iTunes, you're just creating a list of references to pictures in your **Library**. The original picture remains in your **Library** so you can add it to multiple albums if you want.

You can't add the same photo multiple times to an album; if you're not sure whether or not you've added a photo into an album already, go ahead and drag it—it will just snap back into place if it's already in the album.

4 Create a Slideshow from the Album

First select the album you just created, and then click the **Slideshow** button at the bottom of the iPhoto screen to create a slideshow from that album.

iPhoto switches to **Edit Slideshow** mode, showing you all the photos in the album in a scrolling bar at the top, the current photo in the main window, and a toolbar of configuration options at the bottom.

5 Customize Slideshow Settings

At any time, you can click **Play** to start the slideshow with its current, automatically set options. You can also, however, fine-tune the slideshow to display exactly the way you want, with any of a variety of elaborate effects. For example, start by dragging photos back and forth in the bar at the top to change their display order.

One by one, select the photos from the bar at the top, or step through them using the **Left** and **Right** arrows; you can then specify an **Effect** to apply on-the-fly (make the photo black-and-white or sepia-tone), and a **Transition** effect to use in switching to the next photo in the slideshow.

The *Ken Burns effect*, named for the PBS documentarian made famous by his signature pans over Civil War photos, lets you set up similar pan effects. First select the **Ken Burns Effect** check box, then drag the photo and use the **Zoom** slider to set how the photo should look at the beginning of the pan, and then click the **Start/End** switch and use the same pan and zoom controls to set the endpoint of the pan.

89

▶ **TIP**

Click the **Preview** button to see how the photo will display and how the transition to the next photo will look.

▶ **KEY TERM**

Ken Burns Effect—A technique for specifying a combined pan and zoom effect over a still photo; used in iPhoto slideshows and iMovie.

The **Adjust** icon opens a palette that allows you to fine-tune the transition settings, including the photo's duration and special options for certain kinds of transitions, as well as the duration of the transition itself.

Finally, pick a song to play in the background of your slideshow using the **Music** icon, which brings up a navigator sheet that shows you your iTunes Library and all your playlists. Use the **Search** box to zero in on a song by name, and the **Play** button to preview it. Click **OK** to finalize your music selection.

▶ **TIP**

If you don't want any music to play along with your slideshow, deselect the **Play music during slideshow** check box.

When you're satisfied with your global slideshow settings, switch to any other view in iPhoto, such as your **Library**. Your slideshow settings are saved as soon as you adjust them.

6 Play a Slideshow

You can view your slideshow at any time by selecting it in the **Source** pane and clicking **Play**. The screen fades to black, and then the slideshow begins, featuring all the album's photos in the configuration you painstakingly defined.

Press **Escape** to quit the slideshow.

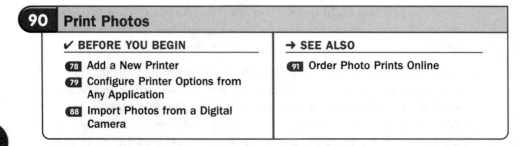

90 **Print Photos**

✔ **BEFORE YOU BEGIN**

78 Add a New Printer
79 Configure Printer Options from Any Application
88 Import Photos from a Digital Camera

→ **SEE ALSO**

91 Order Photo Prints Online

89

It's all well and good to have your photos in your computer so that you can browse them in iPhoto and show them off in slideshows. But something is missing from digital photography: the ability to hold a physical photograph in your hands, turn it around in the light, and look at it along with a stack of other photos you hold in your hand while you sit with a loved one on the couch.

You might be one of those lucky souls who owns a photographic printer, one that can print digital images directly onto heavy photo paper. But even if you're not, you can make printouts of your photos that do a reasonably good job of re-creating the experience of physical photographs, without having to order any professional prints. All you need is a good inkjet or laser printer, preferably with color capability. iPhoto does the rest.

1 Select Photos to Print

Select a photo album or a group of photos in the Photo **Library**. If you don't select any photos, all the photos in the current view are printed. To select multiple photos, press ⌘ or **Shift** while clicking photo *thumbnails*.

2 Click Print Button

Click the **Print** button at the bottom of the iPhoto window. The **Print** setup sheet opens, in which you define how you want your photos to be printed.

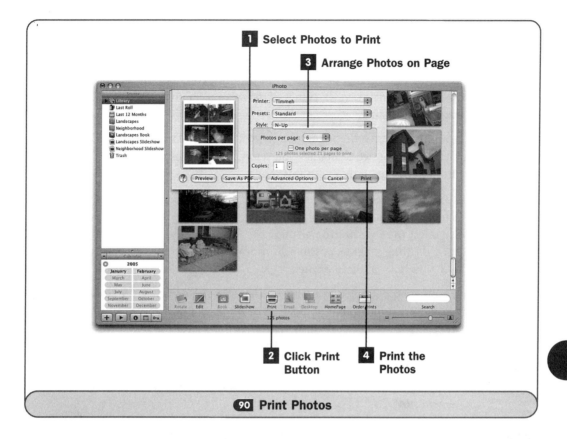

1 Select Photos to Print

3 Arrange Photos on Page

2 Click Print Button

4 Print the Photos

90 Print Photos

90

3 **Arrange Photos on Page**

iPhoto provides a number of useful ways to print your photos, all accessible using the **Style** drop-down list in the **Print** sheet:

- **Contact Sheet**. Prints all the selected photos in a grid in thumbnail form. A slider lets you select how many photos are shown on a single page, and thus how many pages iPhoto has to print.

- **Full Page**. Uses the entire 8.5"×11" sheet size to print a single photo. A slider lets you define how wide the margins should be.

- **Greeting Card**. Prints each photo on a single page, using half the sheet so that the page can be folded over and a message written on the inside.

▶ **NOTE**

iPhoto automatically rotates each photo to maximize the useful space on the page. For instance, in **N-Up** mode, all photos are printed in either horizontal or vertical orientation, depending on how they fit best.

- **N-Up**. Lets you print a certain number of photos on each page. You can select anything from 2 to 16 photos per page, as well as whether iPhoto should print **One photo per page**—in other words, if there are six photos printed on each page, iPhoto will print six copies of the first photo on the first page, then six copies of the second photo on the second page, and so on.

- **Sampler**. Prints multiple photos on each page, in varying sizes according to which of two templates you select. You can also choose the **One photo per page** option with this mode.

- **Standard Prints**. Lets you select a standard print size, such as 4×6 inches or 8×10 inches, and prints the photos to match those sizes. Unless you select the **One photo per page** check box, iPhoto prints the photos using as little paper as possible. **Standard Prints** mode is especially useful if you have a photo printer.

Select the printing options that match your needs. You can click the **Preview** button in the **Print** dialog box to open the sequence of printed pages in Preview.

90

4 Print the Photos

Click the **Print** button in the **Print** sheet or in the Preview window, and the print job will start.

---

91 **Order Photo Prints Online**

✔ BEFORE YOU BEGIN	→ SEE ALSO
30 Configure Networking Manually	**92** Create an iPhoto Book
45 Sign Up for .Mac	**93** Create an Online Photo Album
88 Import Photos from a Digital Camera	

If you aren't satisfied with how your photos look when they come out of your inkjet printer, never fear—iPhoto isn't done closing the loop of digital photography yet. Apple has partnered with the Kodak Print Service, an online photo printing company, to take orders from iPhoto users and print their photos—exactly as they have digitally cropped, enhanced, and retouched them—and send them back in the mail. With today's fast shipping, you can have physical photographs on genuine photo paper in your hands in nearly as little time as it takes the drug store to process and return your film photos to you.

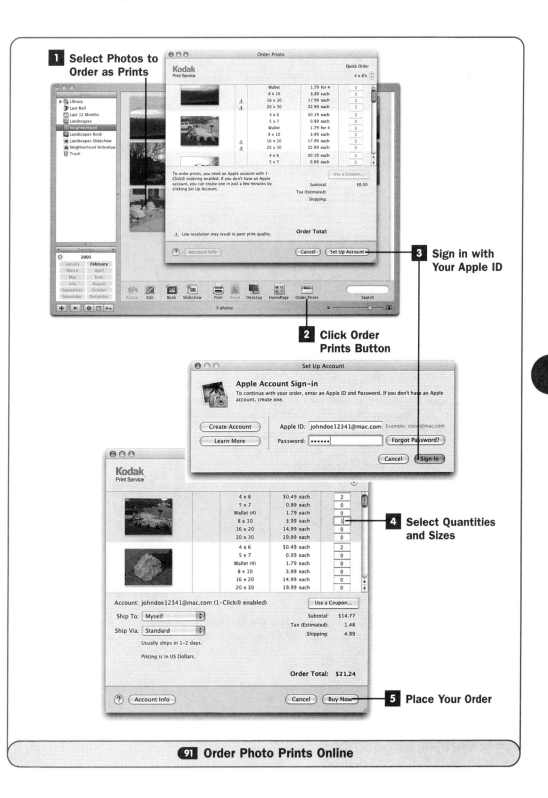

1 Select Photos to Order as Prints

2 Click Order Prints Button

3 Sign in with Your Apple ID

4 Select Quantities and Sizes

5 Place Your Order

91

91 Order Photo Prints Online

When you've finished retouching your photos and are ready to print them, use the **Order Prints** button at the bottom of the iPhoto window. After you sign in using an Apple ID (which you can obtain for free), you can specify exactly what kind of photo prints you want and how many of each. When you place your order, the high-resolution photos are processed by iPhoto and uploaded to the Kodak Print Service, where they are transferred to photographic paper and mailed back to you using the shipping service you specify. The end result is just like using film—except that you never have to leave your house!

1 Select Photos to Order as Prints

Select a photo album or a group of photos in the **Photo Library**. If you don't select any photos, all the photos in the current view are included in the order form.

2 Click Order Prints Button

Click the **Order Prints** button at the bottom of the iPhoto window. This brings up the **Order Prints** form, in which you specify how many of each photo you want printed, and at what sizes.

91

> ▶ **NOTE**
>
> You must be connected to the Internet before you can order photo prints. Also, the Kodak Print Service (and iPhoto's online ordering capability) is available only in the United States and Canada.

3 Sign In with Your Apple ID

To use Apple's online ordering system with iPhoto, you must have an Apple ID with 1-Click ordering turned on.

Click **Set Up Account**. In the **Set Up Account** dialog box that opens, enter your Apple ID and password and click **Sign In**. If you don't have an Apple ID, click **Create Account** to sign up for one.

> ▶ **TIP**
>
> If you have a .Mac account, you can use your **@mac.com** email address as your Apple ID. You might, however, have to fill in your shipping and billing information as prompted by iPhoto.

A three-step process begins if you haven't provided Apple with the necessary shipping and billing information. Fill out the forms as requested. In the first screen, answer the security question associated with your Apple ID or .Mac account. On the second screen, enter your credit card billing information, and in the third, enter your shipping information.

You can define multiple shipping addresses, which can be useful if you want to ship photos to a friend or family member, or if you want to specify whether photos should be sent to you at work or at home. Select **Add New Address** from the **Address** drop-down list to define additional addresses.

After completing the three-step process, you are signed up and able to order photos online with a single click of the **Buy Now** button.

4 Select Quantities and Sizes of Prints

Scroll through the pricing options for each of the photos in your order selection. Each photo is available in any of six sizes, ranging from wallet-sized up through poster-sized. Enter the quantities of each size of each photo you want to order; with each number you enter, the **Order Total** price is dynamically updated.

▶ **NOTE**

If any of your selected photos are too small to print at a certain size or larger, a yellow triangular "warning" sign displays on the photo thumbnail. This means that the Kodak Print Service can't guarantee that the photo will look good at these large sizes. Most modern cameras have sufficient resolution that their photos can be printed on very large paper without becoming unacceptably blocky. However, low image resolution can become a concern if you're working with older photos from early, low-resolution digital cameras, or if you've cropped a small portion from a full-resolution picture.

91

The most commonly ordered photo print size is 4×6 inches. You can use the **Quick Order** button to request copies of all your photos at that size; simply click the **Up** arrow at the top of the **Order Prints** dialog box once to request one copy of each photo at 4×6 inches. Click the **Up** button again for each additional copy you want. Click the **Down** arrow to reduce the number of copies ordered.

Select a shipping destination and a shipping method from the menus at the left. If you select **Express** shipping, the **Order Total** is increased by several dollars.

5 Place Your Order

When you're satisfied with your order, click **Buy Now**; the order is placed, your photos are uploaded to the Kodak Print Service (this might take several minutes, depending on the speed of your connection), and your credit card is charged. You will receive your photos in a few days, depending on the shipping method you selected.

92 | Create an iPhoto Book

✔ BEFORE YOU BEGIN	→ SEE ALSO
45 Sign Up for .Mac	**93** Create an Online Photo Album
88 Import Photos from a Digital Camera	
89 Create an iPhoto Album or Slideshow	

92

Apple's not content with making digital photography merely the equal of film photography; they had to come up with something additional, some feature that was compelling in its own right, that was possible only with digital photography and iPhoto. That feature is the iPhoto Book.

Using iPhoto, you can take any selection of photos and compose them into a book. This book can take on any of a number of different formats or styles ("themes"), and you can lay out the photos on the pages according to various different artistic schemes. The books include text derived from the **Title** and **Comments** fields on each photo in iPhoto, and you can adjust the text until you've got a professional-looking sequence of pages just the way you want them to look. Finally, with a couple of clicks, you can send these pages to Apple, where the book will be professionally printed and bound in hardcover or paperback (depending on the style you select), printed on acid-free glossy paper with a linen binding and a cover color that you choose. This book is then delivered to you using the shipping information defined in your Apple ID account. The whole process costs no more than $30 or $40, though the price can rise depending on the shipping options you choose or if you use more than the baseline 10 pages.

1 Select an Album to Make into a Book

To make a book, you must first select an album. Click any album in the **Source** pane of the iPhoto window to select the photos you want to turn into a book.

2 Choose a Book Style

Click the **Book** button under the right pane to create a book and switch iPhoto into **Edit Book** mode.

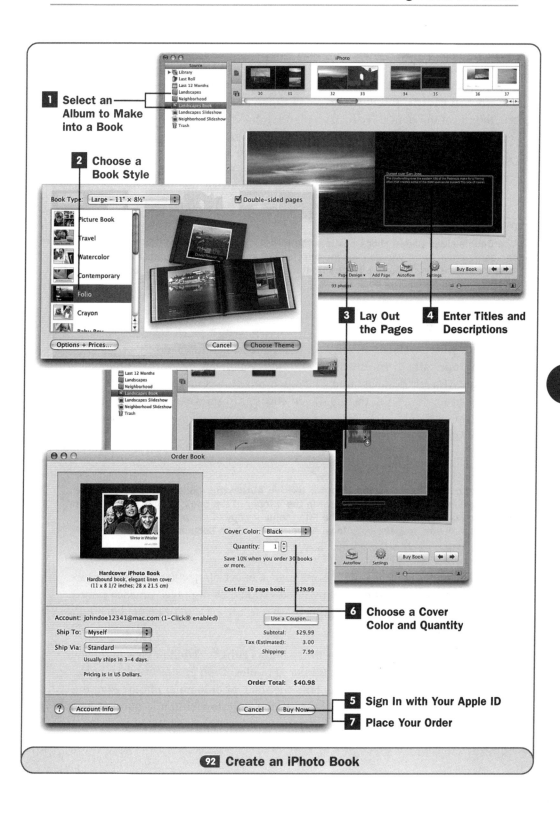

1 Select an Album to Make into a Book

2 Choose a Book Style

3 Lay Out the Pages

4 Enter Titles and Descriptions

6 Choose a Cover Color and Quantity

5 Sign In with Your Apple ID

7 Place Your Order

92

92 Create an iPhoto Book

From the sheet that appears, choose a format and layout style for your book. Click each of the options in turn to see what each style looks like. The **Story Book** theme, for instance, uses rotation and overlaps to create a "fun" look, whereas **Classic** and **Portfolio** create dignified, elegant layouts maximizing the use of the paper. **Travel** uses photos rotated slightly and placed within informal borders to develop a travelogue-like layout. **Picture Book** uses full-bleed printing to extend the photos to the very edges of the pages, and has no text. Pick the style that best matches your photos and the kind of book you want to create.

▶ **TIP**

The **Double-sided pages** check box lets you fit twice as many photos into the book for the same price; but if you go over the baseline 10 sheets of paper, double-sided pages cost more. Use the **Options + Prices** button to go to a website that describes all the pricing options for various book types.

3 Lay Out the Pages

In the next sheet, choose whether to lay the book out **Manually** or **Automatically**. If you choose **Manually**, you are given a series of blank pages with "drop zones" into which you can drag your photos from the scrolling bar (or "shelf") at the top. If you choose **Automatically**, iPhoto arranges your photos onto pages for you; you can rearrange them yourself if you want by dragging and dropping.

▶ **TIP**

The first photo in your selected album is used in **Automatic** mode for the cover of the book. If you want this photo to appear in the interior of the book as well, select the first photo and choose **Duplicate** from the **File** menu. A copy of the photo appears at the end of the album; drag the copy to wherever in the album sequence you want it to appear.

Next comes the pleasantly absorbing task of deciding which photos to place on which pages, and how many photos should be displayed on each page. Use the **Page Type** drop-down menu to select what kind of layout each page should have.

The "shelf" at the top of the window shows either a scrolling view of all your book's pages, or a view of all unplaced photos. Drag photos from the book pages in the main window up onto the shelf, or drag other photos from the shelf into blank spots in the book. Use the **Autoflow** button to automatically place all remaining photos on the shelf into new pages in the book.

92

4 Enter Titles and Descriptions

Most book styles provide areas for you to enter titles, comments, and page numbers. The titles and comments come from the contents of those fields on each of the pictures in the **Organize** view; now do you see why it was a good idea to assign titles and comments to all your photos?

You can change the titles and comments for each of your pictures in **Edit Book** view. Click a **Title** or **Comments** field on any of the layout pages; iPhoto highlights the field so you can type in it. Use the **Zoom** slider to magnify the area in which you're typing.

5 Sign in with Your Apple ID

When you're ready, click the **Buy Book** button at the bottom of the window. Your book is assembled digitally into an uploadable package, which can take a few moments; then you are presented with an order form screen, similar to the one you get when you order photo prints.

▶ NOTE

You must be connected to the Internet to order a photo book.

92

To order a book, you must have an Apple ID with 1-Click ordering turned on. If you have not set up an Apple ID account, refer to **91** **Order Photo Prints Online** for the procedure for setting up your account and billing information.

6 Choose a Cover Color and Quantity

For hardcover books, you can select from four different cover colors: black, burgundy, light gray, or navy. The preview image shows you what the book will look like in each color.

Use the **Up** and **Down** arrows next to the **Quantity** field to select how many copies of the book you want to order. The **Order Total** price is updated dynamically as you adjust the **Quantity** field. Select the shipping destination and method from the menus at left; if you select **Express** shipping, it will cost a few dollars extra.

7 Place Your Order

Click **Buy Now** when you're ready to order your book. The image data is uploaded to the server; this might take a few moments, depending on the speed of your connection. Your credit card is charged, and the book will be delivered to your shipping address in a few days.

93 Create an Online Photo Album

✔ BEFORE YOU BEGIN	→ SEE ALSO
45 Sign Up for .Mac	**46** Share a Slideshow Screen Saver
88 Import Photos from a Digital Camera	**47** Create a .Mac Web Page
89 Create an iPhoto Album or Slideshow	

93

The synthesis of digital and traditional photography comes in iPhoto's ability to take your photos and transform them instantly into an online album that everybody can view, no matter where they are. With an online album in the form of a web page, your photos can reach all your friends and family in the comfort of their own desks or laptops; you don't have to show them a slideshow in iPhoto, nor do you have to physically send them photographs in an envelope. All you have to do is email them a URL.

To create a HomePage photo album, you must have a .Mac account. Use the **.Mac Preferences** pane to sign up for a .Mac account if you don't have one (see **45 Sign Up for .Mac**) or to enter your .Mac account information if you have already signed up.

◼ Select a Group of Photos to Publish

Select a group of photos, either in the main **Photo Library** or in an album; if you don't select any photos, the HomePage function uses all the photos in the current view. Be careful—if you have hundreds of photos in your **Photo Library**, you could end up publishing a photo album page with hundreds of pictures on it!

For best results, try to keep your album limited to 20 or 30 pictures at most.

◼ Click the HomePage Button

Click the **HomePage** button at the bottom of the iPhoto window. This brings up the Publish **HomePage** dialog box in which you can configure your online album page before uploading it to your .Mac account.

▶ NOTE

You must be connected to the Internet to create an online album.

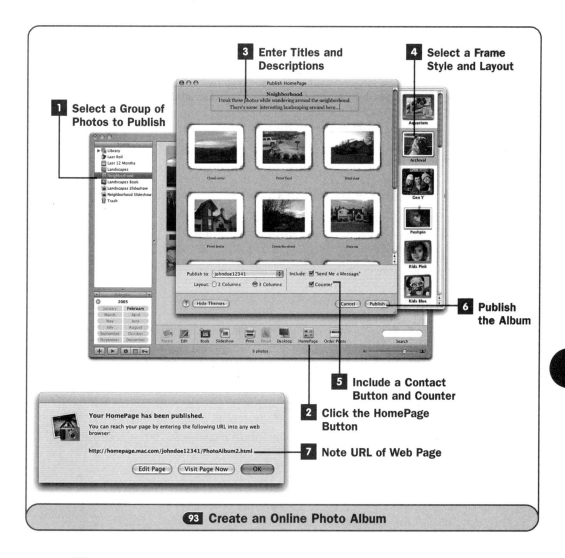

3 Enter Titles and Descriptions

4 Select a Frame Style and Layout

1 Select a Group of Photos to Publish

6 Publish the Album

5 Include a Contact Button and Counter

2 Click the HomePage Button

7 Note URL of Web Page

93 Create an Online Photo Album

3 Enter Titles and Descriptions

The album page provides several editable text fields—the title at the top, a block of descriptive text for the whole page, and titles for each of the pictures on the page. Click to edit each field, being careful to keep the text limited to the size that iPhoto enforces. The descriptive text field for the entire page, for example, can be no more than 150 characters in length.

4 Select a Frame Style and Layout

In the drawer at the right of the **Publish HomePage** dialog box, click any of the 22 frame and background styles to choose a theme for the page. Each of the frames changes the font to a common typeface appropriate to the page style.

▶ **TIP**

.Mac's **HomePage** function provides many more themes than what is available in iPhoto. If you want, after you have published your photo album, you can visit the .Mac website (**http://www.mac.com**) and log in to the iPhoto online album, which is listed among your other HomePage pages. Select one of the other themes available through .Mac to spruce up your album page even more.

Use the radio buttons to choose whether the page should have two or three columns of pictures.

5 Include a Contact Button and Counter

Apple provides a couple of useful options you can enable if you want: a **Send Me a Message** button, which people can use to contact you by email, and a page **Counter**, which lets you keep track of how many people have viewed your page. Select one or both of these check boxes.

6 Publish the Album

When you're done fixing the page the way you want it, click **Publish**. The pictures are scaled down appropriately and thumbnails are created; the images and the web page are then uploaded to the .Mac server.

7 Note the URL of the Web Page

When the album has uploaded successfully, iPhoto reports to you the URL for the online album. Copy this URL into an email message so that you can send it to all your friends and family!

93

13

Data Management: Desk Accessories, Address Book, iCal, and iSync

IN THIS CHAPTER:

Modern computing involves a lot more than simply running applications and browsing the Web. These days, the Internet lifestyle includes not just the computer on your desk, but your laptop, your other computer at work, your Personal Digital Assistant (PDA), your iPod, your cellular phone—a whole belt full of devices that all serve to organize the ocean of digital information that washes around you. Hundreds of names, email addresses, phone numbers, fax numbers, scheduled events, Internet bookmarks, and other pieces of assorted data flood through your head as well as your computer—and every one of your devices, including multiple computers if you have them, can all use the same kinds of data. Your cell phone and PDA can both store directories of contacts and scheduled items—and wouldn't it be great if those directories could match what's stored in your computer?

Address Book, iCal, and iSync are three of the utilities that allow you to manage your data and keep the contents of your digital devices synchronized, with a minimum of effort on your part. These utilities work in conjunction with larger applications such as Mail and Safari, corralling your contacts and bookmarks and transmitting them from device to device while you work. Address Book keeps track of all your email correspondents, friends, family, and business associates; iCal allows you to schedule events and To Do items. iSync keeps all your devices—Palm-compatible PDAs, iPods, and cell phones—synchronized whenever they're connected to your Mac so that you can grab them at any time and access the most up-to-date versions of all the pieces of data that make up your online life. Finally, if you have a .Mac account (see **45** **Sign Up for .Mac**), Mac OS X operates in the background, using Apple's central servers to keep each of your computers' data synchronized with each other at all times so that the same information is always available no matter which computer you use.

Mac OS X Tiger comes with a variety of small applications designed to help you accomplish small everyday tasks: a calculator, a dictionary, a translation tool, a weather monitor, a unit converter, an iTunes controller, and yellow sticky notes on which you can jot text messages to yourself, among many other such examples. These little tools—*desk accessories*—are not applications that stand alone in their own right, but exist in a separate layer that you can think of as floating just out of the range of sight, in a space known as *Dashboard*. With the touch of a key, you can summon Dashboard onto your screen, bringing with it all your desk accessories that you have activated. This is the most convenient way yet to summon a calculator to perform some quick math or to post a sticky note to remind you of something you have to do.

▶ KEY TERMS

Desk accessories—Small software tools for performing quick tasks such as calculation or jotting down quick notes, always active and accessible through Dashboard. Also known as *widgets*.

Dashboard—A special "layer" over your Desktop where your desk accessories are stored, and that can be summoned with a keystroke (**F12** by default).

94 | Access Your Desk Accessories (Dashboard)

→ **SEE ALSO**

6 Grab the Window You Want

95 Add a Person to Your Address Book

New in Mac OS X Tiger is a feature called *Dashboard*, which is a special layer over your Desktop where all your *desk accessories*—a calculator, a dictionary, a weather monitor, a unit converter, yellow sticky notes, and more, including accessories you can download from the Internet and add to Dashboard—are stored. Operating in much the same manner as Exposé (see **6** **Grab the Window You Want**), Dashboard is summoned with a single keystroke, click, or mouse movement, depending on how you configure it.

When Dashboard is invoked, all your active desk accessories swoop into view, overlaid on top of your Desktop, which becomes dimmed. Desk accessories, which are also known as *widgets*, can be activated immediately and placed anywhere on your screen; the next time you invoke Dashboard, the widgets you had previously activated are still right where you left them, with the same contents and active data you had left them with. This makes performing simple, quick tasks such as calculating basic math, jotting down a quick note, looking up a word, or controlling your iTunes music into a simple, instant operation, instead of having to navigate into the **Applications** folder to launch a tiny utility which must be laboriously launched and quit.

1 Open the Dashboard & Exposé Preferences

By default, Dashboard is invoked by clicking the **Dashboard** icon near the left end of the Dock; but a convenient "shortcut" to do the same thing is to press the **F12** key. This can be changed; if you prefer to use **F12** for another function, or if you accidentally hit it a lot during normal typing, you can change the keystroke that summons Dashboard to something more appropriate.

94

1 Open the Dashboard & Exposé Preferences

2 Choose the Keystroke or Mouse Button to Invoke Dashboard

5 Close a Widget

4 Open and Use a Widget

3 Summon Dashboard and the Widget Bar

6 Get More Dashboard Widgets

94

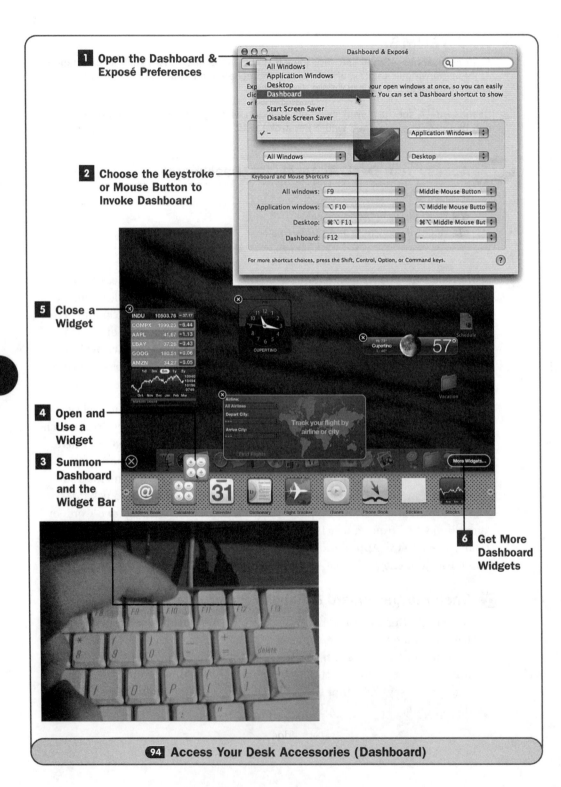

94 Access Your Desk Accessories (Dashboard)

Open the **System Preferences** application (under the **Apple** menu); click the **Dashboard & Exposé** icon to open the **Dashboard & Exposé Preferences** pane.

2 Choose the Keystroke or Mouse Button to Invoke Dashboard

Dashboard is configured the same way as Exposé; you can assign a certain Active Screen Corner to Dashboard so that it's invoked when you move the mouse into that corner, or you can define a dedicated mouse click (such as clicking the middle mouse button) as the command that summons Dashboard. You can configure any combination of Active Screen Corners, keystrokes, or mouse clicks to suit your needs.

Additionally, you can customize the keystroke or mouse click for invoking Dashboard by adding modifier keys, if you don't want to invoke the feature too easily or inadvertently. To assign a compound keystroke (such as **Shift+F12**), hold down the desired modifier keys while you open either of the two menus next to the **Dashboard** label in the **Keyboard and Mouse Shortcuts** section of the window. (The first menu defines a keystroke, and the second menu defines a mouse command.) The symbols for the modifier keys you hold down are shown next to the available function keys you can assign. Select the key combination you want to use. Close the window when you're done.

94

3 Summon Dashboard and the Widget Bar

Press the key combination that you specified. (Alternatively, click the **Dashboard** icon near the left end of the Dock.) The Dashboard layer zooms into view, while the Desktop and all application windows become dimmed. Any desk accessories (widgets) that had previously been in use appear in the positions in Dashboard where you had left them.

At the bottom left corner of the screen is a circular + icon; click this to reveal the **Widget Bar**, a horizontal area at the bottom of the screen (similar to the Dock) that acts as a launcher for your desktop accessories. All the available widgets are shown in the bar, scrolling horizontally with arrow buttons at the right and left ends if there are more widgets in the bar than your screen can show.

Click the + icon again to close the Widget Bar; press the same key combination to dismiss Dashboard as you used to summon it (or simply click on any unused area of the Desktop). You're now acquainted with the techniques necessary to move through the various levels of Dashboard; all that remains is to actually activate and use some widgets.

4 Open and Use a Widget

With the Widget Bar expanded, click the name of any widget that you would like to activate. The desk accessory pops into view in the middle of the screen; if your computer is powerful enough, a "water ripple" effect announces the widget's arrival.

▶ TIP

Alternatively, drag a widget from the Widget Bar to any place on the screen where you want it to appear. The widget transforms as you drag it from its icon guise to its appearance as an active utility; this is a great little trick to show off to people.

Click and drag the widget anywhere on the screen that is most convenient for you. If you leave the widget active when you dismiss Dashboard, the widget will reappear in the same position the next time you invoke Dashboard.

Use the widget in whatever way is appropriate to it. For instance, operate the Calculator by clicking in the display window to activate it, then pressing keys on the numeric keypad. To enter text in a sticky note, click in the note and begin typing.

Some widgets have preferences that can be modified; click the small "i" icon (usually in the bottom-right corner) to flip the widget around and work with the widget's options. For instance, you can change the color of your sticky notes to indicate different importance levels, or configure the Weather widget to reflect your hometown or to display Celsius units rather than Fahrenheit.

▶ NOTE

You may need to move the mouse pointer near the lower-right corner of a widget for the "i" icon to appear that indicates it can be flipped over; otherwise, the icon is invisible. This behavior varies from widget to widget.

5 Close a Widget

To close a widget, hold down the **Option** key as you move your mouse over the widget; a circled **X** icon appears near the upper-left corner of that widget. Click the **X**. The widget disappears into the circle, taking with it any information it had displayed (each time you activate a widget, its information is cleared).

▶ TIP

If the Widget Bar is open, the **X** icon appears on all open widgets, without your having to hold down **Option**; this makes it easier to close them all one by one.

94

6 **Get More Dashboard Widgets**

Open the Widget Bar, then click the **More Widgets** icon that appears in the lower right above the Widget Bar to launch a Safari window and visit the website run by Apple where you can download new widgets. After downloading any widget, move it into the **Widgets** folder in your **Library** folder (inside your **Home** if you want to install the widget only for yourself, or inside the **Library** folder at the top level of the disk to install it for all users). The next time you invoke Dashboard, the new widget appears in the Widget Bar.

95 **Add a Person to Your Address Book**

✔ BEFORE YOU BEGIN	→ SEE ALSO
54 Configure a New Mail Account	**100** Synchronize Your Information Using .Mac

Email deserves its reputation as an instant, easy-to-understand communication system—but without a simple way for you to keep track of people's email addresses, email is all but useless. Who has the memory to keep an entire catalog of cryptic, frequently changing addresses straight?

The answer, of course, is *a computer.*

Address Book is a small application that works as an adjunct to Mail but that is integrated throughout Mac OS X so that all its contents—contact names, phone numbers, email addresses, home page URLs—are available to any application capable of using that information. As you use Mail, you can continually add names and addresses into Address Book with a single click, so that sending messages to the people you know becomes faster and easier all the time.

Each entry in Address Book is known as a *card* (or a *contact*). A card can contain nearly a dozen different kinds of information about a person, including a picture. A card can be for a person or a business (you make the distinction using a check box). At any time, you can edit a card by selecting it in Address Book and clicking the **Edit** button at the bottom of the window.

▶ **TIP**

An additional way to organize your contacts is to use *groups*. Create a new group in Address Book by clicking the + button at the bottom of the **Group** column and enter a name for the new group that appears. You then populate the group by dragging cards into it. Now you can quickly send email to an entire group of people by simply typing the name of the group into the **To** field in Mail. The names in the group are automatically resolved, and the message is addressed to all the members of the group at once.

Hold down **Option** while creating a new group to create a **Smart Group**, which is a saved Spotlight query defined on several useful criteria and automatically contains all matching cards.

94

95

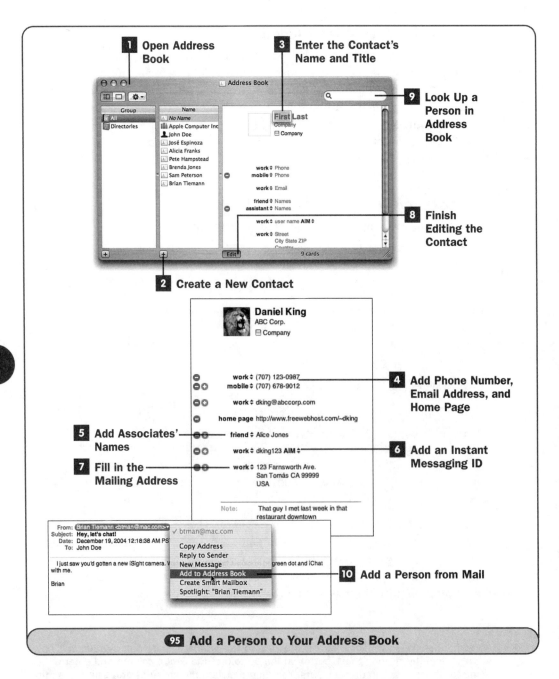

1 Open Address Book

3 Enter the Contact's Name and Title

9 Look Up a Person in Address Book

8 Finish Editing the Contact

2 Create a New Contact

Daniel King
ABC Corp.
Company

work ⬍ (707) 123-0987
mobile ⬍ (707) 678-9012

work ⬍ dking@abccorp.com

home page http://www.freewebhost.com/~dking

friend ⬍ Alice Jones

work ⬍ dking123 AIM ⬍

work ⬍ 123 Farnsworth Ave.
San Tomás CA 99999
USA

Note: That guy I met last week in that restaurant downtown

4 Add Phone Number, Email Address, and Home Page

5 Add Associates' Names

6 Add an Instant Messaging ID

7 Fill in the Mailing Address

From: Brian Tiemann <btman@mac.com>
Subject: Hey, let's chat!
Date: December 19, 2004 12:18:38 AM PS
To: John Doe

✓ btman@mac.com

Copy Address
Reply to Sender
New Message
Add to Address Book
Create Smart Mailbox
Spotlight: "Brian Tiemann"

I just saw you'd gotten a new iSight camera. V   green dot and iChat
with me.

Brian

10 Add a Person from Mail

95 Add a Person to Your Address Book

You can add contacts to Address Book from the Mail application, or you can
enter all of a person's contact information manually. Either way, that information is immediately available to Mail and to the rest of your online applications.

1 Open Address Book

 Navigate to the **Applications** folder in the Finder and double-click the **Address Book** icon. Alternatively, you can click the **Address Book** icon in the Dock.

2 Create a New Contact

There are + buttons underneath both the **Group** column on the left and the second **Name** column (which by default shows all the contacts in the **All** group). Click the + button under the **Name** column to create a new contact.

3 Enter the Contact's Name and Title

In the right pane, a blank contact card appears. The name of each field appears in gray so that you know what is supposed to go in the fields.

▶ **TIP**

You can assign a custom picture to any person's card in Address Book. Simply find a picture file in the Finder and drag it into the square picture area next to the person's name. You can do this whether or not you're in Edit mode. (You can tell whether you're in Edit mode by whether the **Edit** button below the card information is pressed.)

95

Type the person's first and last name. If the person is a business contact, enter their company name and business title as well. Use the **Tab** key to move between fields. Be sure to put the first and last name in the two separate fields provided for them rather than simply typing the whole name into the first field. Separating the contact's name helps Address Book sort the names properly; you can tell Address Book to alphabetize your contacts based on their first or last names in the **General** pane of the Address Book **Preferences** window.

▶ **TIP**

If the card you're entering is for a company rather than a person, select the **Company** check box next to the picture and under the company name. This reverses the positions of the person's name and the company name, placing the company name in large bold letters.

4 Add a Phone Number, Email Address, and Home Page

Each contact in your Address Book can have as many phone numbers, email addresses, and home pages associated with it as you want. The default template, which you are using now, has space for work and mobile phone numbers, a work email address, and a home page. You can add more of any of these pieces of information if you want or change the label on each field. For instance, you can change the **work** email address to a **home** address by selecting the new label from the drop-down list (click the up/down arrow icon next to the label to access the list of label options). When you have entered text into one of the fields, a + button appears next to the entry; click the + button to create space for a second entry of the same type. This way, you can create dozens of contact addresses for each person.

▶ **TIP**

Select **Custom** from the label menu on any entry to type a custom label for the entry.

After you have finished specifying the information for a person, you can use Address Book to quickly access a person's home page, phone number, or email address. Click the label for one of these entries to see a contextual menu of appropriate options. An email entry gives you access to commands for sending email to the person or sending an automatic email with your new contact information if you should change it. If the person is a .Mac user, you can iChat with the person, visit his home page, or open his iDisk right from Address Book.

95

▶ **TIP**

Click the label for a person's phone number and select **Large Type** from the contextual menu to show the address in huge letters across your screen; this can be very useful if you need to dial a phone that's across the room from your computer.

5 Add Associates' Names

You can add the names of the person's friends, family members, assistants, managers, or any of several other relationships. Select the relationship you want to add from the list of label options, and type that person's name.

If the associate's name that you type matches any card in Address Book, you will later be able to jump to that associate's Address Book card by clicking the label and selecting the **Show "John Doe"** option from the contextual menu.

6 Add an Instant Messaging ID

Address Book allows you to specify the instant messaging address or user ID for any contact. You can enter an AIM, Jabber, MSN, ICQ, or Yahoo! address. You will only be able to contact the person using iChat if you enter an AIM address, and then click the location label next to the Instant Messaging entry in the Address Book card, or click the green dot next to the person's picture (which indicates that he is online in iChat or AIM).

7 Fill in the Mailing Address

Enter the information for the person's mailing address, using all the available fields that you know: street address, city, state, ZIP, and country.

Clicking the mailing address label later in Address Book and selecting **Map Of** from the contextual menu when you're in Safari pops up a map (using the MapQuest service) of that address.

▶ **TIP**

You can use different countries' mailing address styles, if you want. Click the mailing address label and choose **Change Address Format** from the contextual menu; from the submenu, select the country for the format you want to use for that card. To change the format that is used globally for all cards, open the Address Book **Preferences** dialog box and click the **General** tab; select the country you live in from the **Address Format** menu.

8 Finish Editing the Contact

When you're done editing the person's card, click the **Edit** button to exit Edit mode. This contact's card is added to Address Book and the contact's name appears in the **Name** column in the Address Book screen.

95

9 Look Up a Person in Address Book

You can browse for a person's name alphabetically in the **Name** column in Address Book. Alternatively, if you know the person's first or last name (or, indeed, any other piece of information, such as the person's phone number or mailing address), type it into the **Search** box. As you type, only the cards with contents that match what you've typed appear in the **Name** column. When you've narrowed it down to a single card, that card appears in the right pane.

10 Add a Person from Mail

Click the down arrow next to any person's name in the headers of an email message in Mail. Select **Add to Address Book** from the contextual menu to automatically create a new card with that person's name and email address. You can then select **Open in Address Book** from the same menu to go to the new card and add any further contact information you might know.

---

96 **Synchronize with an Exchange or Directory Server**

✔ **BEFORE YOU BEGIN**	→ **SEE ALSO**
30 Configure Networking Manually	**54** Configure a New Mail Account

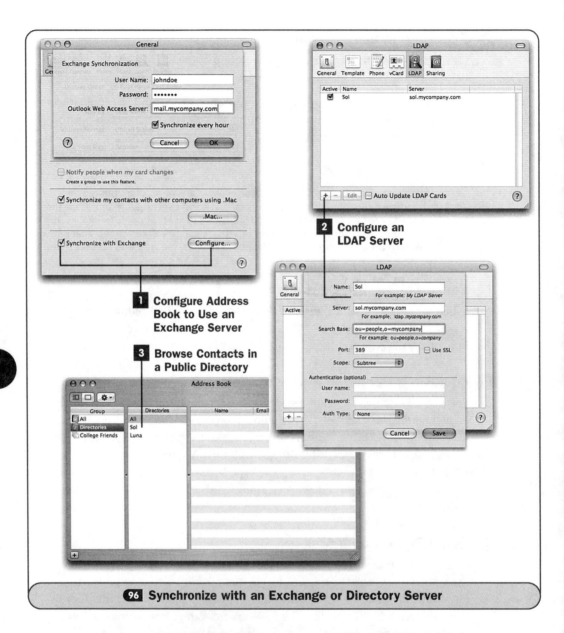

1 Configure Address Book to Use an Exchange Server

2 Configure an LDAP Server

3 Browse Contacts in a Public Directory

96 Synchronize with an Exchange or Directory Server

If you're in a corporate network environment, chances are that you and all your co-workers have Windows Networking user names and passwords that you use to access the Windows-based network—and there is equally likely a Microsoft Exchange server or *Lightweight Directory Access Protocol (LDAP)* server available, making it a breeze to access the contact information for any of your co-workers. You don't even have to enter their information yourself—all you have to do is tell Address Book where the server is, and it will do all the work for you.

There are subtle differences between an Exchange server and a directory server. With an Exchange server, Address Book must connect to the server every so often (generally once per hour) and synchronize its cards with the ones on the server. A directory server, on the other hand, doesn't insert its contents into your Address Book; rather, you browse the contents of the directory over the network as you would a group in your Address Book.

Before configuring Mac OS X to synchronize your Address Book with the Exchange server, make sure that your computer is connected to the corporate network, and that you know your Windows Networking user name and password. Consult your company's network administrator for assistance if you don't know this information.

▶ **NOTE**

When you configure Address Book to synchronize itself with an Exchange server, Address Book is actually passing off the synchronization duties to iSync. While you update contacts in Address Book, iSync operates in the background, finding new and changed entries in the Exchange server and propagating them into your Address Book.

1 **Configure Address Book to Use an Exchange Server**

96

Open the Address Book **Preferences** window; select the **General** tab. Select the **Synchronize with Exchange** check box and then click the **Configure** button to specify the Exchange server.

Enter your Windows Networking user name and password. Then put the server's hostname or IP address in the **Outlook Web Access Server** box. Select the **Synchronize every hour** check box to keep your Address Book in sync at all times, and then click **OK**.

▶ **NOTE**

If you configured an Exchange email account in Mail, Address Book takes its Exchange server settings from that account. See **54** **Configure a New Mail Account** for details on accessing an Exchange server.

The first synchronization process takes place immediately. After the sync process is complete, your Address Book is populated with all your co-workers' names, email addresses, and phone numbers. Mac OS X will check the server every hour for changes; this way, you will always have the most accurate information at your fingertips.

2 **Configure an LDAP Server**

You can also subscribe your Mac to a directory server, also known as an LDAP server. Use the **LDAP** pane of the Address Book **Preferences** window to configure an LDAP server, using the server information provided to you by your network administrator.

Click the + button to add a new directory server. In the sheet that appears, enter a descriptive name for the server, the hostname or IP address, and the "search base"—a string that your network administrator will be able to provide for you.

▶ TIP

Select the **Auto Update LDAP Cards** check box to allow Address Book to automatically update any changed information in a card you access from a directory server.

Click **Save** to close the configuration sheet and then close the **Preferences** dialog box.

3 Browse Contacts in a Public Directory

Back in the Address Book, select the **Directories** entry in the **Group** column; all your configured directory servers appear in the second column. Click a directory to browse the names inside it.

96

97 Create an iCal Event	
✔ BEFORE YOU BEGIN	→ SEE ALSO
25 Set the Time and Date	98 Subscribe to a Shared iCal Calendar
	100 Synchronize Your Information Using .Mac

It's one of the great modern ironies: As you work with your Mac in a business or home environment, your time will likely become still more of a precious resource than it was before—even though computers are supposed to be time-*saving* devices! Inevitably, you'll need a way to manage your time in a more elegant and automatic fashion than simply relying on your memory or Post-It notes.

iCal, Apple's calendaring system, is engineered to be a hassle-free and intuitive way to schedule important events in your life and notify you when they're approaching so that you never have to miss an appointment or meeting.

1 Launch iCal

Navigate to the **Applications** folder in the Finder and double-click the **iCal** icon. Alternatively, click the **iCal** icon in the Dock.

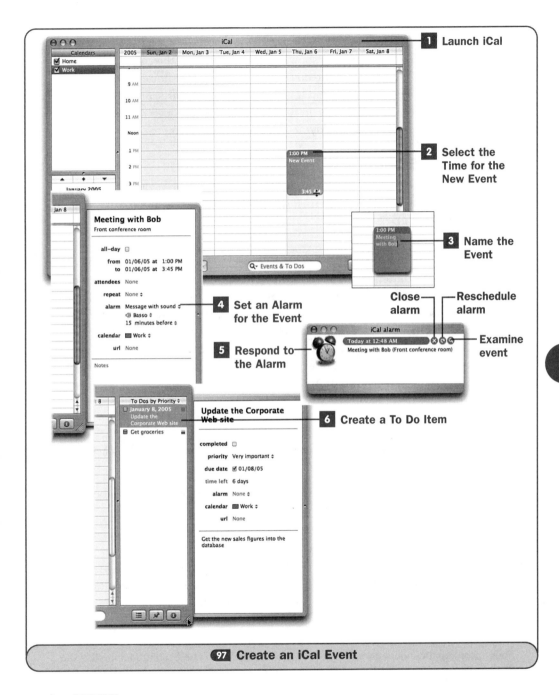

1 Launch iCal

2 Select the Time for the New Event

3 Name the Event

Close alarm — Reschedule alarm

4 Set an Alarm for the Event

5 Respond to the Alarm

Examine event

97

6 Create a To Do Item

97 Create an iCal Event

▶ **NOTE**

iCal's icon in the Dock dynamically updates to reflect the current date. Because the automatic update happens only while iCal is running, you might choose to leave iCal running at all times to keep the display accurate, if your computer has the resources to spare.

2 Select the Time for the New Event

iCal opens into the Week view, showing you each day in the current week as a column, with the hours of the day shown as horizontal lines. Create a new event by clicking on the day and time when the event starts, and dragging to the point where the event ends. In this example, I've dragged into existence an event that starts on Thursday at 1:00 and ends at 3:45.

3 Name the Event

The name for the new event is selected so that you can immediately type a new descriptive name. Press **Return** when you've done this; the new event is registered in iCal.

4 Set an Alarm for the Event

Click the **Info** button in the lower-right corner of the iCal window to open the information drawer for the new event. Set an alarm for the event by clicking the up/down arrows to access the **alarm** drop-down list. You can select from a number of different types of alarms, from a simple pop-up message on your screen a specified number of minutes or hours before or after the event, to a message with a sound effect, or even an email message sent to an address of your choice from your card in Address Book.

97

▶ NOTE

iCal doesn't have to be running for it to send you alarms when your events approach. Feel free to set up your events and then quit iCal; your alarms will appear as scheduled whether iCal is running or not.

Click the various parts of the specification to the right of the alarm label to configure the alarm to your exact preferences.

5 Respond to the Alarm

When the alarm goes off, if you've set it to pop up a message before the event, you will be given options to close the window, reschedule the alarm to go off again in a few minutes, or examine the event.

▶ TIP

Your upcoming iCal appointments are shown in the **Date & Time** System Menu (click the time display in the upper-right corner of the screen to see them).

6 Create a To Do Item

Another kind of scheduled item in iCal is a To Do item. These are not sched-uled events, but rather free-form notes to yourself that relate to tasks you have to accomplish. A To Do item doesn't have to have a due date associated with it, but it can; you can also (optionally) assign a priority level that helps you sort your To Do items according to their importance.

Click the thumbtack button in the lower-right corner of the iCal window to show the To Do list. To create a new To Do item, double-click anywhere in the To Do list pane. A new item named **New To Do** appears, and you can immediately type in a more descriptive name for the item.

▶ **TIP**

Click the **Info** button in the lower-right corner of the iCal window to open the information drawer; for To Do items, this drawer lets you set the priority or due date for a To Do item, as well as a few other options.

98	**Subscribe to a Shared iCal Calendar**

✔ **BEFORE YOU BEGIN**	→ **SEE ALSO**
30 Configure Networking Manually	**99** Publish Your iCal Calendar
97 Create an iCal Event	**100** Synchronize Your Information Using .Mac
	54 Configure a New Mail Account

97

Because iCal is part of Apple's networked data management suite of utilities, you can publish the events on your calendar to a central server, subscribe to other people's iCal calendars so that you can see their schedules, and even seek out public calendars that are published as services for the iCal-using community.

An excellent starting point for finding shared calendars is choosing **Find Shared Calendars** from the **Calendar** menu; this takes you to a shared calendar clearinghouse page hosted by Apple, full of calendars to which you can subscribe.

▶ **NOTE**

iCal uses the industry-standard VCAL format when publishing or exporting its calendar data. This means that you can share calendars with Exchange/Outlook users, as well as with any other application that uses the VCAL format.

▶ **WEB RESOURCE**

http://www.icalshare.com

iCalShare is a site dedicated to allowing iCal users to publish their calendars to a browsable directory. You can seek out and subscribe to a calendar of events in which you're interested, no matter whose iCal it's actually part of.

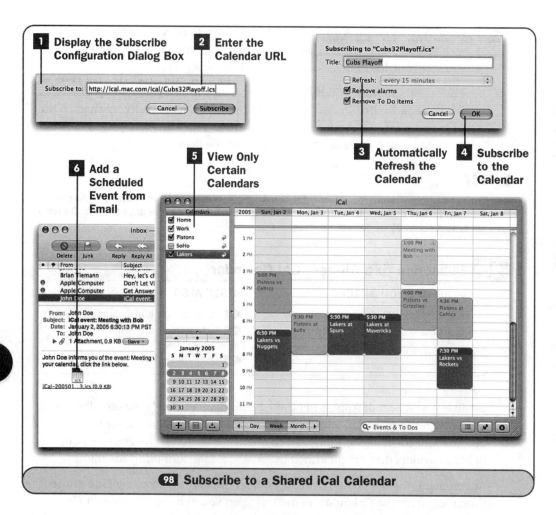

1 Display the Subscribe Configuration Dialog Box

2 Enter the Calendar URL

Subscribing to "Cubs32Playoff.ics"

Title: Cubs Playoff

☐ Refresh: every 15 minutes
☑ Remove alarms
☑ Remove To Do items

5 View Only Certain Calendars

3 Automatically Refresh the Calendar

4 Subscribe to the Calendar

6 Add a Scheduled Event from Email

98 Subscribe to a Shared iCal Calendar

1 Display the Subscribe Configuration Dialog Box

Select **Subscribe** from the iCal **Calendar** menu to display the **Subscribe** address entry dialog box.

2 Enter the Calendar URL

Enter the URL of a calendar that's published on .Mac or a *WebDAV server*. If the calendar was published by a fellow .Mac user, she will be able to give you the URL for the calendar (the URL will have been reported to the person when the calendar was published).

▶ **KEY TERM**

WebDAV server—A type of server, often found on a corporate network, that provides certain kinds of information and upload and download services (such as iCal publishing). iDisk also operates over WebDAV.

Alternatively, visit Apple's iCal calendar library at **http://www.apple.com/ical/library/** or iCalShare at **http://www.icalshare.com** to find an interesting public calendar to subscribe to. These sites present links you can simply click; when you do this, the URL of the calendar in question appears in the **Subscribe** configuration dialog box.

3 Automatically Refresh the Calendar

You can have iCal automatically query the iCal server periodically to check for updates. Select the **Refresh** check box and select a refresh interval—anything from 15 minutes to once a month. The more frequently you have iCal refresh its calendars, the more accurate they'll be—but the more frequently your work might be slowed by iCal's background sync process (or interrupted by any error messages that might result from it).

4 Subscribe to the Calendar

Click the **Subscribe** button at the bottom of the configuration dialog box to add the specified calendar to your **Calendars** pane in iCal. The new calendar is assigned a unique color, and the events in it are overlaid with your existing personal calendar events.

5 View Only Certain Calendars

Use the check boxes in the **Calendars** pane to select which calendars you want to see. Hide the calendars (deselect their check boxes) that don't interest you at a given time to reduce clutter in your iCal window and let you see how much free time you really have.

6 Add a Scheduled Event from Email

Someone can send you an iCal event by email. If you receive an iCal event as an attachment in an email message, simply double-click its link to import it into your iCal.

▶ TIP

To send an iCal event to another person in an email attachment, right-click or Control+click the event in your calendar and select **Mail event** from the contextual menu. A new Mail message opens, with the iCal event packaged into it as an attachment.

iCal will prompt you about which of your calendars to put the new event into; select the calendar you want to use and click **OK**. The new event is added into the selected calendar.

98

99   Publish Your iCal Calendar

✔ **BEFORE YOU BEGIN**	→ **SEE ALSO**
30 Set Up Networking Manually **45** Sign Up for .Mac	**100** Synchronize Your Information Using .Mac

iCal lets you publish any one of your calendars to a central server so that others can see what your schedule is and plan their own events accordingly. You can publish your calendar to .Mac if you have a .Mac account; other .Mac users can then subscribe to your calendar on the .Mac server. If you have a **WebDAV server** on your corporate network, you can publish your iCal calendar to that server, eliminating the need for .Mac in your calendaring.

.Mac even provides the ability for you to publish your calendar to a static web-based calendar on a web server on which you're able to post web pages. This form of the calendar is visible to anybody with a web browser, whether they're on a Mac or not. When you publish a calendar to .Mac, iCal tells you both the URL that others must use to subscribe to your calendar in iCal, and the URL for viewing the calendar with a standard web browser.

1   Display the Publish Configuration Dialog Box

Select **Publish** from the iCal **Calendar** menu to display the **Publish** configuration dialog box.

2   Specify the Calendar Name

Enter a descriptive name for your published calendar. You can leave it as the default (the same name as the calendar has in your local iCal window), or you can give it a more specific or appropriate name for the benefit of others.

3   Select Where to Publish the Calendar

You can publish the calendar either to .Mac or to any WebDAV server to which you have access. Select the destination for your calendar from the **Publish calendar** drop-down list.

4   Publish the Calendar

Click the **Publish** button at the bottom of the configuration dialog box to send your calendar to the specified server.

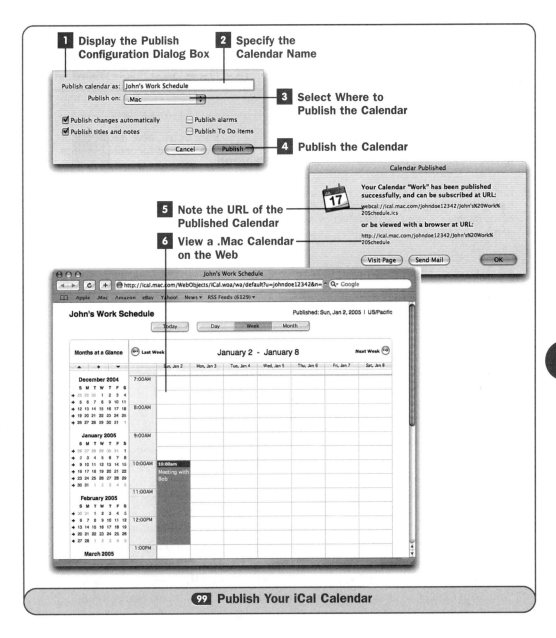

99 Publish Your iCal Calendar

5 Note the URL of the Published Calendar

iCal will report two URLs for the calendar you just published: the URL other users must use to subscribe to the calendar, as well as the URL for viewing the calendar in a web browser.

Click **Send Mail** on the **Calendar Published** dialog box to create a new mail message that automatically includes both these URLs in it; all you have to do is fill in the recipients' names and click **Send** to email these URLs to the people who need to view or subscribe to your published calendar.

▶ TIPS

You can send another email message later as well, if you want to tell more people about the location of your calendar. Select **Send publish email** from the iCal **Calendar** menu to bring up a new Mail message containing the calendar URLs.

---

iCal lets you publish more than one calendar if you want—each calendar you create (using the + button at the bottom left) can be shared, at your discretion. A shared calendar is denoted in the **Calendars** list by a "broadcast" icon to the right of the calendar's name.

6   View a .Mac Calendar on the Web

Click the **Visit Page** button on the **Calendar Published** dialog box to open the static version of the calendar in your web browser.

Alternatively, right-click or **Control**+click the name of a calendar in the **Calendars** pane in the iCal window and select **View Calendar on .Mac** from the contextual menu to open the calendar in your web browser.

99

100   Synchronize Your Information Using .Mac

✔ BEFORE YOU BEGIN	→ SEE ALSO
30 Configure Networking Manually	**51** Keep Your iDisk in Sync
45 Sign Up for .Mac	

The power of synchronizing your computer's information really becomes apparent if you have a .Mac account and more than one Mac. Using Mac OS X Tiger, you can subscribe each computer to the .Mac server and choose certain classes of data to keep synchronized; Mac OS X then works behind the scenes, gathering your data together from disparate locations such as Address Book, Safari, Mail, and iCal, as well as the saved passwords in your Keychain, and constantly compares it against your contacts, bookmarks, passwords, and calendar events that are stored on the .Mac server. Whenever it finds any discrepancies, it automatically makes the change in whichever system is more out-of-date.

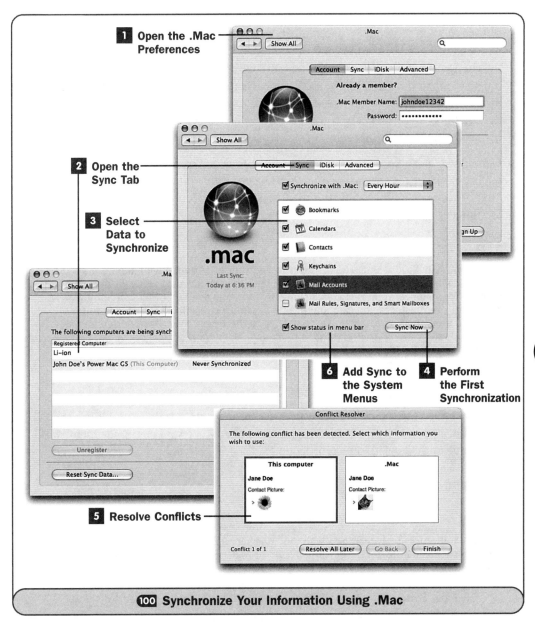

1 Open the .Mac Preferences

2 Open the Sync Tab

3 Select Data to Synchronize

6 Add Sync to the System Menus

4 Perform the First Synchronization

5 Resolve Conflicts

100 Synchronize Your Information Using .Mac

► **TIP**

Because .Mac synchronization depends on each Mac being set to the correct date and time for it to be able to tell which computer's information is the most up-to-date, it's very important for you to make sure that all your Macs' clocks are accurate. See **26** **Enable Automatic Time Synchronization (NTP)** for instructions on how to make sure each of your Macs always has the correct time.

If you add a contact or a bookmark on one Mac, the sync process publishes that change to .Mac. On your second Mac, its own sync process notices that there are newer changes on .Mac than on that computer. It downloads and incorporates the changes from .Mac, thereby propagating your most current information from the first Mac to the second. And the best part is that this is all done transparently, in the background—you don't even ever have to know that it's happening. All that matters to you, the user, is that all your most current information is always available on all your Macs.

Before Mac OS X can do this service for you, however, you must configure it to do so. This involves registering each of your Macs with the .Mac server, so that each Mac's sync process knows how many other Macs it's negotiating with and how recently each one's information has been synchronized.

▶ **TIP**

Even if you only have a single Mac, synchronizing your information with .Mac is a good thing to do, because it protects your valuable data in case it's lost from your own computer. If, for instance, your Mac crashes or you get a new computer, you can immediately restore all your contacts and calendar events by simply subscribing the computer to .Mac and synchronizing the data. To do this, go to the **Reset Sync Data** button on the **Advanced** tab of the **.Mac Preferences** pane and configure it to replace **All Sync Info** on this computer with information from .Mac.

100

1   Open the .Mac Preferences

Open the **System Preferences** application (under the **Apple** menu). Click the .**Mac** icon to open the .**Mac Preferences** pane. Make sure your .Mac member name and password are correctly entered.

2   Open the Sync Tab

▶ **NOTE**

Mac OS X attempts to synchronize with the .Mac server only when you have an active network connection. To set up synchronization or register your Mac, you must be connected to the Internet.

Click the **Sync** tab; this validates your .Mac account settings, registers your computer with .Mac, and shows the .**Mac Sync** settings screen.

To see all the computers registered with your .Mac account, click the **Advanced** tab. This can be helpful in showing you which computers have been synchronizing successfully and which ones have the most up-to-date information.

3 Select Data to Synchronize

The **.Mac Sync Preferences** window now shows you the status and configuration of your .Mac synchronization. Using the check boxes, choose what kinds of data you want iSync to keep updated. You can select or deselect your Safari bookmarks, the contact cards in Address Book, the saved passwords in your Keychain, the events and To Do items in iCal, and the settings of your accounts in Mail.

Select the **Synchronize with .Mac** check box and choose a time period from the drop-down list to tell Mac OS X to attempt to connect to .Mac at regular intervals, and if successful, to synchronize all your data in the background. With this option selected, you should never have to worry about your personal data being out-of-date again.

▶ **NOTE**

Every Hour is a good interval to choose to synchronize your data, especially if you have a permanent Internet connection. If you have an intermittent connection or a low-bandwidth dial-up account, you might choose a longer interval to keep your connection from slowing down every hour as it synchronizes.

100

4 Perform the First Synchronization

When your synchronization options are configured to your liking, click the **Sync Now** button. Mac OS X connects to the .Mac server and exchanges your user information. It downloads the data that's in your .Mac account, compares it to what's in your computer's Address Book, iCal, Mail, Keychain, and Safari, and adds any new entries into them.

5 Resolve Conflicts

If Mac OS X finds *conflicts*—similar but not identical Address Book cards or other items that appear on both your computer and .Mac—it shows you the relevant details of the two items that are causing the problem. Click to select the version you want to keep and then click **Finish**. Mac OS X will have to sync again to finalize the resolved conflicts. Click **Sync Now** in the confirmation dialog box to kick off this cleanup-duty sync process.

▶ **NOTE**

If you don't resolve the conflicts right away or aren't prompted to resolve them during the sync process, the number of conflicts appears in the **Sync Status** System Menu; click the **<#> Conflicts** menu option to resolve the reported conflicts.

Quit **System Preferences**. Your Mac will now synchronize your data automatically every hour, in the background, as long as you have a network connection.

6 Add Sync to the System Menus

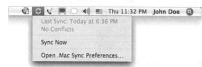

Select the **Show status in menu bar** check box to position the **Sync Status** System Menu in the menu bar above the upper-right corner of the Desktop. Now you can view at a glance when your computer was last synchronized with .Mac, and also run a manual sync process whenever you choose.

---

101 Synchronize Your Palm PDA and Other Devices

✔ BEFORE YOU BEGIN	→ SEE ALSO
95 Add a Person to Your Address Book	100 Synchronize Your Information Using .Mac
97 Create an iCal Event	86 Synchronize With an iPod

100

iSync is a utility designed to keep your data synchronized with any smart digital devices you use to keep track of things and communicate—Personal Digital Assistants, cellular phones, and iPods. iSync can talk to all these devices and keep their data in sync whenever they're connected to your Mac. All you have to do is set them up.

▶ WEB RESOURCE
http://www.markspace.com

Mark/Space is the home of The Missing Sync, a commercial software package ($40) that makes the PDA sync process far more hassle-free and full-featured than even the official Palm software does. It also supports Pocket PC devices; if you have one, The Missing Sync is just what you need.

▶ NOTE

Although you need a .Mac account to synchronize your Macs with each other, you don't need to be a .Mac member—or even have an Internet connection—to synchronize your devices with a single Mac using iSync.

For cell phones and iPods, the process of registering them with iSync is a simple one: Just plug it in and use the **Device**, **Add Device** command to scan for it so that iSync can automatically pick it up. But to use a Palm OS-based PDA with iSync, the process to set it up is rather more complicated.

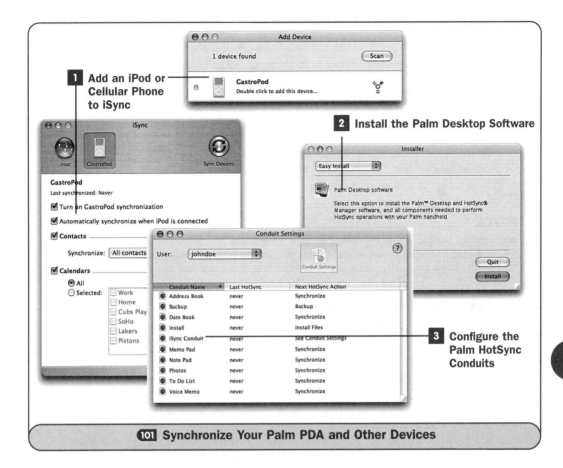

101 **Synchronize Your Palm PDA and Other Devices**

▶ **NOTE**

If you have multiple Macs, you should choose a single one to which to synchronize your PDA, iPod, or cell phone. In other words, don't synchronize the device to your Mac at home, and then again to your Mac at work; the different copies of iSync might become confused, and you may lose data. Instead, make sure that your multiple Macs are synchronized (see **100** **Synchronize Your Information Using .Mac**), and then choose one Mac to use any time you want to synchronize your digital device.

1 **Add an iPod or Cellular Phone to iSync**

Whether you want to add an iPod or cellular phone to iSync, the process is the same. First, plug in the device using FireWire or USB cables as necessary, or Bluetooth if your device and Mac both support it. Open iSync and select **Add Device** from the **Devices** menu.

In the **Add Device** dialog box that opens, click the **Scan** button to scan for connected devices. Any iPods or cellular phones connected to the computer appear in the window. Double-click the icon for each device to add it to iSync.

iPods and different models of cellular phones differ in what kinds of data they can synchronize, but the configuration pane contains controls that let you select from whatever types of data are applicable. Select the check boxes for the data you want to synchronize—contacts, calendars, and other items— and use the **Automatically synchronize when <*device*> is connected** check box to tell iSync to launch a sync process whenever you connect the device to the computer. With this option selected, you never have to open iSync to ensure that your latest data is present on your device; just plug it in and the data is synchronized in the background. To synchronize the new device with the data on your Mac and .Mac server for the first time, click **Sync Now**.

▶ **NOTE**

With certain devices, including newer phones from Nokia and other manufacturers, you are prompted to install an **iSync Config** application on your device to enable iSync configuration. Follow the instructions provided to enable this functionality.

❷ Install the Palm Desktop Software

To add a Palm device to iSync, you must first download the Palm Desktop application suite. Visit the Palm website at **http://www.palmone.com/ software** to locate the Mac OS X version of the Palm Desktop. Register with the website (you must enter the serial number for your handheld device) and download the software.

Double-click the **Palm Desktop Installer** icon to install the Palm software. The installer creates the **Palm Desktop** and **HotSync Manager** applications on your computer, and then presents a brief series of panels that set up your user account, using your Mac OS X user information. When the installation procedure is complete, restart your computer.

❸ Configure the Palm HotSync Conduit

After restarting your Mac, navigate to the **Applications** folder and double-click the **HotSync Manager** icon. The HotSync Manager launches. From the **HotSync** menu, select **Conduit Settings** to bring up the window where you configure the various *conduits*, or mini-applications that transmit data between your Palm device and the Mac.

▶ **KEY TERM**

Conduit—A piece of software hiding under the surface of Mac OS X that transfers a certain kind of information, such as Address Book contacts or iCal events, to and from a digital device such as a PDA.

▶ **NOTE**

If the **Conduit Settings** window doesn't show an **iSync Conduit** entry, you might have to get a newer version of the Palm Desktop software. HotSync Manager version 3.0.1 and earlier might not work properly with iSync 1.2.1 or Tiger.

Double-click the **iSync Conduit** entry in the list in the **Conduit Settings** window. In the dialog box that appears, select the **Enable iSync for this Palm device** check box and click **OK**. iSync will now show the Palm device in the palette at the top of the iSync window. Whenever you connect the Palm device to your computer from now on (either by directly connecting a USB cable or by pressing the **Synchronize** button on the Palm's cradle), iSync will launch a sync process and update the information on the Palm device, just as it does with .Mac and any other devices to which it is connected and registered.

101

PART IV

Making It Work For You

IN THIS PART:

14

Customizing Mac OS X

IN THIS CHAPTER:

Any good operating system exists to be customized. To provide a comfortable operating environment for the user, the system must be flexible enough so that the user can tailor its behavior to suit not just his needs, but his tastes and fancies as well.

Apple has made a business out of the art of user-interface consistency—designing an operating environment in which every application behaves more or less the same way, where (for example) pressing ⌘P always invokes the **Print** command no matter what you're doing when you press it. This kind of consistency is the cornerstone of Apple's vaunted ease of use, but it also means that the Mac OS is a user environment that's harder to customize than a system that imposes no restrictions on the behaviors of component utilities and third-party applications. Windows is supremely customizable, for instance—you can apply *skins* and complete interface overhauls to virtually the entire system—but that's as much a side effect of Windows's flexibility, and therefore its potential to be confusing and unstable, as a virtue in itself.

Mac OS X is not anywhere near as customizable as Windows is. Tiger comes with only a single *theme*, or color and decoration scheme. Apple tightly controls the rules that dictate which applications should use the "brushed metal" look, and which ones should opt for the traditional white-with-pinstripes or smooth gray color schemes. Every Mac application window has the same shape, with the rounded top corners and the consistent drop shadow. Some third-party tools exist to let you tinker with the interface elements, but such tools are "hacks" at best— usually not comprehensive in what they do, and they often pose the risk of destabilizing your system. For most Mac users, the reality is that customizing Mac OS X is limited to what Apple explicitly allows you to do.

▶ KEY TERMS

Skin—A comprehensive alteration in an application's appearance, created by swapping out the default component images that make up the system's visual style for new ones. Applications such as web browsers and audio players are frequently "skinnable."

Theme—Another kind of appearance alteration, featuring customized icons, cursors, window colors, fonts, sounds, and interface elements. Themes are often fully supported by the operating system or application being customized, and can be selected by name.

Aqua—The code name for the user interface style in Mac OS X. Aqua refers to the "watery" theme that pervades the system, with the blue scroll bars and progress meters with their "flowing" effects, the candy-colored buttons, the transparency in menus and icons, and other such elements.

The good news is that what features Apple does permit you to customize are very highly developed. You can do things to your Mac that Windows users can't; if you can't apply a *Lord of the Rings* skin to the *Aqua* interface, so what? You can have your desktop background change smoothly and randomly every five minutes.

Customizing the Mac involves some tradeoffs from what you might be used to in Windows; but you can have plenty of fun with what you can do.

102 Change General Color and Appearance Settings

→ SEE ALSO

76 Install a New Font
103 Change Your Desktop Picture

The most basic kinds of customizations you can make to the operating system are the ones that affect the appearance of the entire system (for your login sessions only, not other users'): fonts, interface element colors, and the items that go into the global **Apple** menu that always appears at the top of the screen no matter what application you're using.

1 Open the Appearance Preferences

Open the **System Preferences** application (under the **Apple** menu); click the **Appearance** icon to open the **Appearance Preferences** pane.

102

2 Select an Appearance Color

Mac OS X has two general color schemes: **Blue** (the standard Aqua color scheme, with blue scroll and progress bars and red, yellow, and green window control buttons) and **Graphite** (which turns all these colored elements gray). Select **Graphite** if you dislike the vivid colors in Mac OS X; this color option makes for a much more subdued user environment.

3 Select a Highlight Color

By default, when you select text in applications, it is highlighted in blue. You can change the highlight color to any of seven predefined tones, or you can select your own highlight color by picking **Other** from the **Highlight Color** drop-down menu and then using the color picker to choose a custom color.

▶ TIP

When selecting a custom color, bear in mind that the black text in most text applications has to show up on top of the color you choose when text is selected. If the color you pick is too dark, the text will be hard to read. Pastel colors work best.

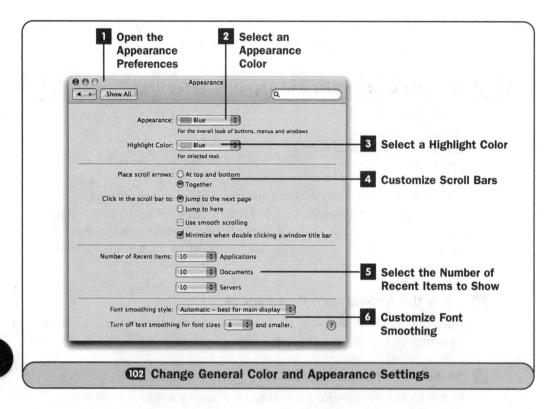

1 Open the Appearance Preferences

2 Select an Appearance Color

3 Select a Highlight Color

4 Customize Scroll Bars

5 Select the Number of Recent Items to Show

6 Customize Font Smoothing

102 Change General Color and Appearance Settings

102

4 Customize Scroll Bars

You can choose to have the arrows on the scroll bars in windows placed at opposite ends of the scroll bar, or together at the bottom or right side of the bar. Arrows are placed together by default; this is usually more comfortable for most users because it involves less mouse movement.

You can also customize what happens when you click in a part of a scroll bar. Select whether you want Mac OS X to jump directly to the part of the window indicated by the part of the scroll bar that you clicked, or to move closer to that position by a single page with each click.

5 Select the Number of Recent Items to Show

By default, the **Recent Items** submenu of the **Apple** menu shows the 10 most recently launched applications, the 10 most recently opened documents, and the 10 most recently connected servers. You can configure the menu to show between 0 and 50 of each.

6 Customize Font Smoothing

Depending on what kind of display (monitor) you have, you might want to modify the style of text smoothing (*antialiasing*) that Mac OS X uses. If you have a CRT display (a deep, heavy, TV-like monitor) or a Mac that uses one (such as an eMac or older iMac), choose the **Standard** option. If you have an LCD (flat panel), choose **Medium** smoothing. You can also make the smoothing sharper (**Light**) or fuzzier (**Heavy**), depending on how you like your text to appear. You may decide to just leave it as **Automatic**, the default setting, which chooses an appropriate antialiasing setting for your display.

▶ KEY TERM

Antialiasing—The technical term for "smoothing," as with fonts or diagonal lines. Sharp differences—*aliasing*—between the colors of neighboring pixels (dots on the screen) are "softened" visually by changing the colors of intermediate pixels to colors somewhere in between. This has the effect of making text look smoother (and readable at much smaller sizes), pictures more appealing, and individual pixels on the screen virtually invisible.

Text smaller than a certain size is not smoothed; you can define that threshold size, between 4 and 12 points, using the **Turn off text smoothing for font sizes <*n*> and smaller** drop-down list.

102

103 Change Your Desktop Picture

✔ BEFORE YOU BEGIN	→ SEE ALSO
102 Change General Color and Appearance Settings	**88** Import Photos From a Digital Camera
	104 Select a Screensaver
	105 Customize a Folder Window

The Desktop picture, which in the Windows world is usually known as "wallpaper," is the largest and most obvious piece of customization available for your computer—aside from putting fins or racing stripes on the case. Very few people leave their desktop looking the way it does when they boot up the computer for the first time. It's really easy to change the background to any picture you want and give your computer an immediate personal flavor.

1 Open the Desktop & Screen Saver Preferences

Open the **System Preferences** application (under the **Apple** menu); click the **Desktop & Screen Saver** icon to open the **Desktop & Screen Saver Preferences** pane. The **Desktop** tab opens by default.

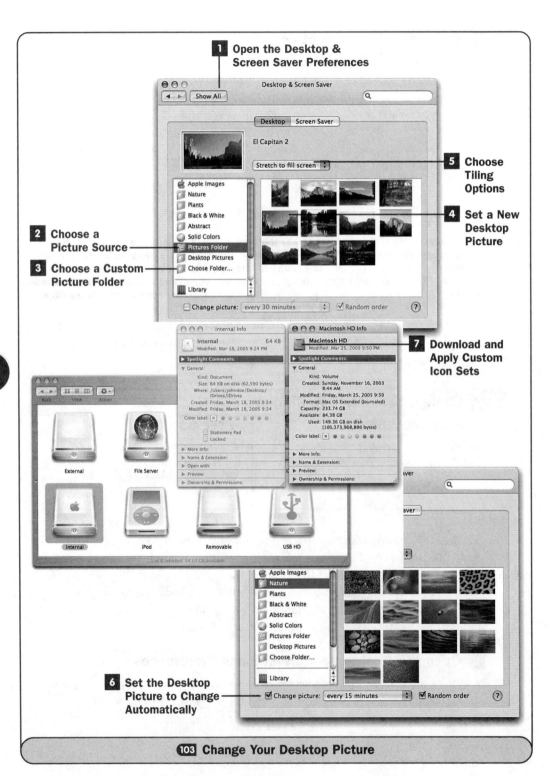

1 Open the Desktop &
Screen Saver Preferences

5 Choose
Tiling
Options

4 Set a New
Desktop
Picture

2 Choose a
Picture Source

3 Choose a Custom
Picture Folder

7 Download and
Apply Custom
Icon Sets

103

6 Set the Desktop
Picture to Change
Automatically

103 Change Your Desktop Picture

2 Choose a Picture Source

Several items appear in the list at the left. Each item is a source for desktop pictures; Apple provides some bundled pictures, available in the **Apple Images** source. You can also choose from several solid colors, or from folders containing collections of picture files.

The **Nature**, **Plants**, **Black & White**, and **Abstract** folders contain themed pictures bundled by Apple. You can also select your own **Pictures** folder. This folder, directly inside your **Home** folder, is where you should ordinarily place image files; choosing it as your picture source lets you select from any of the pictures you've collected. Subfolders of **Pictures** are not searched for valid images.

At the bottom of the list are three or more picture sources that allow you to choose pictures from iPhoto. **Library** shows you all the pictures in your entire iPhoto Library, **Last Roll** lists only the images in the last "film roll" you imported into iPhoto, and **Last 12 Months** includes all pictures taken in the last year.

▶ **NOTE**

As you add more photo albums in iPhoto (see **89 Create an iPhoto Album or Slideshow**), each album is added to the list of sources you can use for selecting your desktop picture.

103

3 Choose a Custom Picture Folder

You can also define a new custom picture source, a folder other than your **Pictures** folder. This is useful if you have a special folder where you keep your desktop pictures. Click **Choose Folder** and use the navigator window that pops up to find the folder you want to use. Click **Choose** after selecting any folder or an item inside it, and the folder will appear among the picture sources.

4 Set a New Desktop Picture

To set a new desktop picture, simply click the one you want to use in the pane on the right. Your computer's Desktop is immediately updated.

Alternatively, if the picture you want is not available in any of the folders or picture sources shown in the list, you can use any picture file anywhere in the system. Simply find the picture file you want to use in the Finder and drag it into the well (the recessed box showing the current Desktop picture) near the top of the **Desktop & Screen Saver Preferences** window.

5 **Choose Tiling Options**

A drop-down list appears next to the well to let you select how an odd-shaped picture should be displayed. Select **Fill screen** to stretch the picture proportionally to fit the entire screen; select **Stretch to fill screen** to stretch it anamorphically (scaling each dimension by a different amount, as necessary to make the picture completely fill the screen in both dimensions). Select **Center** to place the picture in the middle of the screen, or **Tile** to place multiple copies of it all over the screen.

▶ **NOTE**

Because the **Center** option potentially leaves empty space around the edges of the image if it's not exactly the right size to match your screen, a color picker icon appears next to the list if that option is chosen. Use the picker to define what color the leftover space should be.

6 **Set the Desktop Picture to Change Automatically**

You can have Mac OS X automatically change to another picture in the selected source folder after a certain period of time. Select the **Change picture** check box and then select a time period (or an event, such as logging in or waking from sleep) from the drop-down list. Select the **Random order** check box to randomize how the picture is selected; if you don't check this box, the pictures are displayed in alphabetical order, using their filenames.

7 **Download and Apply Custom Icon Sets**

Because Mac OS X lets you set custom icons on files and folders (and even applications), customizing your system can involve collections of custom icons created as "themes." Many websites store massive collections of icon sets, from *Star Trek* to Tolkien to *Tintin*, and with hundreds of abstract design styles to choose from, you'll be able to find icon sets that match your personal tastes.

After you download an icon set, you can apply any icon inside it to an item in your system by using the standard method for copying icons: Open the **Get Info** windows for both the source and the target items, select and copy the icon from the source, and then select and paste it onto the icon in the target window. (See **17** **Change an Icon** for more detailed instructions.) You can do this for folders, hard disks, and any documents or applications in the system.

Many icon sets also allow you to set the default or "generic" icons for items such as folders and disks; to do this, however, involves changing the files within the system itself, and these changes will not survive a system upgrade.

103

If you're adventurous, you can try using any of the various third-party tools that are available for changing your generic icons—but under the same caveats as with "theme" utilities, be aware of the risks to your system's stability.

▶ WEB RESOURCE
http://interfacelift.com/icons-mac

One of the most popular sources for custom Mac OS X icons on the Web, featuring hundreds of user-contributed icon sets, including the **iDrives** set by Wolfgang Bartelme shown in this task.

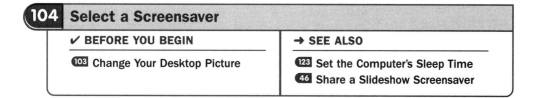

104 Select a Screensaver

✔ BEFORE YOU BEGIN	→ SEE ALSO
103 Change Your Desktop Picture	**123** Set the Computer's Sleep Time
	46 Share a Slideshow Screensaver

Some traditions die hard.

103

Back in the early days of high-resolution color monitors, the concept of a "screensaver" was popularized with the After Dark package, the first widespread piece of software designed to save your monitor from "burn-in" effects resulting from leaving it turned on and showing the same image for hours at a stretch. Simple floating logos and starfields, and goofy animated scenes such as flying toasters, kept the screen from ever showing the same thing from one moment to the next when not in use, lengthening the monitor's useful life. As computing power increased, screensavers became more and more lavish, until the present day, where now our idle monitors show fish tanks that are all but indistinguishable from the real thing, crunch numbers in a distributed effort to find intelligent life in space, and download ads for you to read when you come back to your computer after lunch.

Monitor technology has come a long way since the first screensavers; not just LCD screens, but even the latest CRT monitors are highly resistant to burn-in effects. Screensavers are thus an outdated concept, except for the small fact that they're *cool*. Whether the image on your monitor needs to be kept in motion or not, it's hard to resist configuring a flashy display for your computer to show when you're not in front of it. It doesn't hurt that the screensavers that come with Mac OS X are some of the best and most visually pleasing examples of the craft ever yet produced.

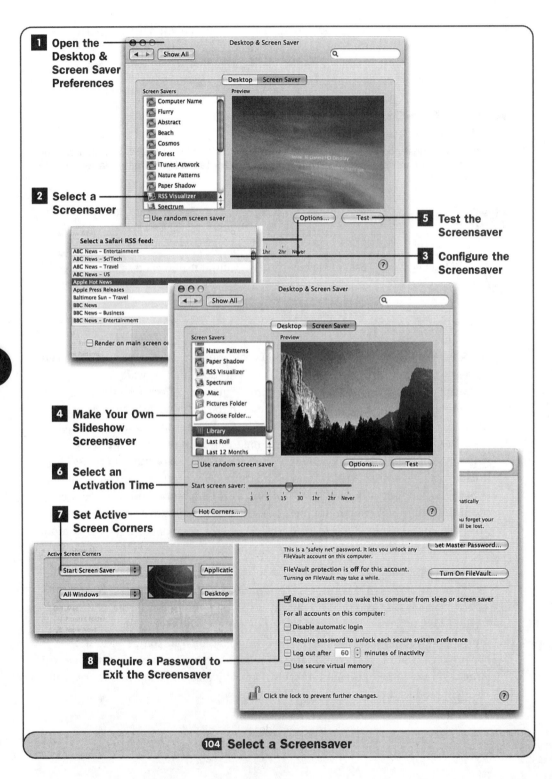

1 Open the Desktop & Screen Saver Preferences

2 Select a Screensaver

5 Test the Screensaver

3 Configure the Screensaver

4 Make Your Own Slideshow Screensaver

6 Select an Activation Time

7 Set Active Screen Corners

8 Require a Password to Exit the Screensaver

104

104 Select a Screensaver

■1 Open the Desktop & Screen Saver Preferences

Open the **System Preferences** application (under the **Apple** menu); click the **Desktop & Screen Saver** icon to open the **Desktop & Screen Saver Preferences** pane. The **Desktop** tab opens by default; click the **Screen Saver** tab.

■2 Select a Screensaver

Choose a screensaver from the **Screen Savers** list on the left. The choices range from the simple **Computer Name** (which displays an Apple logo and the computer's name in various places around the screen) to the beautiful **Abstract, Beach, Cosmos,** and **Forest** slideshows and the new additions **Nature Patterns** and **Paper Shadow;** an automatically updating three-dimensional **RSS Visualizer** ticker that can be customized to show the head-lines from any RSS feed; the understated rolling colors of **Spectrum;** and the mesmerizing **Flurry.** When you click any screensaver in the list, a preview of it appears in the **Preview** panel on the right.

► **TIP**

Many third-party developers have published their own screensavers for Mac OS X; you can add these to your system by moving them (each screensaver has the extension **.saver** on its filename) into the **Screen Savers** folder inside the **Library** folder in your **Home** folder. If you don't have a **Screen Savers** folder inside your **Library**, create it. After moving the **.saver** files into the **Screen Savers** folder, go back to the **Desktop & Screen Saver Preferences** window; the new screensavers should appear in the list.

104

■3 Configure the Screensaver

Most screensavers have several controls and options you can adjust. Click **Options** to open these controls in a sheet; click **OK** when you're done. Generally speaking, because these options don't affect anything but how the screensaver behaves, you can feel perfectly free to tweak any of them howev-er you want. In the case of the **RSS Visualizer** screensaver, the list of avail-able RSS feeds is defined by what feeds Safari knows about; add RSS feeds to your Safari bookmarks to make them available to the screensaver. See **62** **Browse and Organize RSS Feeds** to learn more about RSS feeds.

■4 Make Your Own Slideshow Screensaver

If you like the bundled slideshow screensavers (**Forest** and **Beach** and so on) but you get tired of the same old pictures, you can easily create your own slideshows that work just like them. Mac OS X can automatically create a slideshow screensaver from any folder full of picture files.

Select **Choose Folder** from the **Screen Savers** list and then navigate to the folder containing the pictures you want to use. Click **Choose** when the folder you want is selected. All the pictures in that folder now become part of a smoothly cross-fading and panning slideshow, subject to the options you select in the **Options** sheet.

At the bottom of the **Screen Savers** list are entries for your iPhoto **Library** and **Last Roll**, which let you create slideshow screensavers from your iPhoto Library, just as you can do from the **Desktop** tab (see **103 Change Your Desktop Picture**). Also as in the **Desktop** tab, additional iPhoto albums that you create appear in the list below these entries.

5 Test the Screensaver

To see how the screensaver will look using the full screen, click **Test**. Don't move the mouse after clicking the button; moving the mouse or pressing a key quits the screensaver and returns you to whatever screen was active before the screensaver kicked in.

6 Select an Activation Time

You can have the screensaver activate automatically after a specified period of keyboard or mouse inactivity, from three minutes up to two hours (or never). Drag the slider to select the time period that must elapse before the selected screensaver is activated, or drag it to **Never** to prevent the screensaver from ever activating.

7 Set Active Screen Corners

You can configure *Active Screen Corners* to allow you to start the screensaver immediately, or to prevent the screensaver from activating while you're not moving the mouse or typing (for instance, if you're watching a long QuickTime movie). Click the **Hot Corners** button; use the sheet that appears to define what happens when you move the mouse into each corner of the screen. You can configure some corners to activate *Exposé* functions (see **6 Grab the Window You Want**) and other corners to control the screensaver.

▶ KEY TERMS

Active Screen Corners—Also known as "Hot Corners," this feature allows you to trigger certain functions by moving the mouse pointer into different corners of the screen. Such functions include starting the screensaver or invoking Exposé.

Exposé—A feature that allows you to shrink all your windows so that they all fit on the screen, so you can immediately click to choose the window you want.

104

8 Require a Password to Exit the Screensaver

To protect your computer from the prying eyes of people who walk by after your screensaver has kicked in, you can tell Mac OS X not to allow anybody to reactivate the computer unless they type your account password (see **121** **Change a User's Password** for information on how to manage the account password, which is what a user enters to start a Mac OS X login session). To do this, go to the **Security Preferences** pane (click **Security** in the **System Preferences** application). Select the **Require password to wake this computer from sleep or screen saver** check box.

---

105 Customize a Folder Window

✔ BEFORE YOU BEGIN	→ SEE ALSO
13 Create a New Folder	**17** Change an Icon
	18 Set a Color Label

Because you will be spending a lot of time navigating through the folders in your system and opening the documents in them, it's only natural to want to customize those various folders to reflect your personal tastes. For instance, you might want to navigate the filesystem primarily in the austere but highly functional Column view, but you might want to have your **Pictures** folder be shown in Icon view with each icon cranked up to its maximum size, organized in a grid, sorted alphabetically, and with a special background picture. Mac OS X lets you customize each and every folder in your system if you so desire.

104

▶ **NOTE**

You'll only see your customized folder view if you open a folder directly in a new window—for example, if you have an alias to a folder on your Desktop or in the Dock, or if you double-click the folder in the Finder in Icon view. If you navigate down into a folder using the Finder using List or Column view, the view mode does not change on the fly.

1 Open the View Options Palette

While viewing any Finder window or the Desktop, select **Show View Options** from the **View** menu. The **View Options** palette appears and floats along with the Finder window (it becomes invisible if you switch applications).

With the **View Options** palette visible, you can still click items in the Finder window; if you switch to a different Finder window, the **View Options** palette updates to show the options for the folder shown in the new window.

105

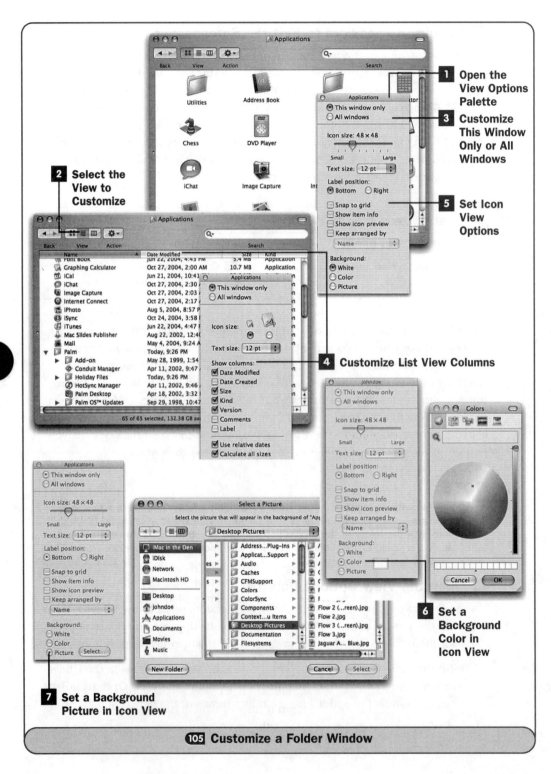

1 Open the View Options Palette

3 Customize This Window Only or All Windows

2 Select the View to Customize

5 Set Icon View Options

4 Customize List View Columns

6 Set a Background Color in Icon View

7 Set a Background Picture in Icon View

105 Customize a Folder Window

2 Select the View to Customize

Click the **view selection buttons** at the top of the Finder window to choose the view mode you want to use for that folder if you open it directly. Note that each view mode has different options shown in the **View Options** palette.

▶ TIP

If you change the view mode for a folder, and then use that same folder window to navigate to another location, the view mode you selected will not be saved for the folder you opened. Changes to the view mode are saved when you close the window; if you want to change the view mode for a folder window you open directly, close the window after selecting the desired view mode. This saves the setting for that folder.

3 Customize This Window Only or All Windows

At the top of the **View Options** palette, no matter what the view mode, are two options that let you choose between setting the options for just the folder window you're customizing, or globally configuring all windows in the system at once.

▶ NOTE

Each view mode's options for each window is set independently. If you set global options for List view, folders that have been set to open in Icon view will still open in Icon view; but if you then switch to List view, the global options take effect. Any specific options you've set for that window override your global settings.

105

4 Customize List View Columns

In List view, you have the option to use large or small icons, to select the font size for document names, and to choose which informational columns you want to show. In the **View Options** palette, select the check box for each column of information you want to see in List view.

You can also reorganize the order in which List view columns are shown on a per-folder basis. In the Finder window for the folder, click a column header and drag it left and right to position it between a different pair of columns. You do not need to have the **View Options** palette open to rearrange the column order.

5 Set Icon View Options

Icon view is the most customizable of the folder views. You can choose how large you want the icons to be (on a smooth scale from 16×16 pixels to 128×128 pixels). You can select whether the filenames should appear below

or to the right of the icons, and whether they should include secondary information about the items' contents (using the **Show item info** check box). You
can force the icons into a strict grid formation, and you can make them sort
themselves alphabetically or according to various other criteria (such as the
time of last modification). If you select the **Show item preview** check box,
documents such as picture files that can be easily represented in a "preview"
form are shown using that preview as a custom icon instead of the default
icon for that document type.

6 Set a Background Color in Icon View

Icon view windows have white backgrounds by default, but you can change
this color. Select the **Background: Color** radio button in the **View Options**
palette for Icon view and click the color box that appears; the color picker
pops up. Use the color wheel and sliders to choose a color.

▶ NOTE

Remember that the black text of the filenames must show up on top of the background
color or you won't be able to read the filenames. Light pastel colors work best as backgrounds for folder windows.

105

7 Set a Background Picture in Icon View

You can use any picture file as a folder window background in Icon view. Select
the **Background: Picture** radio button in the **View Options** palette for Icon
view and click the **Select** button that appears. A navigator window pops up;
navigate to the folder where the picture you want to use is located. Only usable
picture files are selectable; the rest of the items, except for folders, are grayed
out. Double-click the picture file you want, or click it and then click **Select**.

You can remove a background picture by changing the **Background** option
in the **View Options** palette back to **White**.

---

106 | Change the Dock's Position and Behavior

✔ BEFORE YOU BEGIN	→ SEE ALSO
3 Add an Application to the Dock	**4** Control an Application from the Dock
5 Minimize and Restore a Window	

The Dock is the centerpiece of Mac OS X, the flexible and accommodating control
center for your documents and applications. Its ease of use is unprecedented, but
it's also configurable in a number of key ways, a fact that you might find very
welcome as you try to make the Dock work most efficiently for you.

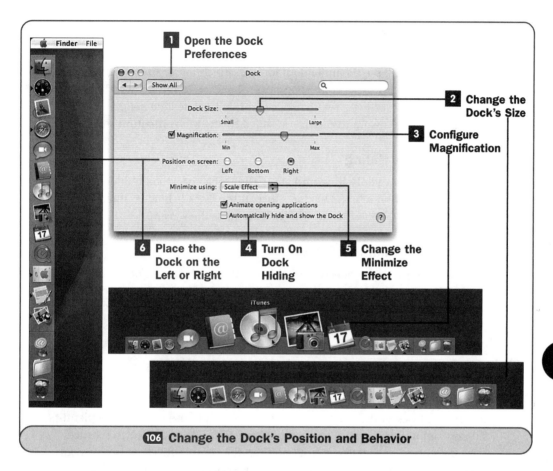

106 Change the Dock's Position and Behavior

1 Open the Dock Preferences

Go directly to the **Dock Preferences** pane by **Control**+clicking or right-clicking the vertical separator bar in the middle of the Dock; select **Dock Preferences** from the contextual menu that pops up. You can also open the **Dock Preferences** by clicking **Dock** in the **System Preferences**, or by choosing **Dock Preferences** from the **Dock** submenu of the **Apple** menu.

2 Change the Dock's Size

Use the **Dock Size** slider to change the size of the Dock. Note that you won't be able to make the Dock larger than the largest size where all icons in the Dock can be shown at once. The Dock's size immediately changes as you move the slider, letting you see the results of your customizations right away.

3 Configure Magnification

One of the Dock's neat features is that even if you make the Dock itself very small, you can still see the individual icons in much larger sizes—because of *magnification*. If you move your mouse over the icons in the Dock with magnification on, the icon you're moving over and its immediate neighbors appear much larger—up to the size specified by the **Magnification** slider.

4 Turn On Dock Hiding

Select the **Automatically hide and show the Dock** check box to hide the Dock from view and regain Desktop space. If the Dock is hidden, it reappears when you move the mouse down to the bottom of the screen.

5 Change the Minimize Effect

There are two minimize effects available in Mac OS X: Genie and Scale. The **Genie Effect** is the default; it's where a minimized window curves and slides into its place in the Dock. The **Scale Effect** simply zooms the window down to its minimized position; you might prefer the Scale effect because of its faster operation.

6 Place the Dock on the Left or Right

By default, the Dock appears at the bottom of your screen. You might not like having the Dock at the bottom; you might prefer it to use up the more plentiful horizontal margin space along the left or right side of the screen (particularly if you have a widescreen display) than the comparatively scarce vertical space at the bottom of the screen. To do this, select either the **Left** or **Right** radio button.

▶ **TIP**

Most of these Dock controls can also be accessed from the Dock itself. Some of the options, such as automatic hiding and left or right positioning, can be selected from the pop-up menu that appears if you **Control**+click (or right-click) the vertical divider bar in the middle of the Dock. You can change the Dock's size by clicking the vertical bar and dragging up and down.

107 Adjust the Format of Numbers and Other Notations

✔ BEFORE YOU BEGIN	→ SEE ALSO
25 Set the Time and Date	108 Change the System's Language

106

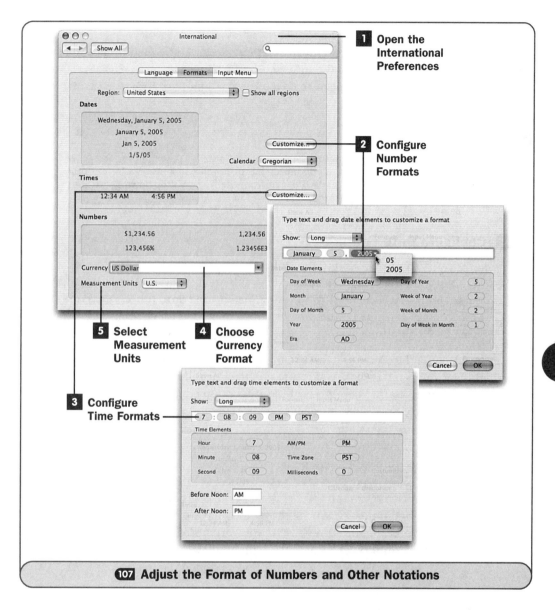

1 Open the International Preferences

2 Configure Number Formats

5 Select Measurement Units

4 Choose Currency Format

3 Configure Time Formats

107

107 Adjust the Format of Numbers and Other Notations

If you're not in the United States, Mac OS X's default behaviors when it displays numbers or dates might appear odd. The operating system supports many different countries' preferred notation formats, and lets you define your own as well (for instance, if you're a U.S. resident who prefers the metric system). Date, time, and number formats can all be changed in the **International Preferences** pane.

1 Open the International Preferences

Open the **System Preferences** application (under the **Apple** menu); click the **International** icon to open the **International Preferences** pane. Click the **Formats** tab to open the page where you can configure the formats of dates, times, and numbers.

▶ TIP

The **Customize** buttons let you manually specify the formats for dates, times, and numbers to match your personal taste. If you prefer, however, you can choose a format profile that matches your country's standard usage from the **Region** drop-down list at the top of the **Formats** page of the **International Preferences** window.

2 Configure Date Formats

Click the **Customize** button in the **Dates** section. The sheet that appears lets you control how a "long date" (using both full and abbreviated weekday and month names, such as **Sunday, January 2, 2005**, and **Sun, Jan 2, 2005**) and a "short date" (such as **1/2/05**) are displayed, as well as other lengths as called for by adjustable listings of dates in applications like the Finder.

To customize the date string format, there are a variety of blue ovals shown in the **Date Elements** box, each representing a meaningful part of the date string: **Day of Week**, **Year**, **Week of Month**, and so on (many of which are more obscurely used than others). Choose a general string style (**Short**, **Long**, **Full**, and so on); then drag these blue ovals from the box into place in the sample string shown above the **Date Elements** box, and drop them into place wherever you want them to appear. To specify a separator character (such as a slash or hyphen), simply click where you want the separator and type the character you want. Most of the date elements also have a white down arrow that appears when you hover the mouse over the oval in the sample string; clicking this arrow shows you variants of the selected element, such as **Jan** or **January**, or **05** or **2005**. With all these options, you can mix and match styles however you wish, creating as standard or as custom a format as you want.

Arrange the date string as desired and click **OK** to go back to the **International Preferences** window.

3 Configure Time Formats

Click the **Customize** button in the **Times** section. In the sheet that appears, you can configure various aspects of how times are displayed beyond what can be configured in the **Date & Time Preferences** pane. For instance, you can choose whether noon and midnight appear as **12:00** or **0:00**; you can

107

have a leading zero placed before one-digit hours (such as **02:00**); and you can enter your own suffixes instead of **AM** and **PM**.

The time string is defined in the same manner as the date string you manipulated in step 4: blue ovals representing time elements, which you can drag into place to develop a string format that suits your fancy. Use the **Before Noon** and **After Noon** text fields to specify what should appear when an identifier like **AM** or **PM** should appear.

Arrange the time string as desired and click **OK** to go back to the **International Preferences** window.

4 Choose Currency Format

Choose a currency format by name from the **Currency** pop-up menu. Nearly every conceivable currency format with a name is represented in the list.

5 Select Measurement Units

Back in the **International Preferences** window, use the **Measurement Units** drop-down list to specify your preferred measurement system (**U.S.** or **Metric**).

---

108 **Change the System's Language**

→ **SEE ALSO**

107 Adjust the Format of Numbers and Other Notations
76 Install a New Font
74 Type §¶éçïà£ ¢hÁràcтérs

Mac OS X supports 83 different languages, all in their own native writing systems, thanks to the massive Unicode character set. Also, because of a unique preference-based cascading localization scheme, you can control which languages are used to run your system. You define what languages are your most preferred; then, whenever you run an application, Mac OS X looks inside it for what *localizations* it supports. A Mac application generally contains several different localizations, defining the contents of text strings and menu options in as many different languages as the application's developer chose to include. Mac OS X goes down your list of preferred languages until it finds one that the application supports, and then it launches the application using that language; this way, you can strike the optimal balance between what languages you want to use and the languages each application has been written to support. All you have to do is set up your **Language Preferences** once.

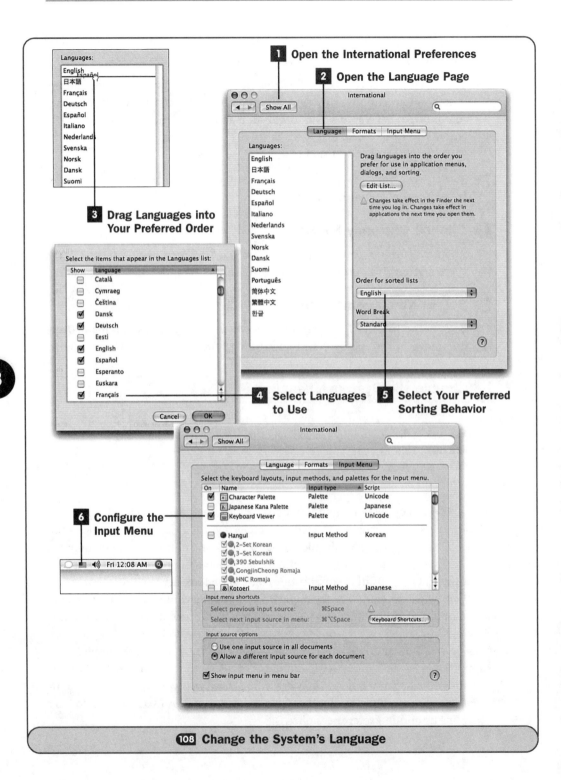

1 Open the International Preferences

2 Open the Language Page

3 Drag Languages into Your Preferred Order

4 Select Languages to Use

5 Select Your Preferred Sorting Behavior

6 Configure the Input Menu

108 Change the System's Language

▶ **KEY TERM**

Localization—Mostly a fancy name for "language," a localization also contains definitions for how sort order, numeric formats, and other written styles behave in a given region.

1 Open the International Preferences

Open the **System Preferences** application (under the **Apple** menu); click the **International** icon to open the **International Preferences** pane.

2 Open the Language Page

Click the **Language** tab to open the language configuration page, if it is not already displayed.

3 Drag Languages into Your Preferred Order

In the **Languages** box, click and drag the displayed language names into the order you prefer to use them. The topmost language is used first if it's available in the application; if not, the second language is used, and so on.

▶ **NOTE**

When you change your language preference order, you are defining what language should be used when each application launches. Because currently running applications have already launched and chosen a language, you'll have to quit and relaunch these applications before they can use your preferred languages. This includes the Finder, so you must log out and log back in before the Mac OS X itself switches languages.

108

4 Select Languages to Use

Although Mac OS X supports 83 languages, only 15 are shown in the **Languages** box. If the language you want to use is not shown there, click the **Edit** button to bring up the dialog box that shows all 83 languages Mac OS X knows about.

Only the languages with the check box selected appear in the **Languages** box. Click the check boxes next to whatever languages you want to appear in the box; you can also deselect languages you know you won't be using. Click **OK** when you're done.

5 Select Your Preferred Sorting Behavior

From the **Order for Sorted Lists** menu, choose the language you want to use for alphabetizing items in lists. Many languages without "alphabets" (such as Chinese and Japanese) have their own *scripts* that define how list sorting works.

Additionally, use the **Word Break** menu to customize how Mac OS X should allow text to "flow" within applications, whether it should break words only on spaces or whether it should use other criteria to automatically break to the next line.

▶ KEY TERM

Script—A general style of writing and set of symbols or letters, often shared by many languages. The Roman alphabet is a script, as is Cyrillic, Kanji, or the Arabic alphabet.

6 Configure the Input Menu

Click the **Input Menu** tab to view the list of input styles. Keyboard layouts for many different languages and regions, as well as palettes for all Unicode characters, for Japanese Hiragana/Katakana, or for the **Keyboard Viewer** are available; you can also choose the **Hangul** (Korean), **Kotoeri** (Japanese), or **Simplified** or **Traditional Chinese** input methods, which let you input native characters using special key commands on a U.S.-style keyboard. Many other simple keyboard-based input methods and regional key remappings are available as well. See **74** Type §¶éçïå£ ¢hÁràc†érs for more information on these special input palettes.

Every input style that you select in the list under the **Input Menu** tab appears in the **Keyboard Input** System Menu, in the right side of the system's main menu bar, to the left of the clock (if you're using the U.S. keyboard layout, the menu appears as a U.S. flag). When only a single *input menu* option is selected in the **International Preferences** window (for instance, the U.S. keyboard layout), the **Keyboard Input** System Menu does not appear in your menu bar. However, if you enable other options using the check boxes, the **Keyboard Input** System Menu icon appears among the System Menu icons, and its icon shows the current input method or layout. You can switch from one layout or method to another quickly by using the menu.

▶ KEY TERM

Keyboard Input System Menu or **Input Menu**—A tool that lets you quickly open a palette or switch to a special input method to enter special characters or non-Latin languages. The Input Menu appears among the System Menu icons in the right side of the menu bar.

For instance, to enable the Dvorak keyboard layout, select it using its check box and the **Keyboard Input** System Menu appears at the top-right corner of the screen (if Dvorak is the second input style you've enabled). Select **Dvorak** from the Input Menu, and your keyboard will now operate in Dvorak mode.

108

Use the **Keyboard Shortcuts** button to set up an easy way to switch between input modes while typing; see **132** **Add a Keyboard Shortcut** for more about the **Keyboard Shortcuts Preferences** pane.

109 Set Applications to Launch Automatically at Login

✔ BEFORE YOU BEGIN	→ SEE ALSO
2 Find, Launch, and Quit an Application	**110** Enable and Disable Automatic Login
	114 Automatically Log Out

One final way to customize your Mac OS X user environment is to have one or more applications launch themselves automatically as soon as you log in (or boot the computer, if you have automatic login enabled). You'll find this very useful as you become more familiar with Mac OS X and with the applications you want to have running to be more productive. For instance, in the course of writing this book, it's necessary for me to have Snapz Pro X (the premier screen-capture application for Mac OS X) running at all times. Rather than hunting it down and launching it every time I start the computer, I can have it launch automatically.

108

▶ TIP

An even quicker way to accomplish what's described in this task is to right-click (or **Control**+click) an application's icon in the dock and choose **Open at Login** from the contextual menu; this adds the application to your Startup Items list.

1 Open the Accounts Preferences

Open the **System Preferences** application (under the **Apple** menu); click **Accounts** to go to the **Accounts Preferences** pane.

2 Select Your Account

Your account is the topmost one shown in the list, and is probably already selected. If not, select it. Your account options display, such as your full name and password options.

3 Go to the Login Items

Click the **Login Items** tab.

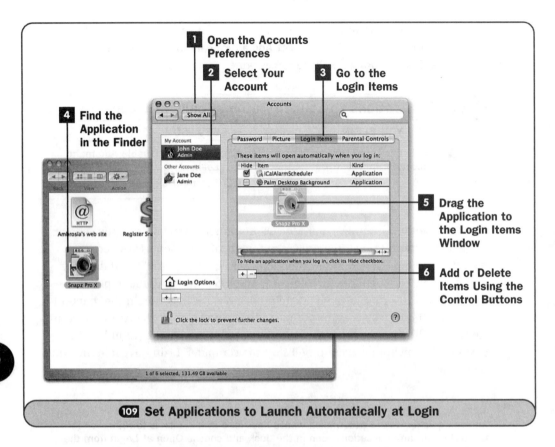

109 Set Applications to Launch Automatically at Login

4 Find the Application in the Finder

Open a Finder window and navigate to the **Applications** folder (using the shortcut in the Finder's Sidebar, for example). Find the application you want to launch at startup or login.

5 Drag the Application to the Login Items Window

Click and drag the application from the Finder window into the **Login Items** list. If there are already items in the list, you can place the new one anywhere in the list you want; the order of the items in the list determines the order in which they are launched. This order might be important, in case some of the items depend on other items already having been launched. If you need to change the order of the listed applications, remove and add applications in the correct order.

▶ **TIP**

You can add other items than just applications to your **Startup Items** list. You can add a document, and it will launch at startup in the application that it's set to open in; or you can add a folder, and the folder window will open at startup. If you add a remote server's icon to the list, Mac OS X attempts to connect to that server as soon as it logs you in, making sure you always have immediate access to items stored there.

6 Add or Delete Items

If you'd rather not drag applications to the **Startup Items** list, you can use the + button below the list box to pop up a navigator sheet you can use to pick the application to add.

To delete an item from the **Startup Items** list, select it and then click the – button. (This action only removes the item from the **Startup Items** list; it doesn't delete it from the computer.)

109

15

Working with Other Users on One Computer

IN THIS CHAPTER:

As a true multiuser operating system, Mac OS X gives you and the other members of your household, classroom, or business a great deal of flexibility in how you all share the use of the computer among yourselves. It also, however, introduces complexities that a single-user operating system lacks.

Security and convenience, it has been said, are mutually exclusive concepts. To make software easier to use and more convenient, software companies sometimes have to sacrifice the security of that software; the reverse is also true. For instance, an email program that automatically opens newly received messages is very convenient, but it is inherently insecure in that it can very easily execute a virus in one of those messages without your lifting a finger.

This principle is especially true when it comes to multiuser operating systems such as Mac OS X. This kind of system allows you to create multiple user environments, each tailored to the tastes of each person who uses the computer, and each secure from all the others on the same machine. But to properly take advantage of this added security and privacy, the users of the computer have to individually log in—instead of simply booting the computer into a single, common working environment as in the Windows and Mac OS systems of old. Indeed, many computer users even in the present day find the task of logging in and out to be too tedious—and they don't use the multiuser features of their computers at all, allowing everybody to share a single user account and working environment. However, this practice—beyond simply lacking security and privacy for the computer's multiple users—misses out on many of the coolest parts of Mac OS X, designed to make the process of switching from user environment to user environment pain-free and convenient.

This chapter discusses the various features of Mac OS X that ease the necessary discomforts associated with a multiuser operating system, allowing users of a single computer to share its resources, exchange files and information with each other, and switch quickly from one login session to another and back. It also discusses the administrative tasks that you, as the owner of the computer, will need to know how to perform—and exactly what makes an "administrator" so special.

110 Enable and Disable Automatic Login

✔ BEFORE YOU BEGIN	→ SEE ALSO
118 Add a New User	**109** Set Applications to Launch Automatically at Login
	112 Switch to Another User

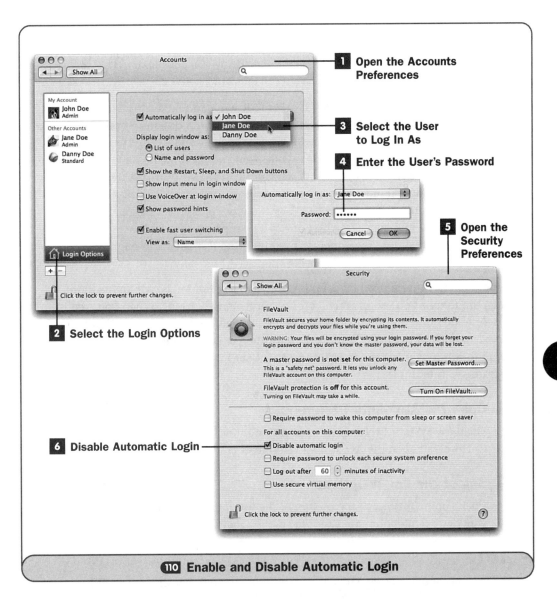

1 Open the Accounts Preferences

3 Select the User to Log In As

4 Enter the User's Password

5 Open the Security Preferences

2 Select the Login Options

6 Disable Automatic Login

110 Enable and Disable Automatic Login

Automatic login is an option that lets your computer act as though it has only one user on it—the user who primarily uses the computer. It's a useful feature if you're the only person who ever uses the machine; it eliminates the need for you to log in to your account when you boot up the Mac, and it logs you directly in to your working environment.

▶ KEY TERM

Automatic login—When you start up a Mac with this option enabled, the computer enters a predetermined user's login session automatically; you don't have to type your password to log in.

If multiple people use your computer, automatic login can be a detriment; after all, you don't want someone else booting up the computer and automatically being dumped into *your* account. He then has to log out and log in to his own account, or he might decide to just use yours—and you'll come home to find all your icons rearranged and a bunch of new music in iTunes that you know you don't listen to. More dangerously, someone using your account can access any of the websites or online systems protected by the passwords saved in your Keychain—including your bank account and your private email. The more you think about it, the more the dangers of maintaining a single login ought to be apparent.

Automatic login is enabled by default until you create more user accounts than the primary one you set up when you first turned on your Mac. When you create a second account, automatic login becomes disabled, so that you must choose an account to log in to after booting; you must then re-enable automatic login if you want to continue using it. See **118** **Add a New User** for more information about working with multiple users.

110

1 Open the Accounts Preferences

Open the **System Preferences** application (under the **Apple** menu); click **Accounts** to open the **Accounts Preferences** pane.

2 Select the Login Options

Click **Login Options** at the bottom of the list of users on the left side of the window. The global options for the system's login behavior appear.

▶ NOTE

You must be logged in as an Admin user to open the **Login Options** pane. See **117** **About Administrative Responsibilities** for more information.

3 Select the User to Log In As

Select the check box next to **Automatically log in as** and open the drop-down list; all the users on the system are in the list. Pick the one you want the system to automatically boot into instead of presenting the login screen.

4 Enter the User's Password

In the sheet that appears, enter the selected user's password and click **OK**. The next time you restart the computer, it will boot directly into that user's working environment.

5 Open the Security Preferences

If you're an Admin user, you can also disable automatic login and force the computer to present the login screen when it boots up. To do this, click **Show All** in the System Preferences toolbar, then click **Security** to open the **Security Preferences** pane.

6 Disable Automatic Login

Click the **Disable automatic login** check box. Automatic login is immediately disabled. To re-enable it, return to the **Accounts Preferences** pane and follow steps 2, 3, and 4 of this task.

---

111 **Log In from the Login Window**

✔ **BEFORE YOU BEGIN**	→ **SEE ALSO**
118 Add a New User	**109** Set Applications to Launch Automatically at Login
110 Enable and Disable Automatic Login	**114** Automatically Log Out

110

With *automatic login* disabled, one screen that you will become very familiar with is the login window. This screen features a box in the middle with a list of all the available users in the system, each with a personalized picture. Any of these users can log in by clicking their name and entering their password when prompted. At the end of your session, when you log out from the **Apple** menu (or if you have Mac OS X set to log you out automatically), you return to the login window.

▶ **TIP**

Security-conscious administrators may choose a different style of login window—one that, instead of a list of available users, presents two text input boxes: a name and a password. You can enter either your full name or your short username, but without the list of users to choose from visually, someone trying to sneak into the system will have a much harder time trying to guess a valid username.

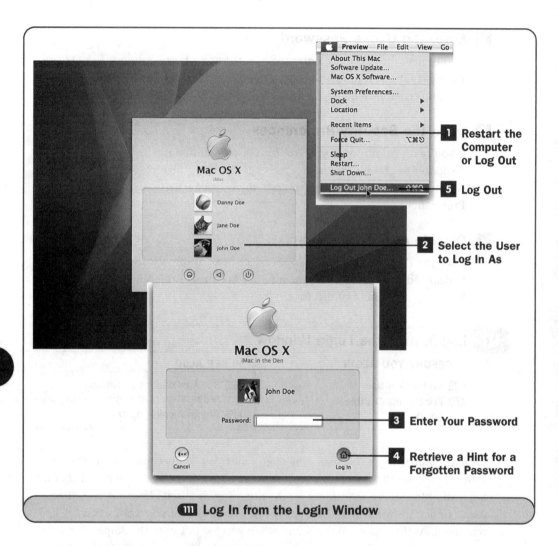

111 Log In from the Login Window

You can even return to the login window without ending your session. If you enable **Fast User Switching** (see **112** **Switch to Another User**), you can call up the login window at any time, log in as another user, or return to your session that's been running in the background.

1 Restart the Computer or Log Out

First make sure that automatic login is turned off (see **110** **Enable and Disable Automatic Login**) to ensure that the computer will present the login window rather than booting automatically into a certain user's account.

Restart the computer; alternatively, select **Log Out <*Your Name*>** from the **Apple** menu and click **Log Out** to confirm the action. When the computer is ready for your input, it will display the login window.

2 Select the User to Log In As

From the list of users, scroll to the user you want to log in as, if necessary, and click on the user's name or picture. The window shifts slightly to give you a password box. Click **Go Back** if you have mistakenly selected the wrong user.

3 Enter Your Password

Type your password into the box and click **Log In**. You are logged in to your user environment; in a few moments, after your Dock and Desktop have been set up and any Startup Items you have configured have executed (see **109 Set Applications to Launch Automatically at Login** for more information), you will be ready to use the computer normally.

4 Retrieve a Hint for a Forgotten Password

It happens to the best of us: You might try to log in, but for the life of you you can't remember your password. Fortunately, Mac OS X has you covered. If you enter an incorrect password three times, you are automatically shown the "hint" that's associated with your account password, which you specified when you first set up your Mac or created the user account you're working with (see **118 Add a New User** for more about password hints). This hint should remind you what password to use.

111

▶ **NOTE**

If you can't remember your password even with the hint, you need to ask the primary user of the computer to reset your password for you, as shown in **121 Change a User's Password**. (Any Admin user can change another user's password.) If you're the primary user and you've forgotten the password for the only Admin account on the computer, you can reset your password by booting the system from the Tiger installation CD or DVD and selecting the **Reset Password** option from the **Utilities** menu rather than going through the installation process.

5 Log Out

When you're done using the computer, choose **Log Out <*Your Name*>** from the **Apple** menu. Click **Log Out** in the confirmation dialog box that appears to quit your applications and log out immediately; if you don't click that button, Mac OS X automatically shuts down all your applications and logs you out after two minutes (120 seconds). After you log out, the Mac returns to showing the login window.

▶ **NOTE**

For privacy's sake, it's always a good idea to log out at the end of each user session if your Mac is in a multiuser environment. You don't want other people to be able to come along and mess around with your files, after all. Consider configuring Mac OS X to log you out automatically (see **114 Automatically Log Out**); or at the very least, make sure that the Mac requires a password if awakened from sleep or the screen saver (**115 Require a Password When Reactivating the Computer**).

112 Switch to Another User

✔ BEFORE YOU BEGIN	→ SEE ALSO
118 Add a New User	**113** Use the Shared Folder
111 Log In from the Login Window	**114** Automatically Log Out

Suppose you're in the middle of typing an important email or working on a movie in iMovie, when your spouse comes in and asks to use the computer "just for a minute." Do you have to quit all your applications, log out, log in to the other account, wait around until it's your turn again, and then log back in using your own account—only to spend another five minutes relaunching all your applications and getting your user environment and your iMovie project back the way you had them? Perish the thought.

The **Fast User Switching** feature lets you immediately switch directly between user environments without the laborious process of repeatedly logging out and logging in as another user. When the feature is enabled, you can select any of the system's users from the **User** menu at the top-right of the screen; when you enter that user's password, you are taken directly to that user environment.

This means that any number of users can be logged in at the same time, all concurrently running their own applications. You can see which users are logged in at any time by opening the **User** menu and seeing which ones are marked with a green check mark. If many users are logged in at once and all running their own applications, the system can run out of memory, which leads to very sluggish performance. It's best to keep simultaneous logins to a minimum, and to avoid using **Fast User Switching** while you're running resource-hungry applications.

▶ **NOTE**

You must have administrative privileges to enable **Fast User Switching**; see **117 About Administrative Responsibilities** for more information. However, after the feature is enabled, any user can switch to any other user, after entering a valid password.

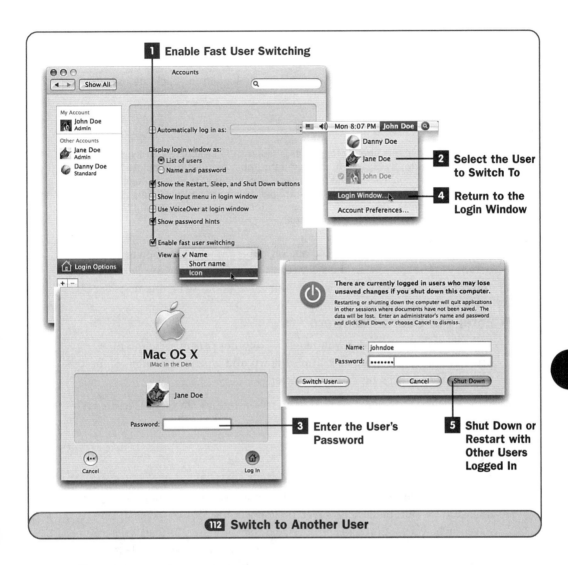

1 Enable Fast User Switching

2 Select the User to Switch To

4 Return to the Login Window

3 Enter the User's Password

5 Shut Down or Restart with Other Users Logged In

112 Switch to Another User

112

1 Enable Fast User Switching

Open the **System Preferences** application (under the **Apple** menu); click **Accounts** to open the **Accounts Preferences** pane. Click **Login Options** and then click the **Enable fast user switching** check box (if it isn't enabled already). Choose also whether to display the list of names as text (the long or short name) or with icons. The menu bar changes to show your name in bold in the upper-right corner, next to the **Spotlight** icon. You can open this **User** menu to switch immediately to any other user.

2 Select the User to Switch To

Click the **User** menu to see the list of available users. If any user is marked with a green check mark, that user is already logged in. Click the user to which you want to switch.

▶ **TIP**

Switching to a user who is already logged in is faster than switching to a user who isn't. If the user is not currently logged in, the computer must perform a complete login operation, starting up any applications the new user has configured to start at login and setting up the user environment with all its trimmings (such as the Dock). This generally takes 10 to 20 seconds. However, if the user is already logged in, switching to her user environment should take only 1 or 2 seconds.

A login dialog box similar to the one on the login window appears in the middle of the screen, with the selected user's name and a password input box. You can click **Cancel** if you change your mind about switching users.

3 Enter the User's Password

Type the user's password; if you're letting another person switch to his account from within yours, let him sit down and type it. It is, after all, best for each user to keep his password secret!

If the password is entered correctly, the screen rotates out of sight and is replaced with the new user's login session.

4 Return to the Login Window

A common scenario might be that you want to take a break from your work and leave the computer running, but you don't want to quit all your applications and log out; neither, however, do you want to lock the screen using a screensaver, preventing others from using the computer. Instead, you can use **Fast User Switching** to simply return to the main login window, leaving your session logged in, but allowing others to log in to their own sessions while you're gone.

▶ **TIP**

When you wake the computer from sleep or a screensaver, if it is configured to prompt you for the current user's password, the dialog box also contains a **Switch User** button. Click this button to log in as another user, leaving the current user logged in in the background.

From the **User** menu, select **Login Window** (the last entry). The screen rotates out of view and is replaced with the login window. Your user session is not suspended or terminated—your applications are still running. You can see this by the green check mark next to your name in the login window. Click your name and enter your password to switch back to your user session.

⑤ Shut Down or Restart with Other Users Logged In

If there are multiple users logged in at once, they might lose unsaved data in their applications if you shut down or restart the computer. To shut down or restart the computer while multiple users are logged in, you must be able to *authenticate* as an Admin user so that you can override the other users' login sessions. Standard users can't force other users' sessions to end.

Select **Restart** or **Shut Down** from the **Apple** menu; a dialog box appears, informing you that there are other users logged in. Type the full name or short username of any Admin user (including yourself, if you are one), as well as that account's password; then click **Shut Down** or **Restart**, depending which you're doing. If the Admin user information is entered correctly, all login sessions are terminated without saving their data.

112

▶ TIP
Naturally, it's best to log out of each user's login session properly before shutting down or restarting. If this is at all possible, switch to each logged-in account and select **Log Out <*User's Name*>** from the **Apple** menu before shutting down the Mac. You should perform step 5 in this task only if there is no other option—if you don't know the other users' passwords, for example.

---

113 Use the Shared Folder

✔ BEFORE YOU BEGIN	→ SEE ALSO
118 Add a New User	**112** Switch to Another User
19 Move, Copy, or Delete a Document or Folder	

Normally, one user cannot rummage around in the folders inside another user's **Home** folder. If there are multiple users on the same machine, you can use the Finder to navigate to another user's **Home** folder (all **Home** folders are inside the **Users** folder at the top level of the startup disk), but with the exception of the **Public** and **Sites** folders, all the user's personal folders are closed to viewing by others.

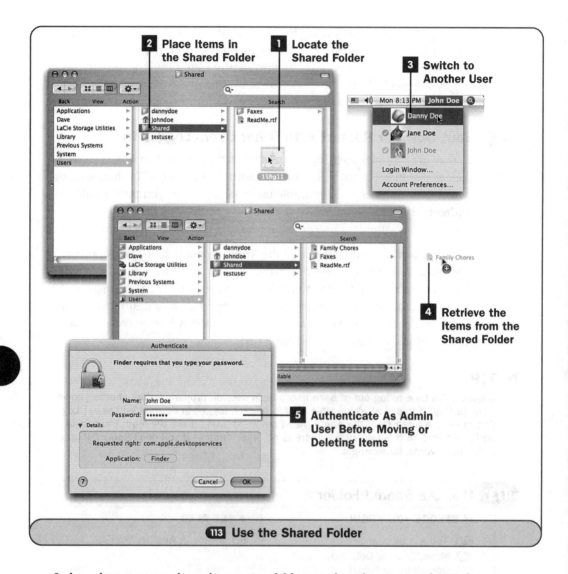

2 Place Items in the Shared Folder

1 Locate the Shared Folder

3 Switch to Another User

4 Retrieve the Items from the Shared Folder

5 Authenticate As Admin User Before Moving or Deleting Items

113 Use the Shared Folder

So how does one user share documents, folders, and applications with another user on the same machine? How can you publish a file so that everybody on the system can access it equally? Using the **Shared** folder, located inside the **Users** folder at the same level as all the **Home** folders. The **Shared** folder has permissions such that any user can place items into it and access items that other users have put there, but only the user who put an item there (or an Admin user) can change it or delete it from the folder.

1 Locate the Shared Folder

Open a **Finder** window and navigate to the **Shared** folder. The easiest way to do this is to click the computer's hard disk icon in the Sidebar (or choose **Go, Computer** and open the disk), switch to Column view, and click the **Users** folder. The **Shared** folder is there inside **Users**.

2 Place Items in the Shared Folder

Drag documents, folders, or applications into the **Shared** folder, or save documents directly into it from your applications.

▶ **NOTE**

If you create an alias to some item in your **Home** folder and put the alias in the **Shared** folder, note that the original item has to be in a publicly accessible folder (**Public**, **Sites**, or any folder you have created yourself at the same level) for other users to be able to use the alias.

3 Switch to Another User

Either use **Fast User Switching** if it is enabled (see **112** **Switch to Another User**) to switch to another user or log out and log in as the other user.

4 Retrieve the Items from the Shared Folder

Navigate to the **Shared** folder. You can access any items placed in that folder, open them in applications, or copy them to your own Desktop simply by dragging (as though they are stored on a different volume).

5 Authenticate As Admin User Before Moving or Deleting Items

If you are an Admin user, you can move other users' items out of the **Shared** folder (by holding down the ⌘ key as you drag it) to your Desktop or the Trash. To make sure that you have the permissions to do this, Mac OS X prompts you for an Admin user's password before it commits such an action.

▶ **NOTE**

If you are the user who placed the items in the **Shared** folder, you can also freely move or delete them without having to authenticate.

113

114 Automatically Log Out

✔ BEFORE YOU BEGIN	→ SEE ALSO
110 Enable and Disable Automatic Login	**112** Switch to Another User
111 Log In from the Login Window	

If you have a shared computer with multiple users, and you're not sure you trust the other users not to mess with your stuff (for example, if the computer is shared at a school or with an inquisitive little brother), it might be a good idea to configure Mac OS X to log out automatically after a certain period of keyboard or mouse inactivity. This ensures that if you get up and walk away from the Mac without properly logging yourself out, a mischievous interloper can't come by an hour later and start pawing through your settings and personal documents. After a period of inactivity that you set, your session will automatically end, and the Mac will return to the login window so that only valid users can access the computer by logging in properly.

114

1 Open the Security Preferences

Open the **System Preferences** application (under the **Apple** menu); click **Security** to open the **Security Preferences** pane.

2 Enable Automatic Log Out

Select the **Log out after** check box to allow Mac OS X to log you out after the default period of 60 minutes of inactivity.

3 Set the Inactivity Time

To adjust how long you want Mac OS X to wait before logging you out, use the up and down arrows to change the period one minute at a time. Alternatively, enter a number of minutes by selecting the existing number and typing. The value you enter must be a number between **5** and **960**. If you enter a larger or smaller number, the value is automatically adjusted to the nearest valid value.

4 Confirm Log Out

When the specified period of inactivity elapses, you will get a dialog box that gives you 120 seconds to cancel logout (or immediately confirm it). If you are running any applications with unsaved data, they will prevent Mac OS X from logging you out. Always make sure that all your data is saved before you get up and walk away!

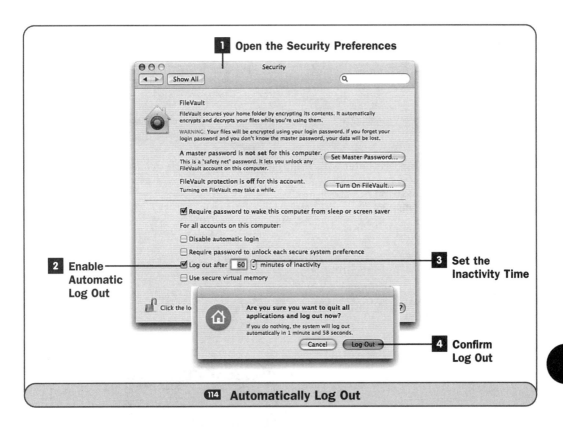

1 **Open the Security Preferences**

2 Enable Automatic Log Out

3 Set the Inactivity Time

4 Confirm Log Out

114 **Automatically Log Out**

114

---

115 **Require a Password When Reactivating the Computer**

✔ **BEFORE YOU BEGIN**	→ **SEE ALSO**
104 Select a Screensaver	**123** Set the Computer's Sleep Time
	116 Lock the Screen
	6 Grab the Window You Want
	94 Access Your Desk Accessories (Dashboard)

In a public working environment, it's always a good idea to make sure that your screen will lock itself if you step away. If you don't want to be automatically logged out after a certain period of inactivity, Mac OS X gives you another option: You can have the system prompt you for a password before it rouses the Mac from sleep or disengages a screensaver that has kicked in.

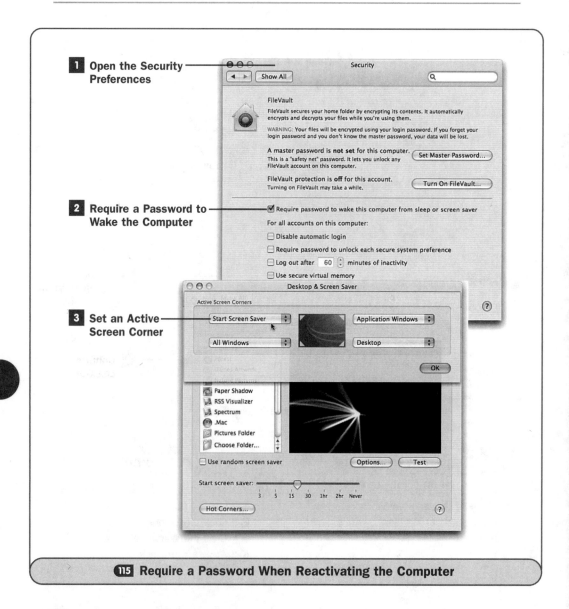

1 Open the Security Preferences

2 Require a Password to Wake the Computer

3 Set an Active Screen Corner

115

115 Require a Password When Reactivating the Computer

1 Open the Security Preferences

Open the **System Preferences** application (under the **Apple** menu); click **Security** to open the **Security Preferences** pane.

2 Require a Password to Wake the Computer

Select the **Require a password to wake this computer** check box. When this option is enabled, Mac OS X prompts you with a username and password input dialog box if you try to wake the computer from sleep or from a screen-saver.

▶ **TIP**

The password you use to wake the computer from sleep is the same as your login password.

③ Set an Active Screen Corner

Open the **Desktop & Screen Saver Preferences** pane (click **Desktop & Screen Saver** in the **System Preferences** window); on the **Screen Saver** tab, click the **Hot Corners** button. In the sheet that appears, pick an unassigned corner and choose **Start Screen Saver** from the list, which also includes Exposé and Dashboard activation modes. From now on, moving the mouse to that corner of the screen immediately starts the screensaver; to reactivate the computer, you (or an intruder) must enter your username and password.

---

116 Lock the Screen

➔ **SEE ALSO**

115 Require a Password When Reactivating the Computer
114 Automatically Log Out
135 Extract a Password from the Keychain

115

An alternative way to lock your screen and to gain access to a number of other security features as well (using *Keychain*) is to enable the **Keychain Status** System Menu and use it to launch a locked screensaver. This System Menu has many other and more subtle uses, as does the Keychain Access utility itself (see **135 Extract a Password from the Keychain** for more information). This task, however, looks only at how to lock the screen using this mechanism.

① Launch Keychain Access

Navigate to the **Utilities** folder inside the **Applications** folder and launch the **Keychain Access** utility.

② Enable the Keychain Status System Menu

Open the **Keychain Access Preferences** (under the **Keychain Access** menu). Under the **General** tab, select the **Show Status in Menu Bar** check box. The **Keychain Status** System Menu appears among your other system menus at the top-right corner of the screen. This menu gives you quick access to the **Keychain Access** utility, as well as one-click shortcuts to locking your current login keychain and the overall system keychain.

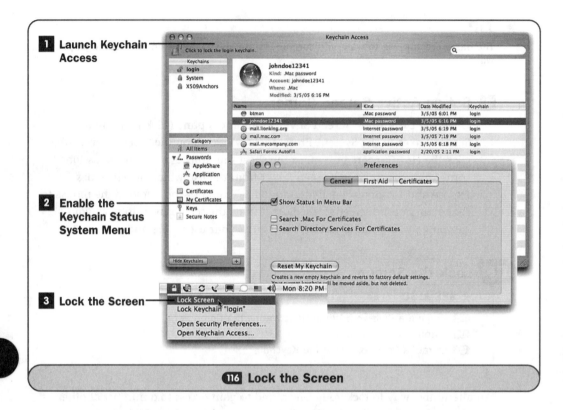

1 Launch Keychain Access

2 Enable the Keychain Status System Menu

3 Lock the Screen

116

116 Lock the Screen

3 Lock the Screen

From the **Keychain Status** System Menu, select **Lock Screen**. The screensaver immediately starts, using the screensaver you most recently selected. When you want to wake the computer by moving the mouse or pressing a keyboard key, you are prompted for a username and password before the screensaver will disengage.

117 About Administrative Responsibilities

There are two kinds of users in Mac OS X: standard users and *Admin users* (or *administrators*). Standard users have limited capabilities; they cannot change global preferences for the computer, modify system files or hardware settings, or install applications. (They can, however, read and burn CDs, play games, and do many other things that require ordinary hardware access.) Admin users, however, have total control over the system's behavior and can change anything they want.

▶ KEY TERM

Admin user—A type of user who is granted the capabilities to change global settings, install applications, and make other changes to the behavior of the entire system.

The first account that was created on your computer, at the time when you first started it up, is an Admin user; unless you have created any other users, this is the account you're using now. You can also grant Admin status to standard users, or revoke it from other Admin users.

The power associated with an Admin user account naturally brings with it the responsibility to use that power wisely, which means using it only where necessary; because an Admin user is capable of changing system files and global settings that a standard user can't modify, such a user also has the potential to wreck the entire system by deleting critical files or mangling system settings. For this reason alone, it's generally desirable to make sure that unless they specifically need to be able to change system settings or install applications, new user accounts that you create (for members of your family or employees at your workplace) are standard user accounts. This greatly reduces the chance that anything will get broken through daily use. (On the other hand, it means you won't have anyone else to blame if anything does go wrong...)

117

Under some circumstances, giving up Admin power for the sake of safety during daily computing is an acceptable tradeoff. You might have a public computer in your living room that anybody can use, for instance; on this computer, you might have a single Admin account that you use only on those rare occasions when you need to install new software or update Mac OS X, and several other accounts—standard accounts—for each of the other members of the household to run their applications and store their personal files.

However, because of the way Mac OS X is designed, it's generally safe to use the computer routinely no matter what kind of account you use. The reason for this is that Mac OS X's security architecture allows any user—even a standard user—to accomplish administrative tasks, provided that that user has the name and password of an Admin user. Mac OS X prompts for this information, in what is known as *authentication*, whenever a user tries to perform a task that requires administrative power (such as changing a global system setting, deleting a file owned by another user, or shutting down while other users are logged in). Thus, as long as there's at least one Admin account on the computer, you can create a standard account for each of the computer's users and even yourself to use on a routine basis, and still be able to accomplish Admin tasks using that account.

You are prompted to authenticate as an Admin user when you attempt to perform certain tasks.

▶ **KEY TERM**

Authentication—When you enter the name and password for an Admin user, you're authenticating as an administrator. If you do so correctly, the system lets you perform a requested administrator-level task. Authentication is usually triggered by clicking a "lock" icon whose appearance ("locked" or "unlocked") indicates whether changes are allowed or prevented. This icon appears in many **System Preferences** panes.

▶ **NOTE**

After you authenticate for any secure task, you have five minutes of free administrative capability (you can issue any new commands that you want without entering your password again) before Mac OS X will again require authentication. Note that this does not apply to moving files that you don't own in the Finder; these operations require authentication on a case-by-case basis.

Similarly, even Admin users must authenticate before certain actions will be executed. The reason for this is that the system must ensure that it's actually a user with Admin privileges requesting the action, not just some random person who sat down at the computer while the real Admin user was away. Admin users can directly manipulate system files (in the global **Library** folder, for example) and change all System Preferences without authenticating, but they must enter their passwords at other critical times, such as when installing new system software. Thus the dangers inherent in routinely working as an Admin user are mitigated, and you generally won't have to worry if your Mac has only a single user account on it, an Admin account, which you use every day.

▶ **TIP**

The security-conscious Mac user might want to extend Mac OS X's cautiousness about installing system software and overriding file ownership to cover the **System Preferences** as well. Open the **Security Preferences** (click **Security** in the **System Preferences**), and select the **Require password to unlock each secure system preference** check box. With this option selected, every time you want to modify any of the locked Preference panes, you will need to click the lock icon in the lower-left corner of the **System Preferences** window to authenticate as an Admin user.

117

If you create additional user accounts, create them as standard user accounts, unless you want the other users to have the same administrative powers that you do. This ensures that while they must rely on you to install new applications or keep the system updated, you're also the only one who can really do any damage to the computer; others can use the system free of worry, leaving the administrative tasks in your capable hands. Aside from the security and privacy benefits discussed earlier in this chapter, having multiple users on a Mac also makes a system a lot easier to administer and keep organized. Particularly thanks to the division of privileges between standard users and Admin users, you can tightly control what kind of important actions take place in the computer, while giving each of your users the freedom to use it according to their own tastes and preferences.

▶ NOTE

Standard users can change their own full names, passwords, and login pictures. They can't, however, change any other user's information.

If you are the system administrator, you can create, delete, and modify all the other user accounts from your own Admin account, including their passwords and login pictures (which appear in the login window and in the **Fast User Switching** menu). All this functionality occurs in the **Accounts Preferences** pane.

117

118	**Add a New User**

✔ BEFORE YOU BEGIN	→ SEE ALSO
117 About Administrative Responsibilities	**119** Grant Admin Capabilities to Another User
	120 Restrict Another User's Capabilities
	122 Delete a User

It's a good idea to create a separate user account for each person who will be using the computer—each member of your family, each student in your class, each employee in your office. It doesn't matter how many accounts your system has; each account's impact on the computer's resources is minimal, consisting of one more **Home** folder hierarchy in the **Users** folder. But making sure that each person has to log in separately into a separate user environment keeps each person's activities from affecting anyone else's documents and settings.

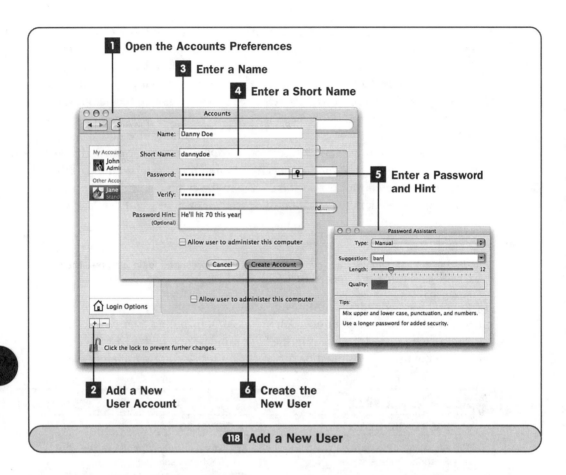

118 Add a New User

Each user must be created in a separate action. To create a user account, you must have the user's full name, his short name (or username), his password, and (optionally) a hint that the person can use if he forgets his password. Ask the person what short name, password, and password hint should be used in creating his new account—or, if you prefer, make them up yourself. Mac OS X will supply a default short name derived from the full name; this short name as a practical matter only appears as the name of the user's **Home** folder.

▶ **TIP**

It's good security practice for every user's password to be as secret as possible—and that means that ideally, even *you* shouldn't know the new user's password. The best way to proceed is to have the other person nearby while you create his account; have him type in his password and hint, so that you don't have to know what it is. Alternatively, set a temporary password (such as **ChangeThis**) and tell the user that he must change his password as soon as possible. See **121** **Change a User's Password** for more information.

▶ **NOTE**

You must be logged in as an Admin user, or able to authenticate as one using the lock icon in the **Accounts Preferences** pane, to create a new user account.

1 Open the Accounts Preferences

Open the **System Preferences** application (under the **Apple** menu); click **Accounts** to open the **Accounts Preferences** pane.

2 Add a New User Account

Click the + icon at the bottom left to create a new user account. The user's account is immediately partially created and appears in the list on the left with no name and a randomly chosen login picture. The right pane contains fields in which you must enter the user's full name, short name, password, and a password hint before the account is fully created.

3 Enter a Name

Type the user's full name. This text entry can contain spaces, apostrophes, and other special characters; it should match how the user naturally writes his full name.

118

4 Enter a Short Name

The *short name* is what's used at the lower Unix level to identify each user and to provide an easy-to-type user ID (such as **jsmith**). The short name is also used as the name for the user's **Home** folder. You won't often have a need to use the short name in Mac OS X (unless you use some of the more advanced Unix features), but if you're logging in at the login window (and you've configured it to require each user to type his name and password rather than picking his picture from the list), you can use either the full name or the short name to identify yourself.

▶ **NOTE**

Short names are generally in all lowercase letters by convention, but you can use capital letters if you want. Logging in using the short name is not a case-sensitive operation, but many of the more advanced Unix features *are* case-sensitive regarding the short name. It's generally best to just stick with all lowercase letters when choosing a short name.

After you enter the user's full name in step 3, Mac OS X automatically choos-es a short name, created by removing any special characters and spaces from the **Name** field and converting it all to lowercase. You can accept the short name that the system picks for you, or you can type any short name that isn't already used by an account in the system. The short name can be as long as you want, but try to keep it under 10 or 12 characters to make it easy for the user to type.

▶ **TIP**

If you are adding a large number of accounts (such as in a business environment), it's a good idea to develop a plan for assigning unique, short, and predictable short names to users. A standard username form might include the first five letters of the last name, followed by the first and middle initials, as in **doejq** for John Q. Doe.

5 Enter a Password and Hint

Type a password for the new user. A good password should be about six to eight characters in length, should not be any word that can be found in the dictionary (or be the same as the short name or anything else that can be guessed easily by someone trying to break in), and should contain at least one special punctuation or symbolic character (such as @, #, or !). A good password scheme might be to pick all the first letters from the title of a favorite song, or to pick a name of a pet and change the occurrences of **S** to **$**, **A** to **@**, and so on.

118

▶ **TIP**

Each user can change her password at will (see **121** **Change a User's Password**), but you might want to at least educate users about what makes a good password. Passwords should be complicated enough to be unguessable, but simple enough for the user to remember easily.

If you need help coming up with a good password to use, click the "**key**" button to open the **Password Assistant** panel. This is a tool that suggests appropriate passwords for you to use according to several different schemes, including **Memorable** (for passwords composed of English words cleverly strung together), **Letters and Numbers**, and **Manual**. Use the **Length** slider to select how long you want the suggested password to be; longer passwords are better and more secure, as indicated by the **Quality** meter below the slider. In **Manual** mode, type a password of your choice into the **Suggestion** box, and the **Quality** meter shows how good the password is; the **Tips** box offers pointers on how to improve your entered password, such as pointing out whether it's derived from dictionary words, too short, or otherwise too easy to guess. Try to pick a password where the quality meter is long and green rather than short and red, and where the **Tips** box has no improvements to suggest.

▶ **NOTE**

The Password Assistant utility automatically fills in its suggested password into the **Password** field of the sheet in the **Account Preferences** pane; however, it doesn't fill it into the **Verify** field. You have to type that yourself, to make sure the password has been entered correctly and memorized.

Enter the chosen password twice—once in the **Password** field, and again in the **Verify** field. Entering the password twice helps ensure that the password is entered correctly, because it's hidden as you type it.

To assist the user in remembering his password, you can enter a "hint," which is text that appears if the user tries several times to enter the password unsuccessfully. The hint should suggest what the password is to the user, but shouldn't make it too obvious to the uninformed. For instance, if your password is **C@mpbell**, you can make the hint **Mother's maiden name with @ for A**. You can also elect not to enter a hint at all.

6 Create the New User

After you've entered a full name, short name, and password, click anywhere else in the **Account Preferences** pane—on another user in the user list, on the **Picture** tab, or on the **Login Options** icon, for instance. When you do this, the new account is created, along with its **Home** folder.

118

▶ **TIP**

If you make a mistake or change your mind about creating the new user account, click the – button under the user list to cancel the operation.

---

119 Grant Admin Capabilities to Another User

✔ BEFORE YOU BEGIN	→ SEE ALSO
117 About Administrative Responsibilities	**120** Restrict Another User's Capabilities (Parental Controls)
118 Add a New User	**122** Delete a User

Your own account, created when you first started up your Mac, is an *Admin account*; it has the inherent capabilities necessary to change any of the **System Preferences**, install software, and perform many other system-modifying actions. Every new user account you create begins life as a standard user, without any of those administrative capabilities. However, you can grant Admin status to any other users you select if you want to share that administrative authority. When you do so, the other users you empower can modify other user accounts, install software, and change pretty much anything about the system.

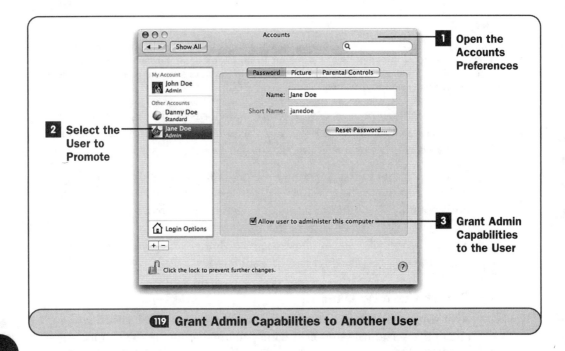

1 Open the
Accounts
Preferences

2 Select the
User to
Promote

3 Grant Admin
Capabilities
to the User

119 Grant Admin Capabilities to Another User

119

You should not grant Admin status lightly. Allow only those people you trust completely with the computer to be administrators. Granting Admin status to a user of your computer is equivalent to giving them your house or car keys and the implicit permission to do whatever they want with them.

▶ NOTE

You must be logged in as an Admin user, or able to authenticate as one using the lock icon in the **Accounts Preferences**, to grant Admin capabilities to another user. Also, you cannot perform this operation on a user who is currently logged in. The user must log out first.

1 Open the Accounts Preferences

Open the **System Preferences** application (under the **Apple** menu); click **Accounts** to open the **Accounts Preferences** pane.

2 Select the User to Promote

From the list of users on the left, select the user you want to promote to Admin status. Then click the **Password** tab if it is not already shown.

3 **Grant Admin Capabilities to the User**

Select the **Allow user to administer this computer** check box. The user is immediately promoted to Admin status, and the **Limitations** tab becomes disabled (because Admin users have no limitations).

---

120 | **Restrict Another User's Capabilities (Parental Controls)**

✔ BEFORE YOU BEGIN	→ SEE ALSO
117 About Administrative Responsibilities	**122** Delete a User
119 Grant Admin Capabilities to Another User	

Under some circumstances, you might want to configure a user account to have even more than the standard limitations on what can be done with the computer. For instance, you might have your Mac acting as a public computer for a classroom of unruly kids. In such a case, you might want to restrict them to pick from only a few approved applications, or to prevent them from downloading hundreds of MP3 files to fill up your disk. Mac OS X lets you apply these kinds of parental-control limitations to specific users. You can also require any user to use the Simple Finder, a simplified version of the Finder that uses large icons and single clicks to make the system more accessible to younger (or vision-impaired) computer users.

119

▶ **NOTE**

You must be logged in as an Admin user, or able to authenticate as one using the lock icon in the **Accounts Preferences**, to restrict another user's capabilities. Also, you cannot perform this operation on a user that is currently logged in. The user must log out first.

1 **Open the Accounts Preferences**

Open the **System Preferences** application (under the **Apple** menu); click **Accounts** to open the **Accounts Preferences** pane.

2 **Select the User to Restrict**

From the list of users on the left, select the user whose privileges you want to modify. Then click the **Parental Controls** tab to reveal the various options for restricting the user's privileges.

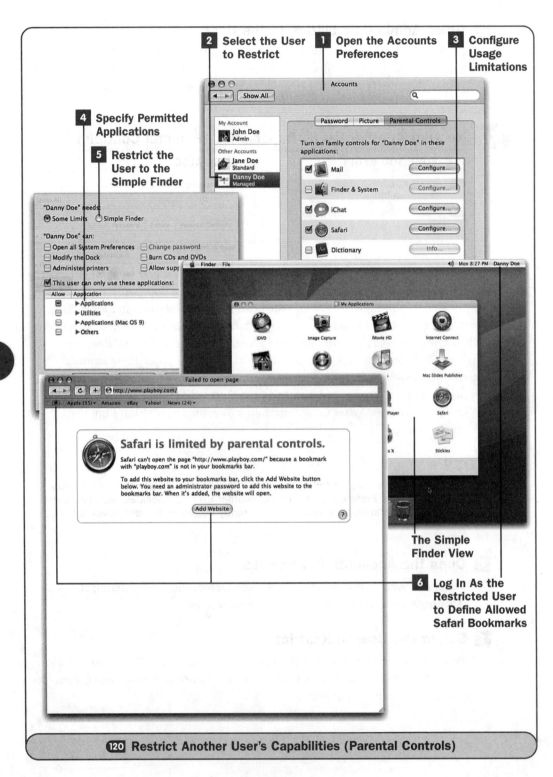

2 Select the User to Restrict

1 Open the Accounts Preferences

3 Configure Usage Limitations

4 Specify Permitted Applications

5 Restrict the User to the Simple Finder

The Simple Finder View

6 Log In As the Restricted User to Define Allowed Safari Bookmarks

120 Restrict Another User's Capabilities (Parental Controls)

▶ **NOTE**

You cannot restrict the privileges of an Admin user; only standard users have an active **Parental Controls** tab.

③ Configure Usage Limitations

Enable parental controls for one of the areas of the system (**Mail, Finder & System, iChat, Safari,** or **Dictionary**) by selecting the check box next to it. Until the check box is selected, that area of the system is unrestricted to the user. After the check box is selected, however, each of these applications becomes configurable in several areas. For example, Mail and iChat can be restricted by only allowing the user to communicate with certain approved partners, defined by adding them one-by-one to an approved list. The **Finder & System** area has many configurable options, as discussed in the next step. The **Dictionary** application can be restricted so that it doesn't show any dirty words. (Technology might change, but kids never do…)

Open an application's configurable restrictions by clicking the **Configure** button next to it.

▶ **CAUTION**

Be aware that if you restrict a user's iChat communications or Safari browsing, the user will still be able to communicate or browse using other similar applications (such as ICQ or Camino). If you take the trouble to set up approved iChat partner lists and Safari browsing locations, be sure to disallow access to other kinds of communication applications, as shown in step 4.

④ Specify Permitted Applications

In the configuration sheet for **Finder & System,** select the **This user can only use these applications** check box if you want to allow the user to be able to use only those applications you define. All the applications installed in the system are organized in this box; you can open one of the collections (**Applications, Utilities,** and so on) to enable only certain applications, or you can use the check boxes to enable or disable whole collections of applications. By default, for example, all applications in the **Applications** collection (which corresponds to the global **Applications** folder) are enabled for the user, but **Utilities** and the other collections are disabled.

120

▶ **NOTE**

If you restrict which applications a user can run or otherwise limit her capabilities with the **Some Limits** option, the user's status changes from **Standard** to **Managed**. If you don't permit a user to open all **System Preferences** panes, the user will not be able to change her password (because the user has to access the **Accounts Preferences** pane to change a password), and the **Change password** check box is grayed out. A user who is restricted in this way can open only those Preference panes that manage how her own login experience behaves, not any of the panes that affect the system.

If a **Managed** user tries to run an application that you haven't designated as an allowed application for the user, a dialog box informs her that she doesn't have permission to run it.

5 Restrict the User to the Simple Finder

The **Simple Finder** option is a heavily restricted user mode you can use to give certain users a very simplified, easy-to-use view of the system. It's especially tailored for younger users. When a **Simplified** user (one configured to use the Simple Finder) logs in, only the applications you administratively specify are available. When the user clicks the **My Applications** folder icon in the limited Dock, the applications are presented in a large window in the middle of the screen. The only other Dock items are the **Documents** and **Shared** folders in which the user can save files. Applications can save files to other folders, but the Simplified user won't be able to access them.

Effectively, a Simplified user can run only the applications you specify, save documents only in the **Documents** and **Shared** folders, and log out.

Click **OK** to commit the changes to the restrictions on the user.

6 Log In As the Restricted User to Define Allowed Safari Bookmarks

Perhaps the most obvious area of need for parental controls is the Web. The way Mac OS X handles this is that if a user's web browsing is under parental control, and the user tries to browse to a site that is not listed in the Bookmarks bar, Safari instead presents a screen warning that the site is disallowed because it's unknown, along with an **Add Website** button so that an administrator can enable access to it by simply entering a password. This means the only sites that the user can visit are the ones listed in the Bookmarks bar. As the administrator in charge of setting up the managed user's bookmarks, you must define these allowed bookmarks for the user.

Log in as the managed user (using Fast User Switching; see **112 Switch to Another User** for more information). Notice that the Bookmarks Library icon in the Bookmarks bar has a "lock" icon on it, indicating that the bookmarks are managed. Click the icon. You are prompted for your administrator password so that Safari knows an Admin user is trying to get into the Bookmarks.

Set up bookmarks for the managed user as you normally would; see **61 Keep Track of Web Sites with Bookmarks** for more information. Remember to put approved sites directly in the Bookmarks bar, or in folders that appear in the bar. Log out of the user's account. From now on, the user won't be able to reach any sites except the ones you've set up as permitted. How's that for peace of mind?

▶ **TIP**

Mac OS X's parental controls are good for more than just managing small children's web browsing. It's also potentially very useful if you run a company with "kiosk" computers in the lobby; this way you can control the information that walk-up customers can browse. This functionality, unique to Mac OS X, might make a Mac as attractive to your business as to your household...

121 **Change a User's Password**	
✔ **BEFORE YOU BEGIN**	→ **SEE ALSO**
117 About Administrative Responsibilities	**122** Delete a User
118 Add a New User	

120

All users (except those under parental controls) can change their own passwords. This is an essential part of conscientious computer usage. As a rule, you should change your password every six months or so, just as a precaution (and more frequently, such as every 30 days, in a business environment where the information on your computer is more sensitive). And as an Admin user, it will be your task to change users' passwords on a fairly regular basis, often because the users have forgotten them.

To change your own password, you have to re-authenticate to make sure that you are the person who is currently logged in. Making you *authenticate* as the signed-in user is a precaution against someone sitting down at your login session and changing your password so that you can no longer log in. However, if you're an Admin user, you can change other users' passwords without authenticating.

1 **Open the Accounts Preferences**

Open the **System Preferences** application (under the **Apple** menu); click **Accounts** to open the **Accounts Preferences** pane.

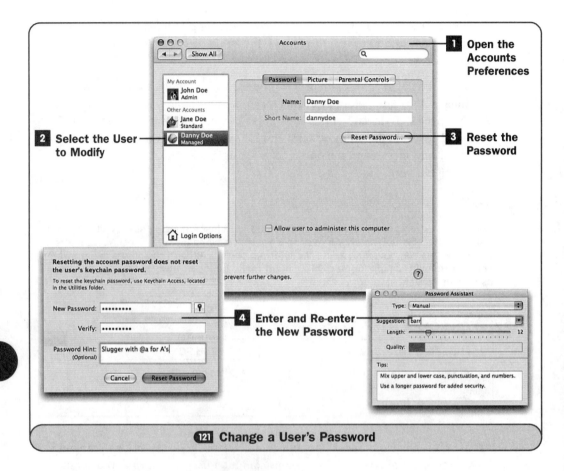

121 Change a User's Password

2 Select the User to Modify

From the list of users on the left, select the user whose password you want to change. (If you're changing your own password, click your account name at the top of the list, under **My Account**.) Then click the **Password** tab to reveal the name and password configuration pane.

3 Reset the Password

Click the **Reset Password** button. This opens a sheet that lets you enter a new password for the user, as well as a hint. You are not prompted to authenticate yourself during this procedure.

4 Enter and Re-enter the New Password

After you have authenticated, type your new password in the **Password** and **Verify** fields. Click another user or tab to save the new password.

If you need help coming up with a good password to use, click the "**key**" button to open the **Password Assistant** panel. This is a tool that suggests appropriate passwords for you to use according to several different schemes, including **Memorable** (for passwords composed of English words cleverly strung together), **Letters and Numbers**, and **Manual**. Use the **Length** slider to select how long you want the suggested password to be; longer passwords are better and more secure, as indicated by the **Quality** meter below the slider. In **Manual** mode, type a password of your choice into the **Suggestion** box, and the **Quality** meter shows how good the password is; the **Tips** box offers pointers on how to improve your entered password, such as pointing out whether it's derived from dictionary words, too short, or otherwise too easy to guess. Try to pick a password where the quality meter is long and green rather than short and red, and where the **Tips** box has no improvements to suggest.

▶ **NOTE**

The Password Assistant utility automatically fills in its suggested password into the **Password** field of the sheet in the **Account Preferences** pane; however, it doesn't fill it into the **Verify** field. You have to type that yourself, to make sure the password has been entered correctly and memorized.

Bear in mind, importantly, that the user's *Keychain* password *is not changed* to the newly set password. The user must open the **Keychain Access** application (in the **Utilities** folder) and enter the old password to unlock the Keychain and reset it to the newly set password. See **135** **Extract a Password from the Keychain** for more information about the Keychain.

This does not apply if you're changing your *own* password; the Keychain password is updated to match your newly entered password. For this reason, it's preferable to have each user reset his password himself, rather than having you do it from within your own login session.

▶ **TIP**

If you're an advanced Unix user, resist the temptation to change your password using the command-line **passwd** command; this command does an incomplete job of updating your password in all locations throughout the system, including your Keychain.

121

122 │ **Delete a User**

✔ **BEFORE YOU BEGIN**

▣ **About Administrative Responsibilities**
▣ **Add a New User**

Deleting a user is an essential housekeeping duty. You'll have to remove user accounts that are no longer used, delete accounts as a punitive measure against abusive users, or clean out user accounts to return the system to a pristine state if you sell your computer to someone else.

Mac OS X lets you delete any user account except for your own. When you delete a user, you can also either delete the user's account immediately (removing the user's **Home** folder and everything in it permanently) or package the user's **Home** folder into a disk image you can then browse later.

▶ **NOTE**

You must be logged in as an Admin user, or able to authenticate as one using the lock icon in the **Accounts Preferences**, to delete another user.

122

1 **Open the Accounts Preferences**

Open the **System Preferences** application(under the **Apple** menu); click **Accounts** to open the **Accounts Preferences** pane.

2 **Select the User to Delete**

From the user list on the left, select the user you want to delete from the system.

3 **Remove the User**

Click the – icon at the bottom of the list of users.

▶ **NOTE**

Don't try to delete a user who's currently logged in. Doing so can result in an "orphaned" user account that can no longer log out until the computer is restarted.

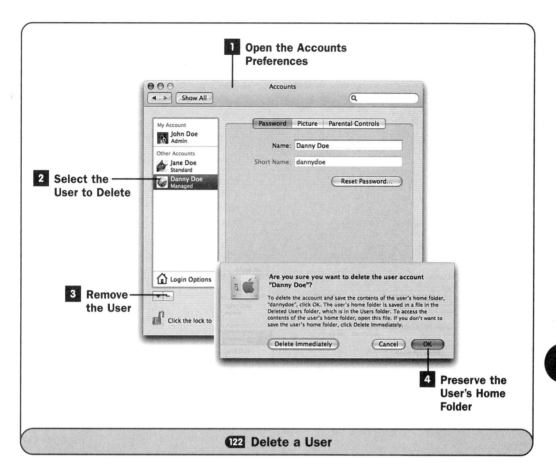

1 Open the Accounts Preferences

2 Select the User to Delete

3 Remove the User

4 Preserve the User's Home Folder

122 Delete a User

4 Preserve the User's Home Folder

A sheet appears asking whether you want to delete the user immediately or archive the user's **Home** folder. Click **Delete Immediately** if you want the user's complete account, including the **Home** folder, to be immediately deleted. Click **OK** if you want the user's **Home** folder to be packaged into a disk image.

If you choose this second option, the user is removed from the system's user database, but the archive of the **Home** folder will appear in a folder called **Deleted Users** inside the **Users** folder. You can mount this disk image by double-clicking it; you can then browse through it to retrieve any important files that the user might have had.

16

Managing Power and Accessibility Options

IN THIS CHAPTER:

"One size fits all" is a statement that never applies to computer users. We all need our computers to do something different, and not just because our tastes in desktop backgrounds vary. Sometimes, our own practical constraints—mobile energy needs, physical accessibility challenges, and so on—dictate that our computers must adapt to us, rather than we to them.

Whether your Mac is a laptop or a desktop computer, the practical fact is that you can't just leave it running all the time. Electricity costs money, and besides, you probably instinctively know that the lifetime of your screen and your hard drive can be extended if they can be shut down occasionally.

Nobody, however, wants to have to boot up their computer from scratch every time they sit down. That's why Mac OS X supports *sleep*, a suspended-activity mode in which the computer uses almost no power, but can be awakened almost instantly by pressing a key or moving the mouse. You already know how to put your computer to sleep or wake it up (choose **Sleep** from the **Apple** menu, or—if your computer is a laptop—simply close the lid); this chapter will discuss some of the finer points of power management, enabling you to tune how your computer automatically deals with inactivity and variable power conditions.Beyond simple power management, Mac OS X has a number of features designed to make life easier for everybody who uses a Mac, under whatever circumstances. Apple has had a long history of making computers that are usable not just by the fully physically capable, but by people who have any of the disabilities or challenges that made traditional computing difficult. The Mac was first to market with text-to-speech synthesis, for example, and there have almost always been ways to control the computer using only the keyboard, rather than relying on the mouse. Mac OS X, with its many graphical and architectural advances, introduces even more accessibility features that depend more heavily on sophisticated graphics and sound processing, under the collective name **Universal Access**. **Zoom** lets you immediately magnify the screen to any level you choose. **Sticky Keys** lets you press multiple modifier keys in sequence rather than at the same time, displaying their floating icons in the upper-right corner of the screen. With **VoiceOver**, you can command your computer by speaking to it, and you can make the computer speak back to you, reading alert messages, information about the system, or even complete documents in a human voice of your choice.

123 Set the Computer's Sleep Time

✔ BEFORE YOU BEGIN	→ SEE ALSO
25 Set the Time and Date	**115** Require a Password When Reactivating the Computer
26 Enable Automatic Time Synchronization (NTP)	**114** Automatically Log Out

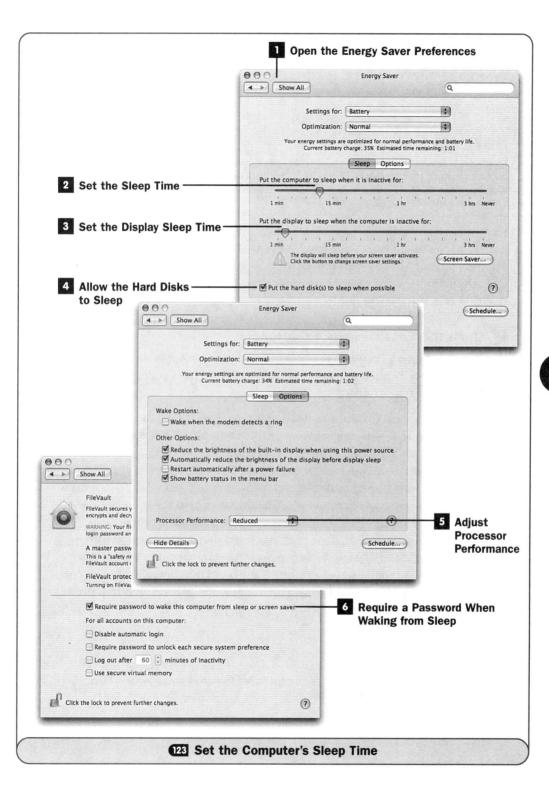

1 Open the Energy Saver Preferences

2 Set the Sleep Time

3 Set the Display Sleep Time

4 Allow the Hard Disks to Sleep

5 Adjust Processor Performance

6 Require a Password When Waking from Sleep

123 Set the Computer's Sleep Time

One of the first and simplest energy-saving things you can do with your Mac is to configure it to put itself to sleep after a certain period of inactivity. If you don't touch your keyboard or mouse for that length of time, the computer will automatically go to sleep; you can then wake it up by pressing a key or moving the mouse.

▶ **NOTE**

There are a few conditions under which your computer won't go to sleep, even if you haven't touched your keyboard or mouse. If a QuickTime movie or a DVD is playing, for instance, Mac OS X will recognize that something's going on and will not dim the screen or put the computer to sleep.

You can also configure separate sleeping behaviors for your display and your hard disk; you might want your screen to turn off after an hour of inactivity, for instance, or your hard drive to spin down, and yet for your computer to not fully go to sleep until another hour has passed. These things are all configurable in the **Energy Saver Preferences** pane.

▮ Open the Energy Saver Preferences

Open the **System Preferences** application (under the **Apple** menu); click **Energy Saver** to bring up the **Energy Saver Preferences** pane. Click the **Sleep** tab if it's not already selected.

If you have a desktop Mac (an iMac, eMac, or Power Mac), the **Energy Saver Preferences** pane will simply show the three tabs for configuring power management behavior: **Sleep**, **Schedule**, and **Options**. However, if you have a laptop (an iBook or PowerBook), the **Energy Saver Preferences** pane has an **Optimize Energy Settings** drop-down menu that lets you select from several predefined energy-saving profiles (optimized for various styles of computer usage) or create your own profile, and a second **Settings for** drop-down menu that lets you configure the settings separately for whether your computer is plugged in or using battery power. You can also show or hide the details of the window, using the **Show Details** or **Hide Details** button in the lower-right corner; when the details are hidden, the only controls that are visible are the ones that let you select an energy profile for your different power sources.

▶ **NOTE**

The illustrations for this task show the **Energy Saver Preferences** pane for a laptop (a PowerBook, to be precise). On non-laptop Macs, the **Show/Hide Details** button is instead a **Restore Defaults** button.

2 Set the Sleep Time

Use the **Put the computer to sleep when it is inactive for** slider to select a sleep time. Mac OS X has different default configurations depending on whether it is running on a laptop or a desktop Mac, or whether the power source is the battery or the AC adapter. On continuous power, it never automatically sleeps, so the slider is in the **Never** position at the far right; on battery power, it is set to sleep after 10 minutes of inactivity. You can disable automatic sleep by moving the slider all the way to the right.

▶ **NOTE**

Notice that the slider's numbering is not linear. At the far left, individual minutes are far apart, so that you can easily select between four and five minutes; but as you move the slider to the right, the numbers increase faster so that you can select up to three hours of inactivity.

3 Set the Display Sleep Time

Normally, your whole computer will go to sleep at once, after the inactivity period you specify has elapsed. However, you can choose to set your Mac to put only its display to sleep, but to keep the computer itself running. This can be useful if you like to keep certain programs running all night long while you sleep, but you don't want to waste energy keeping the screen lit if nobody's looking at it.

Your display will dim (to about half its normal brightness) when the computer has been inactive for half the time it takes to go to sleep or (if you have enabled a separate display sleep time) for the display to sleep. This is useful primarily for laptops, in which the screen is one of the biggest consumers of power; dimming the screen helps reduce power usage. (You can disable dimming using the **Automatically reduce the brightness of the display before display sleep** check box under the **Options** tab.)

Select the **Put display to sleep when the computer is inactive for** check box to enable a separate display sleep time, and set the inactivity period by sliding the pointer to a point to the left of the first slider's pointer. You can reset the display's sleep time to match the system sleep time by moving the second slider to the right until it is in sync with the computer sleep slider. Similarly, if you move the computer sleep slider farther left than your display slider is set, both sliders will move in unison to keep their values synchronized.

123

▶ **NOTE**

If you have a screensaver enabled, Mac OS X warns you if you try to set the system to sleep earlier than how long it takes for the screensaver to kick in. If you set the system to sleep automatically after a certain period of inactivity, visit the **Desktop & Screen Saver Preferences** pane to ensure that the screensaver will activate at an appropriate time. See ⓴ **Select a Screensaver.**

4 Allow the Hard Disks to Sleep

Use the **Put the hard disk(s) to sleep when possible** check box to specify whether or not you want the hard disk to spin down whenever the system determines it's not being used (usually after a few minutes of inactivity). If you allow the hard disk to sleep, its lifetime will be increased; however, it will take several extra seconds for the system to become responsive, as it spins the disk back up again, if you suddenly need to access the disk after it's been shut down.

5 Adjust Processor Performance

Click the **Options** tab. Use the **Processor Performance** drop-down menu to select how fast you want your computer's processor to run. With the processor set to **Highest** performance, the computer will run at full speed, but power consumption will be higher than if you select **Reduced**, which causes the processor to run at a slightly slower speed. Generally this is meaningful only for laptops, but some computers with complex cooling systems (such as the Power Mac G5) also behave differently according to how this option is set.

6 Require a Password When Waking from Sleep

If you have a laptop, especially one with sensitive information on it, it's a good idea to configure Mac OS X to require your password when the Mac wakes from sleep. To do this, open the **Security Preferences** pane (click **Security** in the **System Preferences** application). Use the **Require password to wake this computer from sleep or screen saver** check box to make it so that a thief who makes off with your laptop won't be able to access your sensitive documents. (See ⓰ **Secure Your Files with FileVault** for an additional precaution you can take if your laptop's data is *really* sensitive: encrypting your entire **Home** folder.)

124 Schedule Automatic Startup and Shutdown

✔ BEFORE YOU BEGIN	→ SEE ALSO
㉕ Set the Time and Date	ⓐ Automatically Log Out
㉖ Enable Automatic Time Synchronization (NTP)	

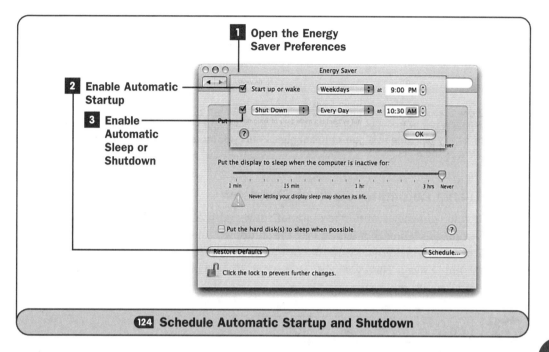

124 Schedule Automatic Startup and Shutdown

124

To make your computer go to sleep, shut down, or start itself up, you don't have to rely on a certain period of inactivity. If you prefer, you can have the computer turn itself off or on at a specific time of day. While the computer is off or sleeping, it's still keeping time and can react according to your needs so that you don't have to remember to put it to sleep at the end of the day or to wait for it to boot up in the mornings.

1 Open the Energy Saver Preferences

Open the **System Preferences** application (under the **Apple** menu); click **Energy Saver** to bring up the **Energy Saver Preferences** pane. Click the **Schedule** button to access a sheet showing the scheduling options.

2 Enable Automatic Startup

Select the **Start up or wake** check box to enable the computer to start up (or wake itself from sleep) automatically at a given time. Then, from the drop-down menu, select whether you want the computer to activate at a certain time every day, on all weekdays, on weekends, or on a single certain week-day.

Finally, set the activation time using the time input fields. Click each number to adjust it, or use the **Tab** key to move between fields; then use the arrow keys, **Up/Down** buttons, or the number keys to set the appropriate time for the computer to activate.

▶ **NOTE**

The settings you specify here are applied when you click the **OK** button to close the configuration sheet.

▶ **TIP**

If you don't want to be awakened by the computer's loud "bong" sound when it wakes up in the next room in the wee hours of the morning, and your external speakers cannot be turned off, try plugging in a pair of headphones; this will mute the sound in the computer's primary speakers.

3 Enable Automatic Sleep or Shutdown

If you want the computer to automatically shut itself down, first select the second check box that lets you set the shutdown time. From the drop-down list, select whether you want the computer to shut itself down completely or to simply sleep. Then you can select a day scheme and a time just as you did with the automatic startup settings.

124

125 Choose a Power-Saving Profile

→ **SEE ALSO**

126 Monitor Your Laptop's Battery Life
43 Create and Configure a Location

If your Mac is a laptop, you will have a variety of different conditions under which you can run it: You might run it off of battery power on an airplane while you watch a DVD, or you might have it plugged into wall power while you play a graphics-intensive game, or you might be stuck in a long meeting taking notes for the whole two-hour duration. Each of these activities places different kinds of demands on the computer and its components, and each scenario is affected by what kind of power is available.

▶ **NOTE**

If your Mac is a desktop model—an iMac, eMac, or Power Mac—the **Energy Saver Preferences** pane does not show the power-saving profile options described in this task. This is because desktop Macs only have a single power source: the wall plug.

If your desktop Mac is asleep, don't unplug it—even sleep mode requires some power! Laptops get their power during sleep from the battery. To shut down your desktop Mac, first awaken it from sleep, and then shut it down using the **Apple** menu.

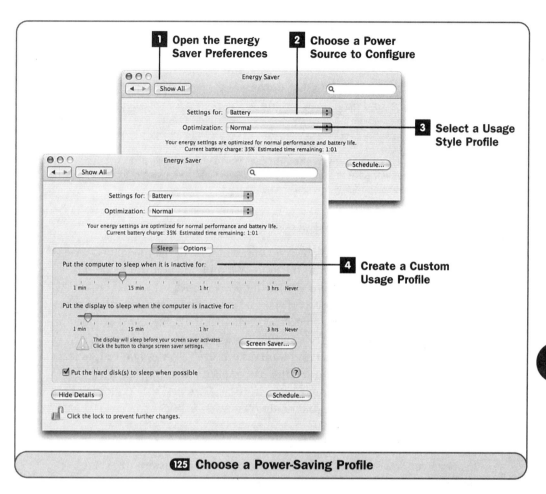

1 Open the Energy
Saver Preferences

2 Choose a Power
Source to Configure

3 Select a Usage
Style Profile

4 Create a Custom
Usage Profile

125 Choose a Power-Saving Profile

The **Energy Saver Preferences** pane lets you select from several usage profiles that correspond to different styles of how you stress the computer and use its available power. Some profiles are designed for high performance; others are designed for long battery life; still others provide a balance between performance and battery life for specific uses. You can also define your own custom-tuned power usage profile if necessary.

1 Open the Energy Saver Preferences

Open the **System Preferences** application (under the **Apple** menu); click **Energy Saver** to bring up the **Energy Saver Preferences** pane. Click the **Show Details** button to show the complete set of Energy Saver controls.

2 Choose a Power Source to Configure

You might want to define different usage settings for whether the computer is plugged in or not. Select the power source from the **Settings for** drop-down list at the top of the window (either **Battery** or **Power Adapter**) and customize the sliders and options according to the power source selected.

▶ **TIP**

Remember that you can select any of the different configuration tabs after having selected one of the power sources; all the tabs and their controls pertain to whichever power source and usage profile is currently selected.

3 Select a Usage Style Profile

From the **Optimization** drop-down menu, select one of the predefined usage profiles, one that corresponds to the kind of computing you will be doing. Explanatory text at the bottom of the window describes what each profile does: **Better Performance** prevents the computer from sleeping and uses the processor at its fastest speed regardless of whether the computer is plugged in (using the power adapter) or not. **Better Battery Life** takes the opposite approach, putting the display and hard disk to sleep after only a couple of minutes of inactivity and running the processor at reduced speed. The **Normal** setting strikes a balance between these extremes, striving for the best mix possible of performance and battery life.

4 Create a Custom Usage Profile

To create your own custom power usage profile, select **Custom** from the **Optimization** menu. Adjust the sliders to achieve the sleep behavior you want. (The profile name changes to **Custom** after you move the sliders regardless of what optimization profile you have currently selected.)

125

126	**Monitor Your Laptop's Battery Life**
✔ **BEFORE YOU BEGIN**	→ **SEE ALSO**
125 Choose a Power-Saving Profile	**43** Create and Configure a Location
	44 Switch to a New Location

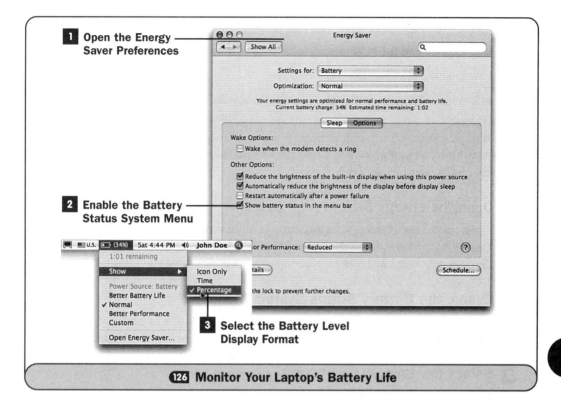

1 Open the Energy Saver Preferences

2 Enable the Battery Status System Menu

3 Select the Battery Level Display Format

126

126 Monitor Your Laptop's Battery Life

If you have a laptop Mac (an iBook or PowerBook), a crucial piece of status information for you to have available at all times is the **Battery Status** System Menu. This icon appears at the top right of the screen and shows your battery's current level and whether the computer is plugged in or not. The icon also gives you access to a menu that shows the battery's status in more detail. You can also use the menu to jump directly to the **Energy Saver Preferences** pane.

Different kinds of computing tasks can use up more battery power than others; some of these tasks might even be occurring without your knowledge. The **Battery Status** System Menu can help you keep an eye on how fast your battery's power is draining; if you're not getting as much life out of your battery as you believe you should be, consider a few of these tasks that may be robbing it of juice unnecessarily:

- AirPort card turned on

- Bluetooth devices active and connected

- Accessing or burning CDs or DVDs

- Heavy network access (downloading large files)

- Processor-intensive operations (such as image or video processing)

- iTunes visualizer running

- Powering an external USB or FireWire device

- Running too many applications at once (heavy disk access)

If your laptop is doing any of these things where AC adapter power is unavailable (such as on a plane), it may be best to wait until you land before you resume your power-hungry work.

1 Open the Energy Saver Preferences

Open the **System Preferences** application (under the **Apple** menu); click **Energy Saver** to bring up the **Energy Saver Preferences** pane. Click the **Options** tab to show the energy-saving options.

2 Enable the Battery Status System Menu

Select the **Show battery status in the menu bar** check box to enable the battery icon among the system menus in the upper-right corner of the screen.

3 Select the Battery Level Display Format

Click the **Battery Status** System Menu to view the current battery status. The menu shows how much longer the battery will last at current power consumption levels, or how much longer it will take for the battery to become fully charged if the computer is plugged in.

The textual readout next to the **Battery Status** System Menu icon can show either the time remaining until the battery is depleted (or fully charged), or the percentage the battery has of its full charge. From the Show submenu, select **Time** to display the time remaining, **Percentage** to show the battery's charge level, or **Icon Only** to show no label at all and rely on the icon to tell you how full your battery is.

---

127 | **Talk to Your Computer and Have It Talk Back to You (VoiceOver)**

→ **SEE ALSO**

129 **Choose How the Computer Alerts You**

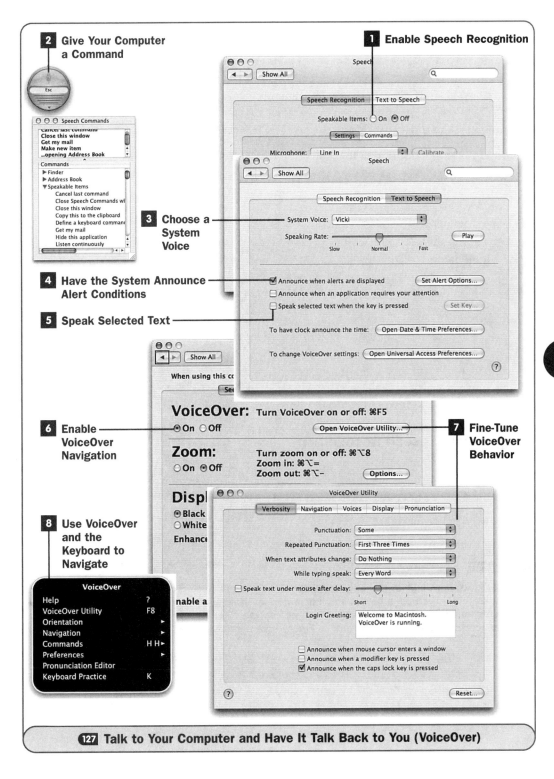

2 Give Your Computer a Command

1 Enable Speech Recognition

3 Choose a System Voice

4 Have the System Announce Alert Conditions

5 Speak Selected Text

6 Enable VoiceOver Navigation

7 Fine-Tune VoiceOver Behavior

8 Use VoiceOver and the Keyboard to Navigate

127 Talk to Your Computer and Have It Talk Back to You (VoiceOver)

Users with difficulty seeing, reading small text, or navigating using the mouse might find it useful to configure Mac OS X to use its advanced spoken user interface, known as **VoiceOver**. This system involves both text-to-speech synthesis (having the computer speak the text of alert dialog boxes, word-processing documents, web pages, and the names of elements of the system that you interact with in everyday operation and navigation), and a comprehensive keyboard navigation system that makes using the hard-to-see mouse unnecessary.

Even fully sighted users can take advantage of Mac OS X's convenience features related to VoiceOver technology. There are a lot of configurable options in the **Speech Preferences** pane that control the many fine-tuning options for these features, such as enabling the system to speak the text of alert messages and selected text, or activating the Mac's built-in voice recognition technology (allowing you to speak commands to the computer and have it respond just as though you were using the mouse or keyboard). You can also choose the spoken interface's voice from many possible "personas" and control its speed, pitch, and volume, even on the fly.

VoiceOver is a sophisticated vocal interface sewn into the very fabric of Mac OS X Tiger, and is designed to tailor itself to your needs or the needs of a user that you're assisting (for example, one with learning disabilities). This book cannot provide a full demonstration of its capabilities; the best way to learn how to use VoiceOver is by trying it yourself. This task introduces you to it by showing you how to activate it and adjust its more important options.

127

1 Enable Speech Recognition

Imagine telling your computer—in your own natural voice—"Get my mail." Imagine the computer firing up Mail, checking for new messages, and waiting for your next voice command, whether it be "Quit this application" or "Tell me a joke." Sound like science fiction? Well, it's not—it's just life with a Mac.

▶ NOTE

Most Macs have built-in microphones that can be used in voice recognition; iMacs, iBooks, and PowerBooks have a small hole next to the display that marks where the microphone is. Power Macs have a line-in jack for an external microphone. Mac OS X also accepts sound input from various FireWire cameras, such as Apple's iSight.

Open the **Speech Preferences** pane (click **Speech** in the **System Preferences** application). Click the **Speech Recognition** tab, if it's not already selected. Click the **On** radio button labeled **Speakable Items**.

A round, floating feedback window appears, with the word **Esc** in its display oval; this indicates that you must press and hold Escape to make the computer listen to you. You can change this default behavior under the **Listening** tab, where you can select a different listening key, choose whether the listening key toggles listening on and off or acts as a "push-to-talk" button, or even define a spoken preamble to make sure the computer knows you're talking to it. "Computer, get my mail," you might say. You can even define a different name for your computer—the Mac will recognize the name as long as you speak it in a clear voice. Just type the name in the **Name** field, if you have selected to have the listening key toggle listening on and off.

2 Give Your Computer a Command

Click the down arrow in the round listening window, and select **Open Speech Commands window** from the menu that appears. This window lists all the built-in speakable commands, and shows you the history of your previous commands.

▶ **NOTE**

The **Speech Commands** window need not be open for voice recognition to work, but it shows you all the available speakable commands, so until you've memorized the commands you want to use, it's a good idea to keep the window open for reference.

Hold down **Escape** (if you are still using the default, "push-to-talk" configuration) and speak the text of any command listed in the **Commands** box. If the Mac recognizes your command, its text appears in the history box, and the command is executed. If the Mac didn't recognize the command, nothing will happen; just try again, speaking as clearly as you can.

▶ **TIPS**

Tell the computer to "tell me a joke," if you like knock-knock jokes.

Also try using voice commands to play the Chess game found in the **Applications** folder. So much for Solitaire, eh?

You can define new commands for any application; just give the command "define a keyboard command" when that application is active, and a window appears that lets you associate a spoken word (which it will interpret as you type it) with a keyboard shortcut that the application recognizes. Try setting up "Play" and "Pause" commands for the QuickTime Player this way, using the **Space** and **Return** key commands (to keep them separate).

3 Choose a System Voice

VoiceOver is the general name of the text-to-speech interface technology in Mac OS X, encompassing a full spoken user interface to aid those with disabilities, as well as a number of convenience features to make anyone's life easier. Without fully enabling the assistive features of VoiceOver, you can tap into its capabilities to have Mac OS X alert you with a certain spoken word or phrase whenever an alert box or sheet appears.

Mac OS X comes with many different "voices" you can use to read your text; **Victoria**, the default, is probably the most natural-sounding one. You can experiment with many others, however; some are "novelty" voices, but many are designed to be as natural-sounding as possible. The System Voice is the default voice that Mac OS X will use when rendering text to speech, unless you specifically choose otherwise within a given feature (such as VoiceOver).

Click the **Text to Speech** tab in the **Speech Preferences** pane. Pick your favorite voice from the **System Voice** drop-down menu, using the **Play** button to preview how each voice will sound.

4 Have the System Announce Alert Conditions

127

Mac OS X can grab your attention when system alerts occur by reading the title of the alert in the voice of your choice, after a specified preamble or by itself. Select the **Announce when alerts are displayed** check box and then click the **Set Alert Options** button to choose the phrase (if any) for Mac OS X to speak before the alert text. You can select a single specific phrase, choose a random or sequential phrase, or even add new phrases of your own, such as "Hey, you!"

▶ TIP

This is text-to-speech synthesis, so you can specify a new phrase by clicking the **Add** button in the **Edit Phrase List** pop-up window and typing the phrase. Mac OS X reads the text you type in the voice you've selected.

Use the **Delay** slider to specify how long the system should wait before speaking the alert text. This can be helpful if you want to be able to respond to alerts yourself within the first 30 seconds or so, but if you also want the system to remind you more forcefully with a spoken alert if you're really busy and have ignored the condition until that time has elapsed. If you dismiss an alert dialog box right away, the system won't speak its text.

Another form of alert is when an application running in the background requires your attention; this often occurs when an iChat buddy sends you a message or Mail is temporarily unsuccessful in logging in to your email account, to take two common examples. Select the **Announce when an application requires your attention** check box to have Mac OS X alert you to these conditions as well.

5 Speak Selected Text

Select the **Speak selected text when the key is pressed** check box to make Mac OS X speak any block of text in the system that you have selected, such as the contents of a text file or an email message, when you give a specified keyboard command.

Click the **Set Key** button to define the key used to make the system speak the selected text. A dialog box appears that allows you to press the key combination you want to use to trigger speech; a good key to use is one of the unused function keys, such as **F8**. Additionally, Mac OS X encourages you to combine this key with one or more modifier keys, such as **Shift** or **Control**. Press the key combination you want to use and click **OK**. (If you specify a single key without modifiers, Mac OS X prompts you to make sure you really want to bind a single key this way; it's generally advisable to use at least one modifier key to prevent accidentally triggering the text-to-speech function.)

6 Enable VoiceOver Navigation

127

To take Mac OS X's spoken user interface to the next level, enable the full assistive features of VoiceOver. Open the **Universal Access Preferences** pane (click the **Universal Access** icon in the **System Preferences** application), and click the **Seeing** tab if it's not already selected. The topmost option is **VoiceOver**; click the **On** radio button to turn on the assistive vocal navigation system.

You will immediately see—or rather hear—how VoiceOver works. The system speaks a brief welcome message and a set of terse phrases that describe what part of the system is currently active: namely, the **System Preferences** application, the **Universal Access** window, and the **Back** button (the first control in the window). This text is spoken using a voice that may or may not be the same as your System Voice (it's set independently).

Move from application to application, clicking various controls and windows; observe how VoiceOver follows your movements and vocally reports what you're doing. This level of VoiceOver functionality can itself provide great assistance to users with vision impairment, enabling them to use the computer more easily than ever before. However, there's still a lot more that can be configured in VoiceOver.

7 Fine-Tune VoiceOver Behavior

In the **Universal Access Preferences** pane, click the **Open VoiceOver Utility** button; alternatively, launch **VoiceOver Utility** from within the **Utilities** folder. This utility allows you to fine-tune the behavior of VoiceOver to an extensive degree. For example, in the **Verbosity** tab, you can control how much of your typing and word-processing commands are reported by VoiceOver. Change the **While typing speak** drop-down menu to **Every Word** to make VoiceOver read everything you type back to you in a more useful manner than the default **Every Character**. You can also change the greeting text that VoiceOver speaks when it's first activated, and enable a feature that speaks the text immediately under the mouse cursor when you hover it there for a brief time (the length of delay is configurable using the slider).

The **Navigation** tab lets you experiment with many check boxes that control subtle behaviors of the system having to do with navigation, cursor tracking, and text selection tracking. Feel free to change these settings until you're comfortable with how VoiceOver reacts to your computing habits.

In the **Voices** tab, choose the default voice that VoiceOver should use when speaking its text; you can even set a different voice for various different aspects of the system, so that (for example) the content of windows can be spoken by a different voice or at a different rate than the titles or attributes of the windows.

The **Display** tab gives you additional assistive features, such as the **Caption Panel**, a floating semi-transparent window that reflects the phrases that VoiceOver speaks as you move through the system, and which can be dragged to any convenient place on the screen and resized using the sliders (or by dragging its lower-right corner). The **VoiceOver cursor** is a rectangle that highlights the currently active control or window, and its contents can be magnified to any comfortable size, further assisting users with impaired vision in getting around the system. The **VoiceOver Menu**, which you will see more of in the next step, is a floating command navigator that gives you access to all of VoiceOver's extensive keyboard commands; it can be summoned by pressing **Control+Option+F7**, and its size can be controlled using the **VoiceOver Menu Magnification** slider.

Finally, the **Pronunciation** tab lets you define certain unusual strings of text (such as acronyms and emoticons or "smileys") that VoiceOver cannot reasonably be expected to pronounce properly. Mac OS X can read practically the entire English dictionary, and a lot of things that aren't in it as well; but if there's some word or construct that it just isn't getting right, you can enter a "substitution" for it by describing to the system how it should pronounce the word phonetically. Several examples are already present to show you the idea.

127

If your VoiceOver settings become too confused, you can click the **Reset** button at any time to revert to the default settings of the vocal navigation system.

8 Use VoiceOver and the Keyboard to Navigate

VoiceOver is intended not just to read the interface to you, but to allow you to easily interact with the interface using some special keyboard commands, rather than the hard-to-see mouse cursor.

There is a comprehensive variety of keyboard commands that are used to move between windows, open and select from menus, click the mouse, and do everything else that normally requires sharp vision. These commands can be accessed using the **VoiceOver Menu**, which is summoned by pressing **Control+Option+F7**. Use the keyboard to move up and down through this floating menu and left and right through the menu hierarchy. Each command (under the **Commands** submenu) is labeled with the key combination necessary to perform basic computing tasks, as are the navigation keystrokes under the **Navigation** submenu. A **Keyboard Practice** option is available to let you become more familiar with the spoken names of every key on the keyboard.

127

At this stage, practice is the best path forward. Use the VoiceOver Menu to discover new keyboard commands, and use the extensive **VoiceOver Help** option (choose **Help** from the VoiceOver Menu) to see a comprehensive tour of the VoiceOver vocal navigation system. Once you have practiced using VoiceOver for a while, you won't need to rely on the mouse—or even your eyes—for a single major aspect of using your Mac.

---

128 Zoom In

→ SEE ALSO

24 Add a Second Display
129 Choose How the Computer Alerts You

Zoom is a feature that lets you instantly magnify the area of the screen in which your mouse pointer is located. The **Zoom** feature lets you immediately clarify small text or point to detailed areas of the screen, which can be very useful for users with limited sight (as well as being a cool feature for anyone to try out and show off). When **Zoom** is enabled, press the ⌘+**Option**+= key combination to zoom in to the configured maximum zoom level. You can keep pressing those keys to zoom in further. Press ⌘+**Option**+– to zoom out to the minimum zoom level, which is most usefully set to the normal non-zoomed display size.

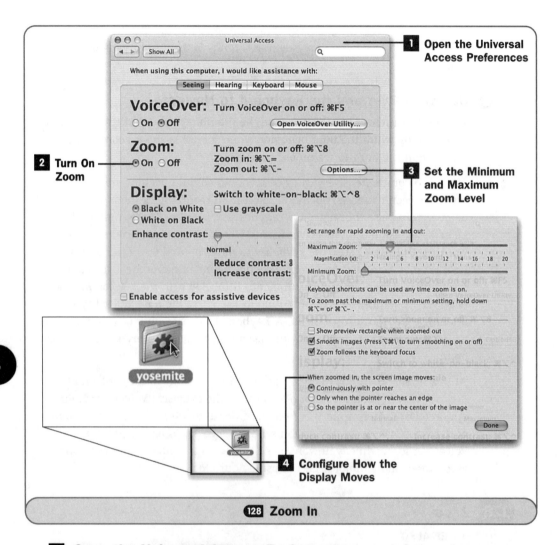

128 Zoom In

1 Open the Universal Access Preferences

Open the **System Preferences** application (under the **Apple** menu); click **Universal Access** to open the **Universal Access Preferences** pane. Click the **Seeing** tab, if it's not already selected.

2 Turn On Zoom

The second large-print item in the window is **Zoom**. Click the **On** button to enable **Zoom** using its default settings. You can now press ⌘+**Option**+= to zoom in on the mouse pointer's location.

③ Set the Minimum and Maximum Zoom Level

Click the **Options** button to display a sheet of zoom configuration options. The **Maximum Zoom** and **Minimum Zoom** sliders at the top allow you to set how far **Zoom** should magnify the screen when you press ⌘+**Option**+=, and to what level it should back off when you press ⌘+**Option**+—. Experiment with the sliders (pressing the triggering key combinations to test them) until you're happy with the **Zoom** behavior.

④ Configure How the Display Moves

Use the radio buttons at the bottom of the sheet to specify how you want the screen to react when you move the mouse in a zoomed-in window. Normally, the mouse pointer moves in the display area to reflect what part of the screen you're in (for example, when you're near the bottom-left part of the Mac OS X Desktop, the mouse pointer appears in the lower-left area of the screen when zoomed in). You can set it instead to move the display only when you push the mouse against the side of the zoomed-in screen, or to keep the mouse pointer at the center of the screen at all times.

Click **Done** when you're happy with your **Zoom** settings.

▶ **TIP**

The **Show preview rectangle when zoomed out** check box allows you to see the area of the screen that will be magnified, before you zoom in.

If the **Smooth images** check box is selected, the zoomed-in screen image will be softened to make graphics appear better and text easier still to read. If it is not selected, each pixel of the normally sized screen is simply made larger, without any smoothing or interpolation. Press ⌘+**Option**+\ (backslash) to toggle between smooth and sharp mode while you're zoomed in.

---

129 Choose How the Computer Alerts You

→ **SEE ALSO**

───────────────────────────────────────

103 Change Your Desktop Picture
128 Zoom In

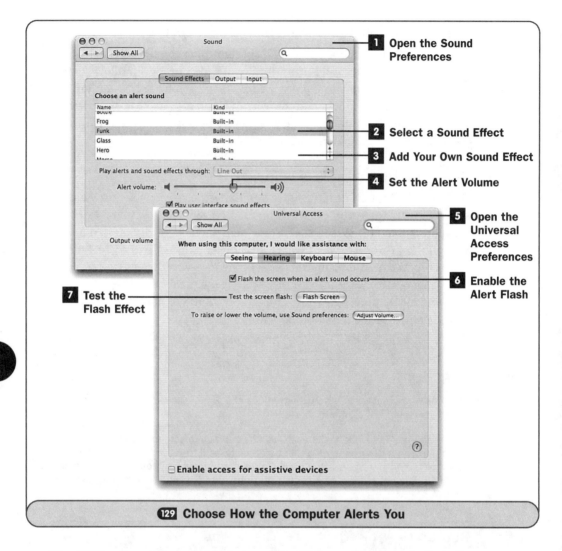

1 **Open the Sound Preferences**

2 **Select a Sound Effect**

3 **Add Your Own Sound Effect**

4 **Set the Alert Volume**

5 **Open the Universal Access Preferences**

6 **Enable the Alert Flash**

7 **Test the Flash Effect**

129

129 **Choose How the Computer Alerts You**

Mac OS X comes with some 14 *alert sounds*, which are short sound effects that play each time an "alert" event occurs. Alerts happen for a variety of reasons: An application might generate an alert if it needs your attention and it's in the background, or if it pops up a dialog box that requires you to enter some information. The system might sound an alert if you enter invalid input or ask it to do something it can't. Depending on your tastes, you can have these events signaled by a soft watery echo (**Submarine**), a short ringing sound (**Glass**), a reedy woodwind (**Blow**), or numerous others. You can even use a sound effect that you provide yourself. When customizing your system, what sound the system makes when something goes wrong is just as important as your desktop picture or the position of your Dock—though tastes, of course, differ.

If you have difficulty hearing, you might not be able to detect audio alerts that occur when Mac OS X notifies you of some important event. One way to work around this problem is to have the system flash the screen in addition to sounding the audio alert. When the flash feature is enabled, the screen goes suddenly white, then fades quickly back to the normal display level.

1 Open the Sound Preferences

Open the **System Preferences** application (under the **Apple** menu); click the **Sound** icon to open the **Sound Preferences** pane. Click the **Sound Effects** tab if it isn't already selected.

2 Select a Sound Effect

You are given a list of the built-in alert sound effects in the system. Click the name of one to hear it played. If you like it, simply close the **System Preferences** window; the alert sound is changed as soon as you click it.

3 Add Your Own Sound Effect

If you have a sound effect you want to add to the system, first make sure it's in AIFF format; then place it in the **Sounds** folder inside the **Library** in your **Home** folder. The next time you open the **Sound Preferences** pane, your sound effect will appear in the list for you to select.

129

▶ **TIP**

Sound files created on Windows machines are often in WAV format; you can use any of a number of different software tools, including iTunes, to convert them to AIFF. In iTunes, first add the sound file to your **Music Library**; then change iTunes's **Importing Preferences** to use the **AIFF Encoder**. You can then select the sound file in the Library, and then choose **Convert Selection to AIFF** from the **Advanced** menu. Select the AIFF file, then choose **Show Song File** from the **File** menu to access it in the Finder and move it to your **Sounds** folder.

4 Set the Alert Volume

Use the **Alert volume** slider to define how loudly the alert sound will play. The alert will never play louder than the master system volume.

5 Open the Universal Access Preferences

To have the Mac flash the screen in addition to playing the alert sound, open the **System Preferences** application (under the **Apple** menu) and click **Universal Access** to open the **Universal Access Preferences** pane. Click the **Hearing** tab.

6 **Enable the Alert Flash**

Select the **Flash the screen when an alert sound occurs** check box. This option enables the flash effect for whenever the system would normally emit an alert sound. (The sound still plays even if the screen is set to flash.)

7 **Test the Flash Effect**

Click the **Flash Screen** button to see what the screen will look like when the alert flash occurs.

---

130 **Use Sticky Keys**

→ **SEE ALSO**

128 Zoom In
131 Control the Mouse Pointer Using the Keyboard

129

Sticky Keys let you more easily use key combinations that involve two or more keys that must be pressed at the same time. If you're only able to press one key on the keyboard at a time, the **Sticky Keys** feature lets you use such key combinations by enabling a "stack" of pressed modifier keys that are all applied to the next regular key you press. For instance, with **Sticky Keys** turned on, you can simulate the ⌘+**Option+M** key combination by pressing first **Command**, then **Option**, and then **M**; the symbols for **Command** and **Option** appear floating on the screen to tell you that they will be applied to the first "regular" key you press—in this case, the **M**.

▶ **TIP**

To remove a pressed modifier key from the displayed list, press that key twice in succession.

1 **Open the Universal Access Preferences**

Open the **System Preferences** application (under the **Apple** menu); click **Universal Access** to open the **Universal Access Preferences** pane. Click the **Keyboard** tab.

2 **Turn On Sticky Keys**

Select the **Sticky Keys: On** radio button. From now on, icons for the modifier keys you press will appear in the upper-right corner of the screen until you press a regular key.

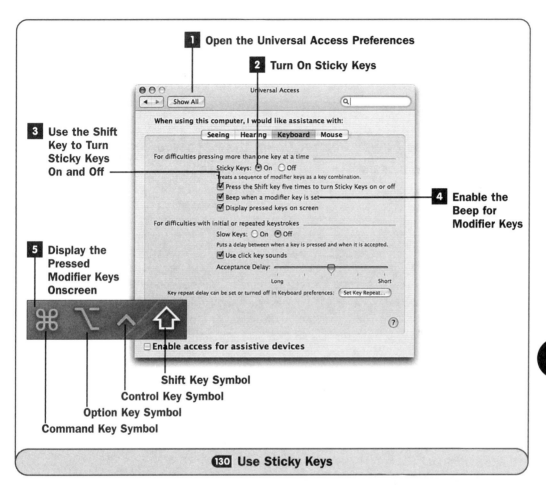

1 Open the Universal Access Preferences

2 Turn On Sticky Keys

3 Use the Shift Key to Turn Sticky Keys On and Off

4 Enable the Beep for Modifier Keys

5 Display the Pressed Modifier Keys Onscreen

Shift Key Symbol

Control Key Symbol

Option Key Symbol

Command Key Symbol

130

130 Use Sticky Keys

3 Use the Shift Key to Turn Sticky Keys On and Off

The **Press the Shift key five times to turn Sticky Keys on or off** check box lets you turn **Sticky Keys** on and off by pressing **Shift** five times in a row. Because this key sequence is very unlikely to be used for any other purpose, it's assigned to the **Sticky Keys** feature and is pretty safe to enable.

4 Enable the Beep for Modifier Keys

When selected, the **Beep when a modifier key is set** check box tells the system to make a soft "key press" sound effect when you press any modifier key. This can be helpful if you have vision difficulties. Deselect the check box if you want the modifier keys to be silent.

5 **Display the Pressed Modifier Keys Onscreen**

If you don't want the pressed modifier keys to be displayed floating in the upper right of the screen, deselect the **Display pressed keys on screen** check box. The **Sticky Keys** feature will still be in effect; you just won't be able to see it in action.

131 **Control the Mouse Pointer Using the Keyboard**

✔ BEFORE YOU BEGIN	→ SEE ALSO
130 Use Sticky Keys	**127** Talk to Your Computer and Have It Talk Back to You (VoiceOver)
	132 Add a Keyboard Shortcut

130

If you don't have a mouse or have trouble using one, you can set up Mac OS X to let you use the numeric keypad instead to move the onscreen pointer. This feature, called **Mouse Keys**, lets you navigate up, down, sideways, or diagonally using the number keys and to use the central **5** key to simulate a click. You can opt to turn the **Mouse Keys** feature on and off by pressing the **Option** key five times in a row.

1 **Open the Universal Access Preferences**

Open the **System Preferences** application (under the **Apple** menu); click **Universal Access** to open the **Universal Access Preferences** pane. Click the **Mouse** tab.

2 **Enable Mouse Keys**

Select the **Mouse Keys: On** radio button to turn on the **Mouse Keys** feature. This option reassigns the numeric keypad's keys so that they control the mouse pointer's movement. Hold down a number key to move the pointer continuously in one direction; tap the button to move the pointer by a very small increment. Press **5** to click the "mouse."

▶ **TIP**

Use the **Cursor Size** slider to increase the size of the mouse pointer. This can be very helpful if you have difficulty seeing the normal-sized pointer on the screen.

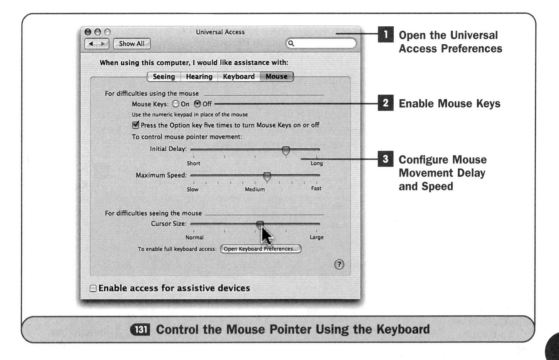

1 Open the Universal Access Preferences

2 Enable Mouse Keys

3 Configure Mouse Movement Delay and Speed

131 Control the Mouse Pointer Using the Keyboard

3 Configure Mouse Movement Delay and Speed

You can specify a delay before the system responds to the numeric keys and moves the cursor; this keeps the cursor from moving immediately if you accidentally touch the numeric keypad's keys. Use the **To control mouse pointer movement** and **Maximum speed** sliders to specify how long the system should wait between the time you press a keypad button and when the pointer begins to move, and to specify how fast the pointer should move when you press a button. The mouse keys' behavior changes immediately when you adjust the sliders so that you can experiment to find where they're most comfortable for you.

132 Add a Keyboard Shortcut

→ SEE ALSO

130 Use Sticky Keys
131 Control the Mouse Pointer Using the Keyboard

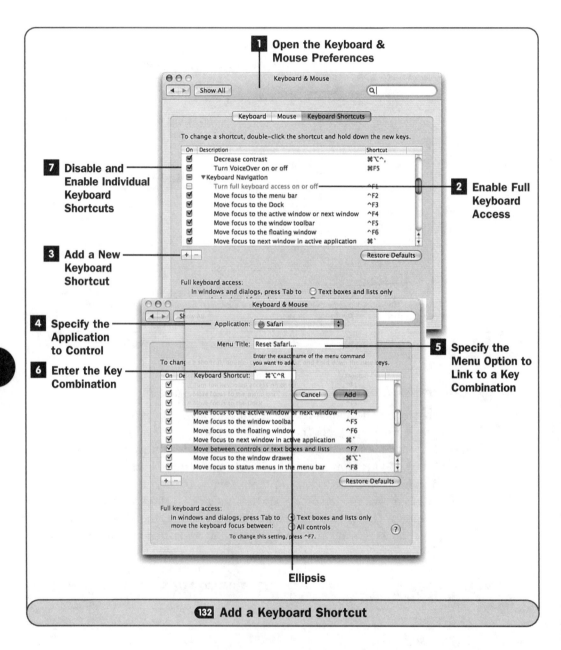

1 Open the Keyboard & Mouse Preferences

7 Disable and Enable Individual Keyboard Shortcuts

2 Enable Full Keyboard Access

3 Add a New Keyboard Shortcut

4 Specify the Application to Control

5 Specify the Menu Option to Link to a Key Combination

6 Enter the Key Combination

132

Ellipsis

132 Add a Keyboard Shortcut

Mac OS X is well instrumented with keyboard shortcuts for most of the popular commands in most applications, and with key commands to replicate most mouse actions (especially useful if you have difficulty using the mouse). However, you may use some application commands or actions frequently that aren't bound to any keyboard shortcuts. Fortunately, you can assign new key commands to certain menu options in any application you like. Keyboard shortcuts are controlled in a registry of key combinations you can configure from the **Keyboard & Mouse Preferences** pane.

1 Open the Keyboard & Mouse Preferences

Open the **System Preferences** application (under the **Apple** menu); click **Keyboard & Mouse** to open the **Keyboard & Mouse Preferences** pane. Click the **Keyboard Shortcuts** tab.

2 Enable Full Keyboard Access

If you want to be able to navigate the Mac OS X system using the **Control** key in conjunction with various function keys (F-keys), you can enable these functions one by one using the check boxes under the **Keyboard Navigation** heading in the list (all specific functions are enabled by default); alternatively, you can use the **Turn full keyboard access on or off** check box to enable or disable all the functions at once.

▶ **TIP**

When **Turn full keyboard access on or off** is enabled, pressing **Control+F1** enables or disables the specific keyboard navigation shortcuts that let you move the *focus* (the active window or control that takes your keyboard input) from one place on the screen to another. Use the radio buttons at the bottom to choose how the **Tab** key should allow you to navigate within windows.

132

3 Add a New Keyboard Shortcut

Suppose that there's a menu option in a certain application to which you want to bind a new keyboard shortcut. To do this, click the + button under the list of keyboard shortcuts to bring up the configuration sheet.

4 Specify the Application to Control

The **Application** menu lists all the applications currently installed on the computer. Select the application you want to control, or select **All Applications** to create a shortcut that applies to a common menu command that appears in lots of different applications.

5 Specify the Menu Option to Link to a Key Combination

Type the name of the menu item to which you want to bind the key combination. This name is the text of the item in the menu itself; it must be entered *exactly as it appears in the menu*, including the ellipsis (trailing dots), if present. Don't include the name of the menu that contains the menu item.

▶ **TIP**

An ellipsis (...) is actually a single character, and you can enter it by pressing **Option+;** (the semicolon).

6 Enter the Key Combination

Click in the **Keyboard Shortcut** input field and then press the key combination you want to bind to the specified menu item. The combination appears in symbolic notation in the field. You can press another combination to replace the one shown in the box.

Click **Add** to create the new keyboard combination. Back in the **Keyboard Shortcuts** tab of the **Keyboard and Mouse Preferences** pane, the shortcut will appear under the application's name under the **Application Keyboard Shortcuts** heading (scroll down to the bottom of the list of shortcuts to see this heading, which contains all the shortcuts you define for your applications in a hierarchical structure).

▶ **TIP**

To reassign a key combination, double-click the shortcut bound to it in the list; then enter the new key combination. You can also double-click the menu item text in the **Description** column of a custom-defined application shortcut to change the menu item bound to that key combination.

132

7 Disable and Enable Individual Keyboard Shortcuts

You can use the check boxes in the list to enable and disable individual key combinations. Click the check box next to an application's name to disable all key combinations assigned to that application; click the check box next to a heading (such as **Application Keyboard Shortcuts** or **Keyboard Navigation**) to disable all the keyboard shortcuts underneath it in the hierarchy.

If an application has more than one keyboard combination assigned to it, you can disable one of them, and the application's global check box will change to a – symbol to signify that some of the application's keyboard shortcuts are enabled and some aren't. This symbol propagates up the hierarchy to higher levels as well.

Click **Restore Defaults** to reset the check boxes for all the keyboard shortcuts except for the ones you've set for individual applications.

PART V

Administering the System

IN THIS PART:

17

Security, Boot Volumes, and Updating the System Software

IN THIS CHAPTER:

As the owner of a computer with a multiuser operating system that's connected to the Internet, you must sooner or later face the unpleasant fact that you are responsible for certain administrative duties that rest on the shoulders of every conscientious computer user. It's the age of viruses, worms, Trojans, and any number of malicious Internet denizens whose sole purpose in life is to make life miserable for the rest of us by breaking into unguarded systems and generally taking advantage of the goodwill of anybody who doesn't keep his system well cared for. Because most of the well-publicized attacks are almost exclusively directed at Windows computers, you can generally rest assured that compared to a Windows user, you've got it easy.

However, Mac OS X is based on Unix, and the only thing keeping most Unix systems on the Internet secure—aside from their relative obscurity—is their ever-watchful system administrators, staying on top of all the latest vulnerabilities in Samba, Sendmail, BIND, OpenSSH, and the other unsung components of Unix. Now that every Mac is effectively a Unix system, Unix-style exploits threaten the consumer computing world, and every Mac user must assume some of the responsibilities of a full-fledged Unix guru. The free ride will end someday, and it's the casual computer users who haven't been keeping a close eye on their computers' security who will pay the highest price.

▶ NOTE

If you use Microsoft Virtual PC to emulate a Windows environment on your Mac, that copy of Windows is susceptible to all the barrages that any Windows computer sustains. Windows viruses and spyware won't affect your Mac system, but you have to keep your Windows installation clean just as any PC user would—and thus you have *two* systems to keep updated, not just one.

The tasks in this chapter explain some of the security features of Mac OS X, features that allow you to operate with transparency and ease while keeping the system buttoned up against possible attacks. You will also learn techniques for booting the computer from alternative volumes such as external disks, which might come in handy if you're managing a complex installation or if you have to troubleshoot a potential security problem. Finally, you will learn how to keep your system software as up-to-date as possible, sealing potential security breaches as soon as Apple and the vigilant Internet security community discover them.

▶ WEB RESOURCE

http://macscan.securemac.com

MacScan is a downloadable utility designed to rid your Mac of spyware (software such as keystroke loggers, remote administration tools, and Trojans that might be installed without your knowledge). Very little spyware is targeted at the Mac these days, so the risk is much lower than with Windows, but this software helps you be appropriately vigilant.

133 Enable or Disable the Firewall

✔ BEFORE YOU BEGIN	→ SEE ALSO
30 Configure Networking Manually	134 Add or Remove Firewall Rules

Mac OS X comes with a *firewall* to protect it from unwanted network traffic. When a firewall is running, for data to be able to travel from your Mac to a host elsewhere on the Internet, that data must match certain criteria, among which is that the data must *originate* from your Mac—in other words, it must be a data transaction that *you* initiate—or, if the data is coming from another computer to your Mac, the data must be one of a few specific types that the firewall knows about, such as web traffic (HTTP).

▶ **KEY TERM**

Firewall—A piece of software that runs at the very innermost level of the operating system (the *kernel*) and serves as a traffic cop for all the Internet communications that travel in or out of your Mac.

By default, Mac OS X ships with the firewall turned off. This means that anybody can send traffic of any kind to your Mac, and the Mac's software must either handle it properly or throw it away according to what kind of traffic it is. When you turn the firewall on, all the traffic but those few exempt types is simply discarded, and your software doesn't have to deal with it at all. This can improve your system's performance, as well as protect it against unsavory characters probing your computer for a weak spot in its defenses.

▶ **NOTES**

You must be logged in as an Admin user, or able to authenticate as one using the lock icon in the **Sharing Preferences** pane, to enable or disable the firewall.

The Internet address space for DSL, cable, and corporate network links use well-known IP ranges; if you are on such a connection, the automated scripts that "script kiddies" use to probe for holes such as the Code Red or Nimda vulnerabilities (which are still being exploited whenever anybody finds an unpatched Windows machine) constantly hit your Mac. Fortunately, Mac OS X is not vulnerable to these Windows-specific attacks, but running a firewall can definitely help you keep them from becoming a drain on your resources.

1 Open the Sharing Preferences

Open the **System Preferences** application (under the **Apple** menu); click the **Sharing** icon to open the **Sharing Preferences** pane. Click the **Firewall** tab.

133

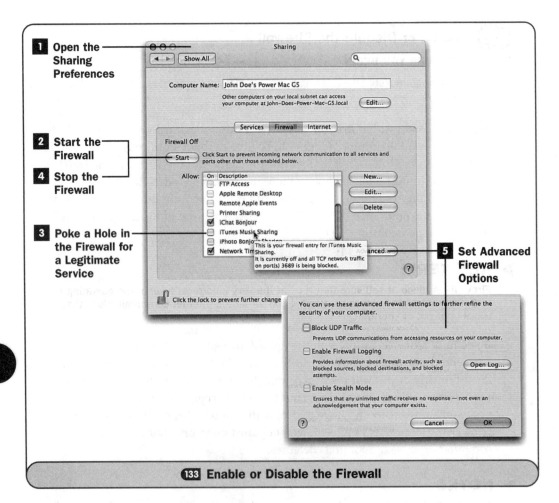

1. **Open the Sharing Preferences**
2. **Start the Firewall**
4. **Stop the Firewall**
3. **Poke a Hole in the Firewall for a Legitimate Service**
5. **Set Advanced Firewall Options**

133 Enable or Disable the Firewall

2 Start the Firewall

To turn on the firewall and begin shielding your computer from attack, click the **Start** button. The button's label immediately changes to **Stop**.

3 Poke a Hole in the Firewall for a Legitimate Service

You won't notice any change in your system's behavior after turning the firewall on; normal Internet traffic such as email and web browsing should continue to work seamlessly. However, there are many other kinds of networked applications—games, file-sharing apps, communication systems such as iChat, and many more—that will be stopped by the firewall when they originate at another computer and are aimed at yours. To allow these types of traffic through the firewall, you must create a "hole" for each one—an explicitly created exception to the general denial rules that block unknown and unwanted traffic.

Many of Mac OS X's built-in sharing services are tied in automatically with the firewall. For instance, if you turn on **Web Sharing**, the *ports*—the numeric identifiers for certain well-known services, such as HTTP or web traffic—associated with the **Web Sharing** service are opened automatically so that traffic using those ports can reach your computer. In the case of the **Personal Web Sharing** service, ports **80** and **427** are made exempt from the firewall so that remote users can connect to your computer with a web browser and view your public documents. One of these "holes" in the firewall is generally known as a *rule*, and your firewall can have any number of rules that describe what kinds of traffic are allowed through and which are prohibited.

▶ KEY TERM

Rule—An entry in the firewall's configuration that tells it to allow or disallow a certain kind of traffic.

There are a couple of extra rule entries in the **Allow** list box, corresponding to popular services you might run on your Mac, that you might find useful to enable. Select the check box for **iChat Bonjour** to allow other people on your local network to send you iChat requests. If you don't enable this exemption, other people won't be able to contact you for voice or video chats in iChat. Similarly, select the check box for **iTunes Music Sharing** to allow other people to browse your shared music in iTunes.

133

▣ Stop the Firewall

If you are having trouble making a connection to some remote host or online service, as might happen with instant-messaging services such as ICQ, your firewall might be getting in the way. It might be a one-time or uncommon occurrence for you to try to use the service in question. By far the best solution is to properly research the behavior of the software in question so you can properly open a firewall hole for it, but in a pinch, it can be easier for you to simply turn off the firewall temporarily to allow a file transfer or other transaction to go through, rather than finding out which specific ports you need to use to allow the traffic through the firewall on a permanent basis. Use this advice with utmost caution!

To turn the firewall off, click **Stop** in the **Firewall** tab of the **Sharing Preferences** pane. Remember to turn it back on by clicking **Start** when you're done using the application that the firewall interferes with!

5 Set Advanced Firewall Options

Click the **Advanced** button. The Mac OS X firewall has three built-in security enhancements you can enable to quickly and cleanly deal with certain kinds of unwanted traffic.

Block UDP Traffic prevents any activity from reaching your computer that uses the UDP protocol, such as is commonly used in Voice-over-IP (VoIP) communications, as well as in tools that attackers often use to probe computers. Don't enable this option if you use VoIP applications, as it could make them stop working.

Enable Firewall Logging writes all information about traffic stopped by the firewall into a log file, which can be read at any time by clicking the **Open Log** button.

Enable Stealth Mode is an option for the super-secure computer, but not for the casual user. With it enabled, any unsolicited traffic will simply be discarded by your Mac, with no acknowledgment sent in response. In other words, the *only* network activity your Mac can engage in is traffic that you yourself initiate, such as web browsing or email. File sharing, FTP access, and other kinds of sharing where other computers access data on your computer are rendered unusable by this option, but it does ensure that no attacker will be able to determine that your computer exists.

133

134	**Add or Remove Firewall Rules**

✔ **BEFORE YOU BEGIN**	→ **SEE ALSO**
30 Configure Networking Manually **133** Enable or Disable the Firewall	**70** Start a Text, Audio, or Video Chat Session **81** About iTunes and Digital Music

Not every network service in the world is available in the standard list of rules in the **Firewall** configuration pane for you to enable and disable at will. A great many more commonly used services won't work properly unless you "poke a hole" in the firewall for them.

Mac OS X's firewall is designed to let you add new exception rules so that certain services can be allowed to contact your machine, even when every other unauthorized form of traffic is blocked.

▶ NOTE

You must be logged in as an Admin user, or able to authenticate as one using the lock icon in the **Sharing Preferences** pane, to add or remove firewall rules.

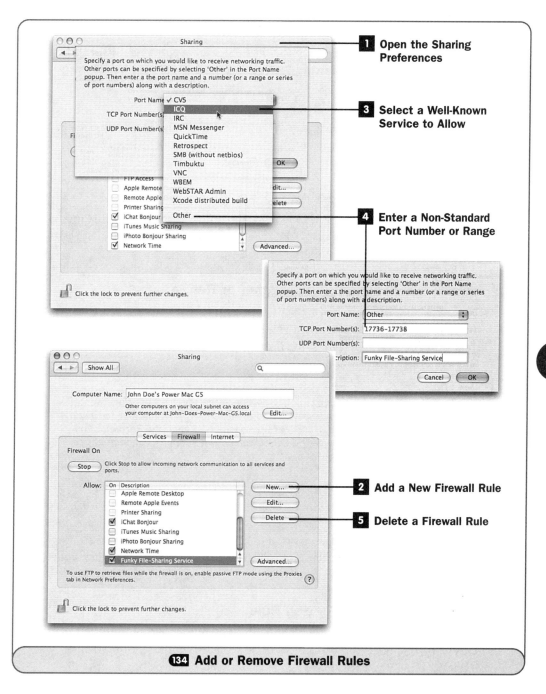

1 Open the Sharing Preferences

3 Select a Well-Known Service to Allow

4 Enter a Non-Standard Port Number or Range

134

2 Add a New Firewall Rule

5 Delete a Firewall Rule

134 Add or Remove Firewall Rules

1 Open the Sharing Preferences

Open the **System Preferences** application (under the **Apple** menu); click the **Sharing** icon to open the **Sharing Preferences** pane. Click the **Firewall** tab.

2 Add a New Firewall Rule

Click the **New** button to the right of the list of services. This brings up a sheet where you can select from a list of commonly used network services with well-known port numbers, or define your own service that isn't in the list.

3 Select a Well-Known Service to Allow

If the service you want to allow to reach your computer is in the **Port Name** drop-down list, select it and click **OK**. The service is now immediately allowed to access your machine through the firewall.

4 Enter a Non-Standard Port Number or Range

For services that aren't in the menu of popular applications, you can enter your own firewall exception rule if you know the port numbers used by the application or service you want to allow.

134

▶ **TIP**

To find out what ports a certain application uses, check the application's documentation or customer support service. Another way to find a well-known port number for a common Internet application is to look in the **/etc/services** file; open the **Terminal** and type `less /etc/services` to browse the list of well-known services, which *might* contain the application you're interested in.

Select **Other** from the **Port Name** drop-down list. In the **Port Number, Range, or Series** field, type either a single port number, a range of ports (separated by a dash), or a list of ports separated by commas. Then enter a name for the firewall rule in the **Description** field. Click **OK** when you're done. Any application whose traffic matches the ports you specified can now reach your computer from a remote source.

5 Delete or Disable a Firewall Rule

To remove a firewall rule that you don't need anymore, select it and click **Delete**. If you prefer, you can simply disable the firewall rule, without deleting it permanently. To disable a rule, just deselect the check box next to the service's name in the list of services to remove that service's exemption.

135   Extract a Password from the Keychain

✔ BEFORE YOU BEGIN

61 Keep Track of Websites with Bookmarks

→ SEE ALSO

121 Change a User's Password
136 Secure Your Files with FileVault

Anybody who has been on the Internet for any length of time knows what it's like to work with account passwords. Every website, every cooperative application, every email account, every online service has a password for you to remember. And your accounts don't even have the decency to all use the same usernames and passwords, because although your favorite username might have been available at one website, at another it might have been taken, forcing you to come up with a new variation on your name. Different websites have more or less stringent requirements for secure passwords, forcing you to think of multiple different passwords for different sites.

Who can possibly keep all these passwords and usernames straight? Mac OS X can, using a feature called the *Keychain*. When you use the Keychain feature, you don't have to remember a single one of your passwords. All you have to remember is a single master password for your Keychain itself. After you've unlocked your Keychain, it will unlock all your individual logins on its own, automatically, when those login passwords are called for. Handily enough, the Keychain is automatically unlocked by the act of your logging in to your Mac OS X account.

As you use Mac OS X, certain applications and websites will ask for passwords. When you enter a password in such a situation, a sheet appears in your browser that contains a **Remember this password in my keychain** check box that offers to add the password information to the Keychain for you. If you select this check box before logging in, the Keychain will fill out the password information for you the next time you open that application or site.

However, you might later have to find out what your password for a given site or application was. You might have to change your password periodically, for example—and everybody forgets passwords. It's just a fact of life. Fortunately, Mac OS X gives you access to the contents of your Keychain, using an application called **Keychain Access**.

135

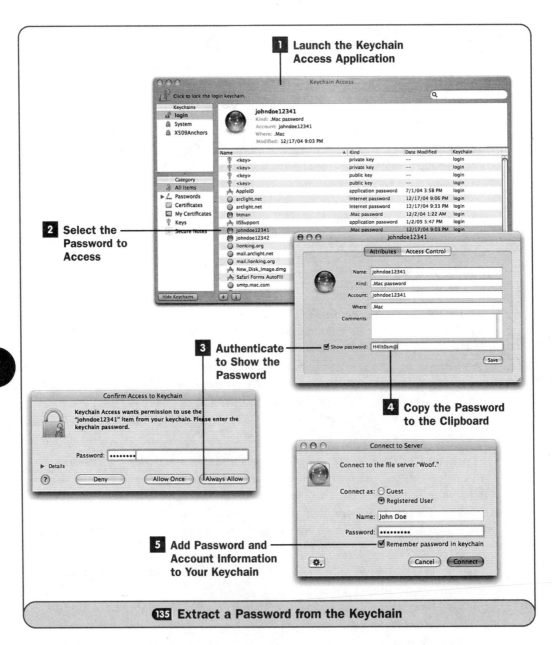

1 Launch the Keychain Access Application

2 Select the Password to Access

3 Authenticate to Show the Password

4 Copy the Password to the Clipboard

5 Add Password and Account Information to Your Keychain

135

135 Extract a Password from the Keychain

▶ **TIP**

There's a lot more you can do with the **Keychain Access** application than simply extracting forgotten passwords; you can lock the system, customize which applications are explicitly allowed to access certain passwords (or "keys"), delete keys, change passwords, or create secure text notes that can be unlocked and read only if you know the Keychain password. Feel free to explore all the features in the **Keychain Access** utility!

1 Launch the Keychain Access Application

In the Finder, navigate into the **Applications** folder and then into the **Utilities** folder; double-click the **Keychain Access** icon to launch the application.

2 Select the Password to Access

All the authentication keys that have been added to your Keychain are visible in the upper pane. Scroll through them until you find the one you want; you can view the details of an item in the lower pane by clicking it.

All different kinds of authentication keys are listed in the **Keychain Access** window; each is listed by its **Kind**, such as **Internet password** or **application password**. Use the **Kind** column or the **Search** box to zero in on the item you want to examine. When you find it, select it; information about that key appears in the fields at the bottom of the **Keychain Access** window when the **Attributes** tab is selected.

3 Authenticate to Show the Password

While viewing the item information, click the **Show password** check box at the bottom of the window. A dialog box appears, prompting you for authentication. This is a security measure, ensuring that you are the rightful owner of this Keychain, and not someone who just came in and sat down at your computer while you were logged in already.

Enter your Keychain password, which is usually the same as your Mac OS X login password (unless your login password was changed by an Admin user).

135

▶ TIP

In Keychain authentication windows such as the one that appears here, you are given three options: **Deny**, **Allow Once**, and **Always Allow**. Click **Deny** to cancel the authentication, denying access to your Keychain to the application requesting it. Click **Allow Once** to authenticate the password for just this one instance (if you try to access the same information again in 10 seconds, you'll have to provide your password again). Click **Always Allow** to give the requesting application permanent access to your Keychain, until the computer is turned off or restarted.

When you have successfully authenticated and unlocked the Keychain, the password for the account is shown in the field at the bottom of the window.

4 Copy the Password to the Clipboard

It can often be easier, especially with cryptic passwords made up of numbers and special punctuation characters, to copy and paste a password rather than having to key it in manually. Select the text of the password and choose

Copy from the **Edit** menu, or press ⌘C, to copy the password into the area of memory known as the Clipboard. If you then switch to another application and choose **Paste** from the **Edit** menu (or press ⌘V), the password is copied from the Clipboard into the application as though you'd typed it yourself.

5 Add Password and Account Information to Your Keychain

As you're using any application that accesses protected services on the Internet—such as Safari or Mail—you may be prompted on occasion to enter your password. In the dialog box or sheet where you type the password, you will usually see a check box labeled **Remember this password in my keychain**, or some similar variation. Select this check box to save the password in the Keychain when you click **OK**. The next time the application tries to access the protected resource, it will be able to get the password automatically from the Keychain instead of having to bug you for it.

If you enter an incorrect password, it is not entered into the Keychain.

135

136	**Secure Your Files with FileVault**

✔ **BEFORE YOU BEGIN**	→ **SEE ALSO**
118 Add a New User	**115** Require a Password When Reactivating the Computer
	121 Change a User's Password

FileVault is a feature that encrypts all the files in your **Home** folder so that they can be accessed only by someone who knows your login password. When you have FileVault turned on, you won't notice any difference in how the system works—by the act of logging in, you've unlocked the FileVault and gained access to your files for the duration of your login session. But if someone else comes along and tries to access your files—even by tearing the computer apart and prying into the hard disk itself—without your password to unlock the files, they'll be beyond the reach of those with ill intent.

▶ **NOTE**

Remember that even with FileVault enabled, someone who knows your login password can still access your files. Always be sure to keep your password secret and unguessable, and change it every few months at least!

▶ **NOTE**

FileVault is designed with corporate laptop users in mind; if a laptop computer full of trade secrets and confidential documents is stolen, the thief could have a gold mine on his hands. But with FileVault, those files are locked up without your login password available to access them.

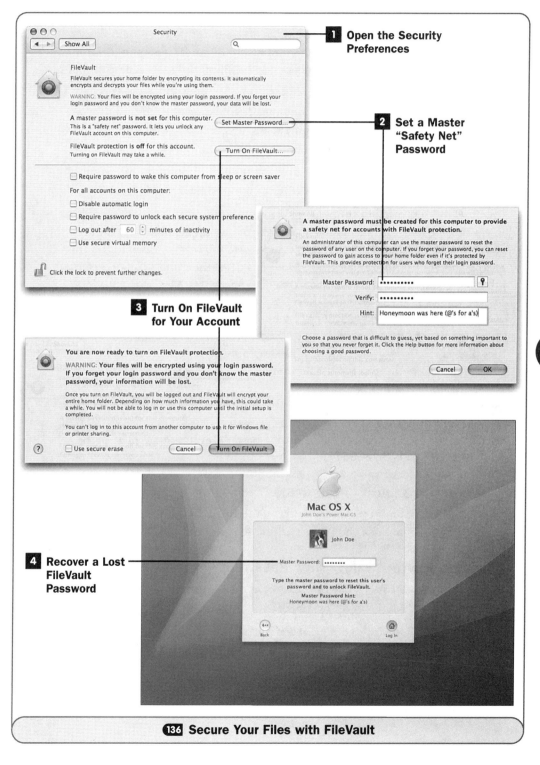

1 Open the Security Preferences

2 Set a Master "Safety Net" Password

3 Turn On FileVault for Your Account

4 Recover a Lost FileVault Password

136 Secure Your Files with FileVault

The tricky part about FileVault is that if any user forgets her password, even the system's Admin user won't be able to restore access to that user's files, because they are all encrypted using that user's forgotten password. Changing the user's login password does not decrypt or re-encrypt the files; they're locked up for good.

Fortunately, FileVault has a safety feature built in: a "master password" for all the FileVault-protected accounts on the computer. If you know the master password, you can regain access to a locked **Home** folder and turn off FileVault so that the user can access her files again.

Before you turn on FileVault for your account, it's very important (and required) that you set this master password. Your users' data depends on it!

One final thing to remember about FileVault is that once it's enabled, everything in your **Home** folder is inaccessible to anyone or any application that doesn't know your login password—and that includes web browsers or other Macs. This means that your **Public** folder (which contains items that others can access from other Macs, as described in ❸❻ **Allow Others to Share Your Files**) and your **Sites** folder (which contains items that others can access using Personal Web Sharing) will no longer be readable. But then, if you're concerned enough about the privacy of your data that you're choosing to enable FileVault, you shouldn't be sharing files publicly from your Mac anyway. Be sure that you absolutely need FileVault protection, and won't miss the ability to share files, before you enable the feature!

136

▶ **NOTE**

You must be logged in as an Admin user, or able to authenticate as one using the lock icon in the **Sharing Preferences** pane, to set a master FileVault password or enable FileVault protection for an account.

❶ Open the Security Preferences

Open the **System Preferences** application (under the **Apple** menu); click the **Security** icon to open the **Security Preferences** pane.

❷ Set a Master "Safety Net" Password

Click the **Set Master Password** button. In the sheet that appears, type a password and type it again in the **Verify** field.

The master password setting can contain a hint; be sure to take advantage of this. Make sure that the hint doesn't give away the game! Your master password should be something that an intruder won't be able to guess, even with the hint. Remember, anybody who can guess the master password can unlock any user's FileVault-protected **Home** folder!

▐3▌ Turn On FileVault for Your Account

When you click **OK** to set the master password, you are automatically prompted to turn on FileVault for your current user account. Click **Turn On FileVault** to begin this process; alternatively, if you're not ready to do so yet, you can click **Cancel** and then click **Turn On FileVault** in the **Security Preferences** pane at a later time.

▶ **TIP**

On the warning sheet that appears when you turn on FileVault, the **Use secure erase** check box enables an additional security feature you might find useful: When a file in the FileVault-protected account is deleted (by emptying the Trash), Mac OS X ensures that its contents can't later be recovered by writing successive streams of random garbage onto the disk location where the file was. This takes longer than normal deletion, but is crucial for sensitive business data.

▶ **NOTE**

Because the act of turning on FileVault involves changing all of your files as they are written on the disk, the process must take place while you're logged out of your account so that you don't touch any files that Mac OS X is working on. For the same reason, any other users must be logged out as well, or Mac OS X will not allow you to turn on FileVault. When you give the command to turn on FileVault for your account, Mac OS X logs you out and prevents you from logging in until all your files have been encrypted. The process might take an hour or longer, depending on how much data you have in your **Home** folder.

136

Enter your login account password when prompted, to verify that you are who you say you are. (If you are not an Admin user, you are prompted to enter the name and password of an Admin user before you can proceed.) Mac OS X gives you a final warning, reminding you that if you lose your password and can't remember the system's master password, you will never again be able to access your files...ever.

Save all your open files and quit all your applications. When you're ready, click **Turn On FileVault**.

Mac OS X logs you out of your account and encrypts your **Home** folder. After the process is complete, you can log back into your account and use the system as you normally would.

▶ **NOTE**

After your **Home** folder has been secured with FileVault, the icon for it in the Finder changes from a regular house to the "safe house" icon representing FileVault. Furthermore, other users can no longer browse the contents of your **Home** folder at all—not even your **Public** folder.

4 Recover a Lost FileVault Password

If you try three times to log in at the login window and can't remember the correct password for your account, Mac OS X presents you with your password hint. If the hint doesn't help you remember your password, and you enter it incorrectly one further time, Mac OS X presents the hint for the master FileVault password. Enter this password to be given the opportunity to unlock your account by entering a new login password for the account.

▶ **NOTE**

Only the administrator of the computer should know the master system password. If you've forgotten your password for a FileVault-protected account, ask the computer's administrator to enter the master password for you.

After you enter the master password correctly and set a new password for your account, you will see a notice that your *Keychain* is still locked using your old login password. You won't be able to access your Keychain unless you remember your old password, but the original Keychain still exists in the new FileVault-protected **Home** folder, in case you remember the old password and want to extract its contents. Otherwise, a new Keychain is started using your new account password.

136

---

137 | **Run Software Update**

✔ BEFORE YOU BEGIN	→ SEE ALSO
1 Install an Application from Disc or Download	**138** Ignore an Update
	139 Schedule Automatic Software Updates

Software Update, a utility accessible either from **System Preferences** or from the **Apple** menu, is Apple's mechanism for checking the central Apple servers for available updates to Mac OS X, its component utilities, and Apple applications such as iTunes, iMovie, and Keynote, as well as firmware revisions for devices like the iPod and iSight. These updates, which generally appear two or three times a month, range in importance from minor revisions to esoteric components such as Bluetooth and Java, all the way up to patches for critical security vulnerabilities and new versions of Mac OS X itself that address flaws in the software that impair its operation.

When **Software Update** detects an update that applies to your system, you can install that update with a couple of clicks. **Software Update** also gives you the option to ignore updates that don't apply to you, or to schedule automatic checking for updates.

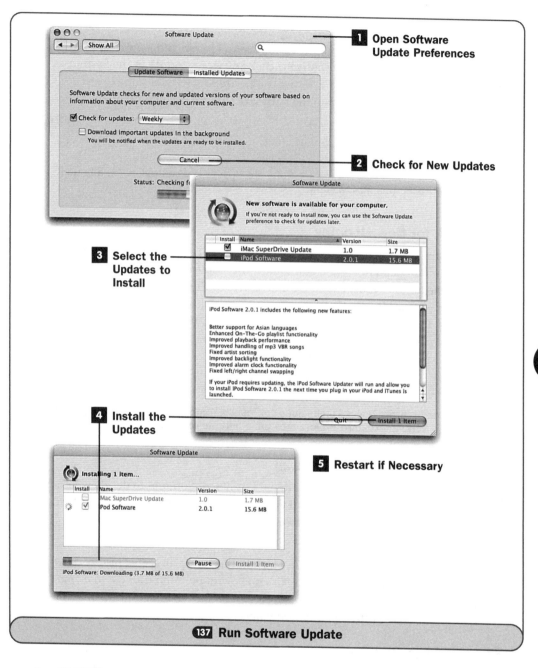

1 Open Software Update Preferences

2 Check for New Updates

3 Select the Updates to Install

4 Install the Updates

5 Restart if Necessary

137 Run Software Update

▶ **NOTE**

You must be logged in as an Admin user, or able to authenticate as one when prompted, to install new software obtained by **Software Update**.

▣ Open Software Update Preferences

Select **Software Update** from the **Apple** menu to launch the **Software Update** utility directly. Alternatively, click **Software Update** in the **System Preferences** application. The **Software Update Preferences** pane opens, which allows you to configure the **Software Update** utility and launch a check.

▶ TIP

Just to make sure that you don't miss it, **Software Update** is also available in a button link from the **About This Mac** window.

▣ Check for New Updates

Make sure that you're connected to the Internet. (The **Software Update** utility can't find any updates if you can't reach the Apple servers.) Then click **Check Now**; the button's label changes immediately to **Cancel**. **Software Update** examines your Mac OS X system and its core applications and compares their version numbers to the updates available on the server. All the applicable updates that the utility finds are listed in the separate **Software Update** window that appears.

▶ NOTE

If the separate Software Update utility does not launch, it means there were no updates available. The **Software Update Preferences** pane informs you of this condition as well.

▣ Select the Updates to Install

Click an update in the results list to read its description and to decide whether you want to install it. For each update you decide to install, select the **Install** check box to the right of the update's name. (Updates are typically selected for installation automatically.)

If the update requires a restart after installation, you will see a "restart" icon to the left of the **Install** check box (it's a leftward-pointing triangle in a small circle). You can install multiple updates that require restarts at the same time and have to restart the computer only once.

▣ Install the Updates

Click the **Install <n> Items** button to install all the updates you have selected. If necessary, a dialog box appears that prompts you to authenticate as an

Admin user. Enter the username and password of an **Admin** user to continue. You may also be required to read and agree to one or more End User License Agreements (EULAs) for various software packages presented for download.

Software Update begins downloading the selected updates. An update can be any size from several hundred kilobytes to a hundred megabytes or more; refer to the **Size** column to determine how large your total download will be and plan the download accordingly. Use the **Pause** button to stop the download; you can then resume the download later without losing your place.

After all the required updates have been downloaded, Mac OS X will unpack and install them. This might require a lot of processor power and system resources, so now is a good time to quit any resource-hungry applications that you might be running, or at least go and get a cup of coffee.

5 Restart if Necessary

If any of the installed updates were marked as requiring a restart, you are prompted to restart the computer. Click the **Restart** button to do so. All your currently running applications will be terminated.

137

▶ **TIP**

If you have unsaved data in any of your applications, the application might prevent the computer from shutting down while it waits for you to confirm whether to quit without saving the changes. Be sure to answer all such confirmation requests promptly or the shutdown process might time out. If this happens, quit all your applications manually and select **Restart** from the **Apple** menu.

It's not a good idea to keep using your system without restarting it after you've installed an update that requires a restart. Chances are that nothing bad will happen, but conflicts between the version of the operating system that's running and the version of the update you just installed might cause some very unpleasant results. Always restart promptly after a major update!

▶ **NOTE**

If you have installed an update to an application such as iTunes or iCal that uses passwords and interacts with your Keychain, the next time you run that application, you may be prompted with a dialog box that informs you that the application has been updated and the Keychain entry associated with it needs to be re-confirmed. Click **Update All** to fix all Keychain entries for that application.

138 | Ignore an Update

✔ BEFORE YOU BEGIN	→ SEE ALSO
137 Run Software Update	**139** Schedule Automatic Software Updates

Sometimes the **Software Update** utility will find software that can be installed on your computer, but that you're not interested in. For instance, there might be an update to iMovie, but you don't use iMovie and don't want to spend the time downloading 80 megabytes of software you won't benefit from. To prevent this iMovie update from appearing in your update list every time you check, you can tell Software Update to ignore it.

1 Check for Updates

Use the **Software Update** utility to check for updates as set out in **137** **Run Software Update**. Review the detected updates to decide which ones you want to install and which ones aren't relevant to you.

2 Select the Update to Ignore

Click to select one of the updates you want to ignore. You can ignore only one update at a time.

3 Ignore the Update

Select **Ignore Update** from the **Update** menu and click **OK** on the confirmation dialog box that appears. The update disappears from the list, and won't ever trigger a **Software Update** launch in the future.

4 Reactivate Ignored Updates

If you want to see your ignored updates again (for instance, if you suddenly develop an interest in video editing and want to try iMovie after all), select **Reset Ignored Updates** from the **Software Update** menu. Any updates that you had previously ignored will appear in the list again.

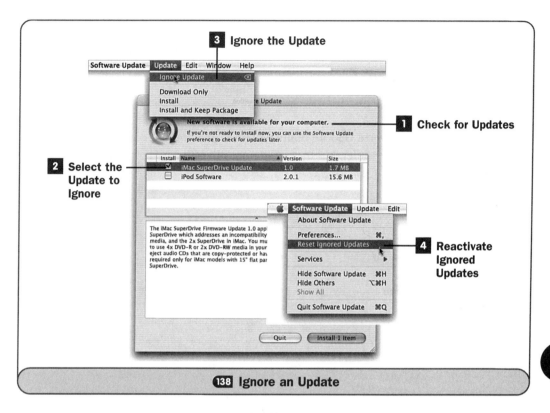

3 Ignore the Update

1 Check for Updates

2 Select the Update to Ignore

4 Reactivate Ignored Updates

138 Ignore an Update

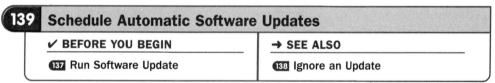

139 **Schedule Automatic Software Updates**

✔ BEFORE YOU BEGIN	→ SEE ALSO
137 Run Software Update	**138** Ignore an Update

The **Software Update** utility can run in the background, performing its maintenance tasks on a periodic basis so that you don't have to worry about it. Better yet, when the utility detects available updates, it can download them in the background while you're busy with other tasks. When the package is finished downloading, **Software Update** notifies you that there's an update ready to install. This can be a big time-saver.

1 **Open the Software Update Preferences**

Open the **System Preferences** application (under the **Apple** menu); click **Software Update** to open the **Software Update Preferences** pane.

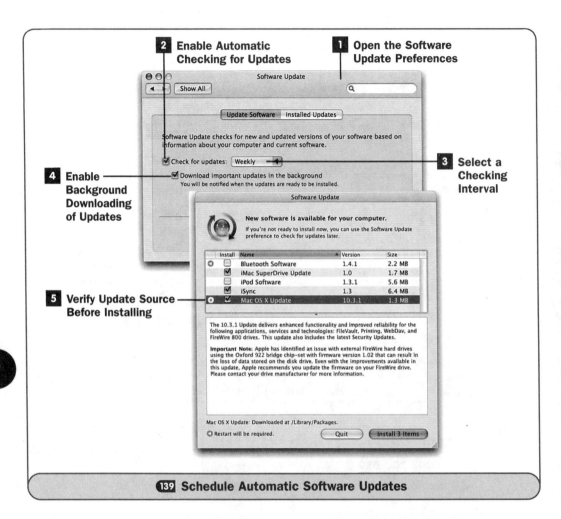

2 Enable Automatic
Checking for Updates

1 Open the Software
Update Preferences

4 Enable
Background
Downloading
of Updates

3 Select a
Checking
Interval

5 Verify Update Source
Before Installing

139

139 Schedule Automatic Software Updates

2 Enable Automatic Checking for Updates

Select the **Check for updates** check box to enable automatic checking on the
default interval, **Weekly**.

3 Select a Checking Interval

Use the drop-down menu to select a checking interval of **Daily**, **Weekly**, or
Monthly. Whichever period you select counts from the time the last check
was performed. For instance, if you last checked for updates at 4:13 P.M. on
Tuesday, the next **Weekly** check will occur at 4:13 P.M. the following Tuesday.

4 Enable Background Downloading of Updates

If you want to enable background downloads, select the **Download important updates in the background** check box. This lets Mac OS X download crucial security updates for you. Applying these patches as soon as they become available is so important that Apple has allowed the operating system software to get that much closer to updating itself automatically. With all these options in place, all you have to do—ideally—is authenticate and confirm the package's installation when Mac OS X prompts you.

▶ **NOTE**

Large and optional updates, such as revisions of iTunes and iMovie, are not downloaded in the background. The background download option is intended only for the most important and critical system updates.

5 Verify Update Source Before Installing

If you do see a dialog box prompting you to allow Mac OS X to install a new update, be sure to confirm that the update is in fact coming from **Software Update**! An easy way for a virus or Trojan to install itself on your system is to pose as a legitimate message from Software Update. However, such a malicious program cannot actually use the **Software Update** mechanism; the utility is tied into Apple's servers and can only report legitimate updates from Apple.

If you get a dialog box prompting you to install a newly downloaded update, make sure that the **Software Update** utility has launched and open it up so that you can view what the update is. If the update isn't listed in the **Software Update** window, then beware—you might be facing a program with malicious intentions.

It's always safer to cancel or quit the dialog box instead of installing a software update. Remember that you can always run **Software Update** again. If there are any legitimate updates remaining to install, **Software Update** will ask for permission to install them.

139

---

140   Select the Boot Volume at Boot Time

→ **SEE ALSO**

If you have multiple copies of Mac OS X (or other operating systems) installed on different volumes on your disk, or on different disks attached to your computer, you can boot from any one of them without having to configure anything in software. This is done through the use of the **Option** key while booting.

1 Restart the Computer

Select **Restart** from the **Apple** menu to restart your computer. If the computer is powered off, start it up.

2 Hold Down the Option Key

Immediately after the "bong" sound, press and hold the **Option** key. Hold the key down until the boot volume selection screen appears.

3 Select the Volume to Boot From

The Mac scans all available disks for bootable volumes. Each such volume that it finds appears as a button-style icon on the screen, along with two buttons for rescanning and booting. The default boot volume—usually the primary partition on the built-in hard disk—is selected by default. If you click the **Boot** button (with a right arrow symbol), the Mac boots from that partition as it normally does.

140

▶ TIP

If you want to boot from an external disk that isn't currently plugged in, and you didn't plug it in in time for the Mac to recognize it during the scan, plug it in now and click the Rescan button. The Mac should recognize the disk this time. If not, restart the computer holding down **Option** again. (You may have to turn off the computer—hold down the Power button for several seconds—and turn it back on.)

To boot instead from a different available volume, wait several moments for the computer to finish scanning for boot volumes (the mouse pointer changes from a stopwatch to a pointer), and then select the volume you want to boot from. This volume can be a hard disk partition, a CD-ROM or DVD, an external FireWire drive, or any of several other devices—and it doesn't have to be Mac OS X, either. You can have Linux or BeOS installed on some of your volumes, and you can select these volumes as well from this screen.

4 Boot the Computer

After you have selected the boot volume you want, click the **Boot** button. The Mac will boot using that volume.

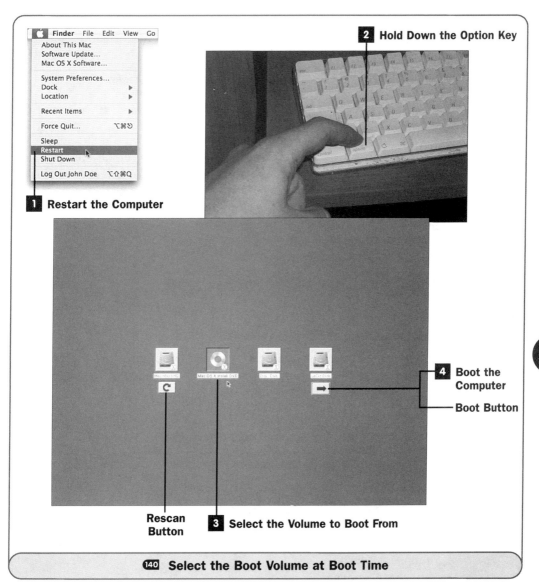

1 Restart the Computer

2 Hold Down the Option Key

140

4 Boot the
Computer

Boot Button

Rescan
Button

3 Select the Volume to Boot From

⓴ Select the Boot Volume at Boot Time

▶ **NOTE**

Using the boot volume selection screen and the **Option** key is a one-time override operation. The next time you boot the computer, it will use the default boot volume it normally
uses.

141   Boot from Different Disks Using Keystrokes

✔ BEFORE YOU BEGIN	→ SEE ALSO
140 Select the Boot Volume at Boot Time	**142** Change the Startup Disk
	22 Partition a Hard Disk

By holding down certain special key combinations at boot time, you can force the Mac to boot from specific devices. These special key combinations can also cause a number of other interesting effects to happen. These key combinations are poorly documented and the subject of folklore, but some are more well-known than others. Memorize the ones you're likely to need, considering your hardware configuration and your work patterns.

1   Restart the Computer

Select **Restart** from the **Apple** menu to restart your computer. If the computer is powered off, start it up.

2   Hold Down the Key for the Device You Want

Immediately after the "bong" sound, press and hold one of the following key combinations, depending on the effect you want.

▶ **NOTE**

Like the boot volume picker screen described in **140** Select the Boot Volume at Boot Time, these key combinations cause a one-time behavior change only. The next time you boot your computer, it boots in the standard manner from the default volume.

Key(s) Pressed	Effect
C	Boot from CD
D	Boot from Internal Hard Disk
N	Boot from Network Server
T	Boot into FireWire Target Disk Mode
⌘+Option+Shift+Delete	Boot from External Disk
⌘+Option+Shift+Delete+<# key>	Boot from SCSI ID #
⌘V	Show Console Messages (Verbose Mode)

▶ **WEB RESOURCE**

http://davespicks.com/writing/programming/mackeys.html

Dave Polaschek compiles a comprehensive list of lots more keyboard shortcuts for use at boot time and later.

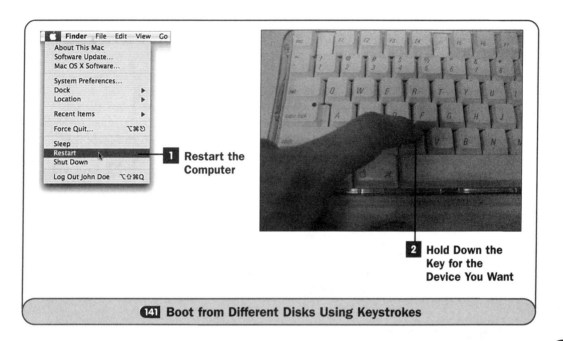

1 Restart the Computer

2 Hold Down the Key for the Device You Want

141 Boot from Different Disks Using Keystrokes

142 Change the Startup Disk

→ SEE ALSO

140 Select the Boot Volume at Boot Time

141 Boot from Different Disks Using Keystrokes

The boot volume selection screen and the many different key combinations you can use to control how your Mac boots are useful indeed, but they're only one-time solutions (see **140** **Select the Boot Volume at Boot Time** and **141** **Boot from Different Disks Using Keystrokes**). If you want to switch permanently to a different boot volume instead of selecting it from the selection screen every time you start up the computer, use the **Startup Disk Preferences** pane to change your default startup volume.

1 Open the Startup Disk Preferences

Open the **System Preferences** application (under the **Apple** menu); click **Startup Disk** to open the **Startup Disk Preferences** pane.

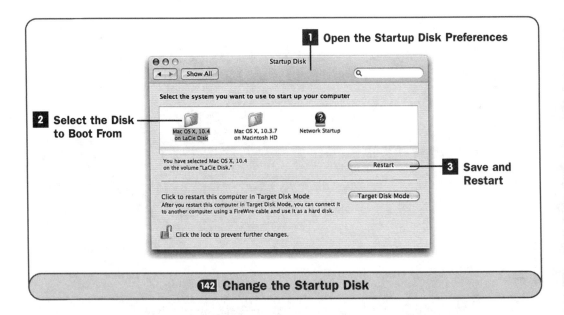

1 Open the Startup Disk Preferences

2 Select the Disk to Boot From

3 Save and Restart

142 Change the Startup Disk

142

2 Select the System to Boot From

Wait a few moments for Mac OS X to detect all the available bootable volumes. All the volumes appear in the window, each one (except the **Network Startup** option or CD/DVD discs) represented as a system folder. Each folder is labeled with an operating system version. The icon representing the volume you normally boot from is selected.

Click the icon representing the volume from which you want to boot. This can be a Mac OS X system, a Mac OS 9 system, or another kind of bootable volume.

3 Save and Restart

When you have selected the boot volume you want, click the **Restart** button. On the confirmation sheet that appears, click **Save and Restart**. When you do this, the Mac saves low-level information that tells it to boot from the new volume the next time it starts up pane.

▶ **TIP**

If you select a Mac OS 9 system as your default boot volume, your computer will boot into Mac OS 9. However, if you then want to switch back to Mac OS X, you must use the **Startup Disk Control Panel** in Mac OS 9—it's available from the **Control Panels** submenu of the **Apple** menu, and it works very similarly to Mac OS X's **Startup Disk Preferences** pane. Bootable volumes are shown in a hierarchical manner; click the icon of your Mac OS X installation, save, and restart back into Mac OS X.

The Mac will restart and should boot into the system installation that you selected pane.

18

Rescue Operations

IN THIS CHAPTER:

Not even a Mac is perfect. The truly die-hard Apple fans might not like to admit it, but even the best-designed computer in the world is a machine—and as such, it's subject to the unpleasant realities that all machines face: mechanical failures, misconfigurations, and obsolescence. That shiny new Mac you brought home and took lovingly out of its elegantly packaged carton is virtually guaranteed to be too old for you to use within a few years. Parts break and have to be replaced. New applications demand more memory, faster video cards, and bigger hard disks. And by the time you've installed a couple of dozen applications on your Mac and built up music and photo libraries to enjoy in your leisure time, the newest software on the market will seem as though it's designed to require a computer just a *little* bit faster than the one you've grown so comfortable with.

Living with your Mac, by necessity, means not just having the skills to operate your software and the operating system to get the most out of them. It also means being able to repair your system when something goes wrong, to upgrade it when you need to extend its lifespan, and—when you finally upgrade to a new Mac—to move your life over to it from your old computer so that you don't have to start over from scratch.

143 | 143 Back Up Your Information

✔ BEFORE YOU BEGIN	→ SEE ALSO
45 Sign Up for .Mac	**144** Move Your Data to a New Mac
30 Configure Networking Manually	**147** Archive and Install a New Mac OS X Version

Apple knows that one of the biggest problems with computers is the fact that they sometimes fail. Hard drives crash, laptops are dropped or stolen, files are accidentally deleted—and for most people, there's no solution but to start over from scratch. Making proper backups is one of those things that everybody knows they *should* do, but very few people have the patience to actually do it. Backup applications can be expensive, as can the media on which the data is stored. It's like insurance: a significant cash outlay designed to buy assurance that in the extremely unlikely chance of catastrophe, the loss of data can be reversed—and nobody likes paying for insurance.

▶ WEB RESOURCE
http://www.dantz.com
Dantz Retrospect is a full-featured backup suite for Mac OS X that gives you more control over your system's data backups than what Apple **Backup** offers.

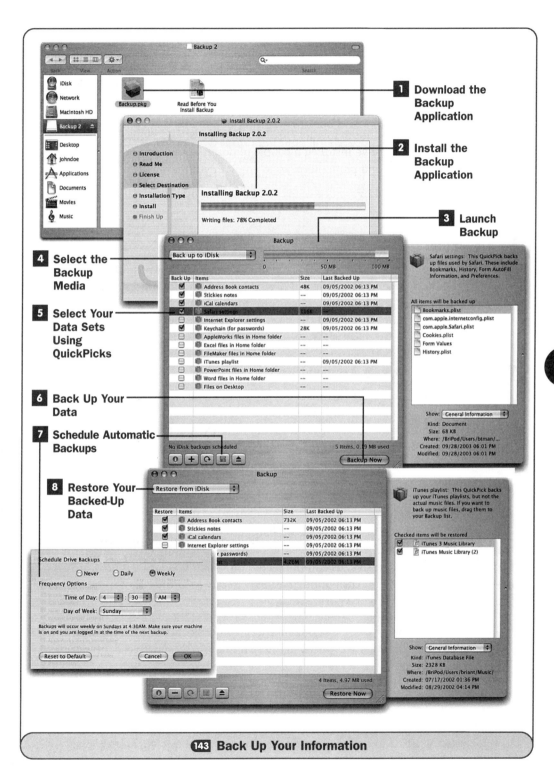

1 Download the Backup Application

2 Install the Backup Application

3 Launch Backup

4 Select the Backup Media

5 Select Your Data Sets Using QuickPicks

6 Back Up Your Data

7 Schedule Automatic Backups

8 Restore Your Backed-Up Data

143

143 Back Up Your Information

▶ **NOTE**

Apple Backup is only one of several data backup applications commercially available for the Mac, and you might decide that it isn't full-featured enough to meet your needs (or you might not have a .Mac account, which is required to take full advantage of Backup's functionality).

That's why .Mac includes a data backup program, and a very good one at that. **Backup**, as it's called, can archive all your important data to CD, DVD, an external or network drive, or to your iDisk if you've purchased enough storage there. If you have a writable CD or DVD drive (or an external FireWire drive) and a paid .Mac account, you don't have much of an excuse for not making regular backups.

143

1 Download the Backup Application

Log in to the .Mac website and click the **Backup** icon in the left panel to go to the **Backup** page. A large site full of step-by-step tutorials and strategies is online here, as is a link (in the upper right) to the download page for the **Backup** application. Download the most recent version available, which at the time of this writing is **Backup 2**.

2 Install the Backup Application

When the disk image has finished downloading (if you're using Safari), it automatically mounts and opens in the Finder; if it doesn't, locate it (on the Desktop, usually) and double-click it to mount it. Double-click the **Backup.pkg** file to run the installer. When prompted about whether the installer can "run a program to determine if it can be installed," click **Continue**.

3 Launch Backup

After the **Backup** application is installed, navigate to it in the **Applications** folder and double-click its icon.

4 Select the Backup Media

The drop-down list in the upper-left corner of the **Backup** application window lets you choose your backup media. You can only choose a media type to which your computer can write; if you don't have a SuperDrive, for instance, but only a CD-R burner, you can't back up to DVD.

To back up to an external or network drive, first make sure that the drive is mounted on your Mac and that you are able to write to it. Then select **Back up to Drive** from the menu, and click the **Set** button to open a sheet where you select whether to open an existing backup location or create a new one.

Click **Create** to make a new backup target. In the navigator sheet that appears, go to the location on the external or network drive where you want to save your backed-up data. Specify a descriptive name for the backup location (such as **FireWire Drive**) and click the **Create** button. Backup is now set to use that location as its target.

▶ **NOTE**

CD or DVD burning in Backup both require a full .Mac account. If you have a trial account, it will not allow backups to CD or DVD to be performed.

5 Select Your Data Sets Using QuickPicks

The main window of the application lists QuickPicks, which are prepackaged collections of data associated with certain conceptual areas that aren't easy to find by simply navigating through the system's folders. For instance, Backup will back up your Safari bookmarks and Keychain passwords, even if you don't know where in the system such things are stored. Just select the check box next to each collection of data that you want to back up.

As you click each QuickPick check box, the usage bar at the top of the window updates to reflect how much space the backup will take if you're backing up to iDisk. The darker orange bar indicates space on your iDisk that is already used; lighter orange is the segment that will be used by the next backup, using the current QuickPicks.

If you back up to CD, DVD, or an external drive, some additional QuickPicks are available—namely, the ones that take up a lot of space, such as your iTunes music and your iPhoto Library. These data collections are likely to be far too large to back up to iDisk, so they're available only for CD or DVD backups.

▶ **TIP**

You can back up different sets of data to different locations. For instance, you can create a small set of critical files to back up daily to your iDisk, and set your huge iTunes **Music Library** to be backed up weekly to an external drive. It's a good idea to set up a more frequent backup scheme for the parts of your system that are changed most frequently.

6 Back Up Your Data

When your backup configuration is complete, click **Backup Now**. If you're using iDisk, your data will be backed up and transferred to the .Mac servers; if you're using CD or DVD, you will be prompted to insert a blank disc. If your backup data set will span more than one disc, you will be prompted again for another disc at the appropriate time.

143

▶ **TIP**

If you schedule automated backups to an external or network drive, make sure that the drive is mounted and available at the time the backup is supposed to run! If **Backup** can't access the drive, it won't be able to back up your data. One way to make sure a network drive is always available is to add it to your Startup Items (see **109** Set Applications to Launch Automatically at Login).

7 Schedule Automatic Backups

You can optionally set up automatic, scheduled backups to iDisk. Click the **Schedule** icon at the bottom-left of the **Backup** window (which looks like a calendar). In the dialog box that opens, choose whether to back up daily or weekly, select a time range (in the middle of the night is a good bet), and click **OK** to set the schedule.

8 Restore Your Backed-Up Data

If you should need to restore from your backups, because of a catastrophic hard drive failure or because you accidentally deleted an important file, the restore process is simple. Just select **Restore from iDisk**, **Restore from CD/DVD**, or **Restore from Drive** from the drop-down list at the top left of the **Backup** window (depending on which type of media you used for your back-up). A list of the files and QuickPicks that were backed up onto the selected media appears. You can navigate to individual files and drag them into the Finder to restore them, or you can click **Restore Now** to restore all backed-up files to their original places on the disk.

▶ **NOTE**

Be especially conscious of your password if you have enabled FileVault (**136** Secure Your Files with FileVault), which encrypts all your data using that password. If you forget your account password, the encrypted data can't be recovered in a usable form—even if it was conscientiously backed up.

---

144 **Move Your Data to a New Mac**

✔ **BEFORE YOU BEGIN**

143 Back Up Your Information
118 Add a New User

If you buy yourself a new Mac, after the first few hours of elation at how much faster it is, there's always the inevitable crash of realization: You have to some-how get all your data from your old computer to your new one. Preferably, you want to be able to get all your applications, all your music, all your photos, and all your documents onto the new system so that you don't have to reconstruct anything before you're back up and running.

Prior to Mac OS X Tiger, transferring (or *migrating*) the data from your old computer to your new one was a lengthy, tedious ordeal involving many steps calling on all the various computing skills you've accumulated to this point, including creating new users, mounting shared drives, synchronizing .Mac settings, and even performing certain operations at the Terminal command line. However, in Tiger, a new utility called **Migration Assistant** makes this operation a straightforward and streamlined affair. This procedure appears during the setup process of a new Mac when you boot it up for the first time, and you can follow the steps in this task to set up your new computer as part of that process. You can run the Migration Assistant utility at any time, though, copying the data and settings from your old computer's individual user accounts as well as global system settings and installed applications whenever it is most convenient for you. You can even use the Migration Assistant utility to transfer your old data from another volume on the same computer, which comes in handy if you're upgrading your Mac to a larger or newer hard disk.

▶ **NOTE**

144

Before beginning this task, be sure to have a FireWire cable handy. FireWire cables can be purchased for $10 or so (though some brands can be unnecessarily expensive) at any electronics store. Be sure to get a cable that has a full-size six-pin connector at both ends, as each end will have to plug into a Mac's FireWire port.

1 **Launch Migration Assistant**

Navigate into the **Utilities** folder within the **Applications** folder on your hard disk. Double-click the **Migration Assistant** icon to begin transferring information from an old Mac to your current one.

An introduction screen appears, outlining the basics of the migration process. After reading the information on this screen, including the note that during the procedure you will be prompted to authenticate as an administrator, click **Continue**.

2 **Choose the Location to Migrate From**

The Migration Assistant gives you two options for migrating your data: You can transfer it from another computer, or you can transfer it from another volume on the same computer. If you choose the latter option, for example if you're upgrading your existing Mac to a larger hard disk, steps 3 and 4 are irrelevant and skipped by the Assistant. Click **Continue** to proceed.

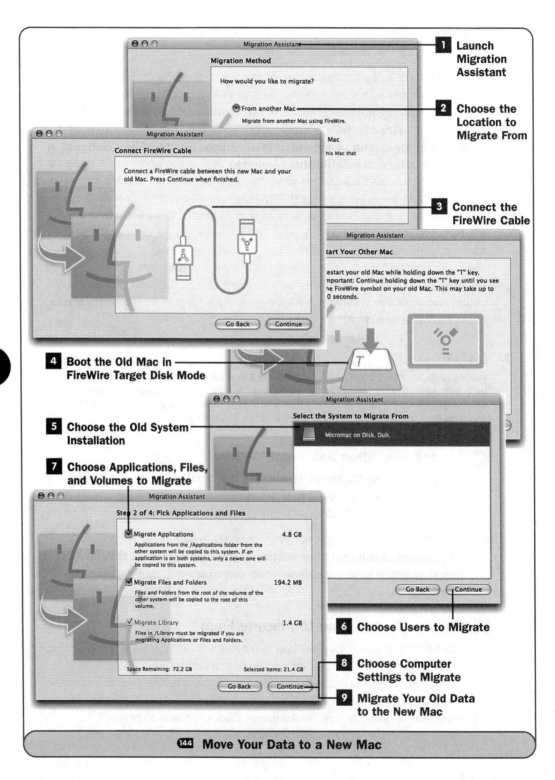

144

1 Launch Migration Assistant

2 Choose the Location to Migrate From

3 Connect the FireWire Cable

4 Boot the Old Mac in FireWire Target Disk Mode

5 Choose the Old System Installation

7 Choose Applications, Files, and Volumes to Migrate

6 Choose Users to Migrate

8 Choose Computer Settings to Migrate

9 Migrate Your Old Data to the New Mac

144 Move Your Data to a New Mac

3 Connect the FireWire Cable

You are now prompted to connect your old computer to the new one using the FireWire cable. (The old computer can be either on or off—it doesn't matter.) The FireWire port, which is on the back of desktop Macs, on the side of laptops, or additionally on the front of the Power Mac G5, can be recognized with a "Y"-shaped icon where two of the arms are dashed and one is solid, as shown in the drawing on the Migration Assistant screen. Click **Continue** when both ends of the cable are connected.

▶ **NOTE**

The FireWire cable can only be inserted one way; don't force it. If the cable connector doesn't go in easily, turn it around and try it with the flat end pointed the other way.

4 Boot the Old Mac in FireWire Target Disk Mode

As directed, boot (or restart) your old computer while holding down the **T** key on its keyboard. Keep holding down this key until the yellow FireWire logo appears on its screen.

The Migration Assistant automatically detects when the old Mac has booted into FireWire Target Disk Mode and a connection is established; the **Continue** button becomes active at this point. Click it to continue.

144

▶ **TIP**

If you're migrating from a laptop Mac (an iBook or PowerBook), it's a good idea to plug it in using the power supply and AC adapter, as the migration process can take several hours—and you don't want your laptop running out of juice in the middle of the data transfer.

5 Choose the Old System Installation

The next screen contains a list of systems installed on the old Mac. (Usually there is only one.) Click the appropriate one to select it, and then click **Continue**.

6 Choose Users to Migrate

In the next screen are listed all the users on the old Mac, along with their pictures and the size of each user's **Home** folder with all its contents. Information at the bottom of the window tells you how much space is left on your new Mac, and how much additional space will be consumed by the items you choose to transfer from the old computer. Select the check boxes next to each user entry to mark them for migration; deselect users you don't want to migrate. Click **Continue**.

7 Choose Applications, Files, and Volumes to Migrate

Next, you are prompted to choose whether to migrate your old Mac's applications and any files and folders in the top level of its hard disk. As with the previous step, each selectable item's size is indicated, and the total is reflected at the bottom of the window.

Carefully consider the implications of what you select here. Applications that don't exist on your new Mac will be copied into its **Applications** folder; however, if an application from the old Mac also exists on the new one, and the one on the old computer was installed more recently, the version on the new computer will be replaced with the migrated copy.

Click **Continue**; the next screen gives you the opportunity to migrate the contents of additional volumes attached to the old Mac, if any. Select the **On** check box next to any volume you want to migrate. Each volume you select will be copied to a folder of the same name as the volume, at the top level of the new computer's hard disk. Click **Continue** to move to the final configuration step.

8 Choose Computer Settings to Migrate

The final screen of options enables you to save yourself the hassle of re-entering the old computer's TCP/IP information or setting up your Sharing configuration the way you had it before. This step is really only useful if you're going through the Migration Assistant as part of the setup of a brand-new Mac; if you're migrating old data to a new computer that you've been using for a while, it's probably a good idea to deselect the options in this screen, or else your working settings will get overwritten by older settings that may not be correct anymore.

9 Migrate Your Old Data to the New Mac

Click **Migrate** to begin the data transfer process. Depending on the amount of data you have to transfer, this can take an hour or more; FireWire transmits data at 400 megabits per second, so if you noted the amount of space required in the **Selected Items** readout in previous steps, you can use that to calculate how much time the transfer will take, although the Migration Assistant gives you a running estimate of the time remaining anyway.

▶ **TIP**

1 GB (gigabyte) is equal to 1024 MB (megabytes); one megabyte is equal to 8 megabits. Remember, there's a calculator in Dashboard (press **F12**).

144

You can't interrupt the migration process once it's going, so be sure your laptop's power supply is plugged in and go get yourself a snack and watch some TV. (It's possible to quit the Migration Assistant entirely if you really want to halt the transfer.) When you come back, the Migration Assistant will have reached its final wrap-up screen, and your new Mac will have the users and applications from your old computer, intact and usable with all their settings. Unplug the FireWire cable and shut off (or restart) the old Mac.

▶ **TIP**

Because your old Mac's data is not affected by this process, you might want to keep it untouched and handy for a few days to make sure that all the data was transferred intact. The Migration Assistant makes migration nearly foolproof, but you can never be too careful when it comes to your most treasured data....

---

145 | **Verify and Repair a Disk**

✔ BEFORE YOU BEGIN	→ SEE ALSO
21 Add a Newly Installed Hard Disk to the System	**146** Restore or Duplicate a Disk
143 Back Up Your Information	

144

Hard disks have a bad habit of deteriorating over time—perhaps more so than any other component in a computer. This is especially problematic in that your hard disk isn't just a component that you can replace; it's the permanent memory for your computer, the place where all your accumulated data and important documents are stored. If you haven't done a backup (and why haven't you?), and your hard disk goes bad, you will likely be willing to do just about anything to get that data back.

The **Disk Utility** application, located in the **Utilities** folder inside **Applications**, provides a handy way to perform quick repair operations on your hard disk—operations that have a surprisingly high success rate in many cases. **Disk Utility** can examine the Unix permissions on your hard disk and detect discrepancies that might cause instabilities in your system; it can also correct those errors for you. What's more, **Disk Utility** can scan your disk for surface defects (the most common cause of data loss from deterioration over time), and even "repair" these errors by recovering the data in the defective regions and copying it to a healthy part of the disk.

▶ **NOTE**

You must be logged in as an Admin user to verify or repair a hard disk.

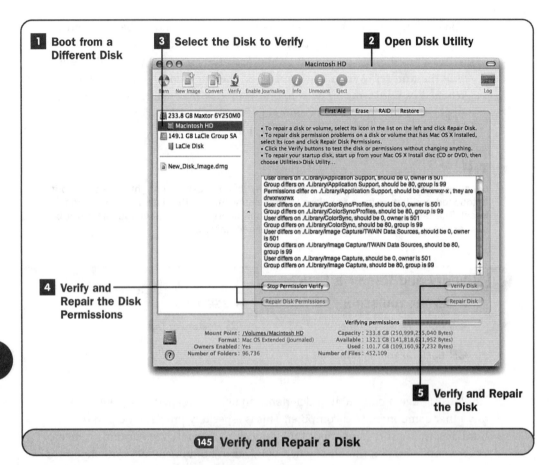

1 Boot from a Different Disk

3 Select the Disk to Verify

2 Open Disk Utility

4 Verify and Repair the Disk Permissions

5 Verify and Repair the Disk

145 Verify and Repair a Disk

1 Boot from a Different Disk

Determine whether the disk you want to inspect is your Mac's startup disk. If it is, you won't be able to do repairs on it while the Mac is booted from it. Boot the system from an external backup disk or from the Mac OS X installation CD to do repairs on your main startup disk. Another method is to use a second Mac, by booting your computer into FireWire Target Disk Mode and connecting it to another computer using a FireWire cable. You can then run Disk Utility on that second computer, operating on your main Mac's hard disk. See **141** **Boot from Different Disks Using Keystrokes**.

2 Open Disk Utility

Navigate into the **Utilities** folder inside the **Applications** folder. Double-click the **Disk Utility** icon to launch the application.

▣ Select the Disk to Verify

From the list in the sidebar of the **Disk Utility** window, select the disk you want to examine for errors. You can select an entire disk or a single volume within that disk. Click the **First Aid** tab to access the disk repair functions.

▣ Verify and Repair the Disk Permissions

Click **Verify Disk Permissions** to begin a scan of the permissions of all the files on the disk. This process will take several minutes; **Disk Utility** reports all its findings in the status window.

▶ TIP

If you notice results in the status window that indicate a possible reason for instability in the system, repair the permissions by clicking **Repair Disk Permissions**. This process, too, can take some time. When the repair is complete, however, your Mac OS X system and its applications might behave more predictably if you've been seeing a permissions-related problem.

▣ Verify and Repair the Disk

To perform a surface scan of the disk, click **Verify Disk**. This process can take several minutes or up to an hour or more. The results of the process are shown in the status window.

145

▶ NOTE

To do a surface scan of the disk, **Disk Utility** must be able to unmount it from the system. Make sure that you are not using any applications or documents on that disk, or **Disk Utility** will report an error and fail to perform the verification.

If **Disk Utility** reports correctable errors in the status window, and you want to recover your disk and make it usable again, click **Repair Disk**. **Disk Utility** will again unmount the disk and attempt to repair any surface inconsistencies that it detected during verification.

When **Disk Utility** has finished the repair process, restart your computer using the regular startup disk (if necessary); with any luck at all, your disk will be back in working order.

However, even if you were able to resurrect your disk using **Disk Utility**, be aware that any surface defect that causes you to do a repair is an indication of an aging disk that should be replaced. Consider buying a new hard disk for your computer, and by all means back up your data using the .Mac **Backup** application as described in ⑭③ **Back Up Your Information**. At the least, copy your files to CDs or DVDs. You'll thank yourself later!

146 Restore or Duplicate a Disk

✔ BEFORE YOU BEGIN	→ SEE ALSO
145 Verify and Repair a Disk	**22** Partition a Hard Disk
143 Back Up Your Information	

Using the **Disk Utility** application, you can quickly and easily make duplicates of entire hard disks or volumes, or restore a hard disk to a known reference "image"—a technique commonly used in computer labs and business environments where a network administrator must be able to ensure that multiple computers are all "cloned" from a known software state.

Disk Utility can start with either a disk image file or a physical disk (either a hard disk or a CD); you can even specify the URL of a disk image to fetch from an Internet location. The application takes a new disk, initializes it, and then writes the contents of the source disk or disk image onto the new disk.

A typical useful application of this technique is if you buy a new disk to replace an aging or deteriorating hard drive; all you have to do is mount the new disk, launch **Disk Utility**, specify the existing disk as the source and the new disk as the destination, and click **Restore**. Then you can boot your system using the new disk, and your system will be as good as new!

146

▶ NOTE

You must be logged in as an Admin user to restore or duplicate a disk.

1 Open Disk Utility

First make sure that the disk to which you want to restore is mounted on the Mac. See **21 Add a Newly Installed Hard Disk to the System** for more information on adding additional disks.

Navigate into the **Utilities** folder inside the **Applications** folder. Double-click the **Disk Utility** icon to launch the application. Click the **Restore** tab at the far right of the **Disk Utility** window to access the **Restore** functions.

2 Select a Source Disk or Disk Image

Determine which disk you want to use as the source for the restoration process. You can select any disk in the system, including your startup disk if you want to clone it onto a new disk. Drag the disk or volume from the left pane of the **Disk Utility** window into the **Source** field to select it.

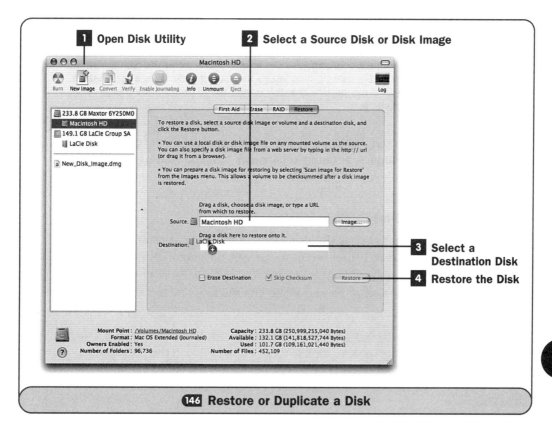

1 Open Disk Utility   **2** Select a Source Disk or Disk Image

3 Select a Destination Disk

4 Restore the Disk

146

146 Restore or Duplicate a Disk

▶ **TIP**

To use a disk image file, click the **Image** button next to the **Source** field and navigate to where the disk image file is in the navigation pane that appears.

3 **Select a Destination Disk**

You can specify any mounted disk in the system as the destination disk, with the exception of your startup disk and any disk (such as a CD-ROM) that is not writable. Drag a disk or volume from the left pane of the **Disk Utility** window into the **Destination** field.

▶ **TIP**

If you're particularly concerned about data integrity, you can elect to have **Disk Utility** do a *checksum*—a mathematical verification of the data written—after the disk is restored. This can be done only if you're using a disk image file. Select **Scan image for Restore** from the **Images** menu and navigate to the disk image file to prepare the image for restoration with a checksum.

If you select the **Erase Destination** check box at the bottom of the **Disk Utility** window (which erases all data on the destination disk), you can select or deselect the **Skip Checksum** check box, which (if selected) saves time by omitting the checksum step, which isn't as necessary if you're erasing the disk.

4 Restore the Disk

When you're ready to copy the source disk to the destination disk, click the **Restore** button. **Disk Utility** begins the process of "dubbing" the first disk to the second. The process might take several minutes to an hour or more, depending on the size of the source disk you're using and the speed of your computer.

When the process is complete, you can browse the destination disk and verify that the duplication process took place correctly. You can then remove the disk and install it in another computer, or remove the old disk from your Mac and use the new one if you're moving your data from an old disk to a new one.

146

147 Archive and Install a New Mac OS X Version

✔ **BEFORE YOU BEGIN**

1 Install an Application from Disc or Download
143 Back Up Your Information

The next version of Mac OS X that you install on your computer, in its default behavior, will install on top of your existing installation (as an "upgrade"). If all goes well, you will put in the disc, go through the guided installation procedure, and then continue using your Mac with the same configuration settings you had been using previously. A standard Mac OS X installation adds new features to your existing system, but doesn't give you any further insight into the upgrade procedure.

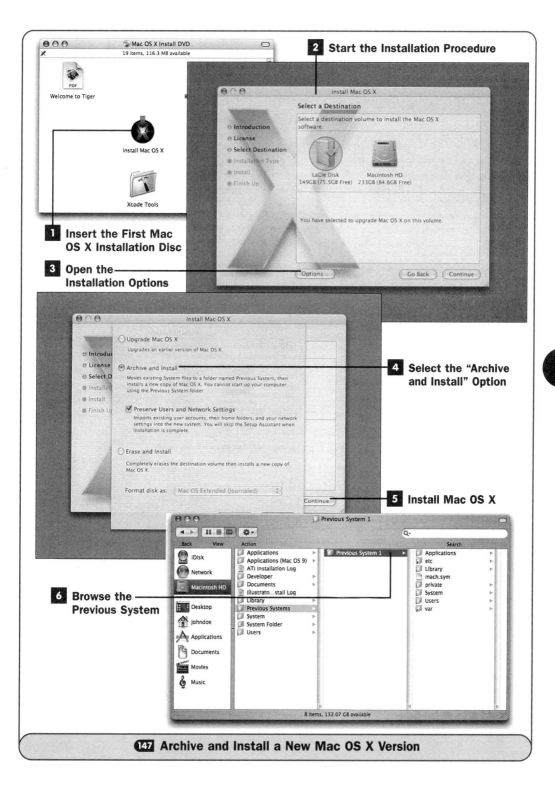

2 Start the Installation Procedure

1 Insert the First Mac OS X Installation Disc

3 Open the Installation Options

4 Select the "Archive and Install" Option

147

5 Install Mac OS X

6 Browse the Previous System

147 Archive and Install a New Mac OS X Version

When troubleshooting an installation of Mac OS X, sometimes it's helpful to be able to examine the files in the previously installed version of the operating system, compare files from one version to another, and revert to earlier versions of the files if necessary. To do this, the Mac OS X **Installer** program provides a helpful option called **Archive and Install**.

▶ **NOTE**

Another installation option is **Erase and Install**, which erases all the contents of your startup disk before installing the new version of Mac OS X on it. This option is helpful for systems that have been repeatedly reinstalled and reconfigured to the point where the new version of the operating system cannot be installed cleanly on top of it. It's also the preferred method of cleaning up a used Mac to be given to a new owner. After an **Erase and Install** procedure, be sure to install the additional software from the Software Restore disc that came with the Mac—this includes software such as iLife and Classic.

When you use the **Archive and Install** option, your old version of the operating system is cleaned from the hard disk—essential in many cases where the old version is full of conflicting files from multiple earlier installations—but it's preserved in a folder on your disk called **Previous Systems**. The new version of Mac OS X is installed cleanly and without conflicts with earlier versions, and it even preserves your user environment, but you can access the old system files (for troubleshooting purposes or to recover important data) by browsing the **Previous Systems** folder.

147

1 **Insert the First Mac OS X Installation Disc**

To begin installing the new version of Mac OS X, insert the CD-ROM or DVD labeled **Mac OS X Install Disc 1** (or something similar).

2 **Start the Installation Procedure**

In the CD-ROM Finder window that opens, double-click the **Install Mac OS X** icon. The **Installer** program opens and prompts you to enter your user password (as a security precaution, to make sure that you aren't an intruder who sat down while a legitimate user was logged in). Then you are asked to click the **Restart** button to begin installing Mac OS X.

3 **Open the Installation Options**

The Mac restarts. After it boots into the **Installer** program on the CD or DVD, you start to go through the introductory screens that tell you what the **Installer** will do.

When you reach the screen where you choose the disk onto which you want to install Mac OS X, select the appropriate disk (generally the Mac's primary hard disk) and then click the **Options** button at the bottom of the screen.

4 Select the Archive and Install Option

Click the **Archive and Install** radio button to select the installation mode that will create a clean Mac OS X installation but preserve your original system for your later perusal.

▶ TIP

If you want to keep your user environment intact (as well as all the files inside your **Home** folder, such as your iTunes music, your digital photos, and your important documents), make sure that the **Preserve Users and Network Settings** check box is selected. If you don't select this option, you will have to go through the **Setup Assistant** screens to set up your primary user account from scratch again, and none of your original files or settings will be available after the installation process completes.

Click **OK** to accept the options.

5 Install Mac OS X

Click **Continue**. Mac OS X installs itself on your system. The computer restarts after the completion of the installation process, and boots into your primary user account (or the login window, depending on your **Automatic Login** settings).

6 Browse the Previous System

To access the files that make up your previous system, navigate in the Finder to the **Previous Systems** folder (at the top level of the disk). Inside this folder are subfolders for each previously installed system, differentiated with numbers (**Previous System 1**, **Previous System 2**, and so on). Select the one you want and browse its contents for the items you want.

147

Index

Symbols

A

D

J-K

Q-R

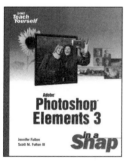

Key Terms

Don't let unfamiliar terms discourage you from learning all you can about Mac OS X. If you don't completely understand what one of these words means, flip to the indicated page, read the full definition there, and find techniques related to that term.

.Mac   *Apple's centralized network service, available for a yearly fee, that allows you to publish the products of your creativity online and make all your Macs operate as one.*   **Page 128**

1-Click ordering   *A technology that allows you to predefine your credit card information at the server, so that you can later purchase items online with a single click.*   **188**

Active Screen Corners   *Also known as "Hot Corners," this feature allows you to trigger certain functions by moving the mouse pointer into different corners of the screen.*   **432**

Admin user   *A type of user who is granted the capabilities to change global settings, install applications, and make other changes to the behavior of the entire system.*   **467**

AirPort   *Apple's brand of wireless Internet connectivity devices.*   **129**

Alias   *A pseudo-file that, when opened, instead opens a real file, application, or folder elsewhere in the system.*   **89**

Antialiasing   *The technical term for "smoothing," as with fonts or diagonal lines.*   **425**

AOL Instant Messenger (AIM)   *One of the leading instant-messaging applications used by millions of people.*   **278**

AppleTalk   *Apple's own networking protocol.*   **145**

AppleWorks   *A suite of productivity tools that includes a word processor, a spreadsheet program, a drawing program, and more.*   **309**

Application   *Also known as a program, any piece of software you run within Mac OS X.*   **18**

Archive   *A collection of documents, folders, or applications packed into a single file, which is usually compressed.*   **44**

Authentication   *To enter a name and password, usually for an Admin user.*   **468**

Automatic login   *When you start up a Mac with this option enabled, the computer enters a predetermined user's login session automatically.*   **452**

Bookmark   *A reference to a favorite website to which you want to return to in the future.*   **Page 256**

Bonjour   *A technology built into Mac OS X that allows applications on your Mac to automatically find network services provided by other computers on the same network.*   **128**

Conduit   *A piece of software hiding under the surface of Mac OS X that transfers a certain kind of information to and from a digital device such as a PDA.*   **416**

Contact sheet   *A group of thumbnail images gathered together onto a single sheet.*   **365**

Cookie   *A piece of information that some websites store on your computer to store your preferences for the site, or your username and password.*   **269**

Disk image   *A file that contains the contents of an entire disk.*   **44**

DNS servers   *Computers on the network that provide a mapping between numeric IP addresses and textual hostnames; this mapping is the Domain Name Service, or DNS.*   **137**

Domain   *Centrally managed groups of Windows computers with centralized password management and administration.*   **162**

Ethernet   *A low-level communication protocol that involves cables that end in RJ-45 jacks, which resemble large phone jacks.*   **129**

Exposé   *A feature that allows you to shrink all your windows temporarily so that they all fit on the screen and you can select the one you want.*   **432**

File Transfer Protocol (FTP)   *A method of transferring files from one computer to another.*   **272**

Firewall   *A piece of software that runs at the very innermost level of the operating system (the kernel) and manages all the Internet communications in and out of your Mac.*   **519**

iLife   *The packaged combination of iTunes, iMovie, iPhoto, iDVD, and GarageBand.*   **334**